Dawn of the Arcana

7

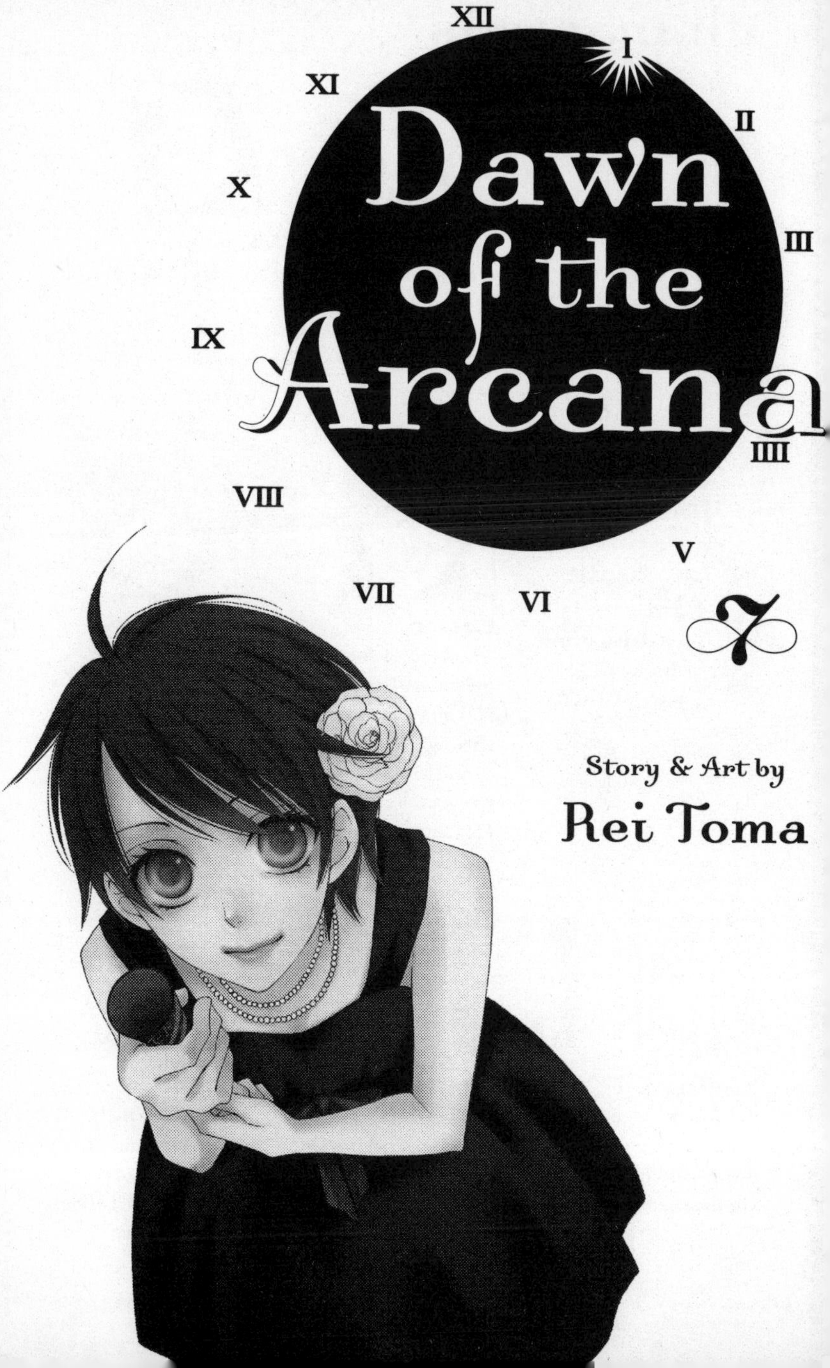

Story & Art by

Rei Toma

characters

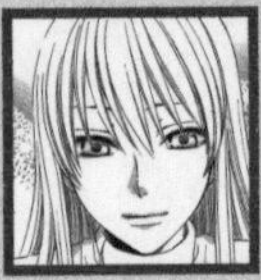

Sara
King Guran's concubine. Deceased.

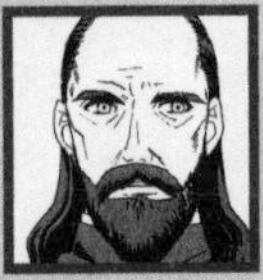

Guran
King of Belquat.

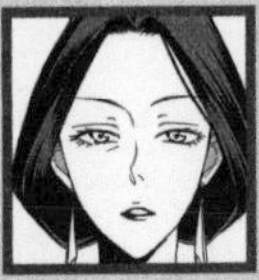

Rosenta
Queen of Belquat.

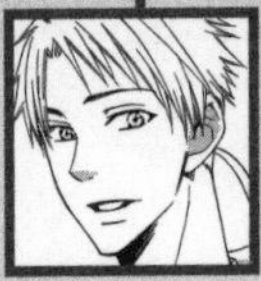

Cain
First-born prince of Belquat. Caesar's brother.

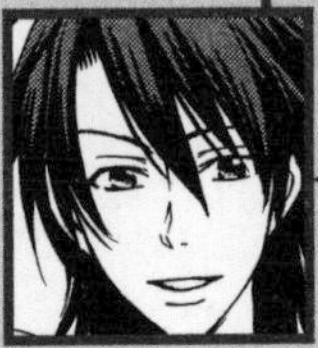

Caesar
The second-born prince of Belquat. Nakaba's husband through a marriage of political convenience. Headstrong and selfish.

Married

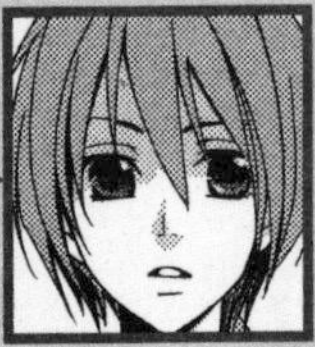

Nakaba
The princess royal of Senan. Strong of will and noble of spirit, she possesses a strange power.

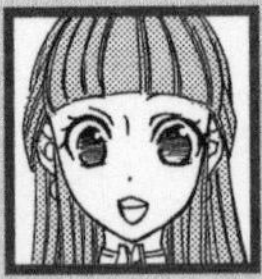

Lemiria
Bellinus's younger sister. Fond of her big brother.

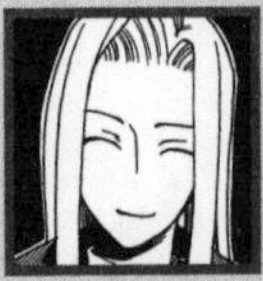

Bellinus
Caesar's attendant. Always cool and collected.

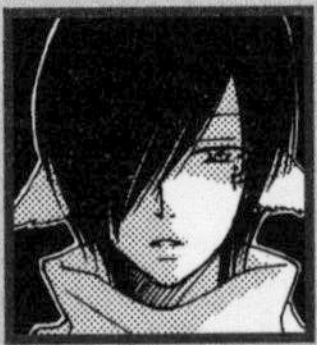

Loki
Nakaba's attendant. His senses of perception are unmatched.

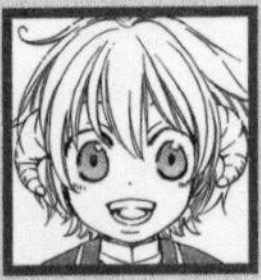

Rito
Nakaba's attendant. Recently arrived from Senan.

story

• Wed to Prince Caesar as a symbol of the peace between their two countries, Nakaba is actually little more than a hostage. Unbeknownst to King Guran, she is a survivor of the race he tried to destroy for fear of their power. Nakaba herself possesses the Arcana of Time, so she can see the past and the future.

Neighboring Kingdoms

Senan
A poor kingdom in the cold north of the island. Militarily weak.

Belquat
A powerful country that thrives thanks to its temperate climate.

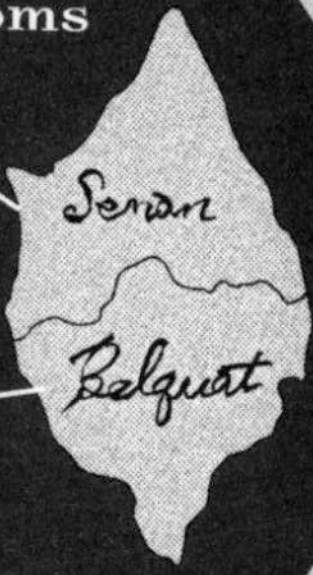
Senan
Belquat

• The political marriage between Nakaba and Caesar gets off to a rocky start, but as they grow to know each other, the gulf between them begins to close. After learning of King Guran's plans to test a devastating new weapon on a demi-human village, Nakaba and Caesar set out to stop the attack under the pretext of a honeymoon.

• They arrive at the demi-human village to find it already beset by the king's forces under command of Prince Cain, Caesar's brother. The village goes up in flames, and any hope of evacuating the demi-humans to avoid conflict is lost. Nakaba puts herself in harm's way to protect Lemiria from the death foretold by the Arcana, forcing Loki to come to Nakaba's aid by killing Prince Cain.

• Knowing her attempts to alter the future were responsible for Cain's death, Nakaba withdraws from her friends. Only Caesar's affection is able to comfort her, and their love grows deeper.

• Nakaba and Ceasar flee to Senan to avoid the pursuit that was sure to come after Cain's death. After crossing the border, they find themselves in the village of Kalika, where they have a chance encounter with Adel, heir to the Senan throne!

Dawn of the Arcana

Volume 7

XII

XI

X

CONTENTS

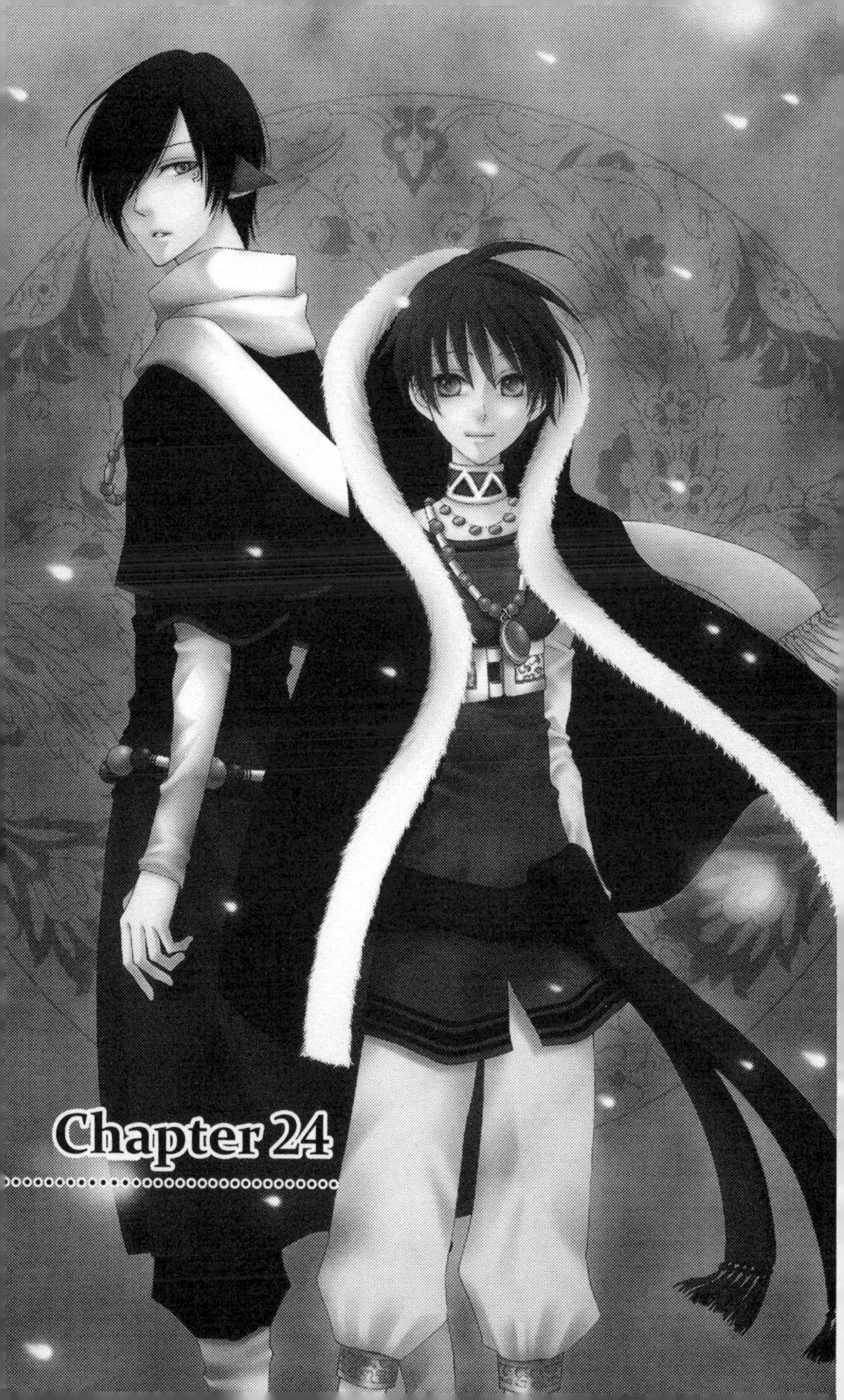
Chapter 24

THIS... IS PRINCE ADEL?
THE CROWN PRINCE?
FOR NOW, MY GRAND-FATHER SITS ON THE THRONE...
...BUT ADEL IS NEXT IN LINE.
...
DON'T TELL ME...

Dawn of the Arcana

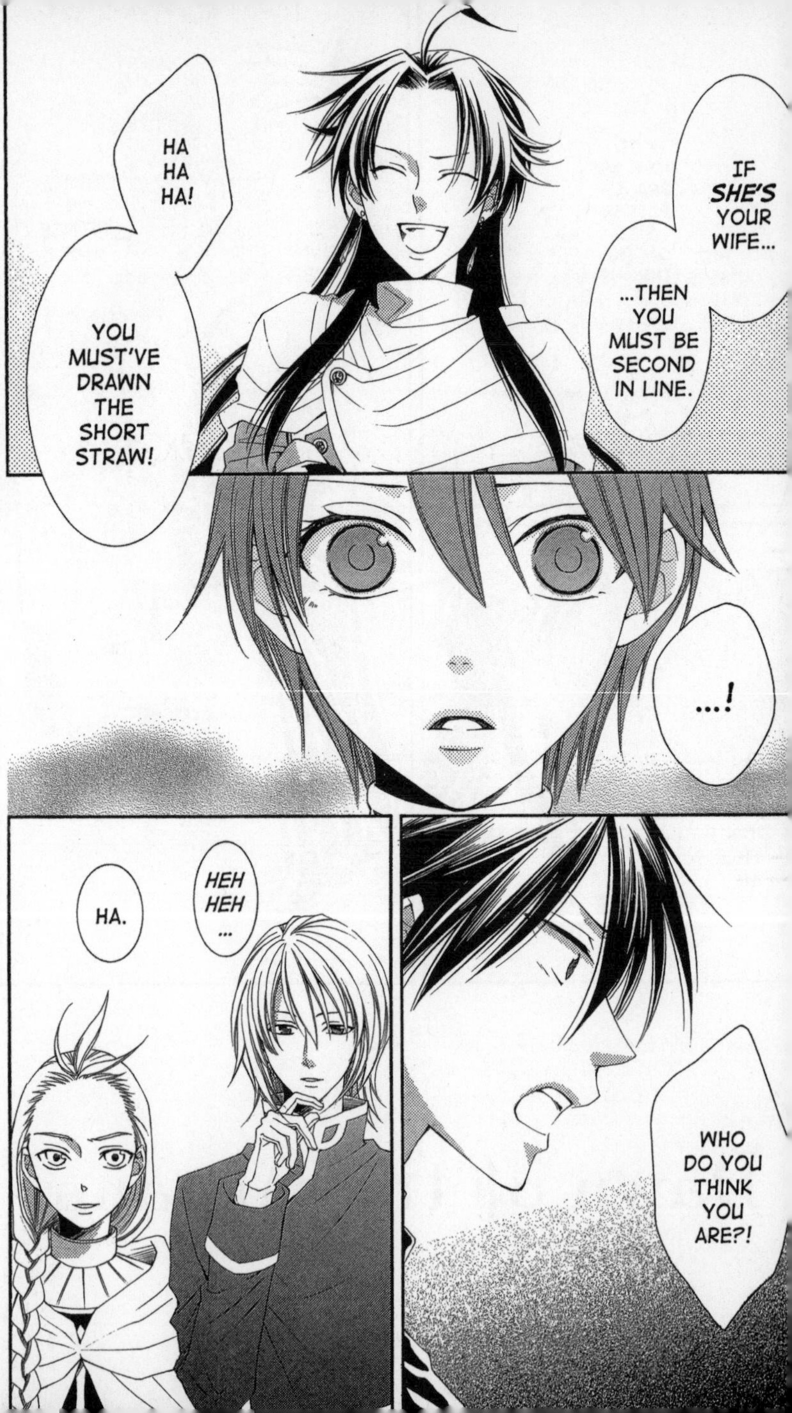
IF *SHE'S* YOUR WIFE...
...THEN YOU MUST BE SECOND IN LINE.
HA HA HA!
YOU MUST'VE DRAWN THE SHORT STRAW!
...!
WHO DO YOU THINK YOU ARE?!
HEH HEH ...
HA.

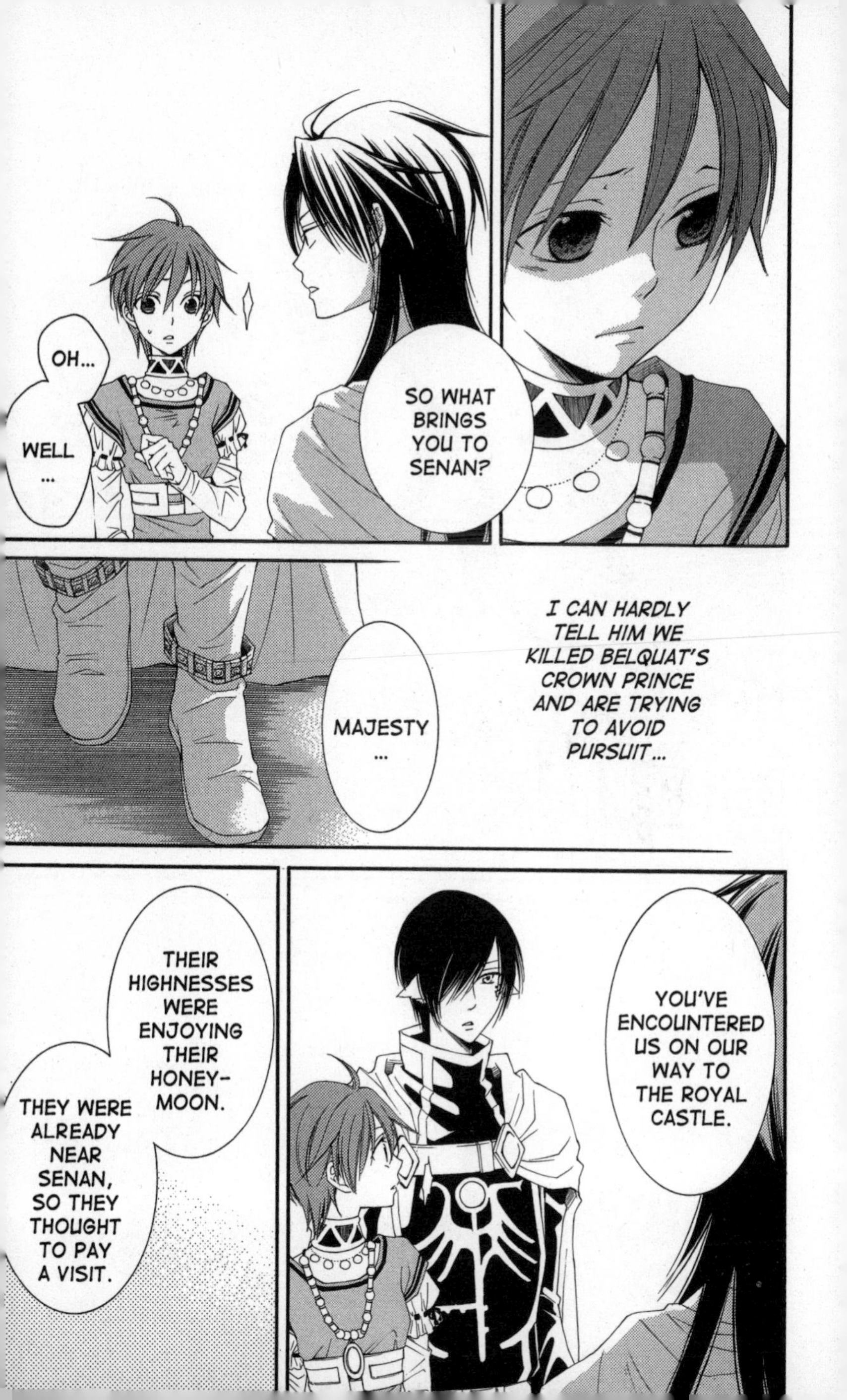
SO WHAT BRINGS YOU TO SENAN?
OH...
WELL ...
I CAN HARDLY TELL HIM WE KILLED BELQUAT'S CROWN PRINCE AND ARE TRYING TO AVOID PURSUIT...
MAJESTY ...
YOU'VE ENCOUNTERED US ON OUR WAY TO THE ROYAL CASTLE.
THEIR HIGHNESSES WERE ENJOYING THEIR HONEY-MOON.
THEY WERE ALREADY NEAR SENAN, SO THEY THOUGHT TO PAY A VISIT.

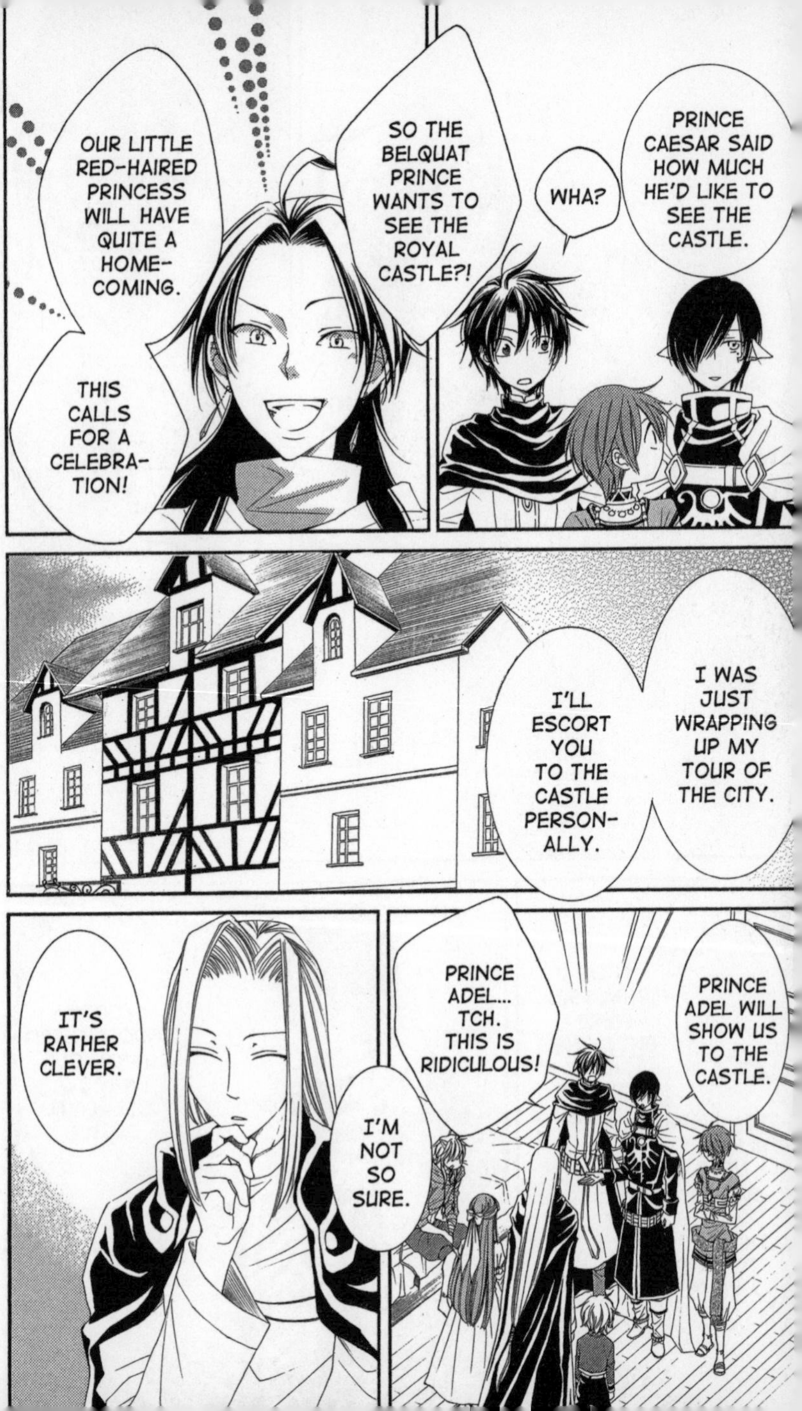
PRINCE CAESAR SAID HOW MUCH HE'D LIKE TO SEE THE CASTLE.
WHA?
SO THE BELQUAT PRINCE WANTS TO SEE THE ROYAL CASTLE?!
OUR LITTLE RED-HAIRED PRINCESS WILL HAVE QUITE A HOME-COMING.
THIS CALLS FOR A CELEBRA-TION!
I WAS JUST WRAPPING UP MY TOUR OF THE CITY.
I'LL ESCORT YOU TO THE CASTLE PERSON-ALLY.
PRINCE ADEL WILL SHOW US TO THE CASTLE.
PRINCE ADEL... TCH. THIS IS RIDICULOUS!
IT'S RATHER CLEVER.
I'M NOT SO SURE.

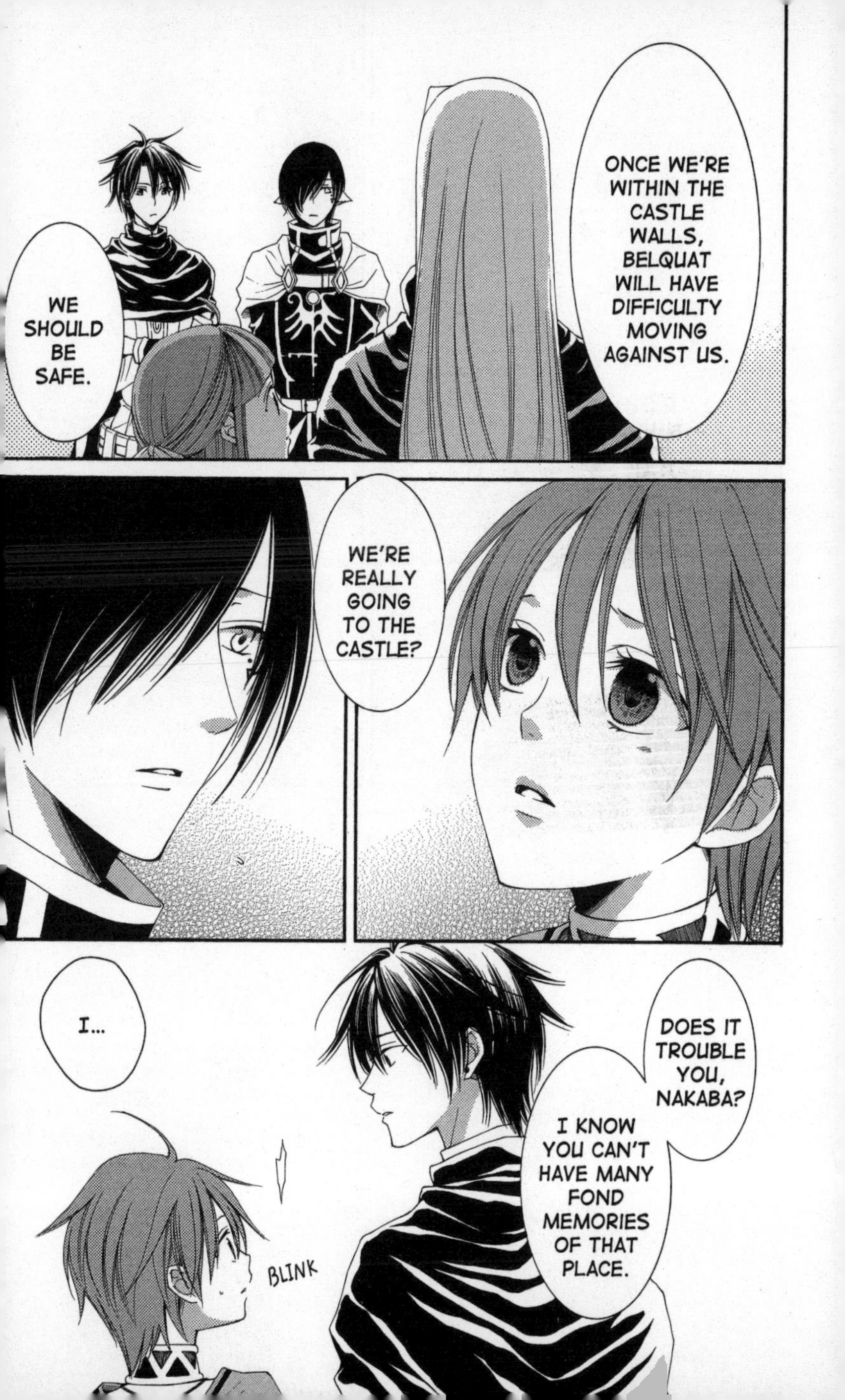
ONCE WE'RE WITHIN THE CASTLE WALLS, BELQUAT WILL HAVE DIFFICULTY MOVING AGAINST US.
WE SHOULD BE SAFE.
WE'RE REALLY GOING TO THE CASTLE?
DOES IT TROUBLE YOU, NAKABA?
I KNOW YOU CAN'T HAVE MANY FOND MEMORIES OF THAT PLACE.
I...
BLINK

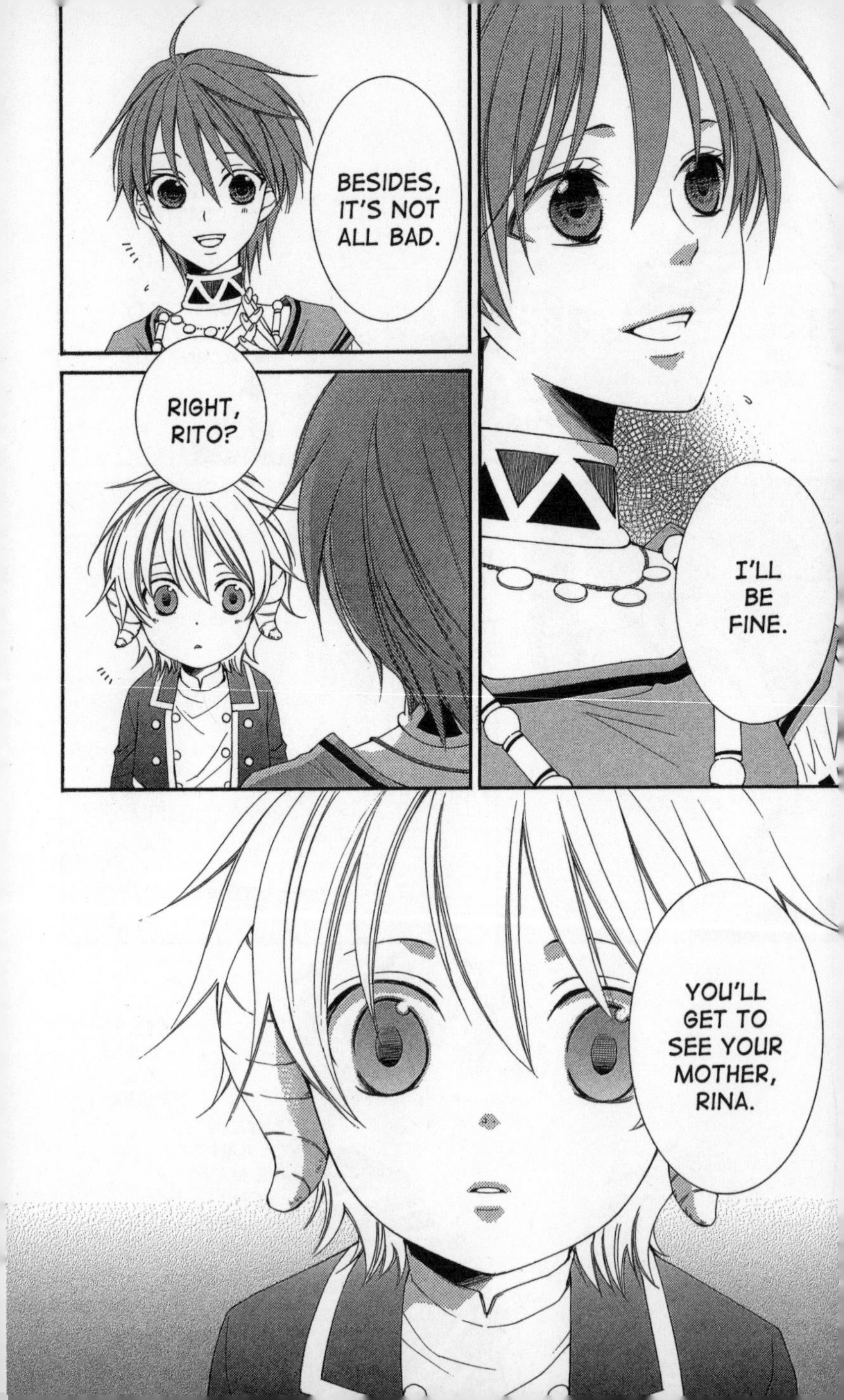
I'LL BE FINE.
BESIDES, IT'S NOT ALL BAD.
RIGHT, RITO?
YOU'LL GET TO SEE YOUR MOTHER, RINA.

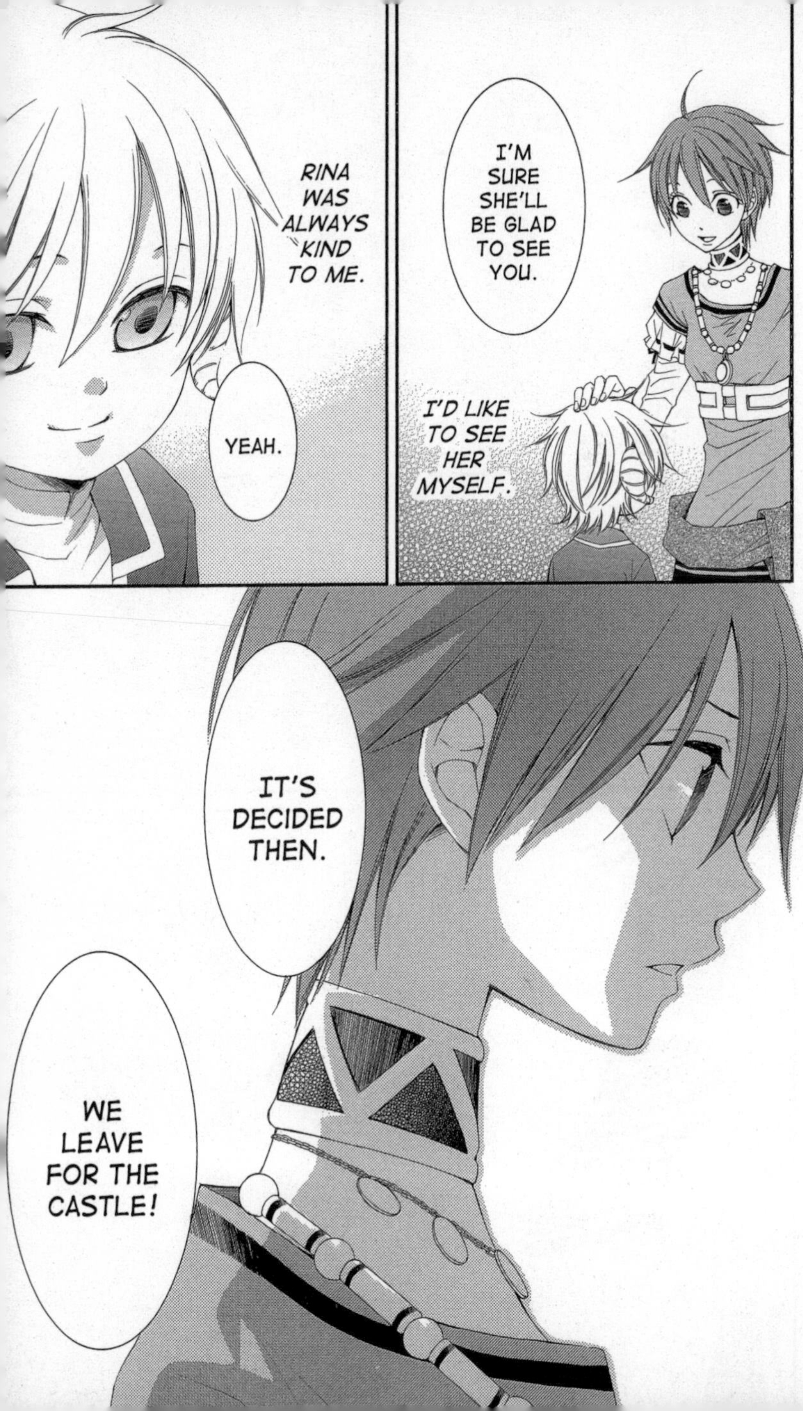
I'M SURE SHE'LL BE GLAD TO SEE YOU.
I'D LIKE TO SEE HER MYSELF.
RINA WAS ALWAYS KIND TO ME.
YEAH.
IT'S DECIDED THEN.
WE LEAVE FOR THE CASTLE!

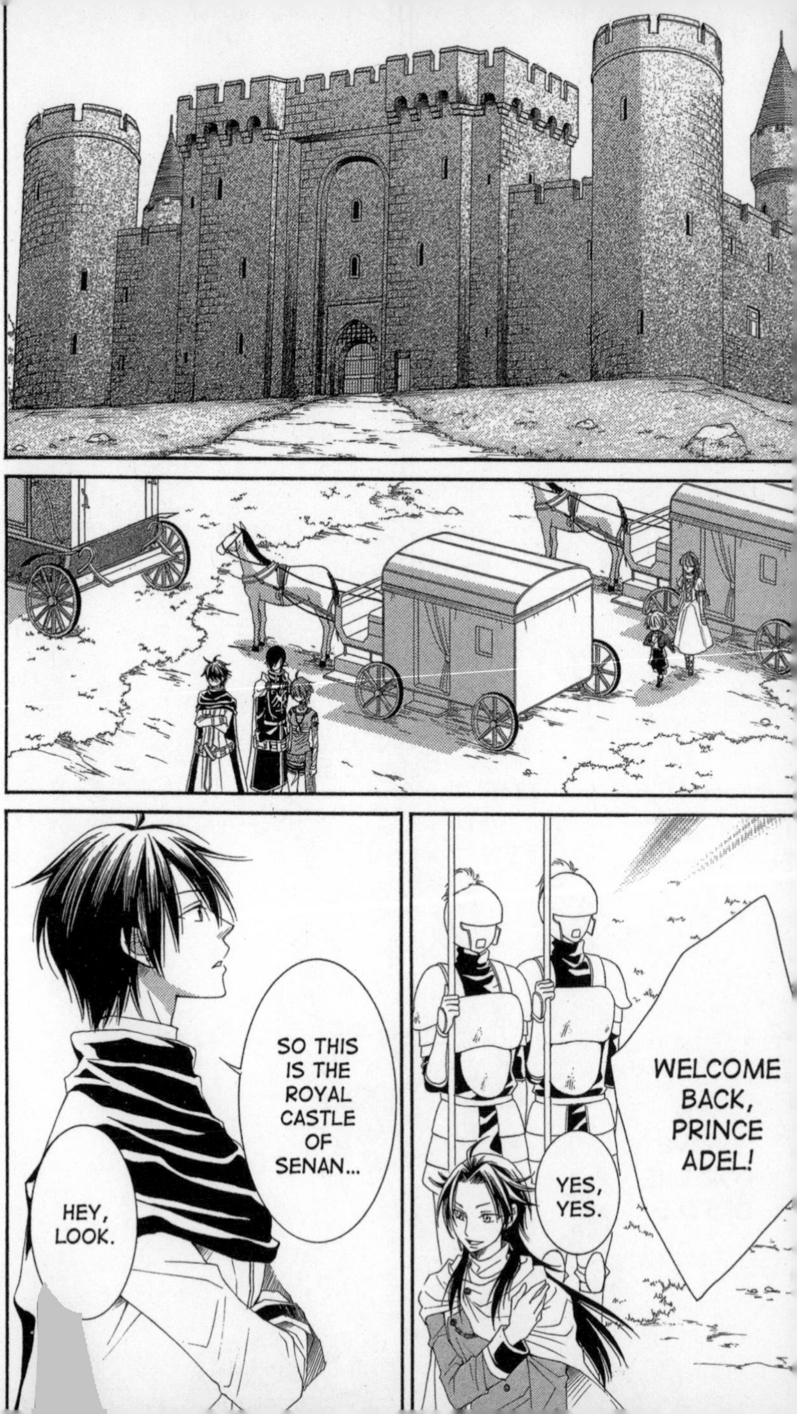
WELCOME BACK, PRINCE ADEL!
YES, YES.
SO THIS IS THE ROYAL CASTLE OF SENAN...
HEY, LOOK.

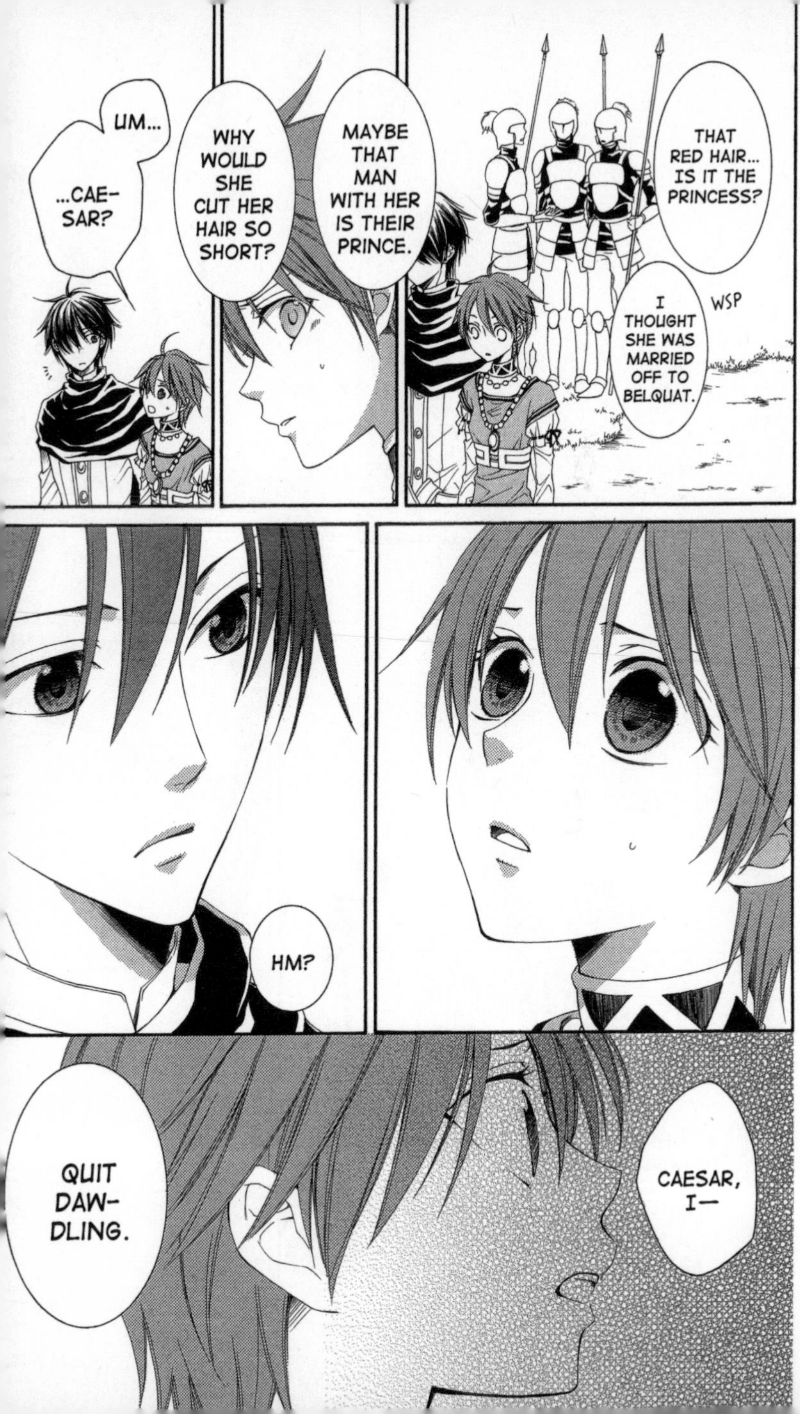
THAT RED HAIR... IS IT THE PRINCESS?
I THOUGHT SHE WAS MARRIED OFF TO BELQUAT.
WSP
MAYBE THAT MAN WITH HER IS THEIR PRINCE.
WHY WOULD SHE CUT HER HAIR SO SHORT?
UM...
...CAE-SAR?
HM?
CAESAR, I—
QUIT DAW-DLING.

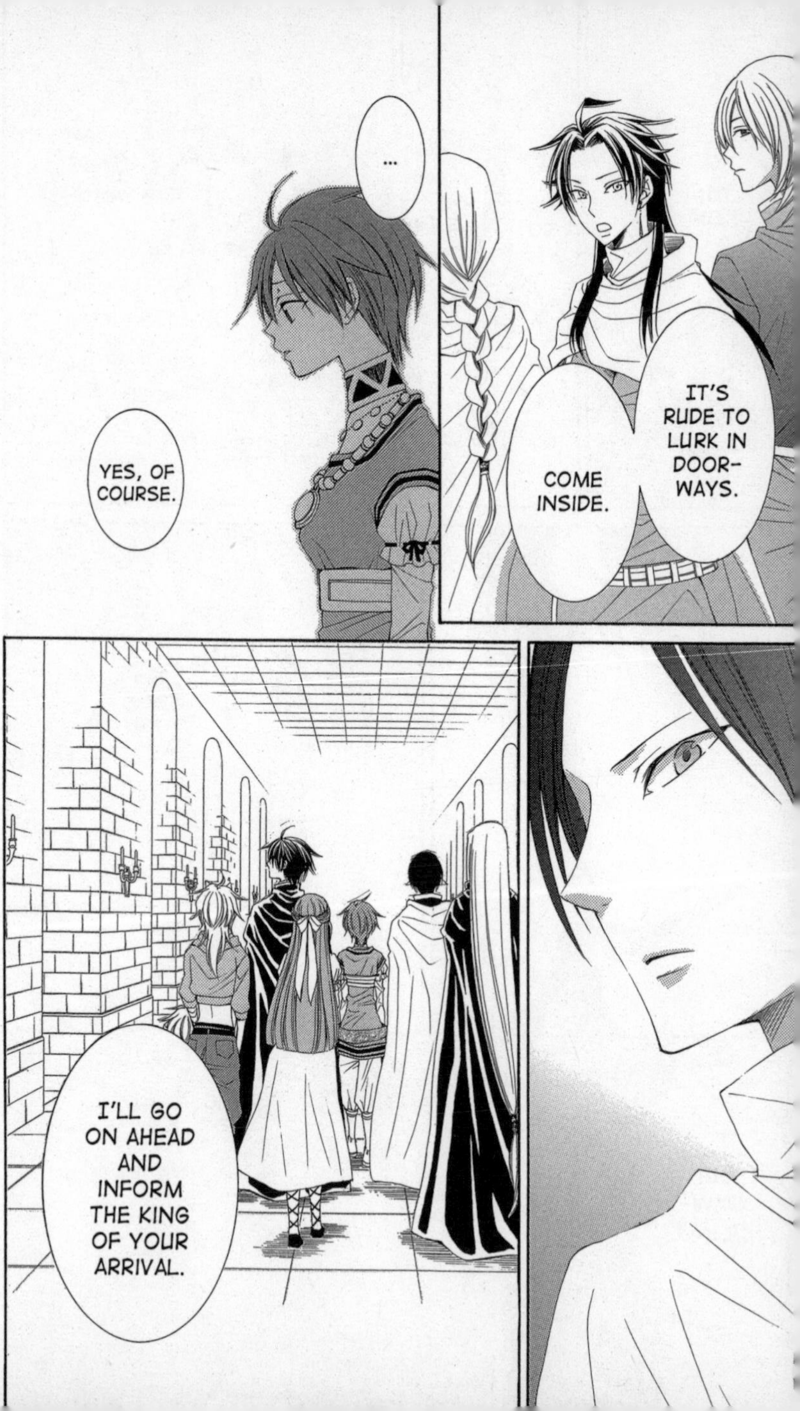
IT'S RUDE TO LURK IN DOORWAYS.
COME INSIDE.
...
YES, OF COURSE.
I'LL GO ON AHEAD AND INFORM THE KING OF YOUR ARRIVAL.

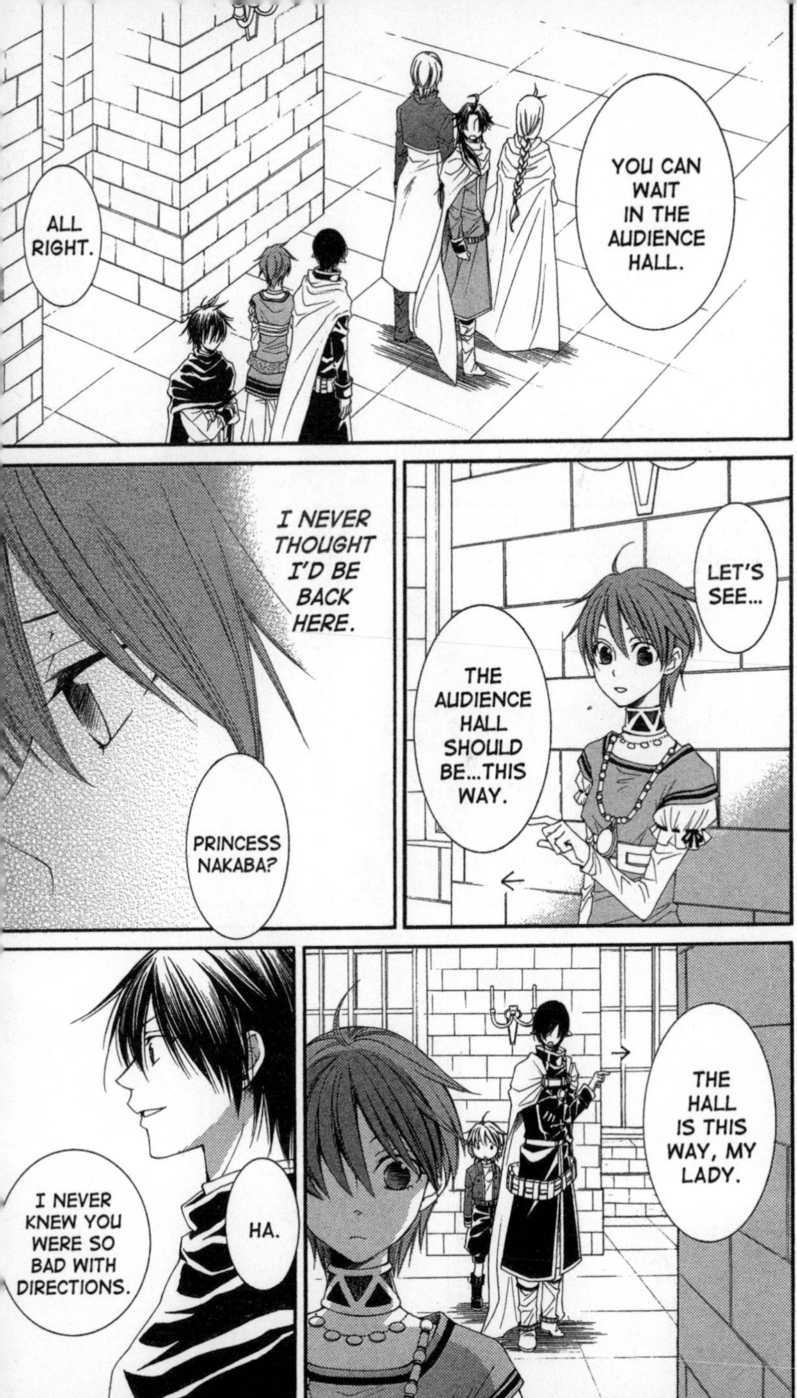

YOU CAN WAIT IN THE AUDIENCE HALL.
ALL RIGHT.
LET'S SEE...
THE AUDIENCE HALL SHOULD BE...THIS WAY.
I NEVER THOUGHT I'D BE BACK HERE.
PRINCESS NAKABA?
THE HALL IS THIS WAY, MY LADY.
HA.
I NEVER KNEW YOU WERE SO BAD WITH DIRECTIONS.

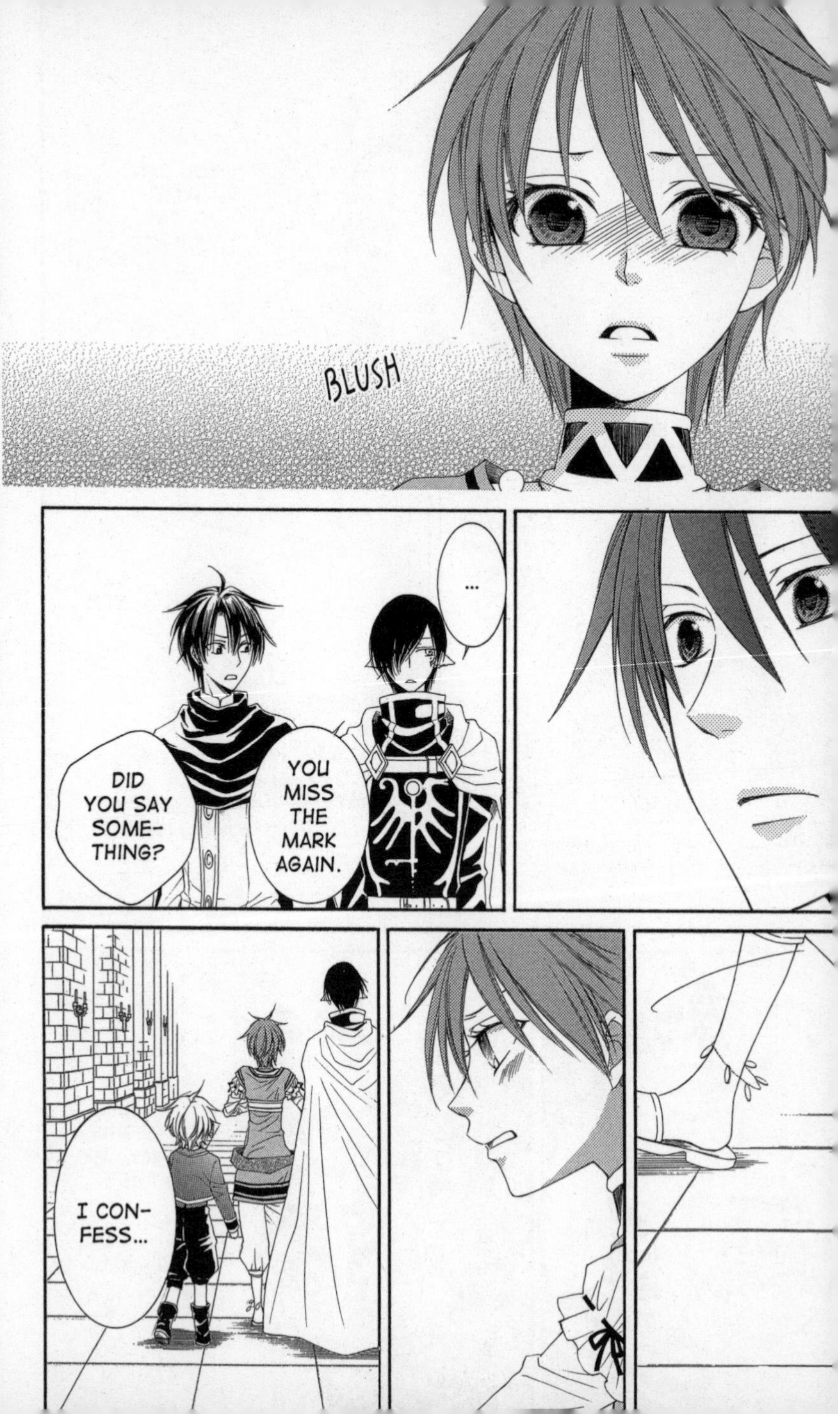

BLUSH
...
YOU MISS THE MARK AGAIN.
DID YOU SAY SOME-THING?
......
I CON-FESS...

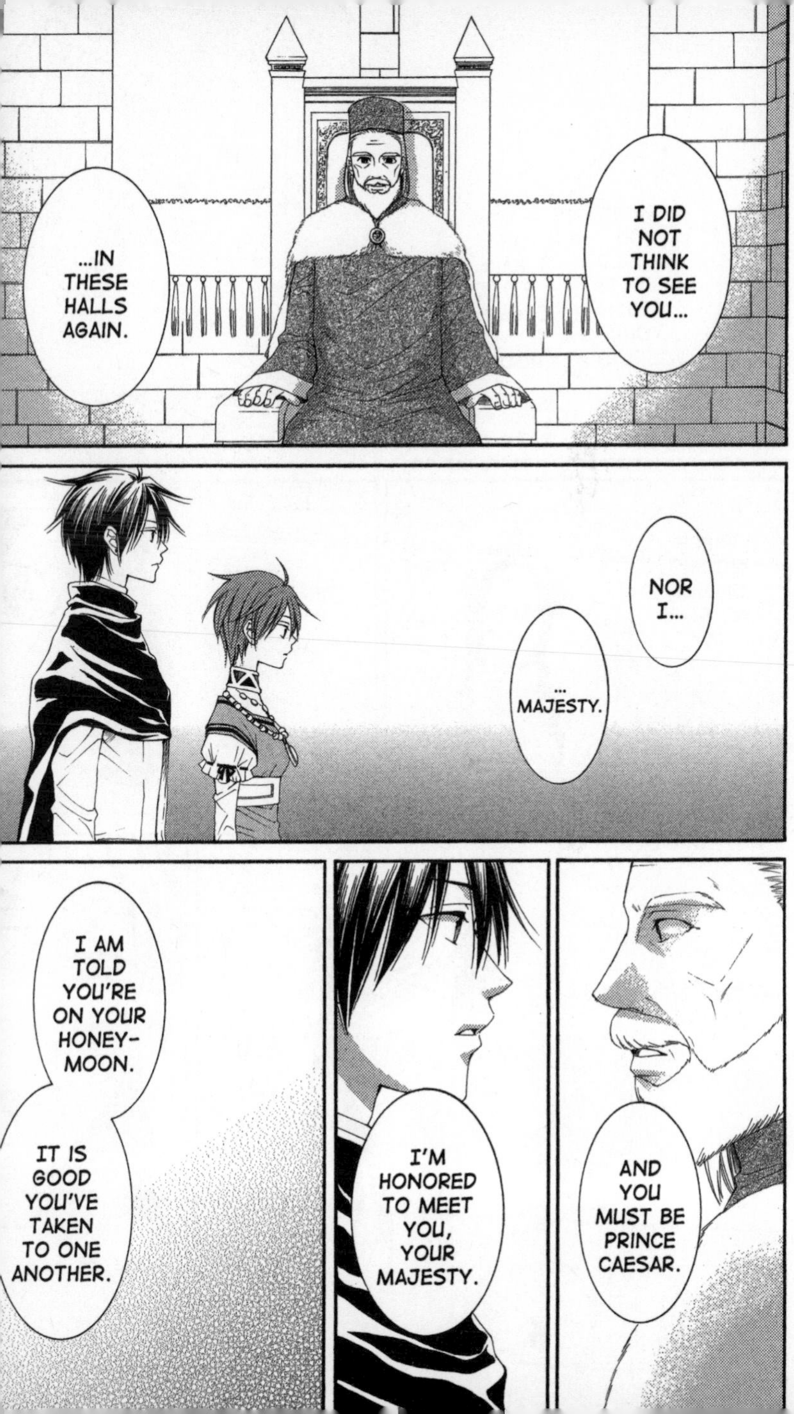
I DID NOT THINK TO SEE YOU...
...IN THESE HALLS AGAIN.
NOR I...
... MAJESTY.
AND YOU MUST BE PRINCE CAESAR.
I'M HONORED TO MEET YOU, YOUR MAJESTY.
I AM TOLD YOU'RE ON YOUR HONEY-MOON.
IT IS GOOD YOU'VE TAKEN TO ONE ANOTHER.

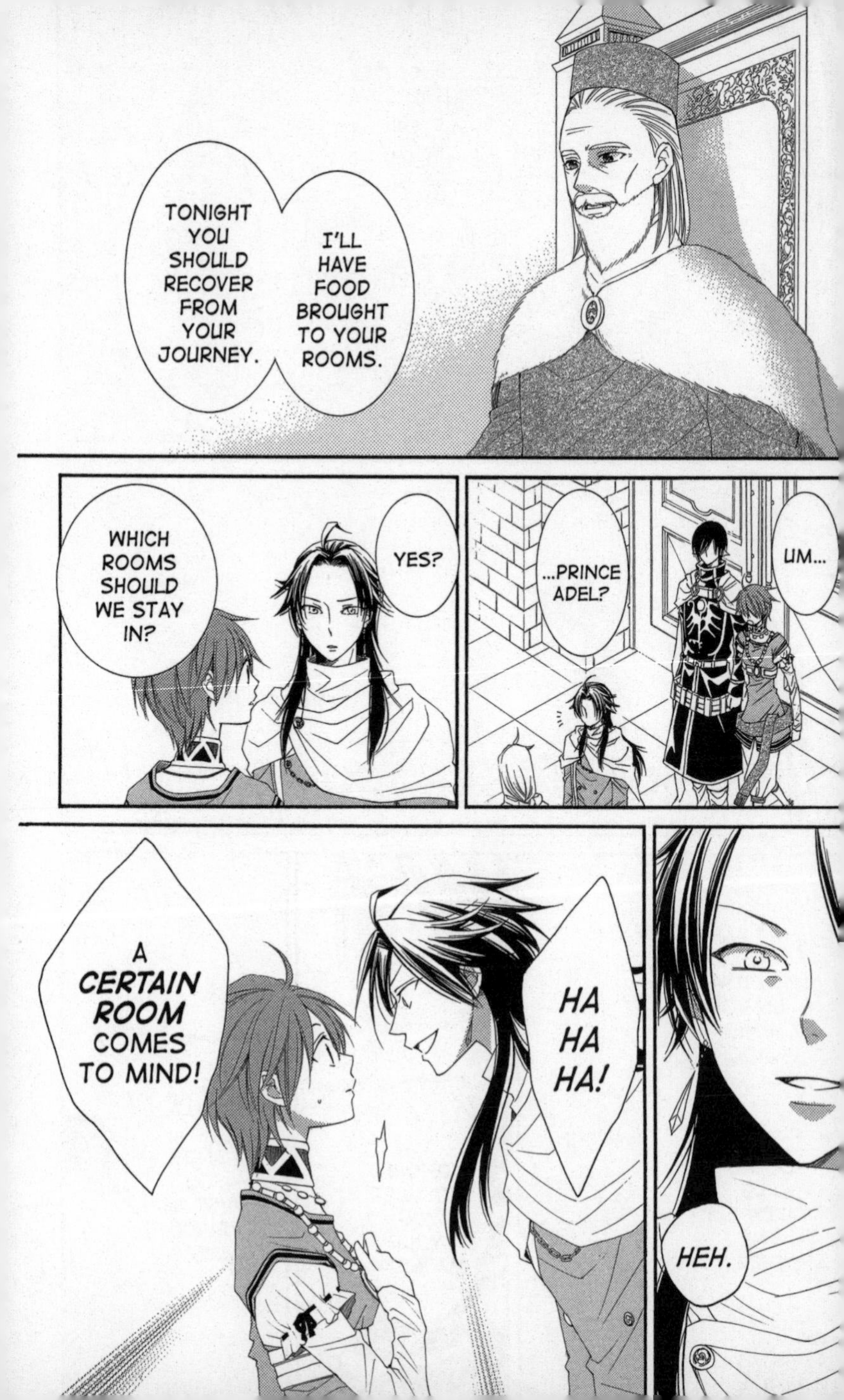
I'LL HAVE FOOD BROUGHT TO YOUR ROOMS.
TONIGHT YOU SHOULD RECOVER FROM YOUR JOURNEY.
UM...
...PRINCE ADEL?
YES?
WHICH ROOMS SHOULD WE STAY IN?
HEH.
HA HA HA!
A CERTAIN ROOM COMES TO MIND!

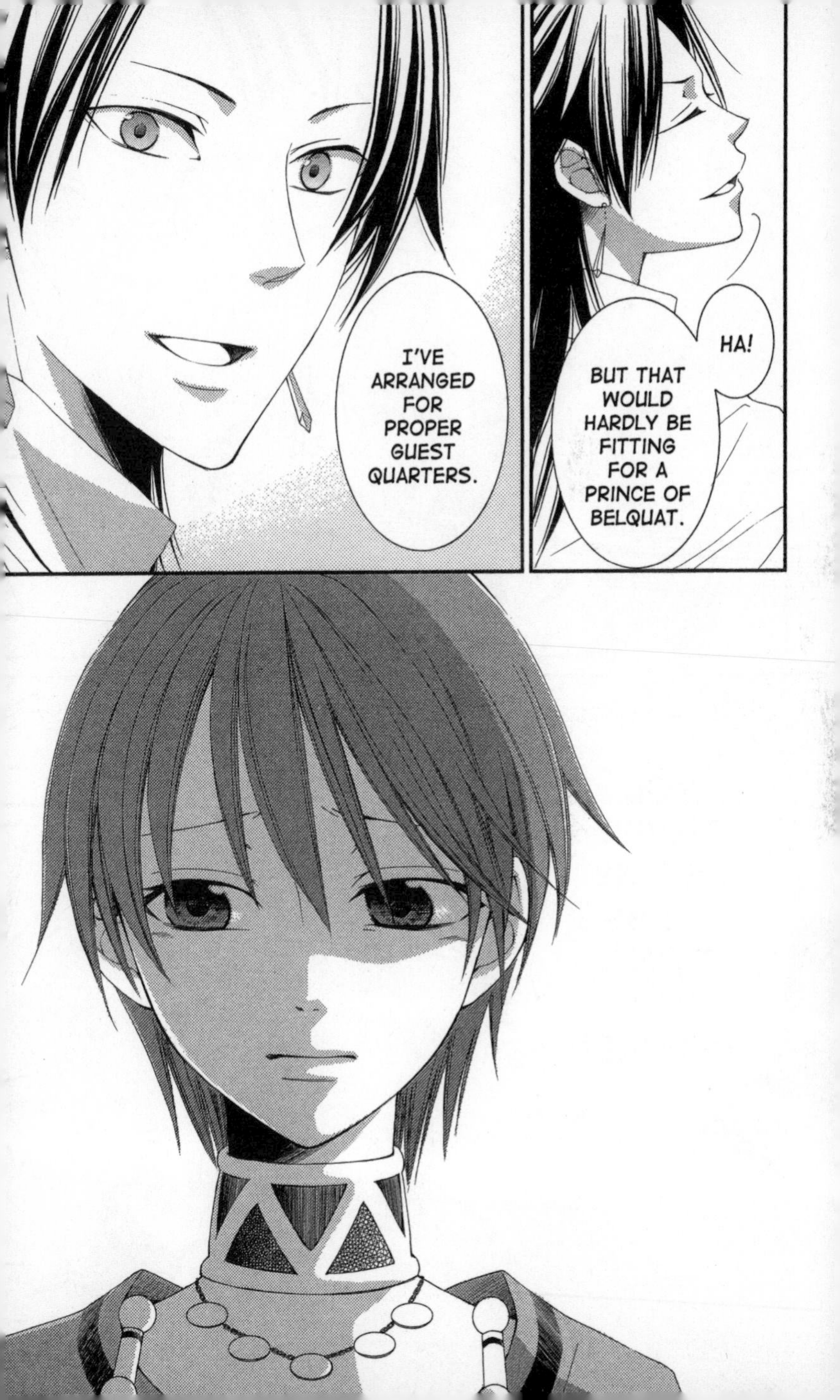
HA!
BUT THAT WOULD HARDLY BE FITTING FOR A PRINCE OF BELQUAT.
I'VE ARRANGED FOR PROPER GUEST QUARTERS.

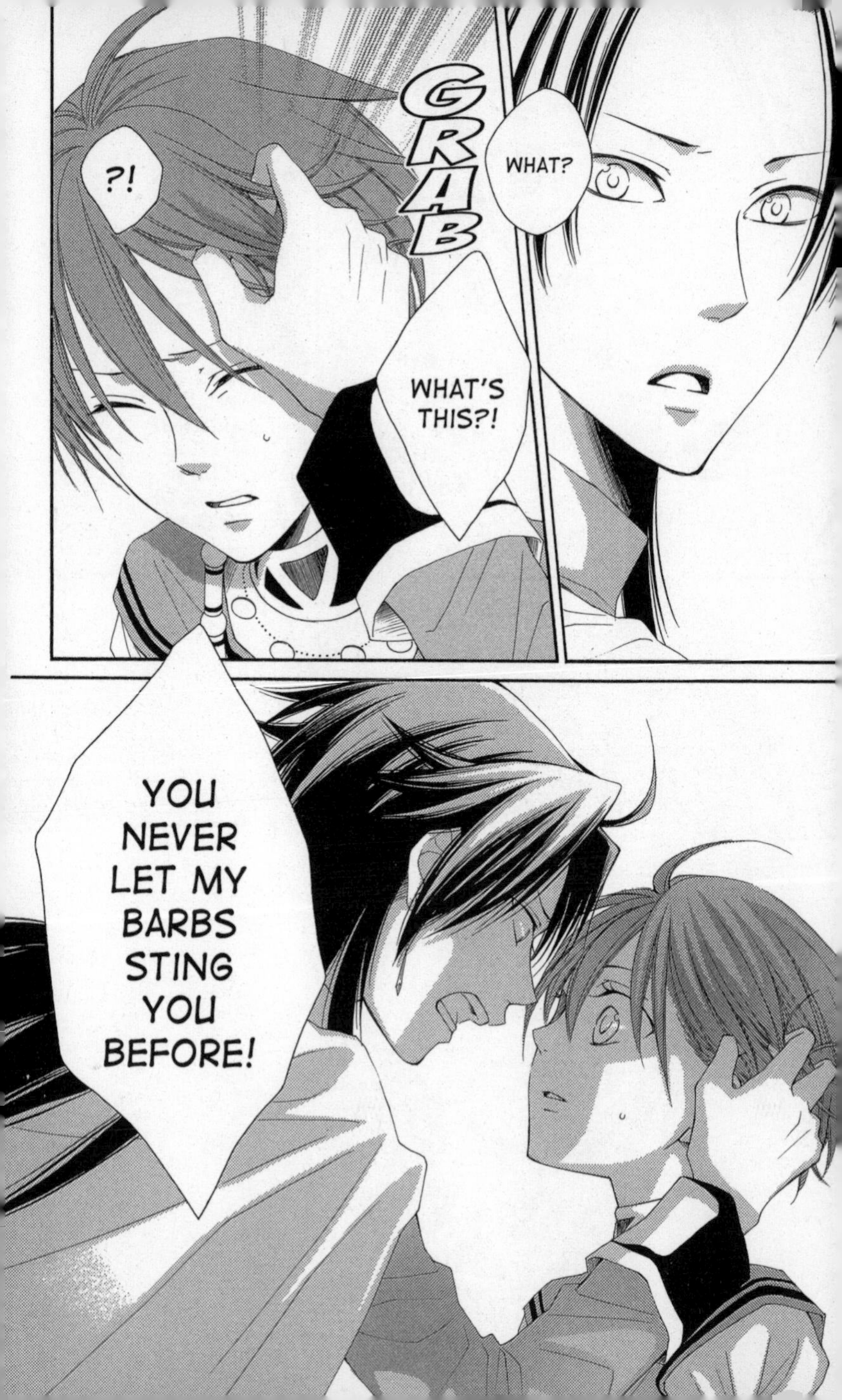
WHAT?
GRAB
?!
WHAT'S THIS?!
YOU NEVER LET MY BARBS STING YOU BEFORE!

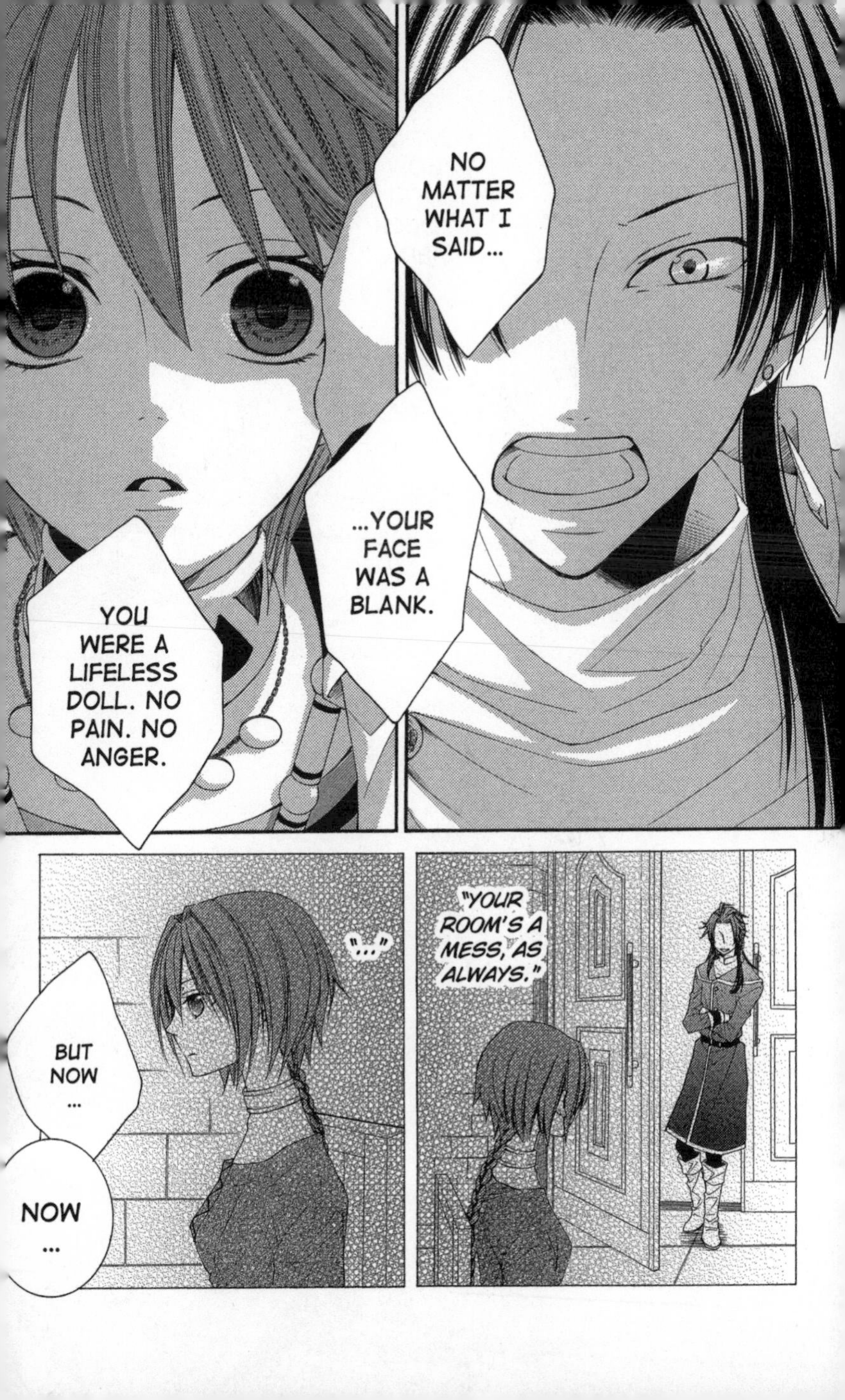
NO MATTER WHAT I SAID...
...YOUR FACE WAS A BLANK.
YOU WERE A LIFELESS DOLL. NO PAIN. NO ANGER.
"YOUR ROOM'S A MESS, AS ALWAYS."
"..."
BUT NOW ...
NOW ...

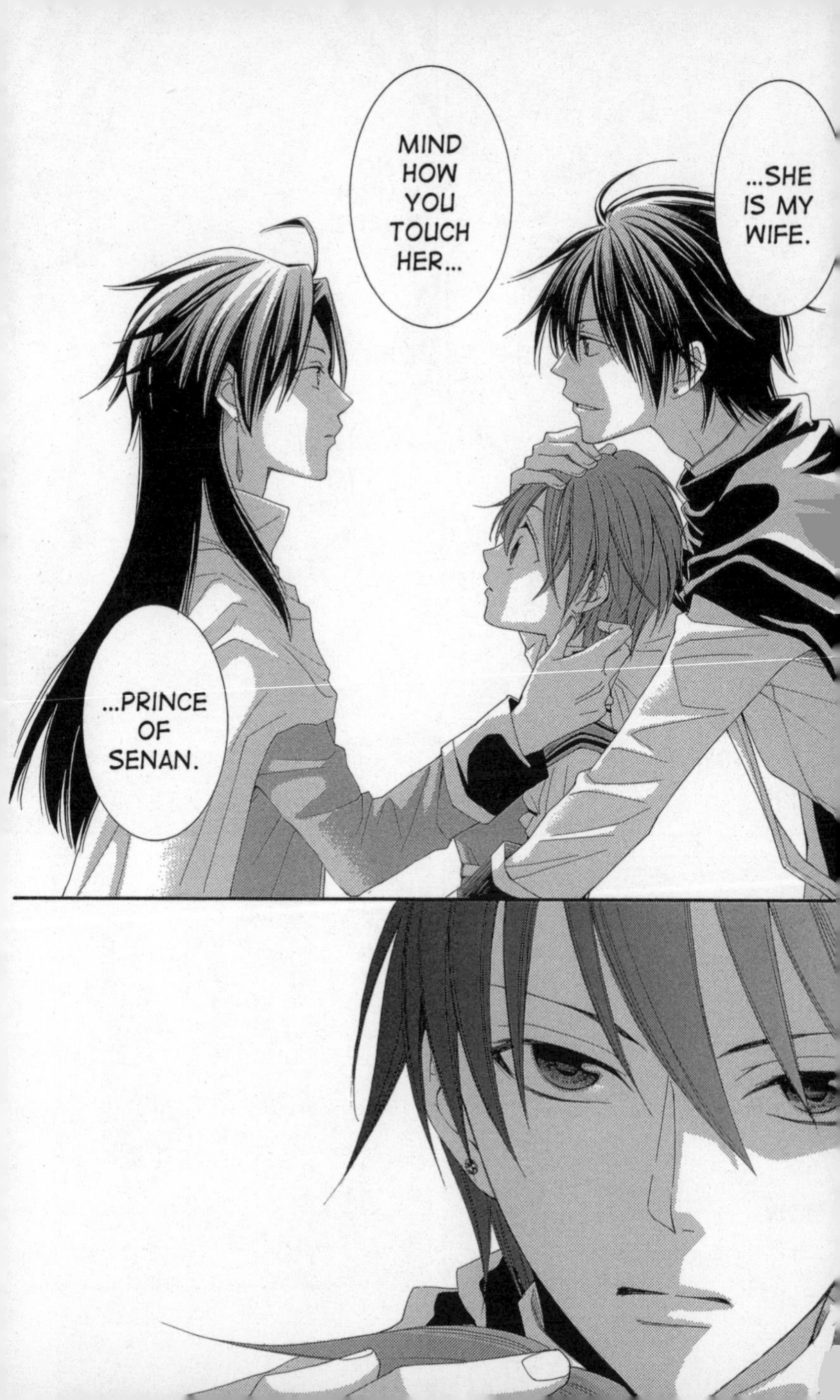
...SHE IS MY WIFE.
MIND HOW YOU TOUCH HER...
...PRINCE OF SENAN.

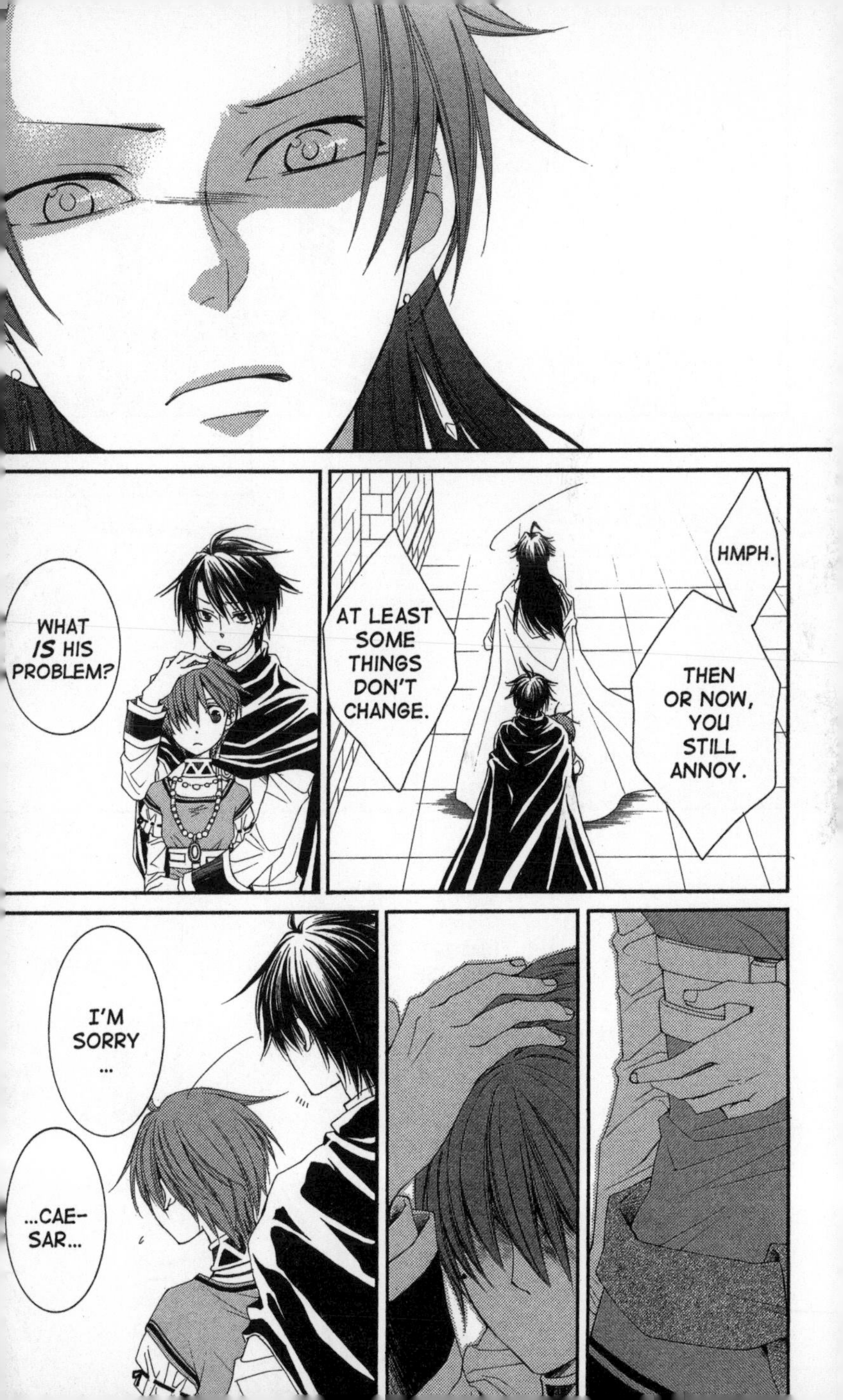
HMPH.
THEN OR NOW, YOU STILL ANNOY.
AT LEAST SOME THINGS DON'T CHANGE.
WHAT *IS* HIS PROBLEM?
I'M SORRY ...
...CAE-SAR...

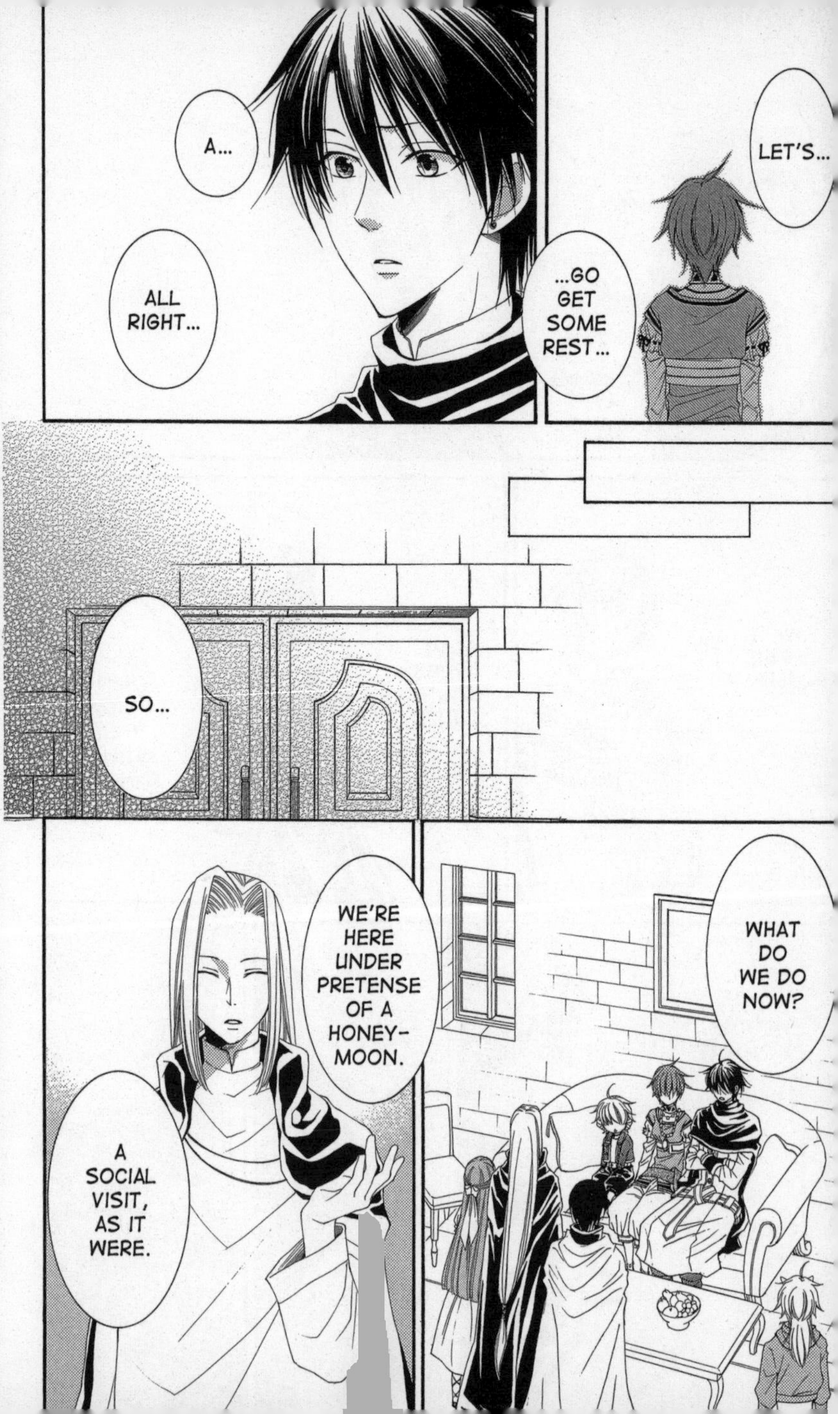
LET'S...
...GO GET SOME REST...
A...
ALL RIGHT...
SO...
WHAT DO WE DO NOW?
WE'RE HERE UNDER PRETENSE OF A HONEY-MOON.
A SOCIAL VISIT, AS IT WERE.

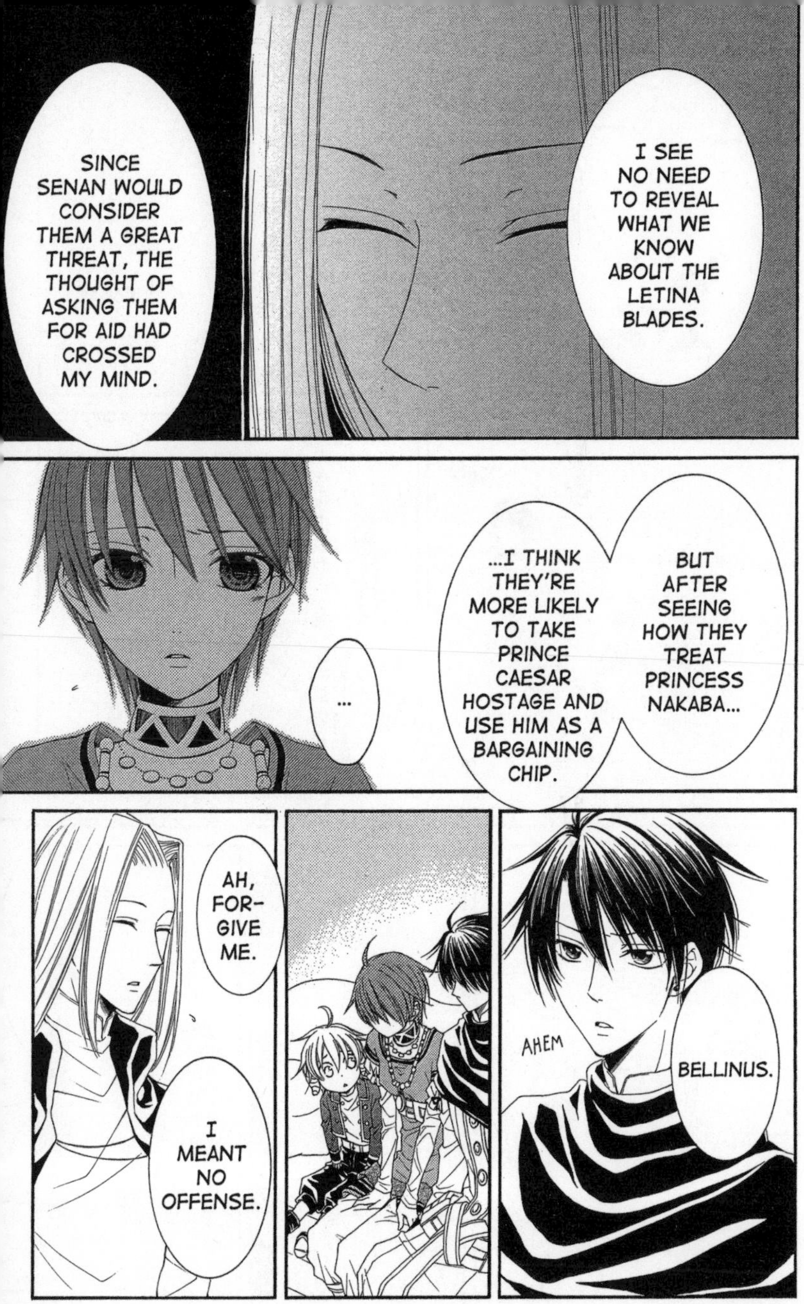
I SEE NO NEED TO REVEAL WHAT WE KNOW ABOUT THE LETINA BLADES.
SINCE SENAN WOULD CONSIDER THEM A GREAT THREAT, THE THOUGHT OF ASKING THEM FOR AID HAD CROSSED MY MIND.
BUT AFTER SEEING HOW THEY TREAT PRINCESS NAKABA...
...I THINK THEY'RE MORE LIKELY TO TAKE PRINCE CAESAR HOSTAGE AND USE HIM AS A BARGAINING CHIP.
...
AHEM
BELLINUS.
AH, FOR-GIVE ME.
I MEANT NO OFFENSE.

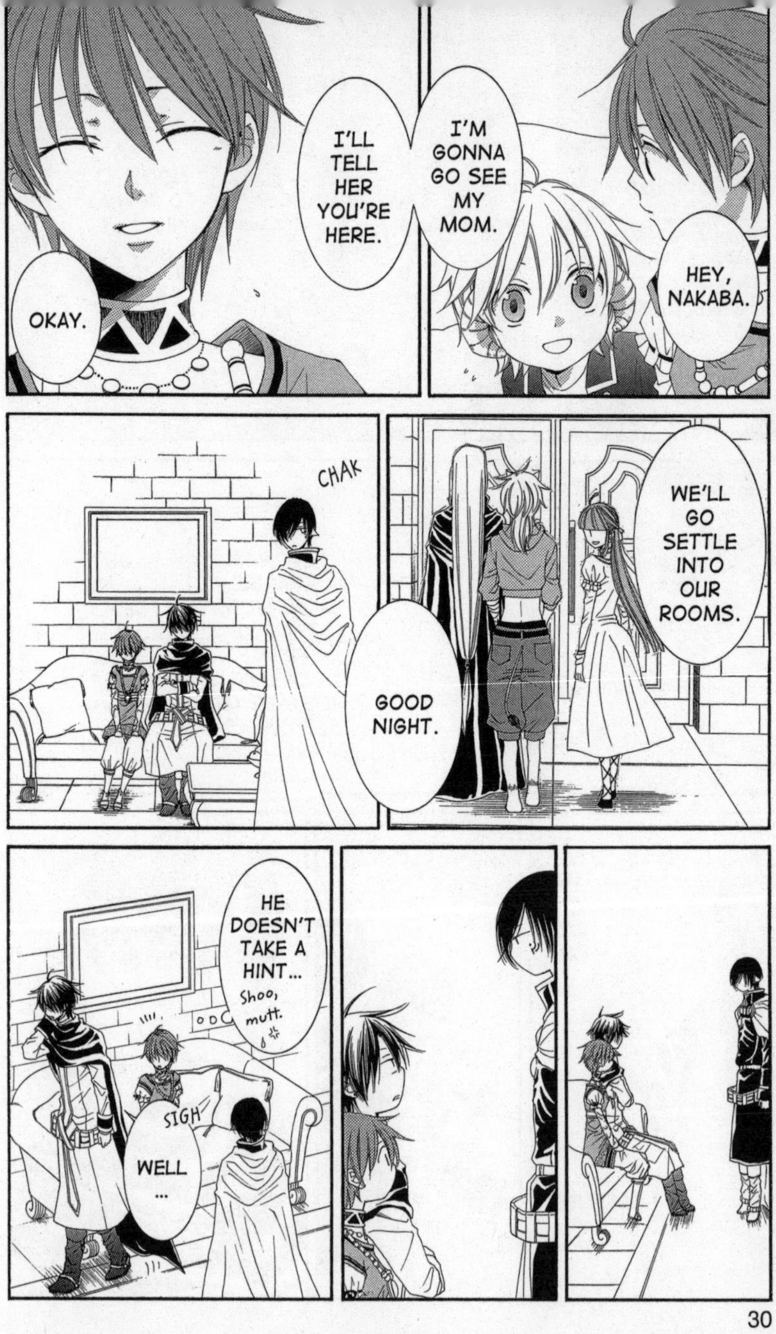
HEY, NAKABA.
I'M GONNA GO SEE MY MOM.
I'LL TELL HER YOU'RE HERE.
OKAY.
WE'LL GO SETTLE INTO OUR ROOMS.
GOOD NIGHT.
CHAK
HE DOESN'T TAKE A HINT...
Shoo, mutt.
SIGH
WELL ...

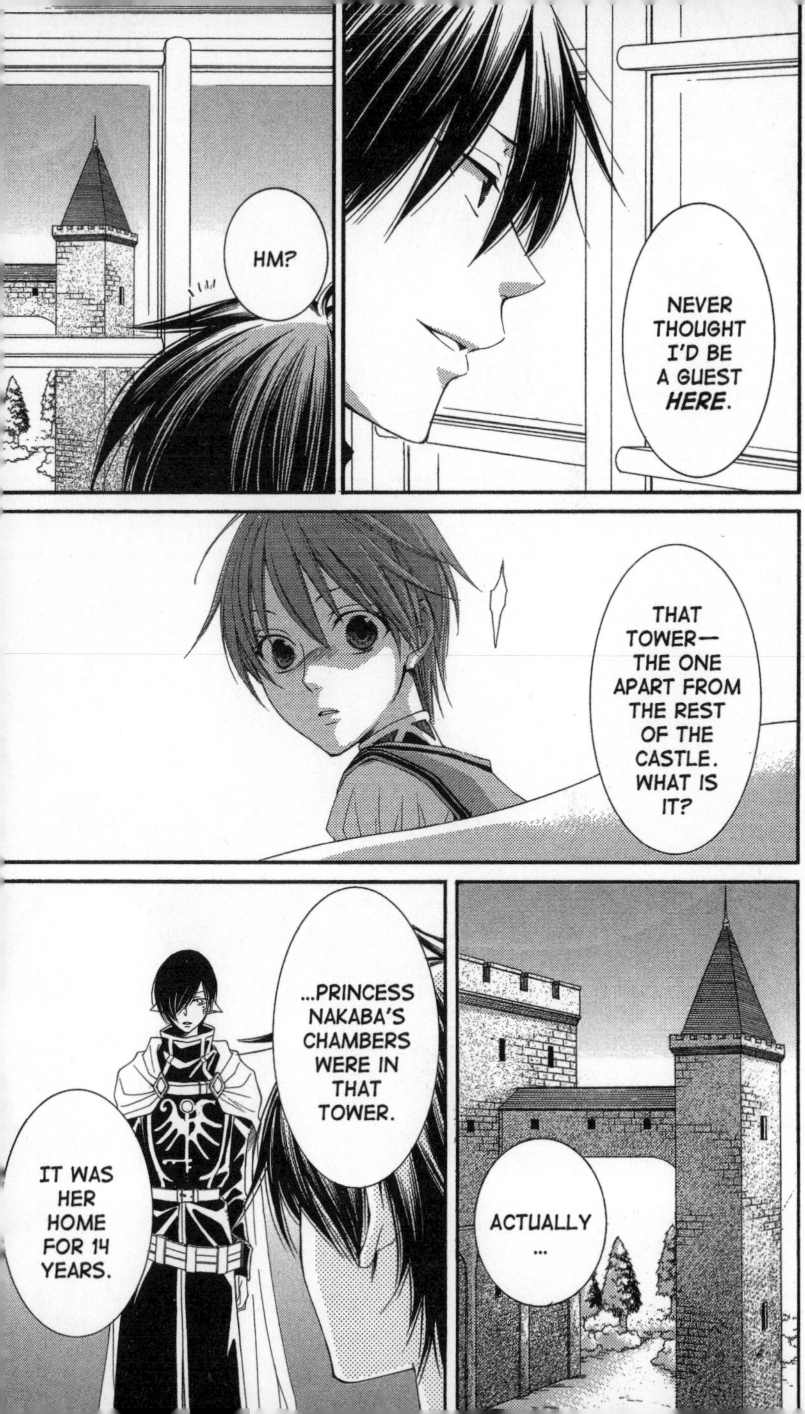
NEVER THOUGHT I'D BE A GUEST *HERE*.
HM?
THAT TOWER—THE ONE APART FROM THE REST OF THE CASTLE. WHAT IS IT?
ACTUALLY ...
...PRINCESS NAKABA'S CHAMBERS WERE IN THAT TOWER.
IT WAS HER HOME FOR 14 YEARS.

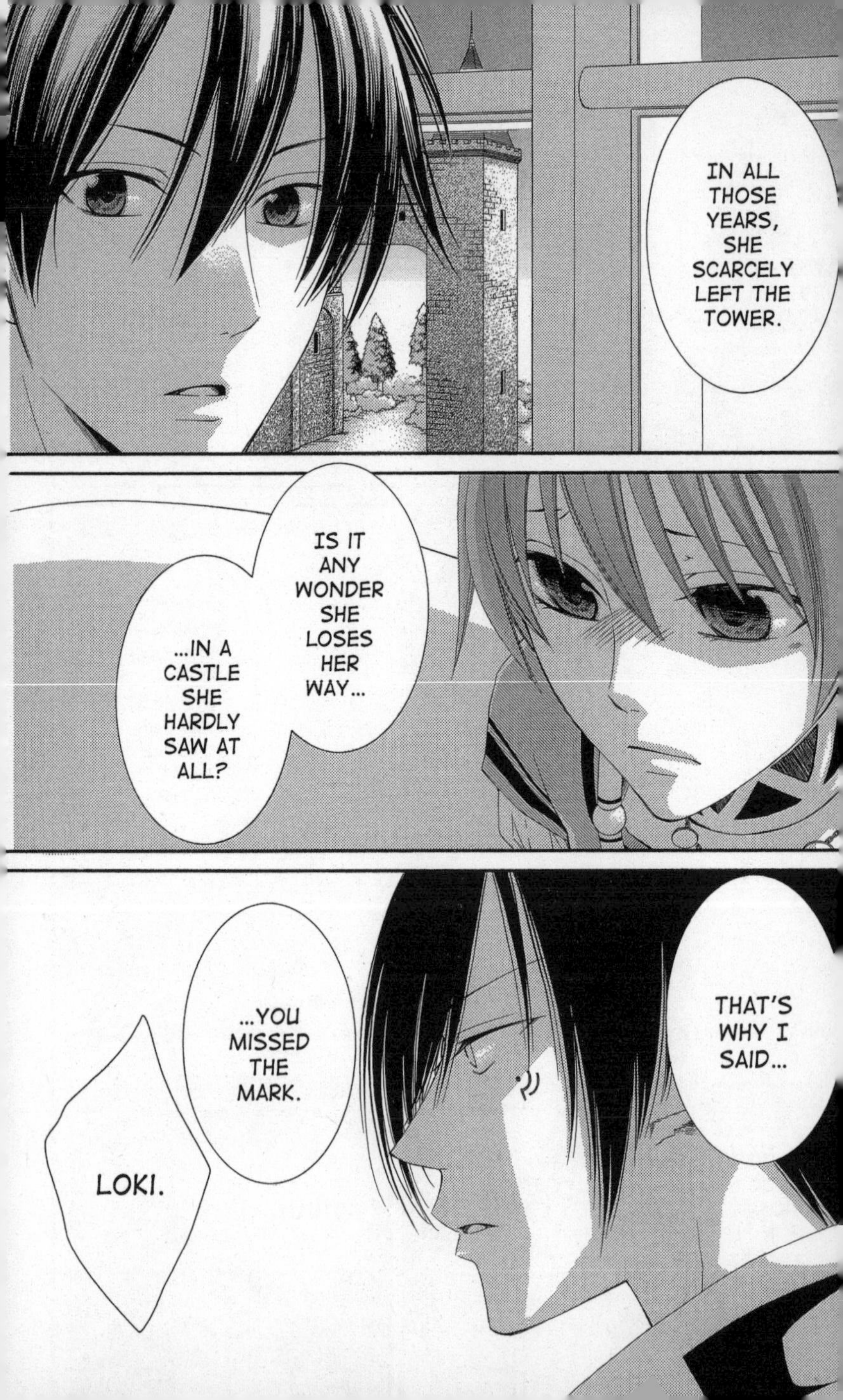
IN ALL THOSE YEARS, SHE SCARCELY LEFT THE TOWER.
IS IT ANY WONDER SHE LOSES HER WAY...
...IN A CASTLE SHE HARDLY SAW AT ALL?
THAT'S WHY I SAID...
...YOU MISSED THE MARK.
LOKI.

PLEASE ...

DON'T SAY ANY MORE!

HEY, WAIT! NAKABA!

DASH

SLAM

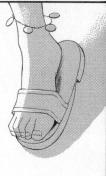

CAESAR KNEW.

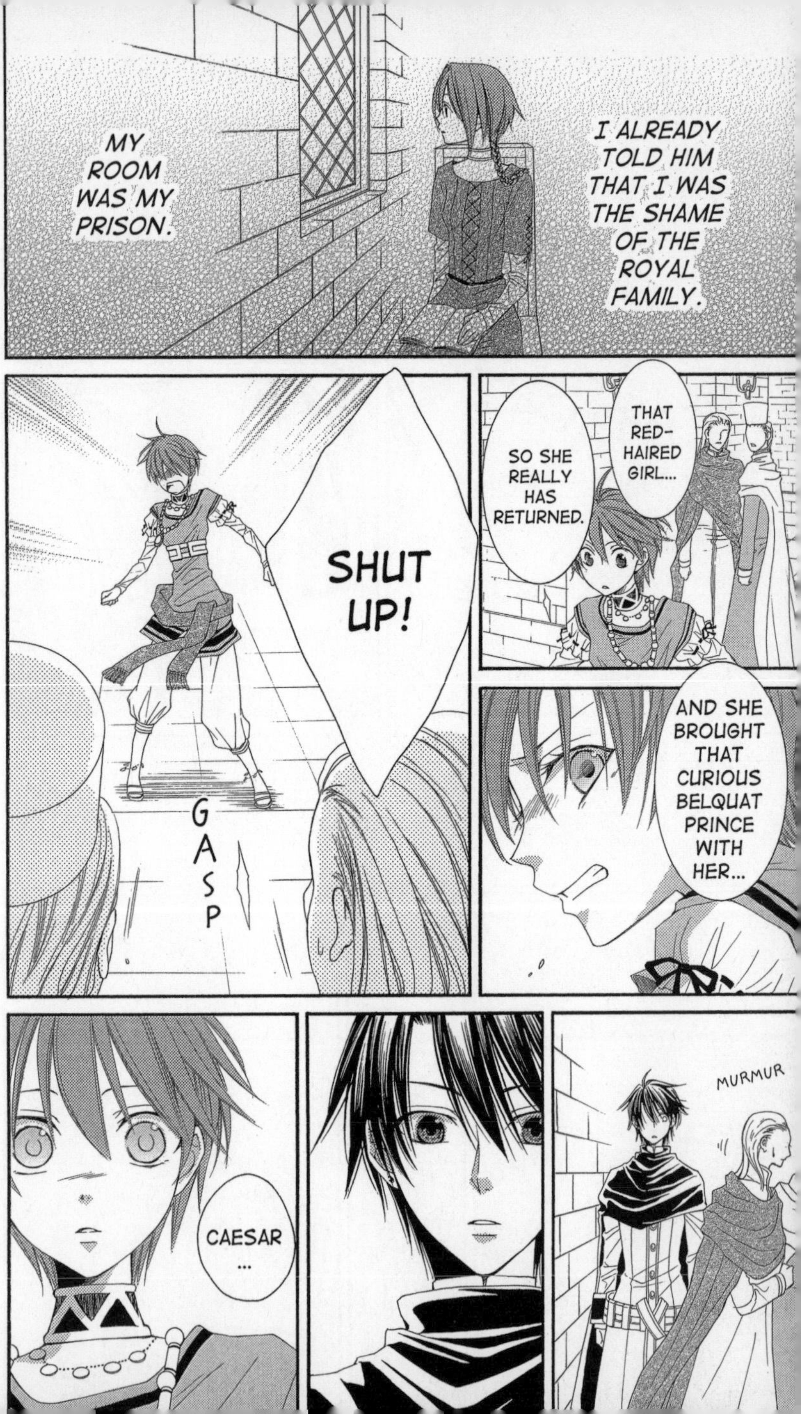
I ALREADY TOLD HIM THAT I WAS THE SHAME OF THE ROYAL FAMILY.
MY ROOM WAS MY PRISON.
THAT RED-HAIRED GIRL...
SO SHE REALLY HAS RETURNED.
AND SHE BROUGHT THAT CURIOUS BELQUAT PRINCE WITH HER...
SHUT UP!
GASP
MURMUR
CAESAR ...

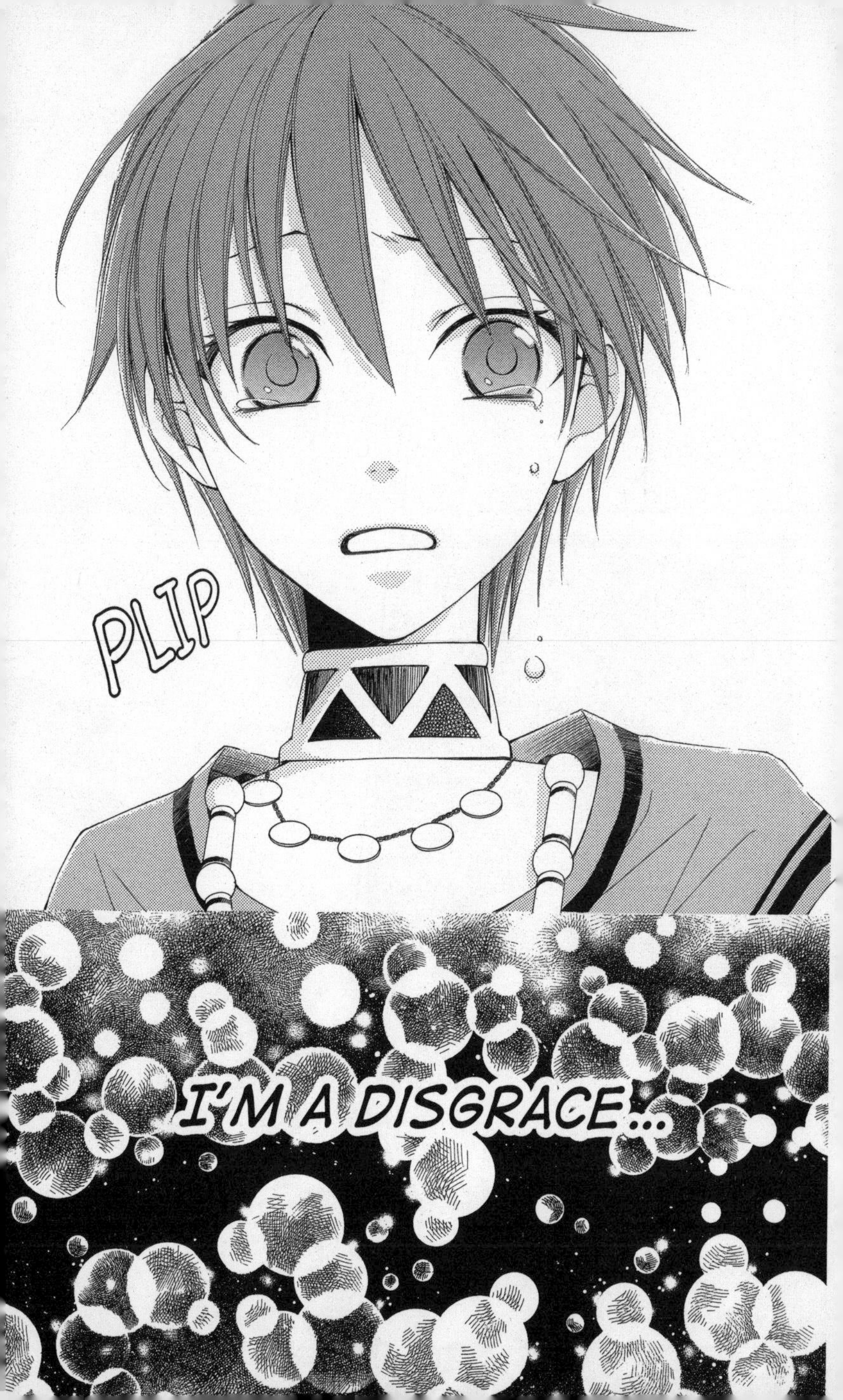
PLIP
I'M A DISGRACE...

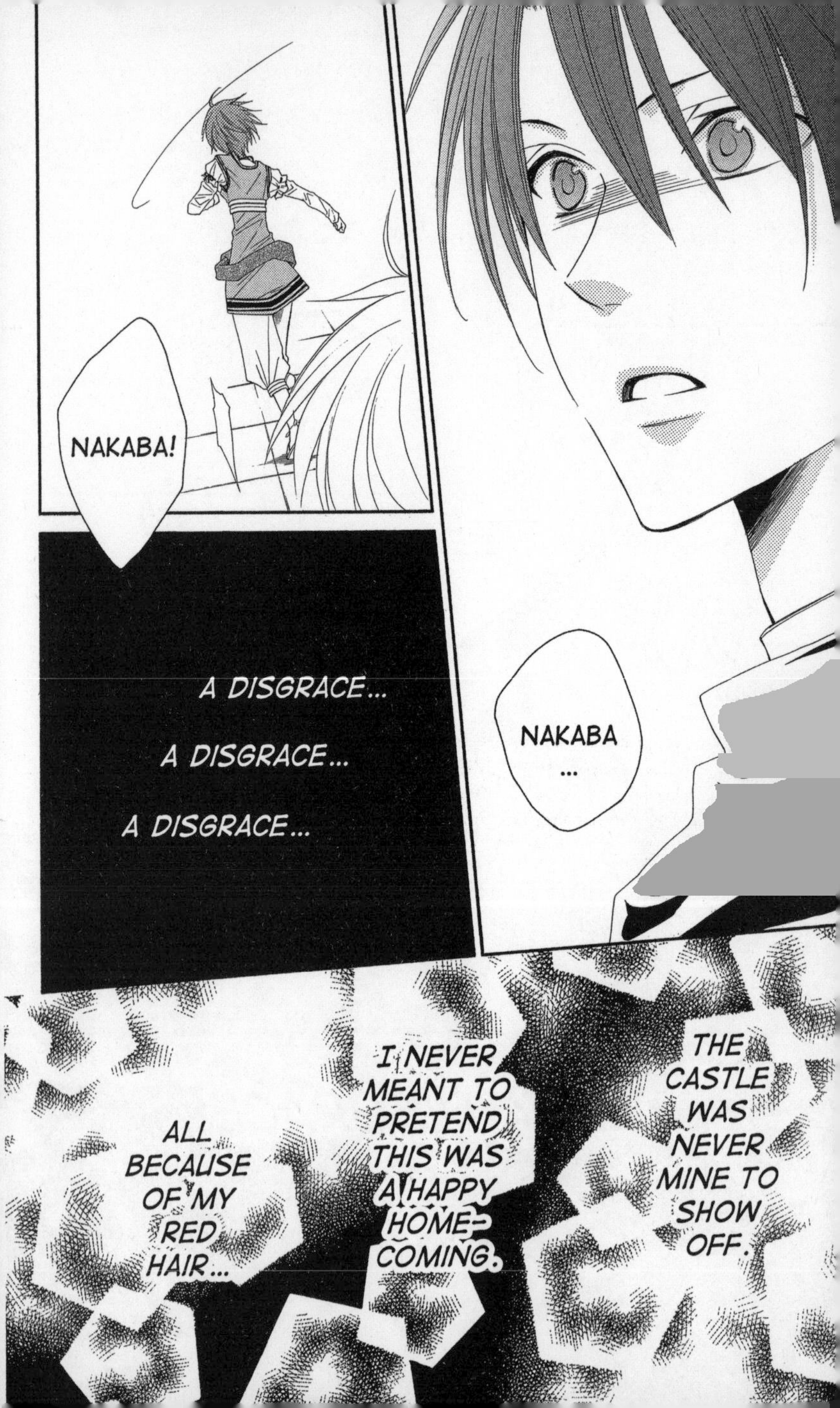
NAKABA...
NAKABA!
A DISGRACE...
A DISGRACE...
A DISGRACE...
THE CASTLE WAS NEVER MINE TO SHOW OFF.
I NEVER MEANT TO PRETEND THIS WAS A HAPPY HOME-COMING.
ALL BECAUSE OF MY RED HAIR...

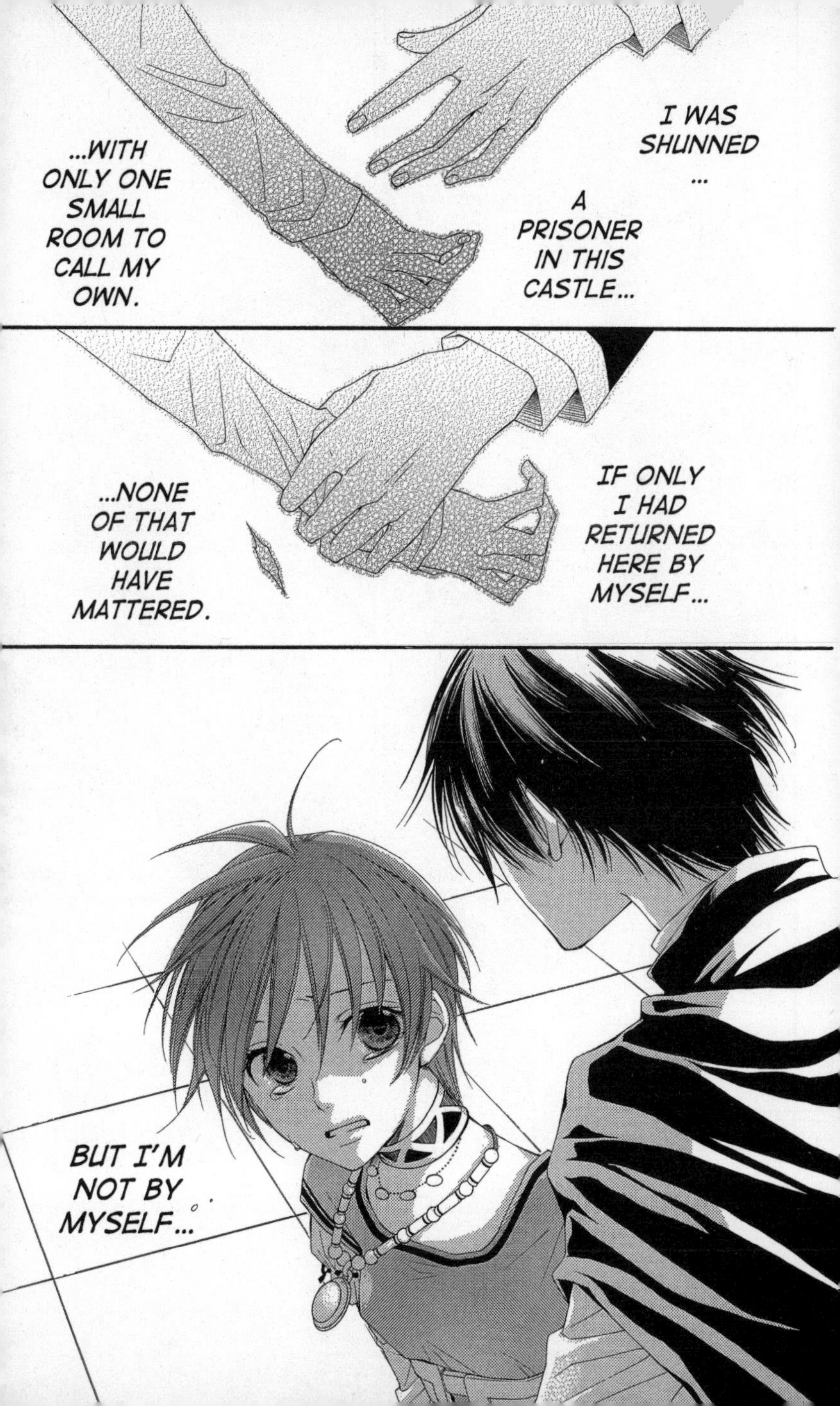
I WAS SHUNNED...
A PRISONER IN THIS CASTLE...
...WITH ONLY ONE SMALL ROOM TO CALL MY OWN.
IF ONLY I HAD RETURNED HERE BY MYSELF...
...NONE OF THAT WOULD HAVE MATTERED.
BUT I'M NOT BY MYSELF...

THEY'RE MAKING FUN OF YOU.

NAKABA?

I'M SORRY.

AND IT'S ALL MY FAULT!

I'M SORRY, CAESAR.

I KNOW...

BUT STILL...

B...

I DON'T CARE ABOUT THAT!

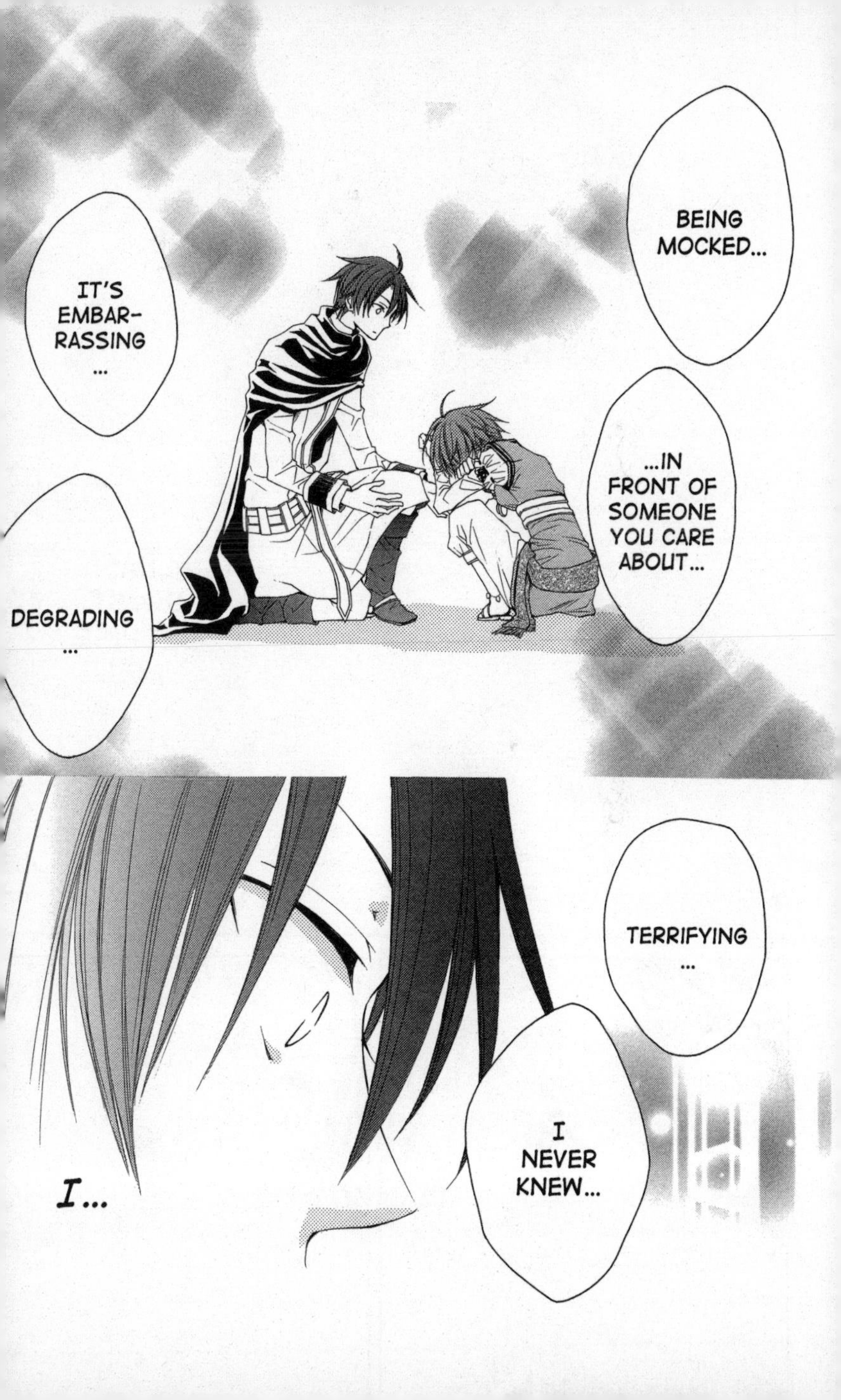
BEING MOCKED...
...IN FRONT OF SOMEONE YOU CARE ABOUT...
IT'S EMBARRASSING...
DEGRADING...
TERRIFYING...
I NEVER KNEW...
I...

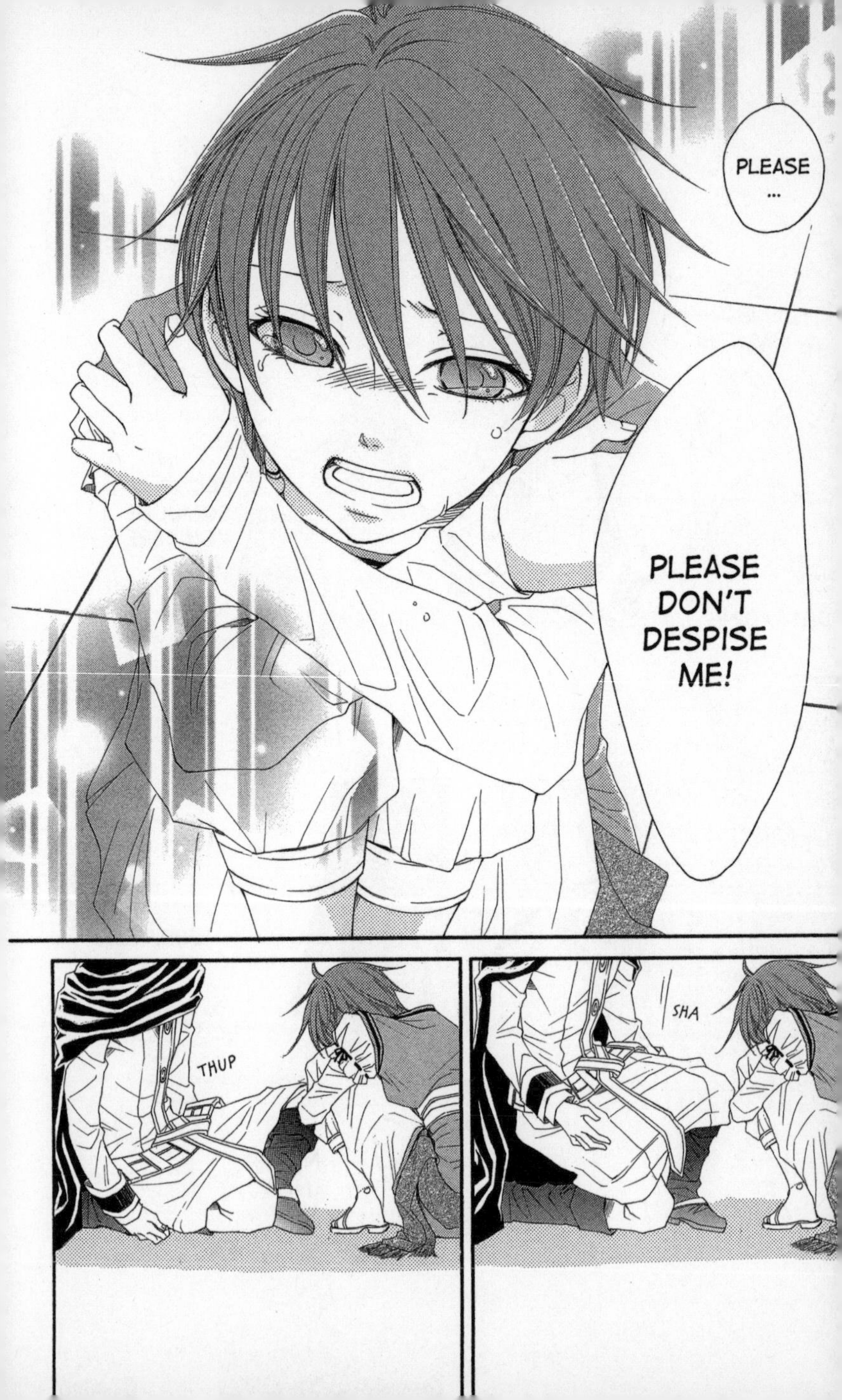
PLEASE ...
PLEASE DON'T DESPISE ME!
SHA
THUP

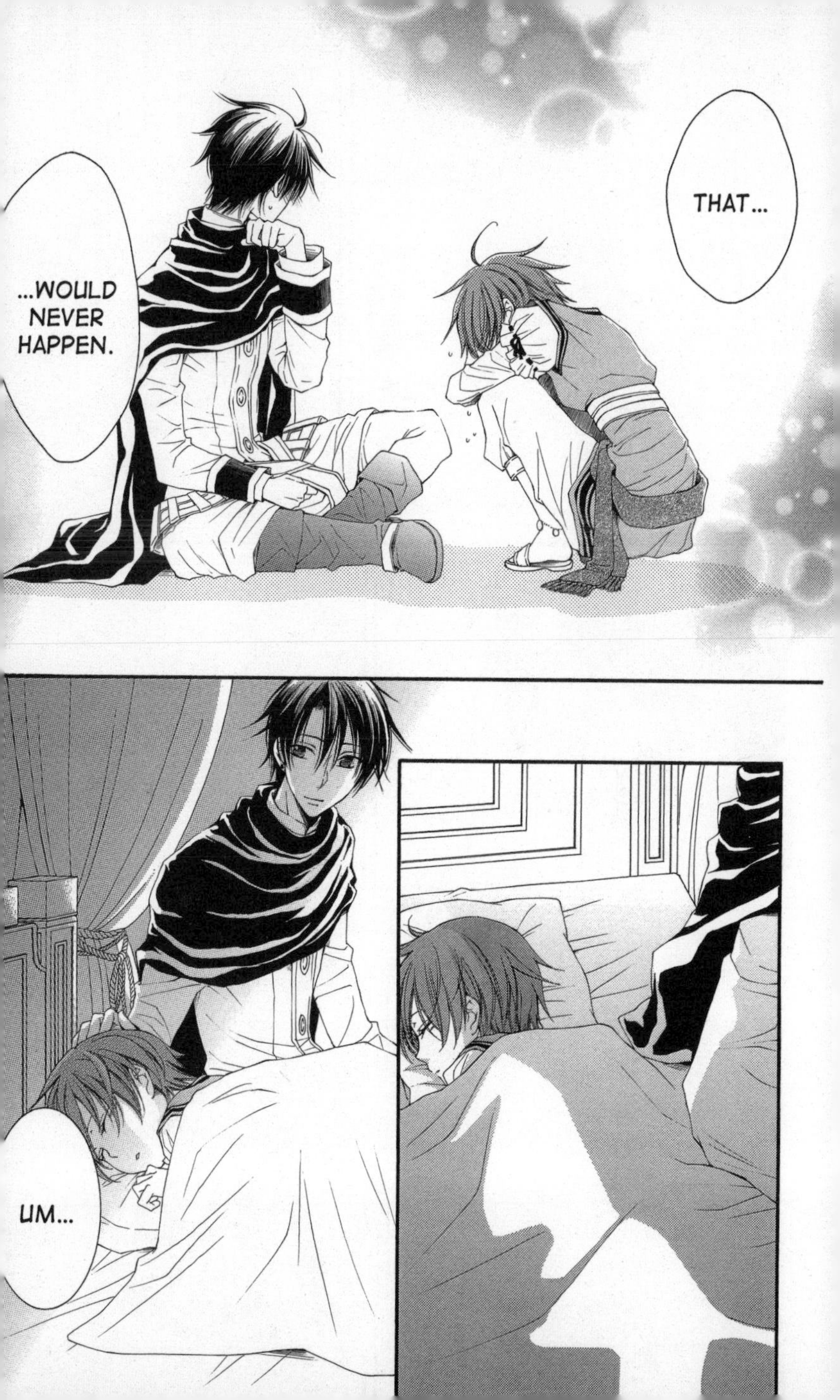
THAT...
...WOULD NEVER HAPPEN.
UM...

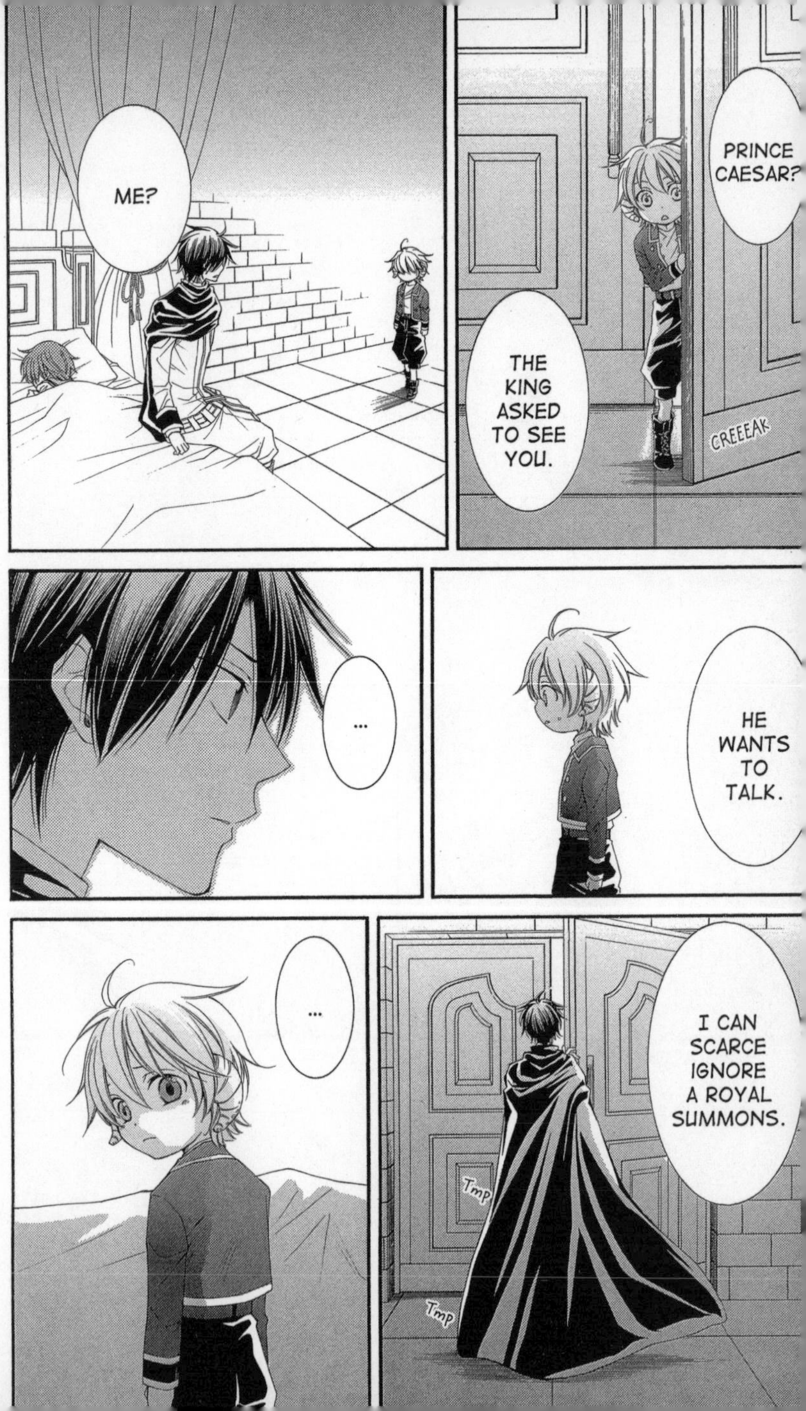
PRINCE CAESAR?
CREEEAK
THE KING ASKED TO SEE YOU.
ME?
HE WANTS TO TALK.
...
I CAN SCARCE IGNORE A ROYAL SUMMONS.
Tmp
Tmp
...

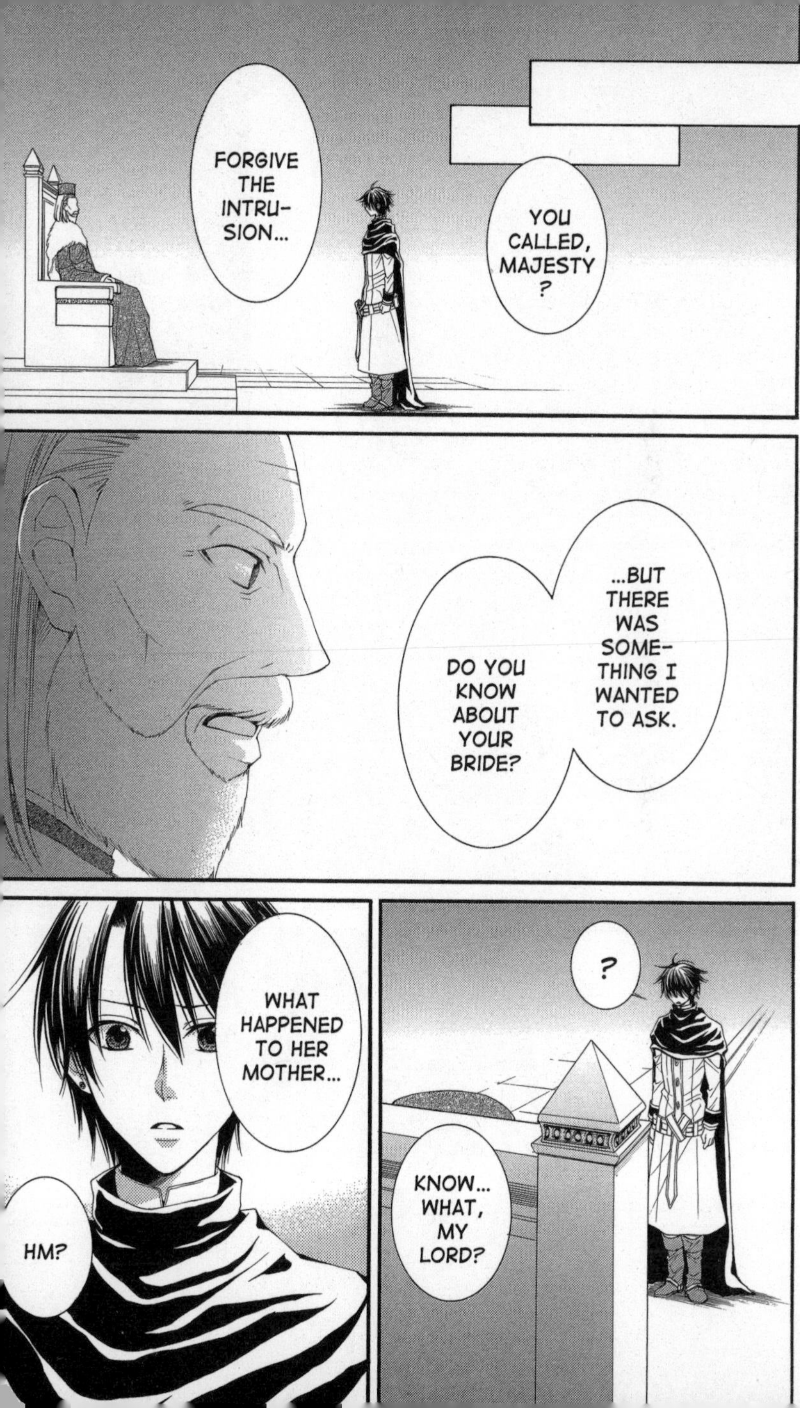
YOU CALLED, MAJESTY?
FORGIVE THE INTRUSION...
...BUT THERE WAS SOMETHING I WANTED TO ASK.
DO YOU KNOW ABOUT YOUR BRIDE?
?
KNOW... WHAT, MY LORD?
WHAT HAPPENED TO HER MOTHER...
HM?

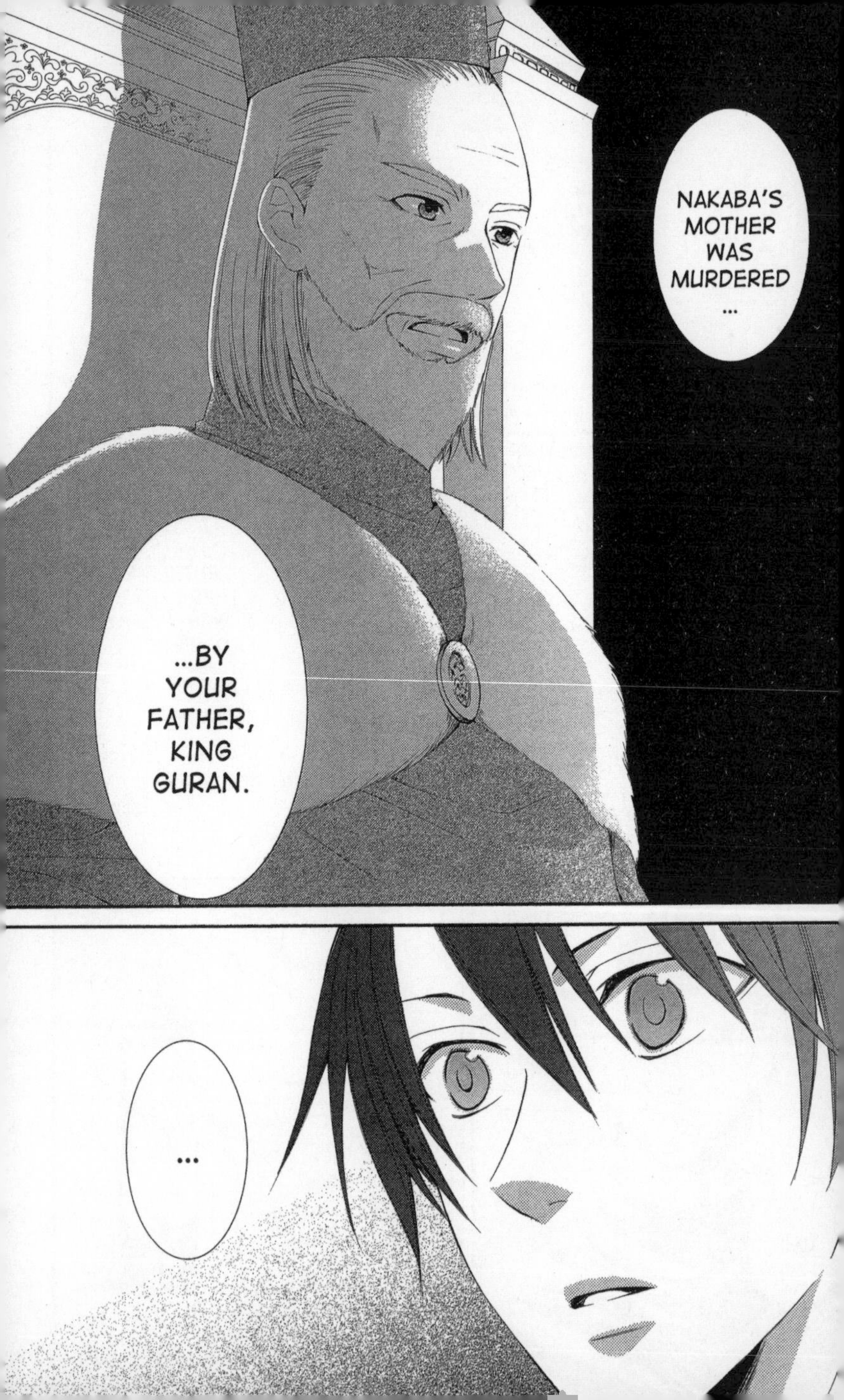
NAKABA'S MOTHER WAS MURDERED ...
...BY YOUR FATHER, KING GURAN.
...

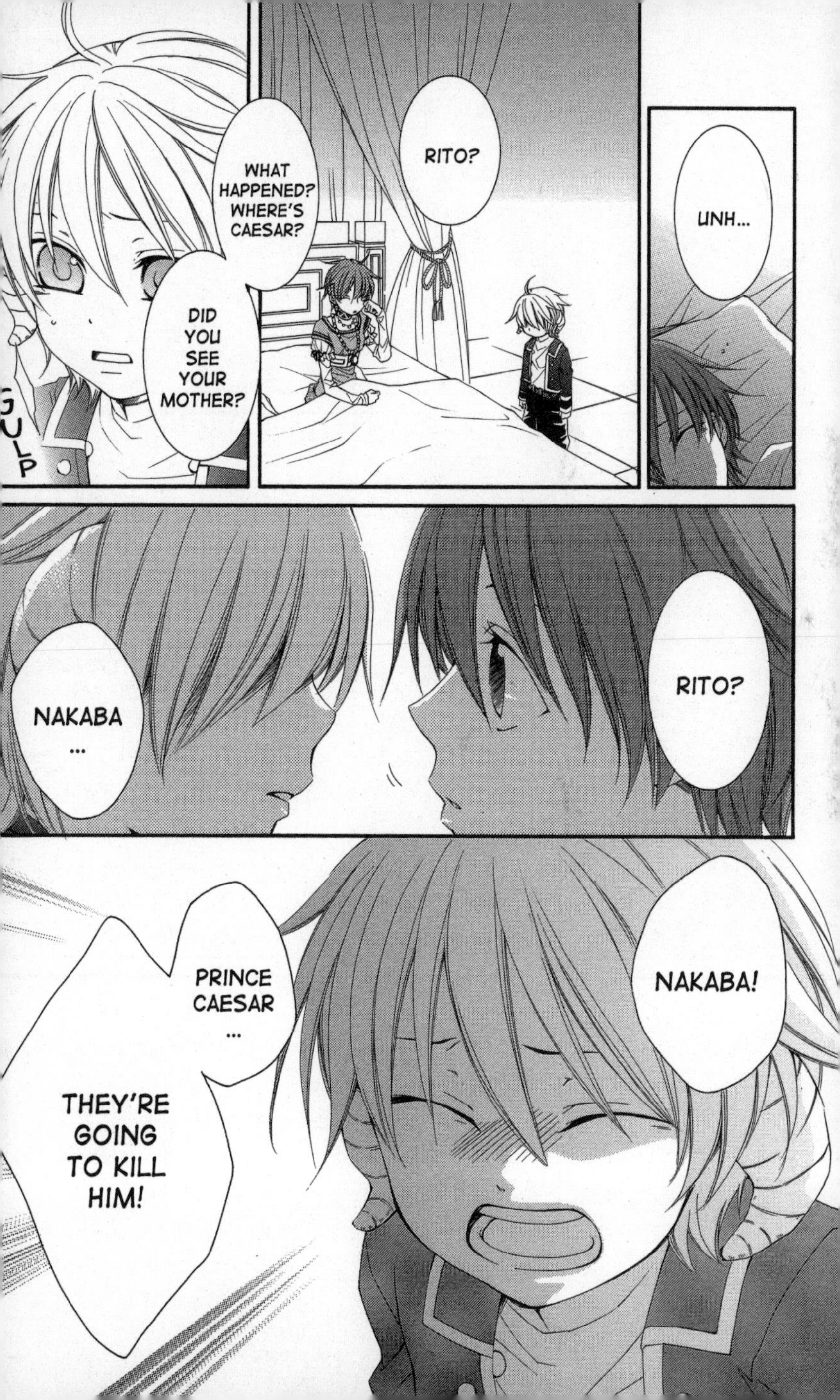
UNH...
RITO?
WHAT HAPPENED? WHERE'S CAESAR?
DID YOU SEE YOUR MOTHER?
GULP
RITO?
NAKABA ...
NAKABA!
PRINCE CAESAR ...
THEY'RE GOING TO KILL HIM!

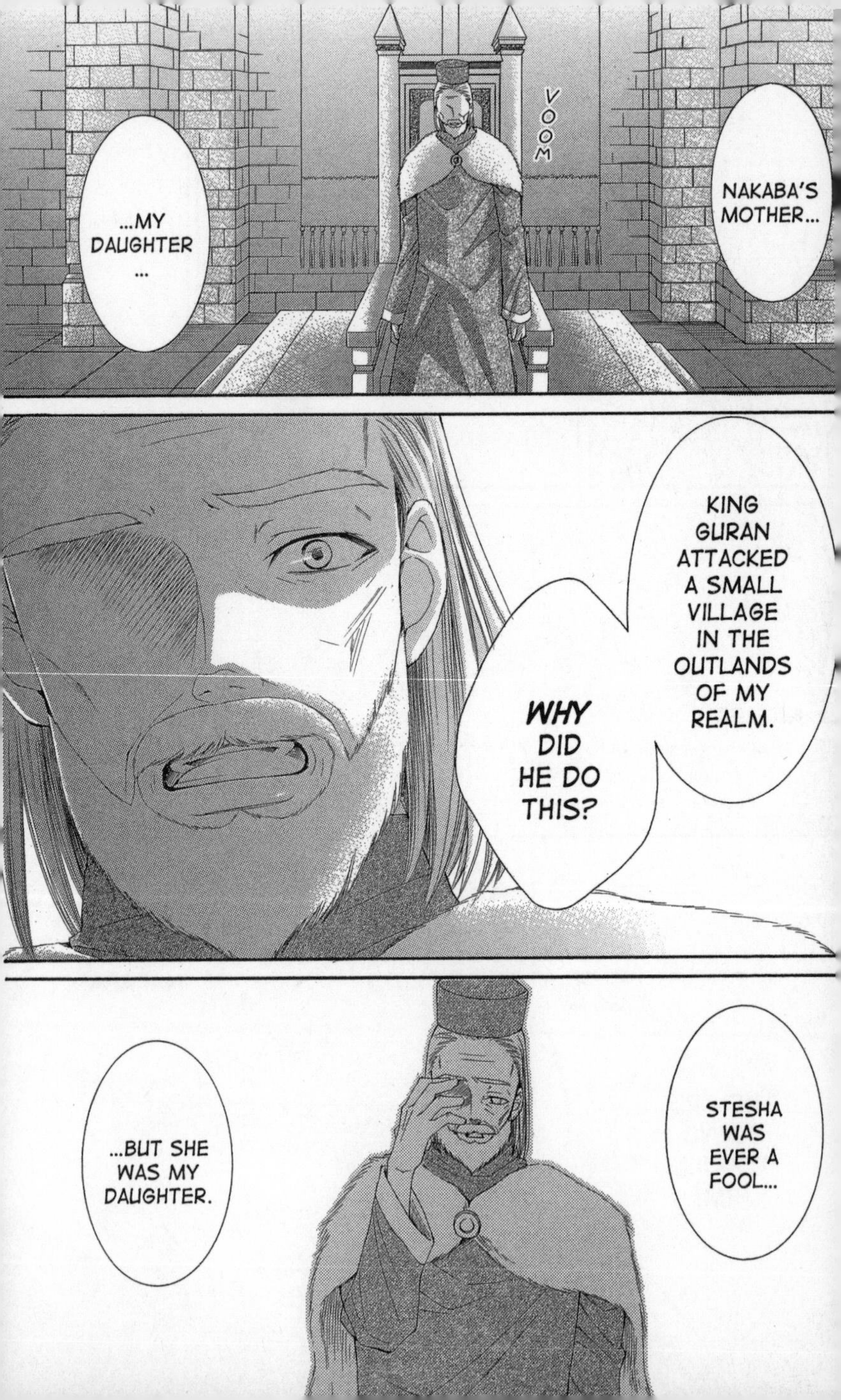
NAKABA'S MOTHER...
VOOM
...MY DAUGHTER ...
KING GURAN ATTACKED A SMALL VILLAGE IN THE OUTLANDS OF MY REALM.
WHY DID HE DO THIS?
STESHA WAS EVER A FOOL...
...BUT SHE WAS MY DAUGHTER.

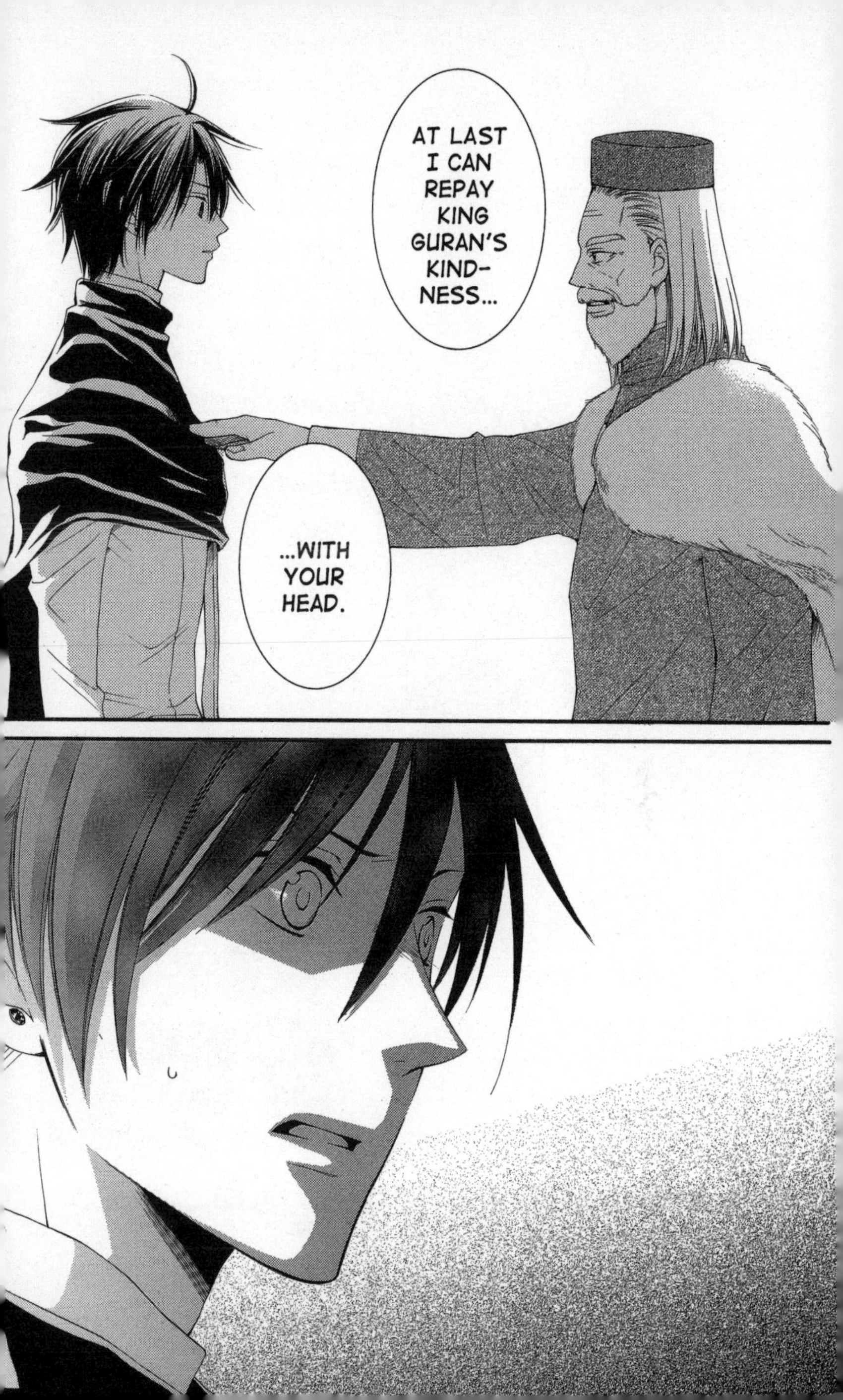
AT LAST I CAN REPAY KING GURAN'S KIND-NESS...
...WITH YOUR HEAD.

Stopgap page filler!!

I had my assistants draw Arcana characters with their hand that's not dominant. ♡

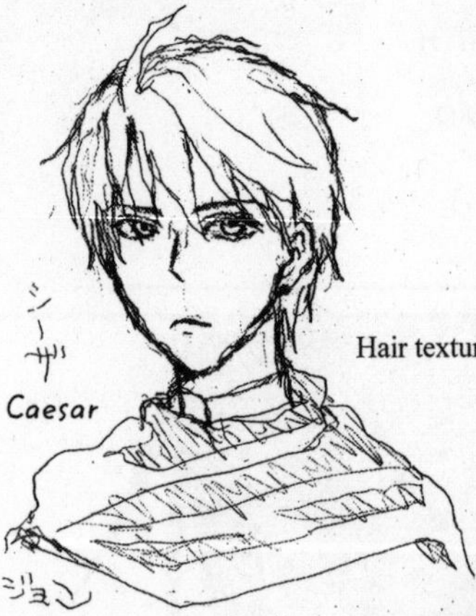
シーザ
Caesar

Hair texture: Seaweed

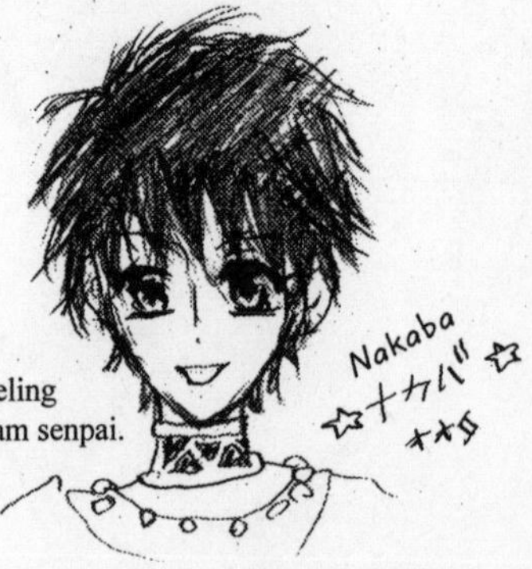
Nakaba
☆ナカバ☆

Specialty: Enduring the grueling training of her volleyball team senpai. Or, a passionate dance.

Chapter 25

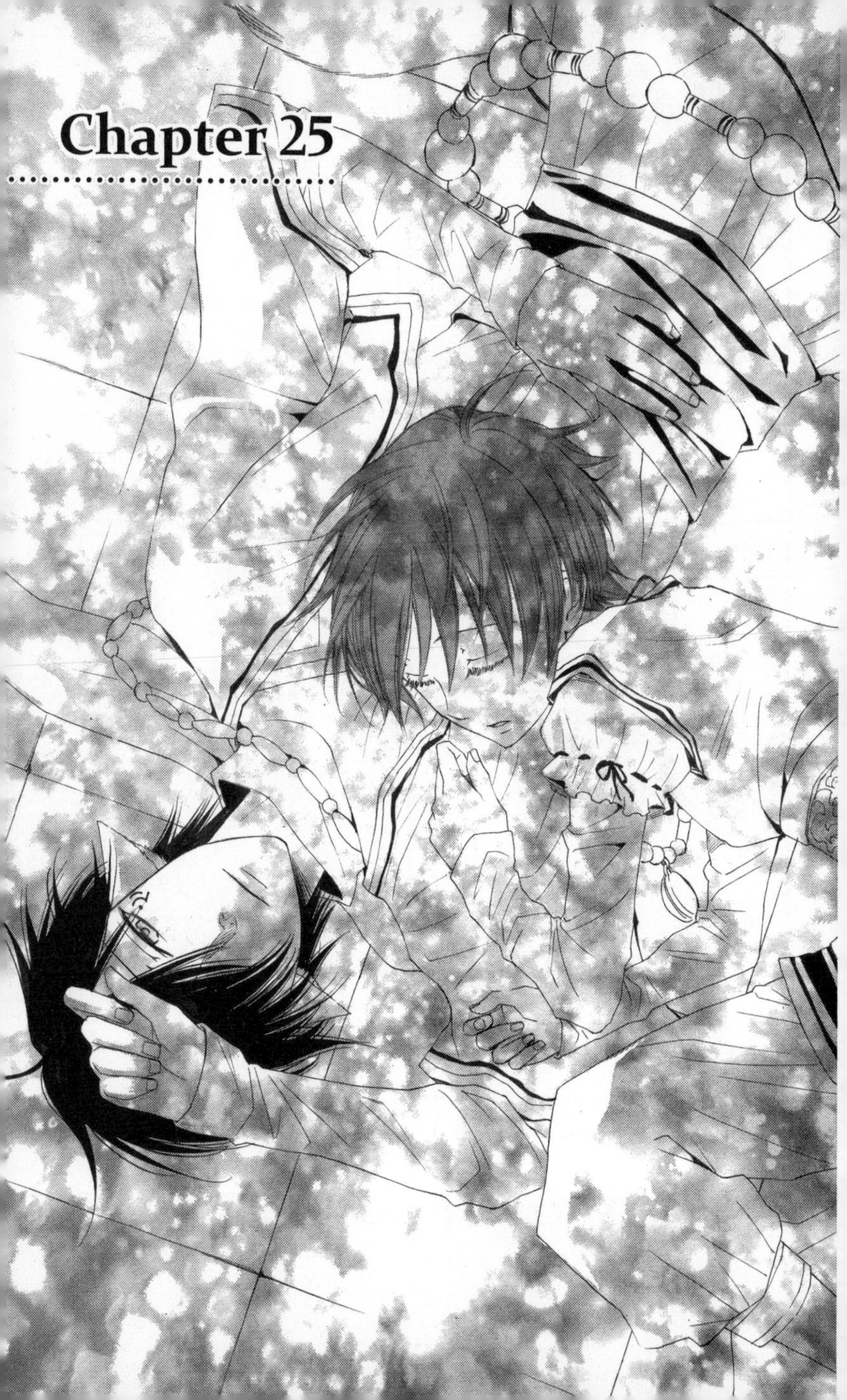

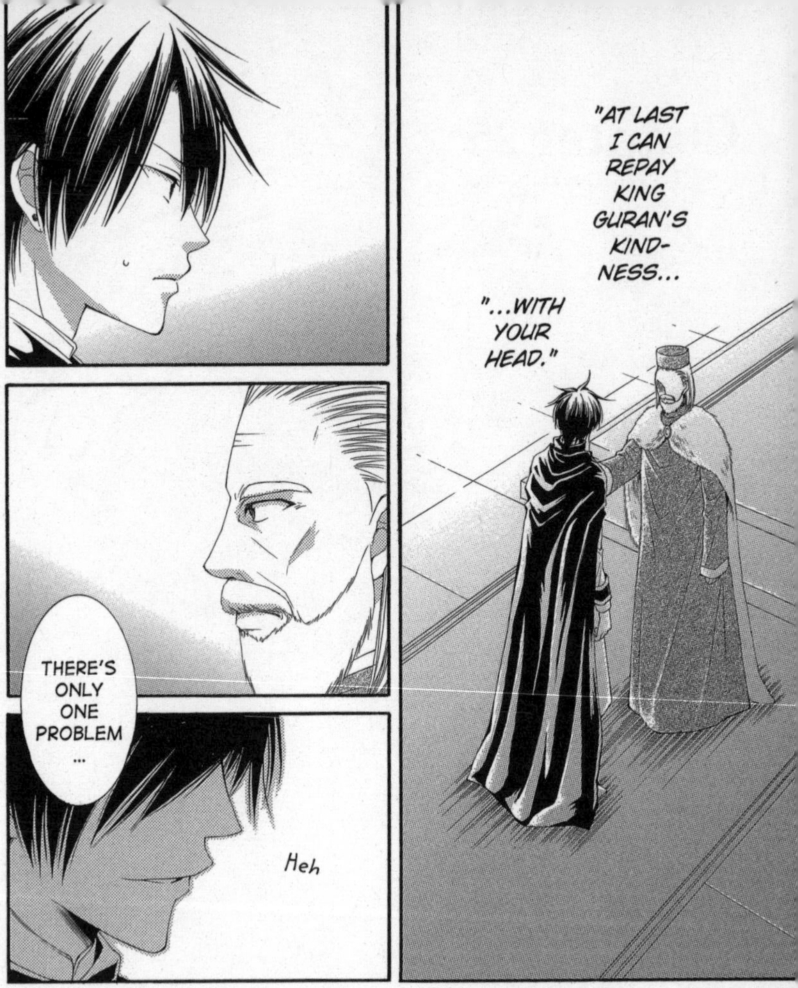
"AT LAST I CAN REPAY KING GURAN'S KIND-NESS...
"...WITH YOUR HEAD."
THERE'S ONLY ONE PROBLEM ...
Heh

Dawn of the Arcana

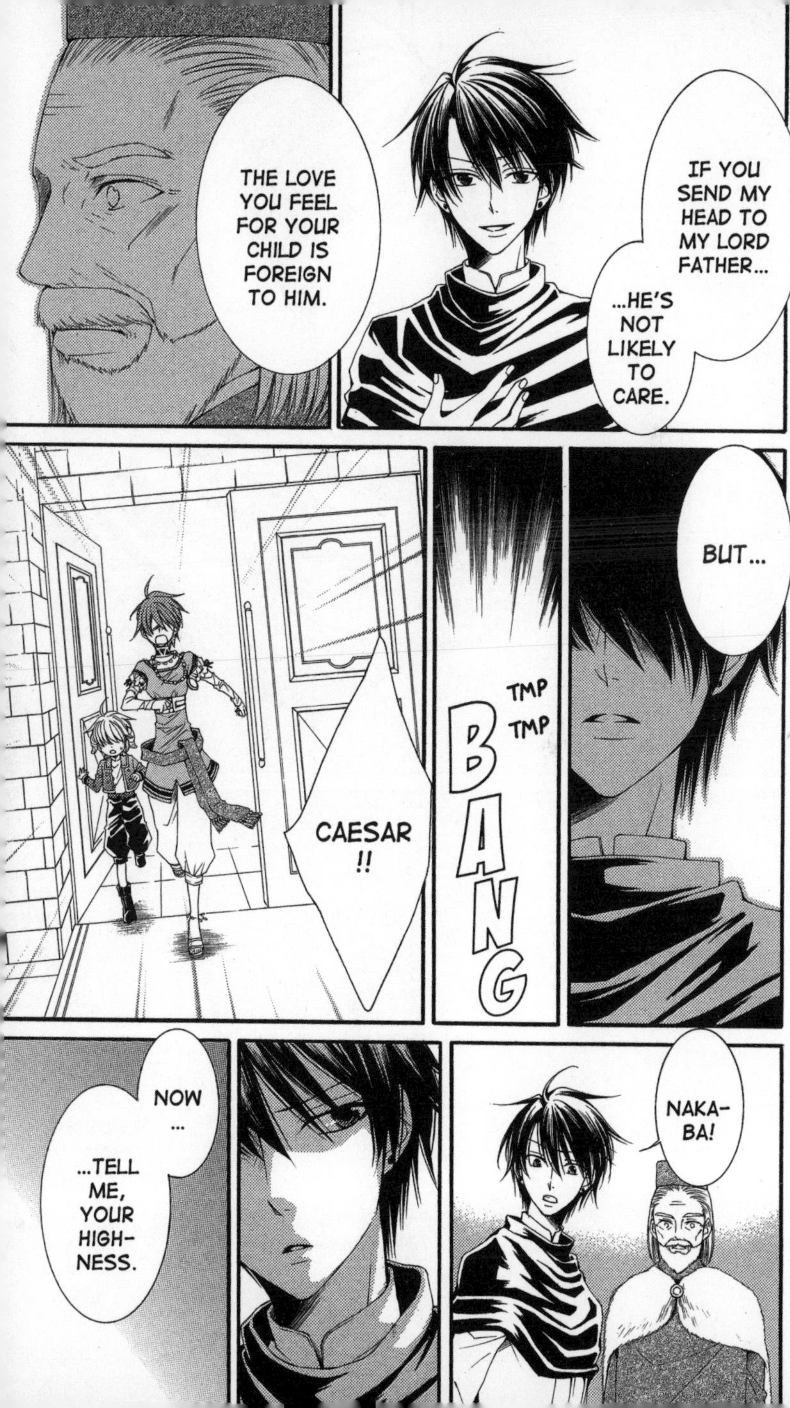
IF YOU SEND MY HEAD TO MY LORD FATHER...
...HE'S NOT LIKELY TO CARE.
THE LOVE YOU FEEL FOR YOUR CHILD IS FOREIGN TO HIM.
BUT...
TMP TMP
BANG
CAESAR !!
NAKA-BA!
NOW ...
...TELL ME, YOUR HIGH-NESS.

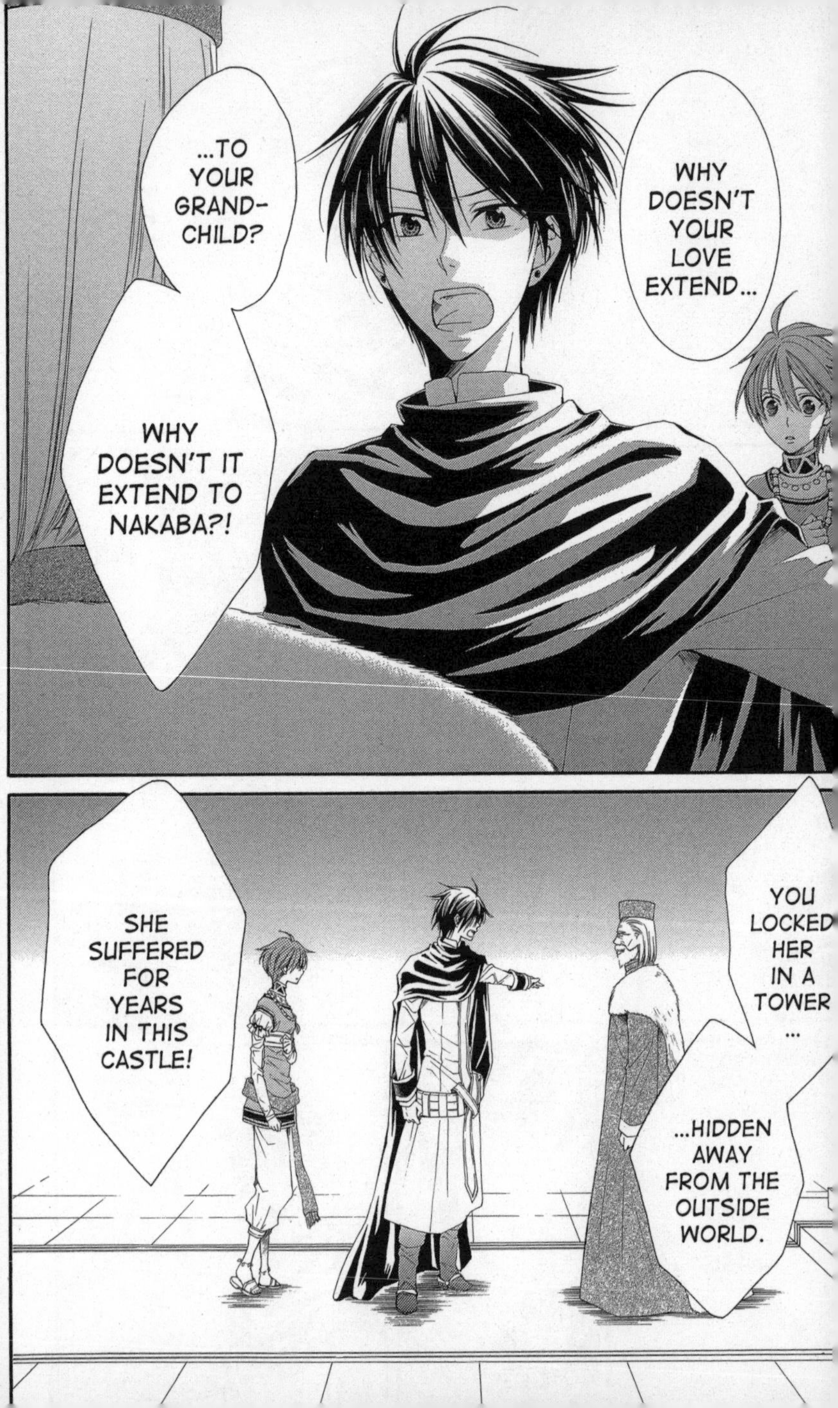
WHY DOESN'T YOUR LOVE EXTEND...
...TO YOUR GRAND-CHILD?
WHY DOESN'T IT EXTEND TO NAKABA?!
YOU LOCKED HER IN A TOWER...
...HIDDEN AWAY FROM THE OUTSIDE WORLD.
SHE SUFFERED FOR YEARS IN THIS CASTLE!

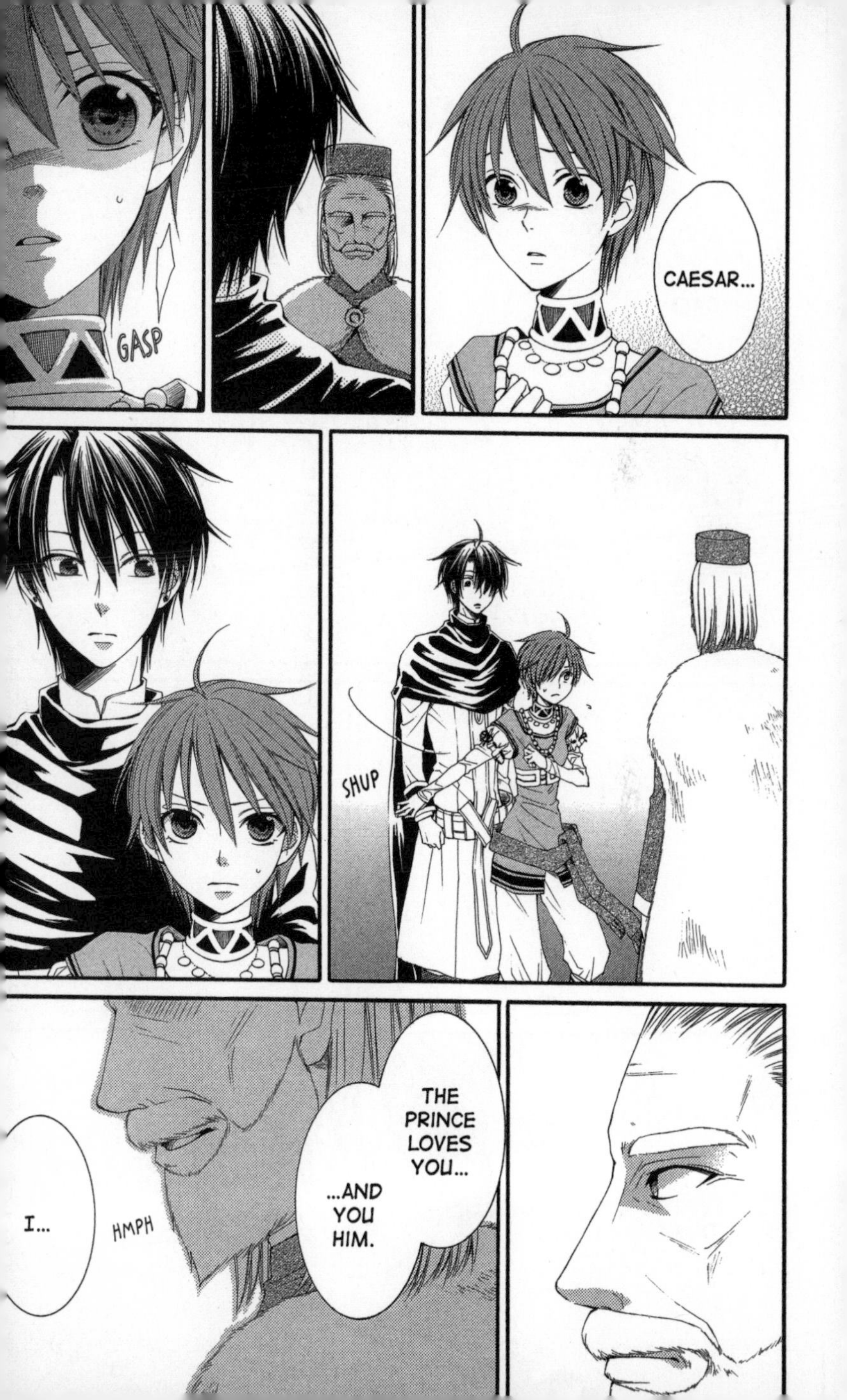
CAESAR...
GASP
SHUP
THE PRINCE LOVES YOU...
...AND YOU HIM.
HMPH
I...

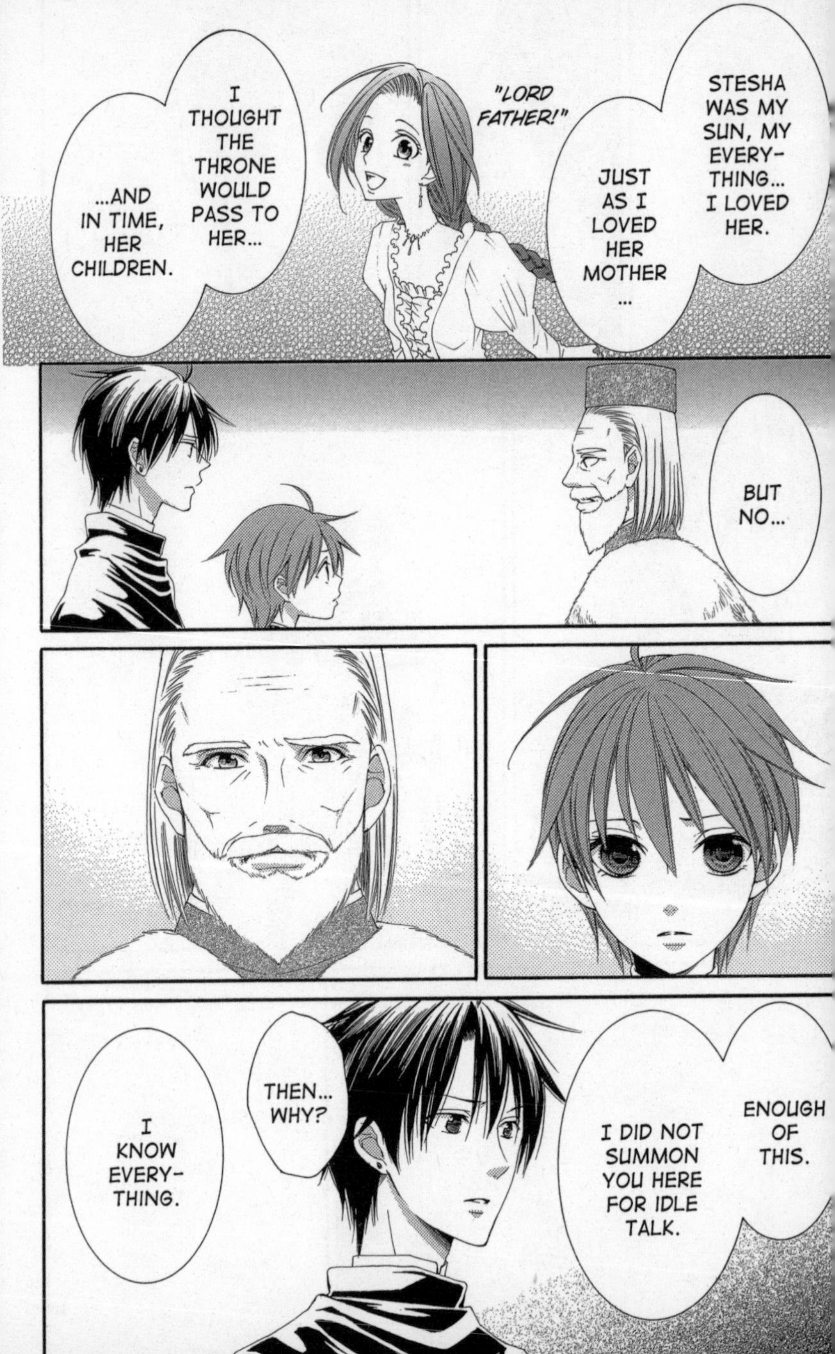
STESHA WAS MY SUN, MY EVERYTHING... I LOVED HER.
JUST AS I LOVED HER MOTHER...
"LORD FATHER!"
I THOUGHT THE THRONE WOULD PASS TO HER...
...AND IN TIME, HER CHILDREN.
BUT NO...
ENOUGH OF THIS.
I DID NOT SUMMON YOU HERE FOR IDLE TALK.
THEN... WHY?
I KNOW EVERYTHING.

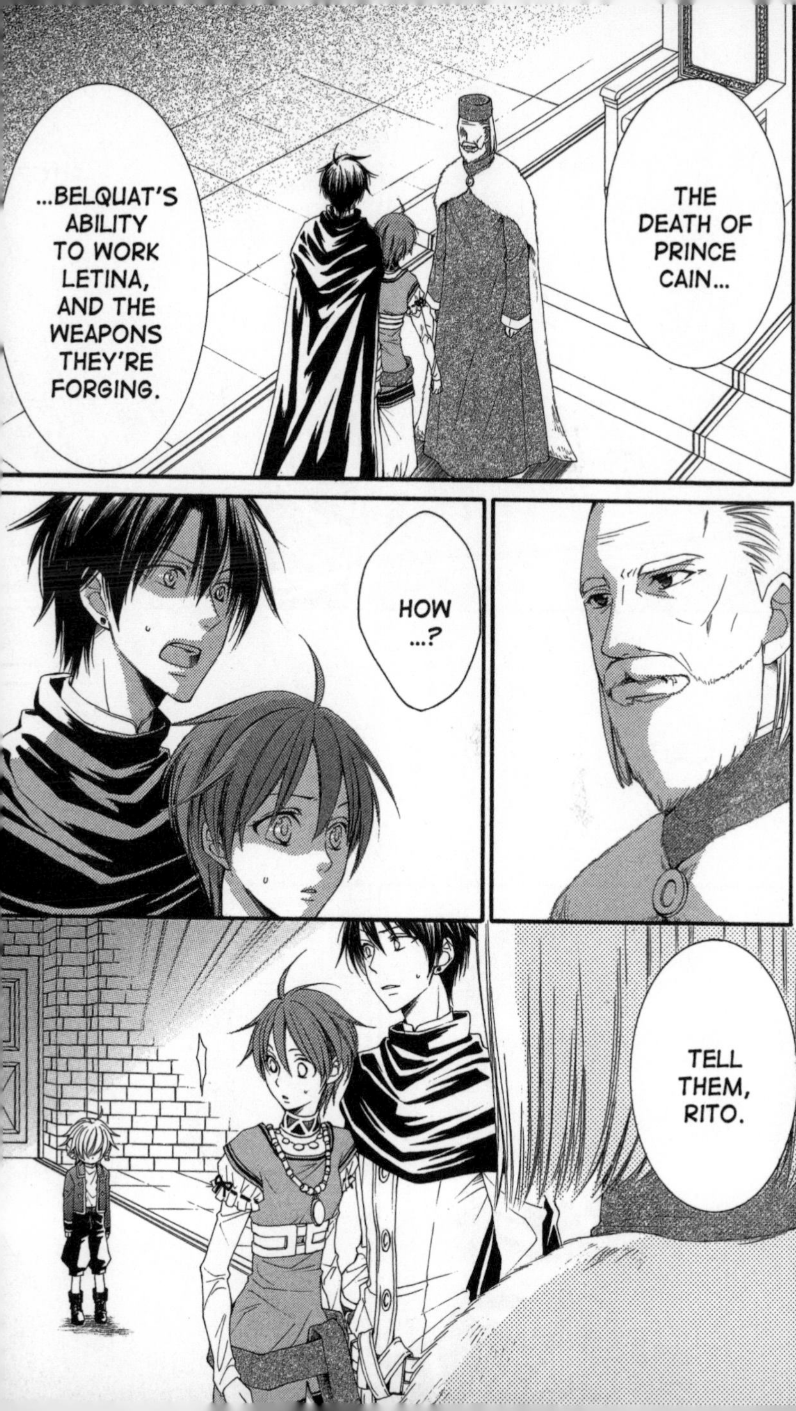
THE DEATH OF PRINCE CAIN...
...BELQUAT'S ABILITY TO WORK LETINA, AND THE WEAPONS THEY'RE FORGING.
HOW ...?
TELL THEM, RITO.

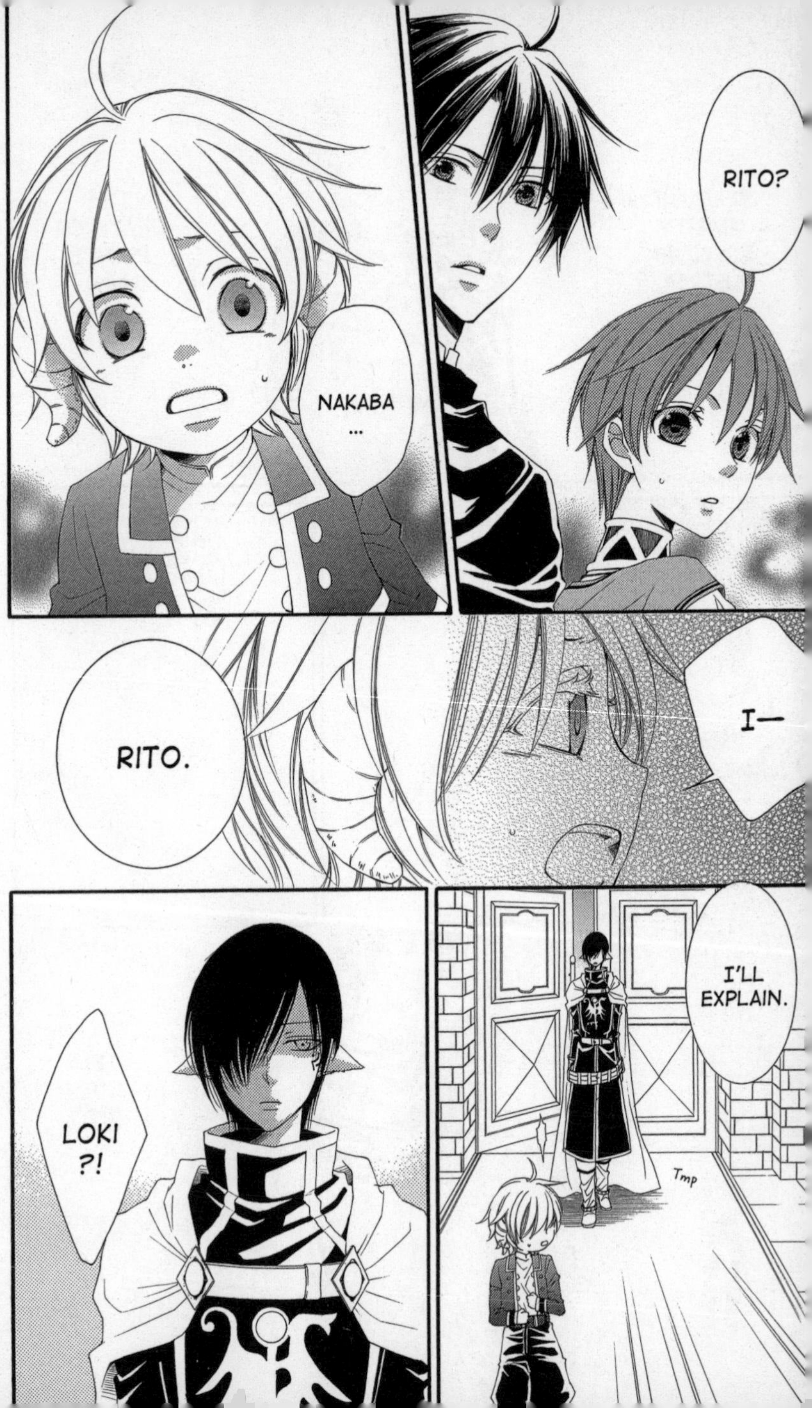
RITO?
NAKABA ...
I—
RITO.
I'LL EXPLAIN.
Tmp
LOKI ?!

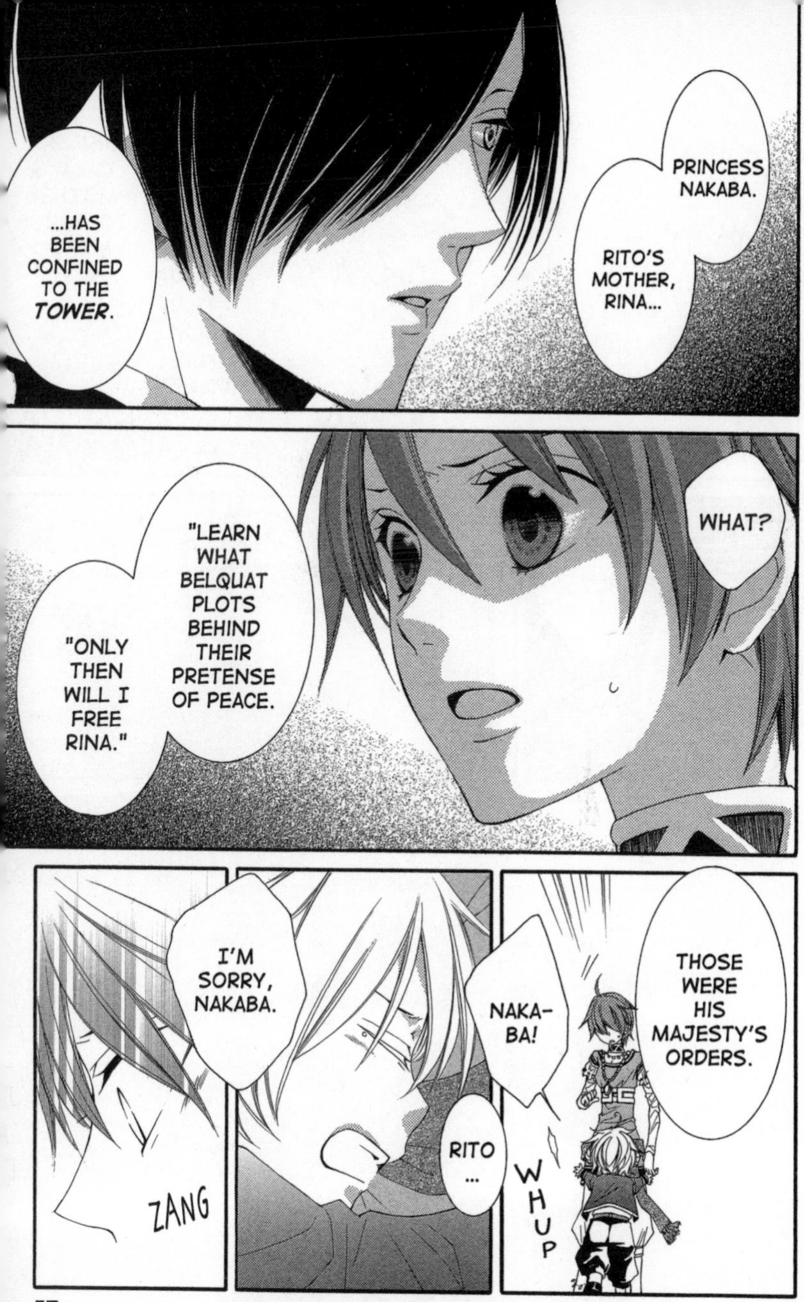
PRINCESS NAKABA.
RITO'S MOTHER, RINA...
...HAS BEEN CONFINED TO THE *TOWER*.
WHAT?
"LEARN WHAT BELQUAT PLOTS BEHIND THEIR PRETENSE OF PEACE.
"ONLY THEN WILL I FREE RINA."
THOSE WERE HIS MAJESTY'S ORDERS.
NAKA-BA!
WHUP
RITO ...
I'M SORRY, NAKABA.
ZANG

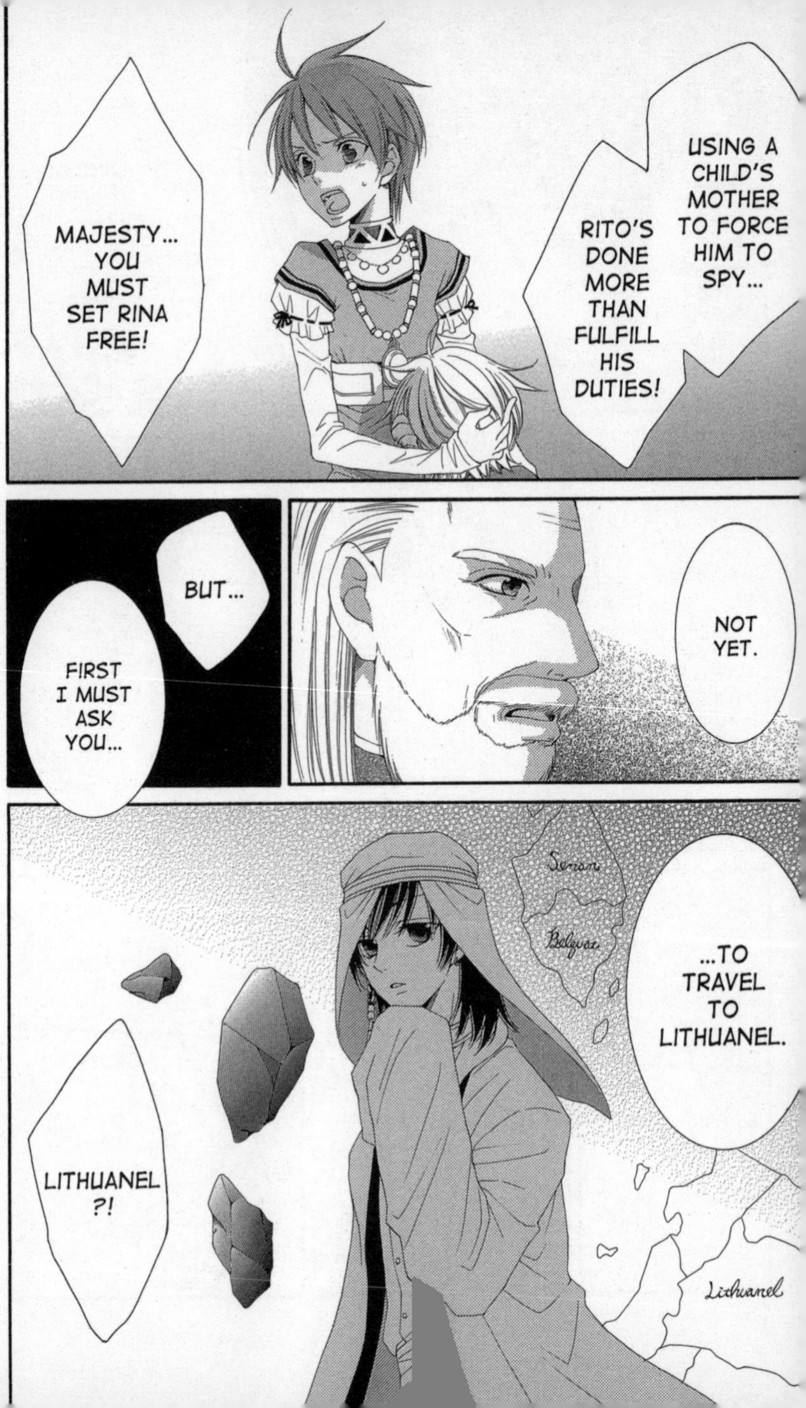
USING A CHILD'S MOTHER TO FORCE HIM TO SPY...
RITO'S DONE MORE THAN FULFILL HIS DUTIES!
MAJESTY... YOU MUST SET RINA FREE!
NOT YET.
BUT...
FIRST I MUST ASK YOU...
...TO TRAVEL TO LITHUANEL.
Lithuanel
LITHUANEL ?!

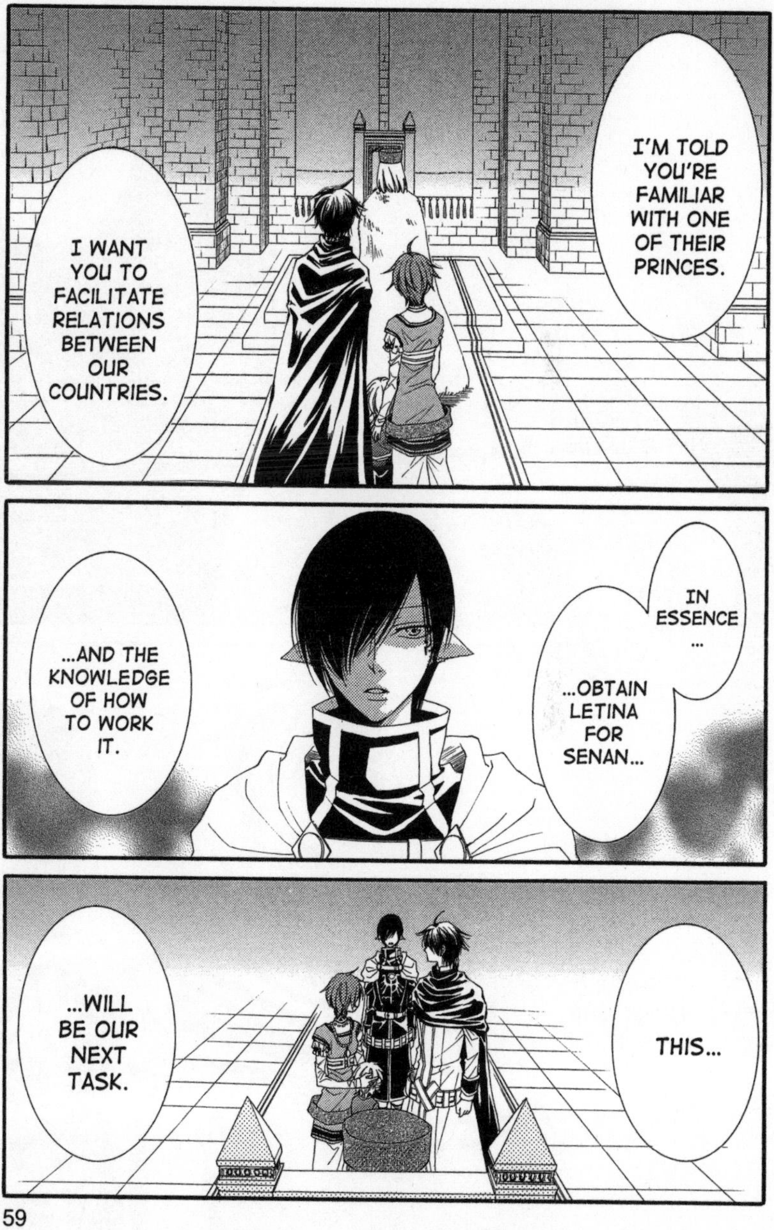
I'M TOLD YOU'RE FAMILIAR WITH ONE OF THEIR PRINCES.
I WANT YOU TO FACILITATE RELATIONS BETWEEN OUR COUNTRIES.
IN ESSENCE ...
...OBTAIN LETINA FOR SENAN...
...AND THE KNOWLEDGE OF HOW TO WORK IT.
THIS...
...WILL BE OUR NEXT TASK.

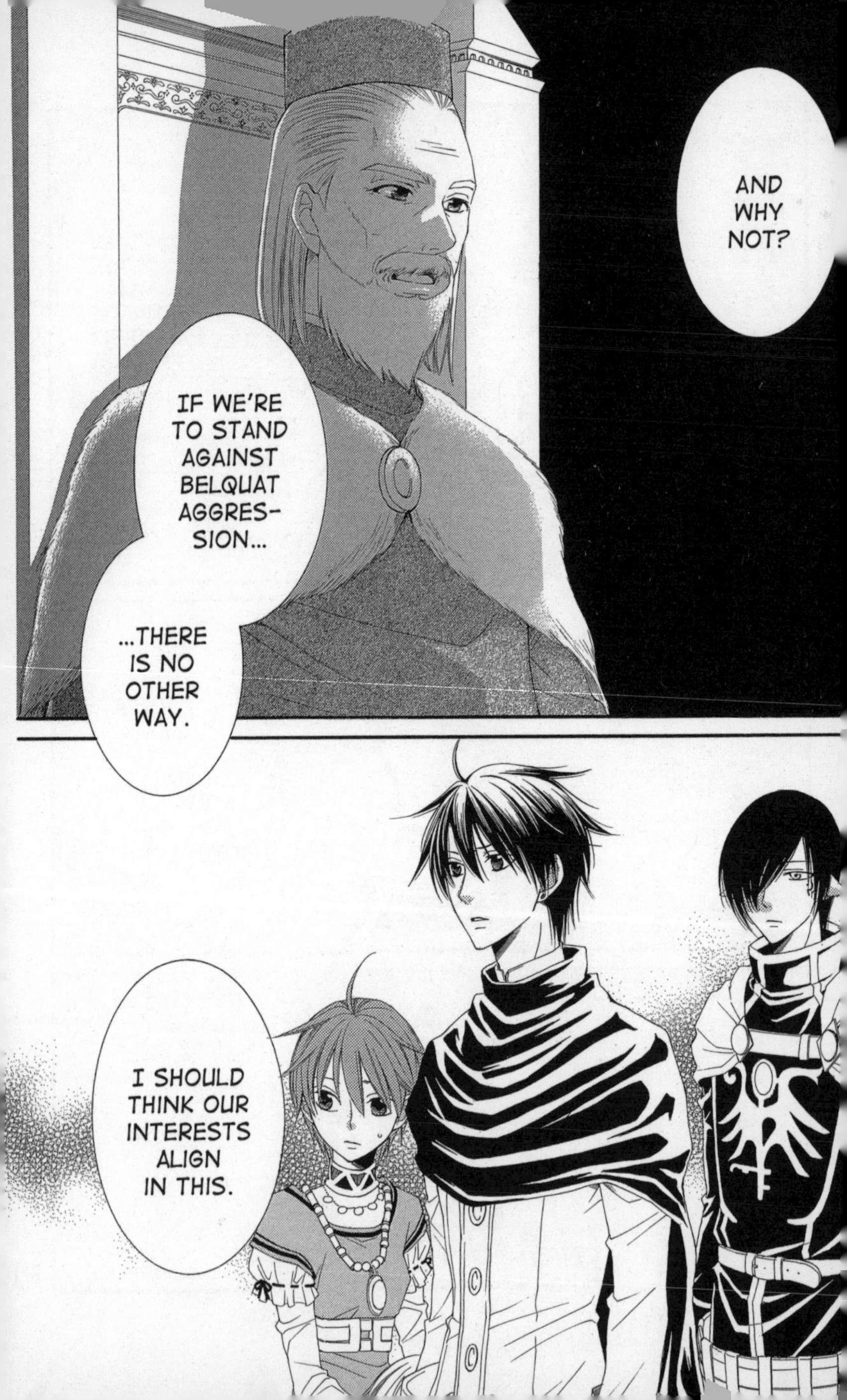
AND WHY NOT?
IF WE'RE TO STAND AGAINST BELQUAT AGGRES-SION...
...THERE IS NO OTHER WAY.
I SHOULD THINK OUR INTERESTS ALIGN IN THIS.

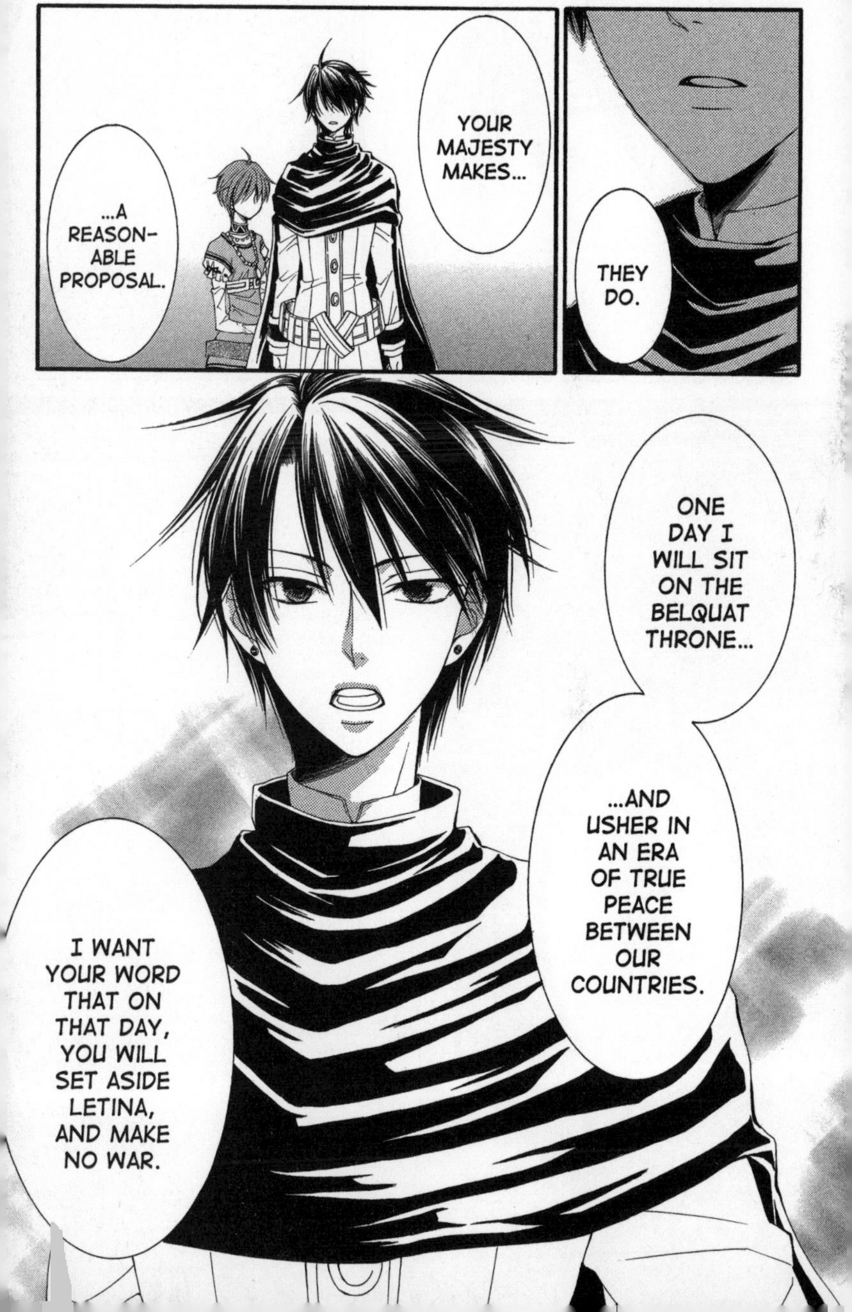
THEY DO.
YOUR MAJESTY MAKES...
...A REASON-ABLE PROPOSAL.
ONE DAY I WILL SIT ON THE BELQUAT THRONE...
...AND USHER IN AN ERA OF TRUE PEACE BETWEEN OUR COUNTRIES.
I WANT YOUR WORD THAT ON THAT DAY, YOU WILL SET ASIDE LETINA, AND MAKE NO WAR.

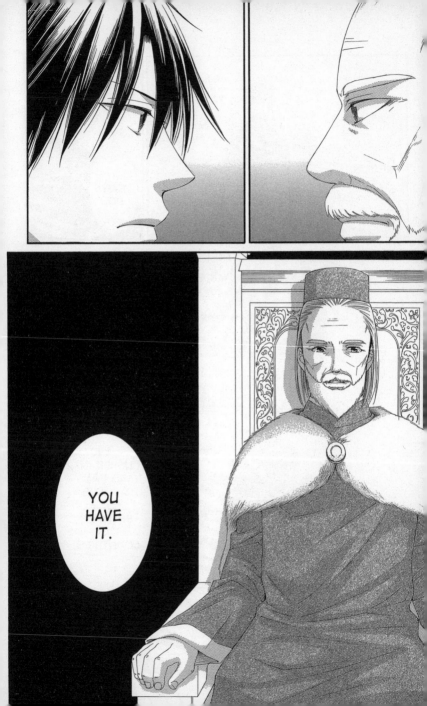

YOU
HAVE
IT.

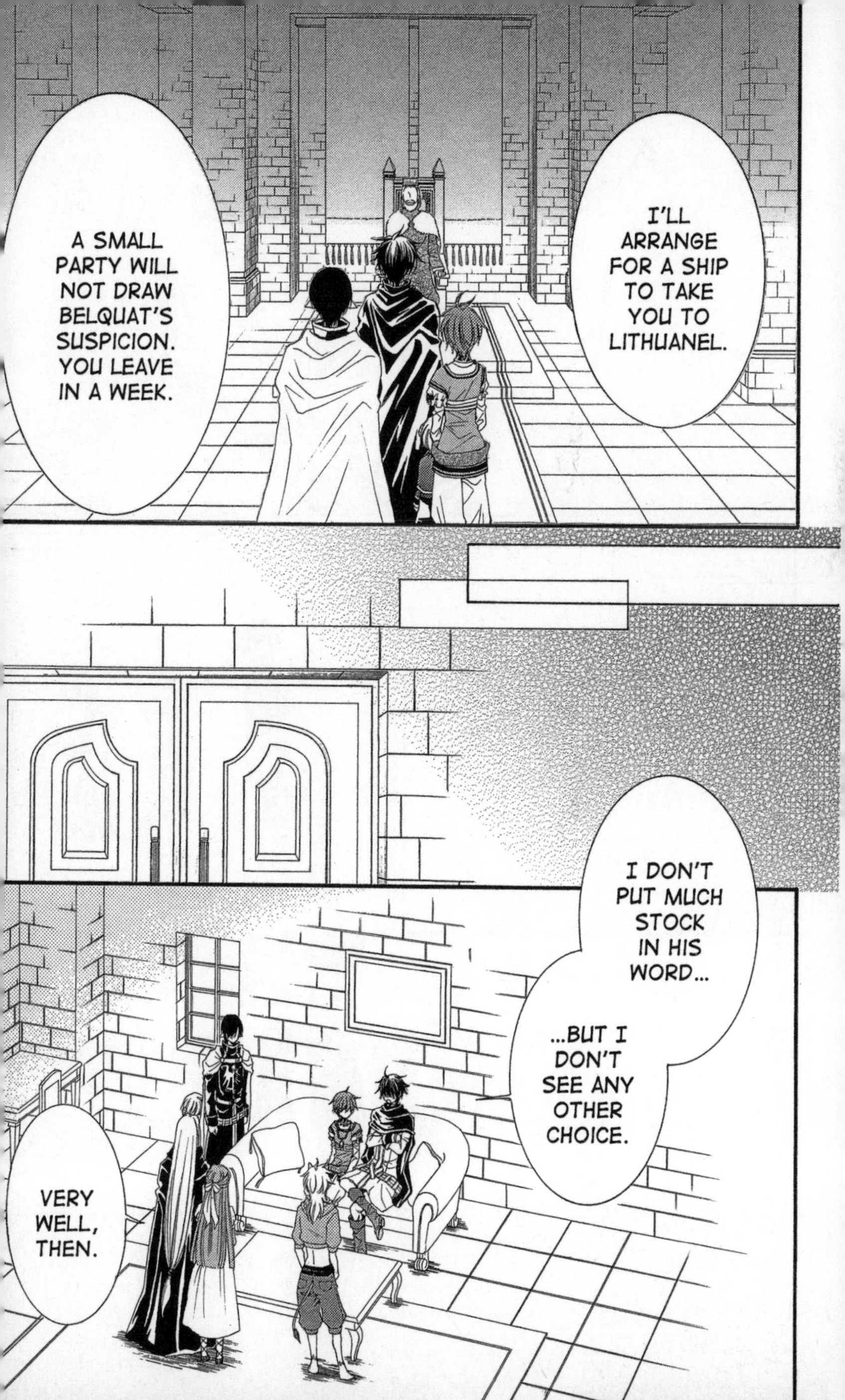
I'LL ARRANGE FOR A SHIP TO TAKE YOU TO LITHUANEL.
A SMALL PARTY WILL NOT DRAW BELQUAT'S SUSPICION. YOU LEAVE IN A WEEK.
I DON'T PUT MUCH STOCK IN HIS WORD...
...BUT I DON'T SEE ANY OTHER CHOICE.
VERY WELL, THEN.

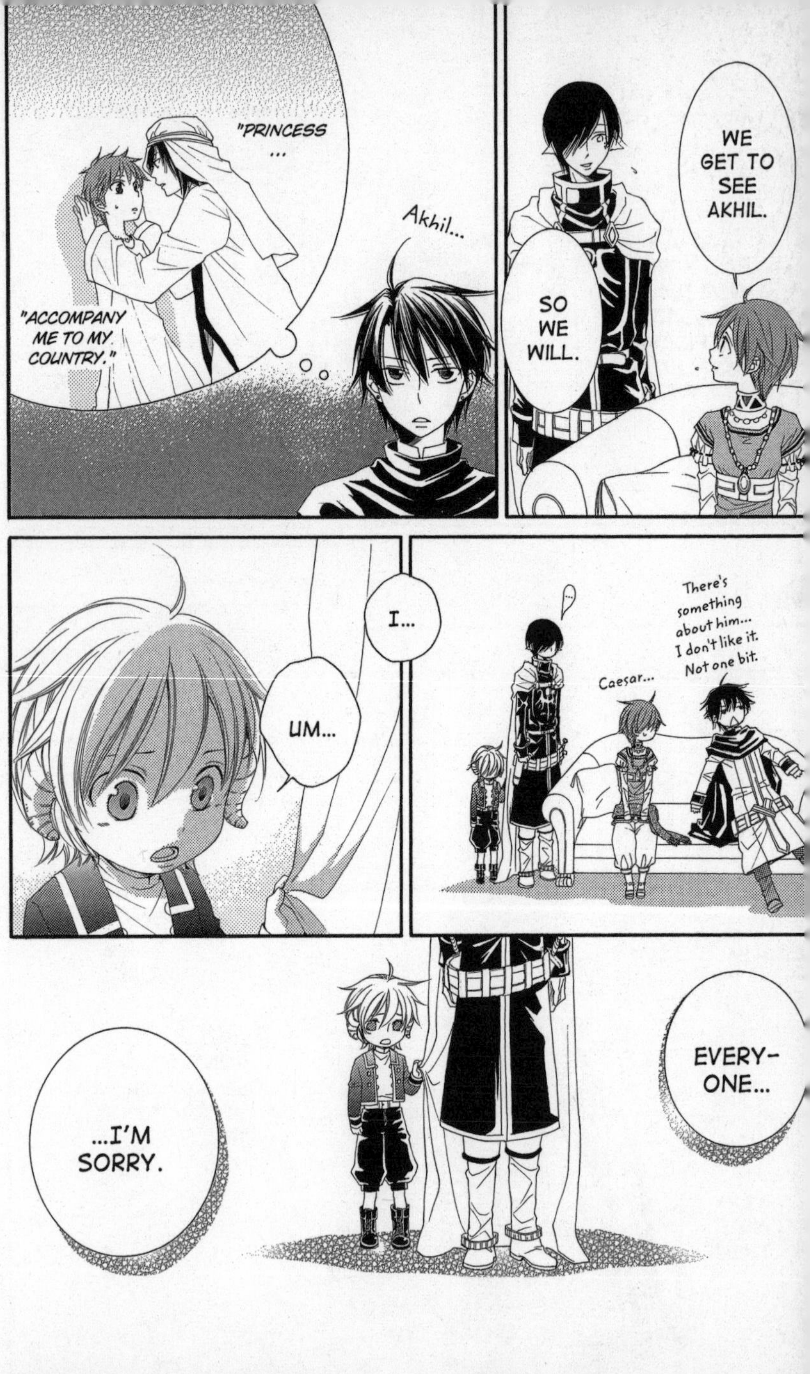
WE GET TO SEE AKHIL.
SO WE WILL.
"PRINCESS ...
"ACCOMPANY ME TO MY COUNTRY."
Akhil...
...
There's something about him... I don't like it. Not one bit.
Caesar...
I...
UM...
EVERY-ONE...
...I'M SORRY.

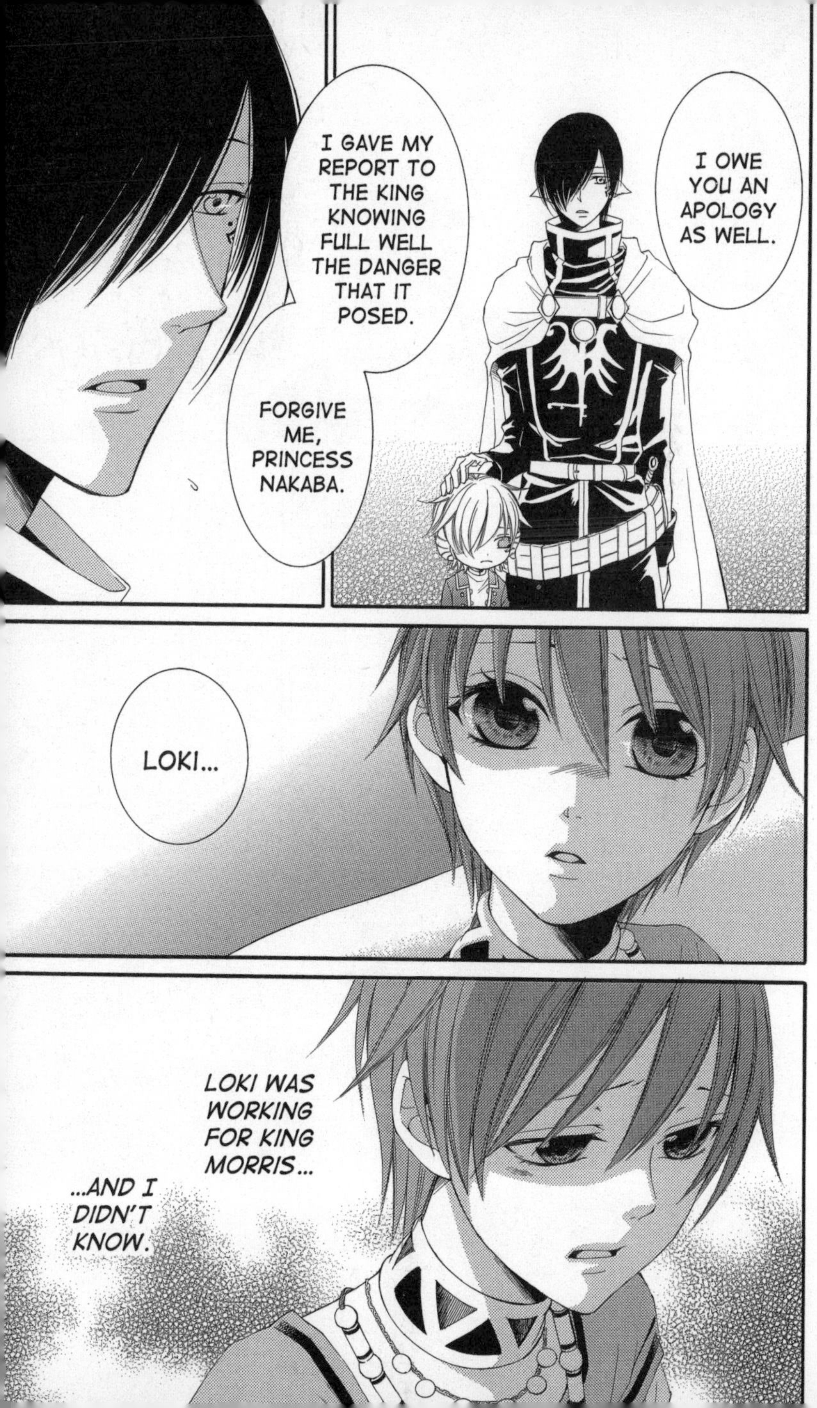
I OWE YOU AN APOLOGY AS WELL.
I GAVE MY REPORT TO THE KING KNOWING FULL WELL THE DANGER THAT IT POSED.
FORGIVE ME, PRINCESS NAKABA.
LOKI...
LOKI WAS WORKING FOR KING MORRIS...
...AND I DIDN'T KNOW.

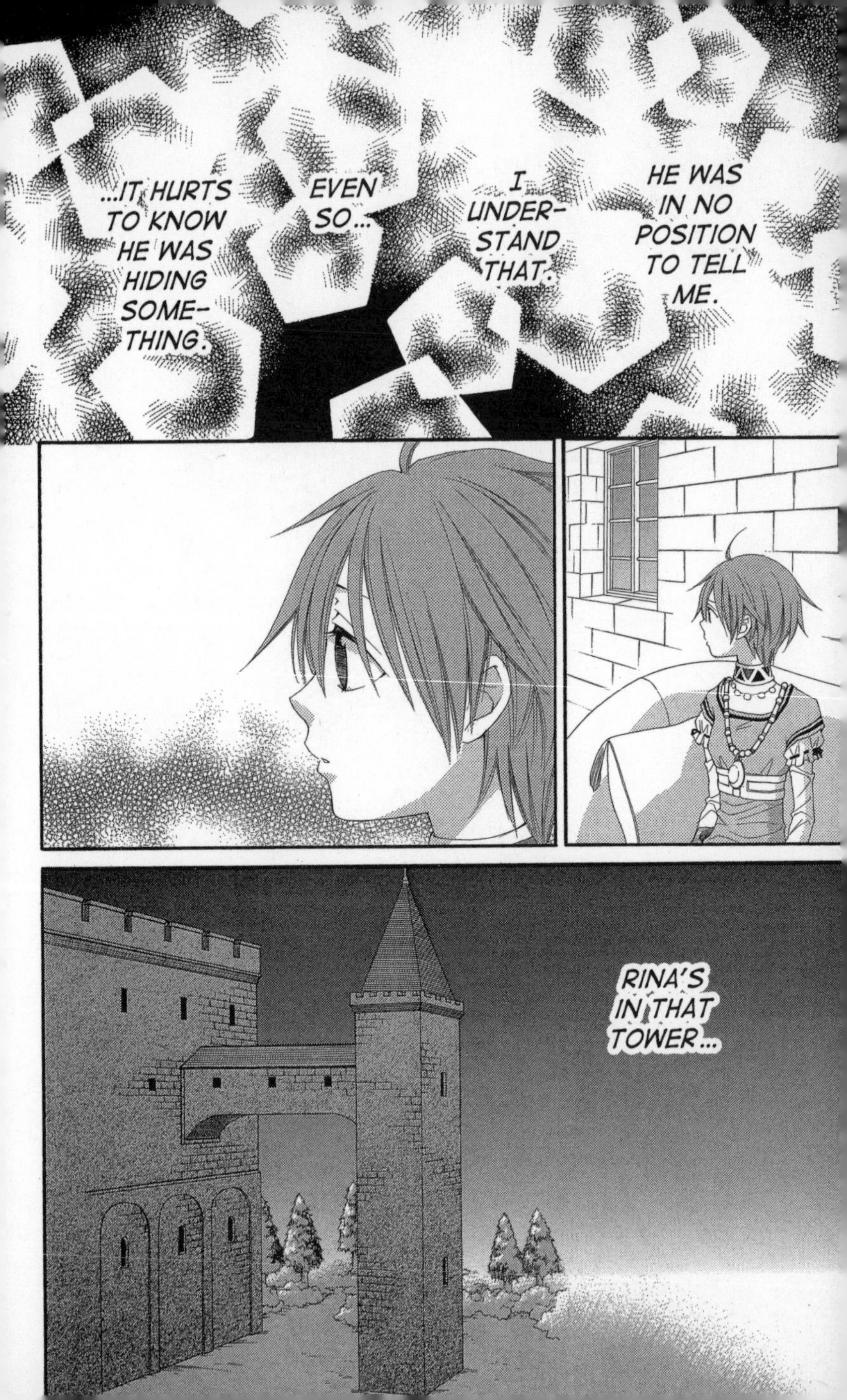
HE WAS IN NO POSITION TO TELL ME.
I UNDERSTAND THAT.
EVEN SO...
...IT HURTS TO KNOW HE WAS HIDING SOMETHING.
RINA'S IN THAT TOWER...

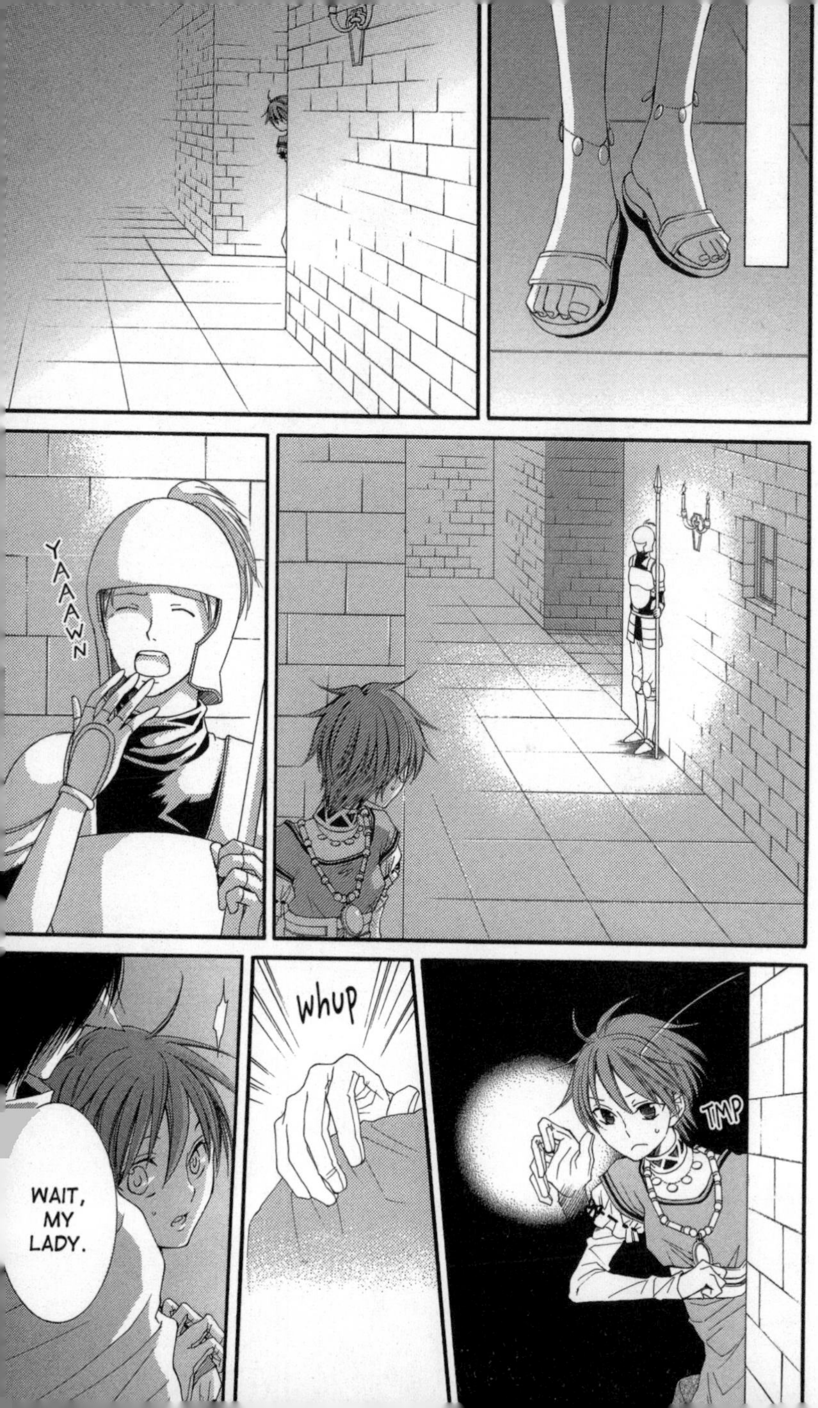
YAAAAWN
TMP
whup
WAIT, MY LADY.

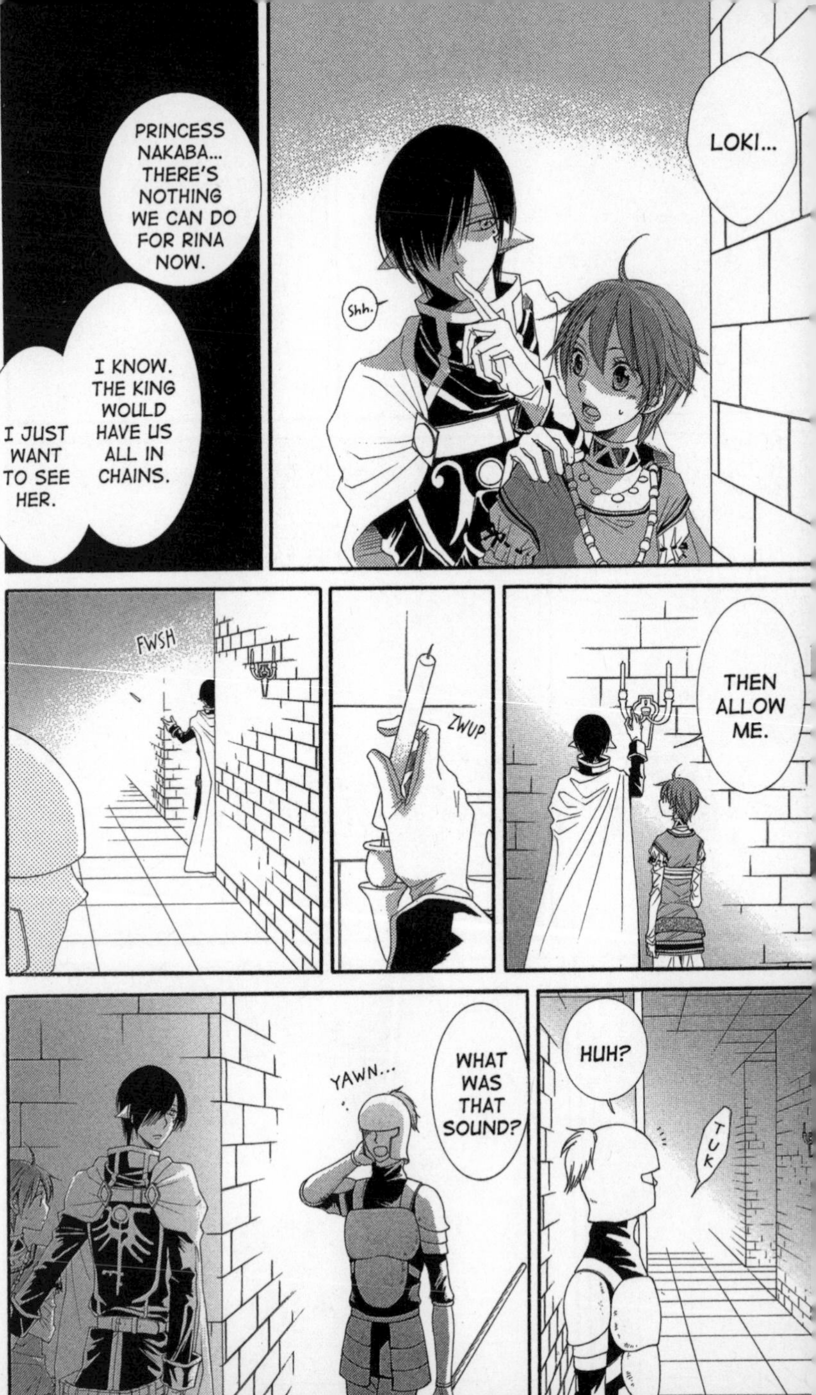
LOKI...
Shh.
PRINCESS NAKABA... THERE'S NOTHING WE CAN DO FOR RINA NOW.
I KNOW. THE KING WOULD HAVE US ALL IN CHAINS.
I JUST WANT TO SEE HER.
THEN ALLOW ME.
ZWUP
FWSH
HUH?
TUK
WHAT WAS THAT SOUND?
YAWN...

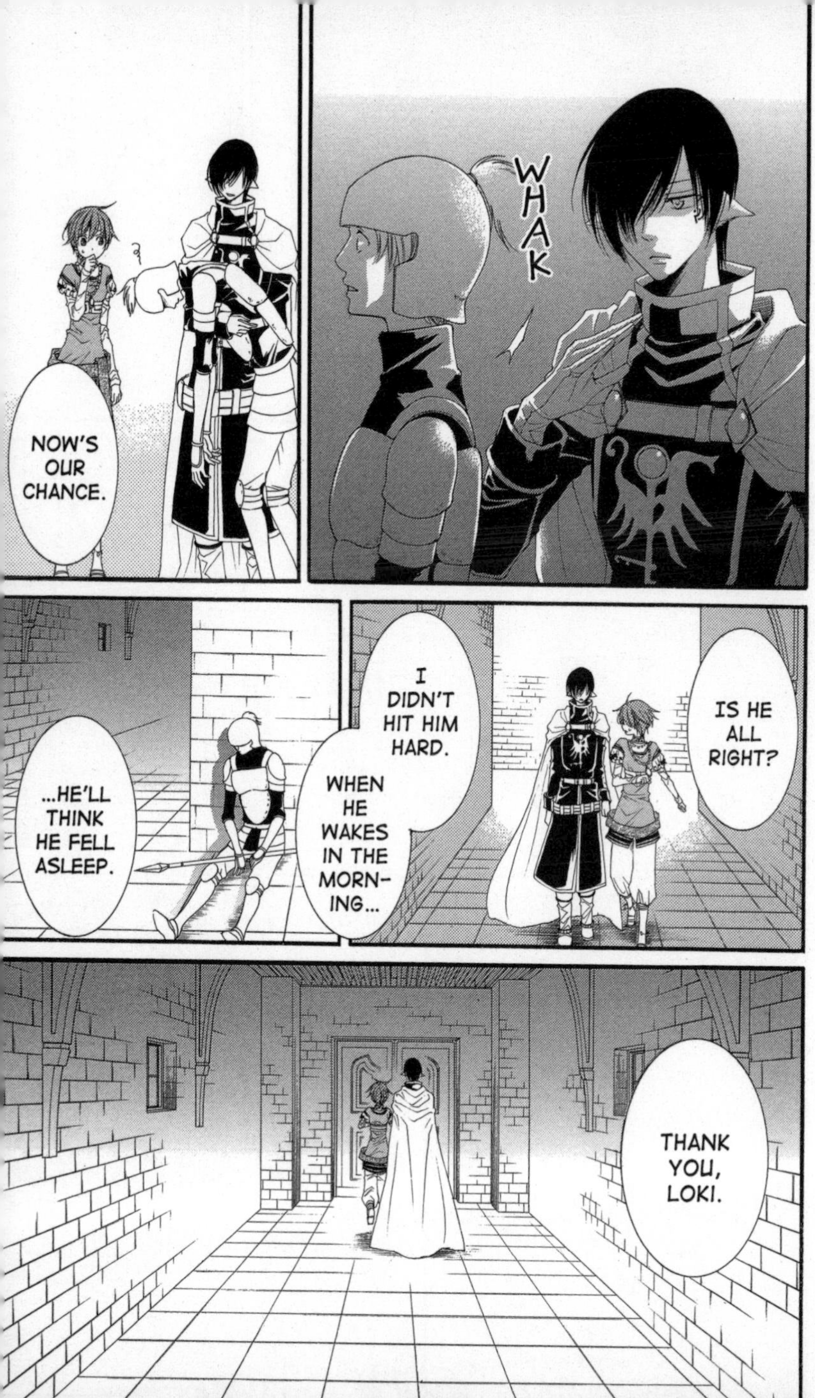
WHAK
NOW'S OUR CHANCE.
IS HE ALL RIGHT?
I DIDN'T HIT HIM HARD.
WHEN HE WAKES IN THE MORN-ING...
...HE'LL THINK HE FELL ASLEEP.
THANK YOU, LOKI.

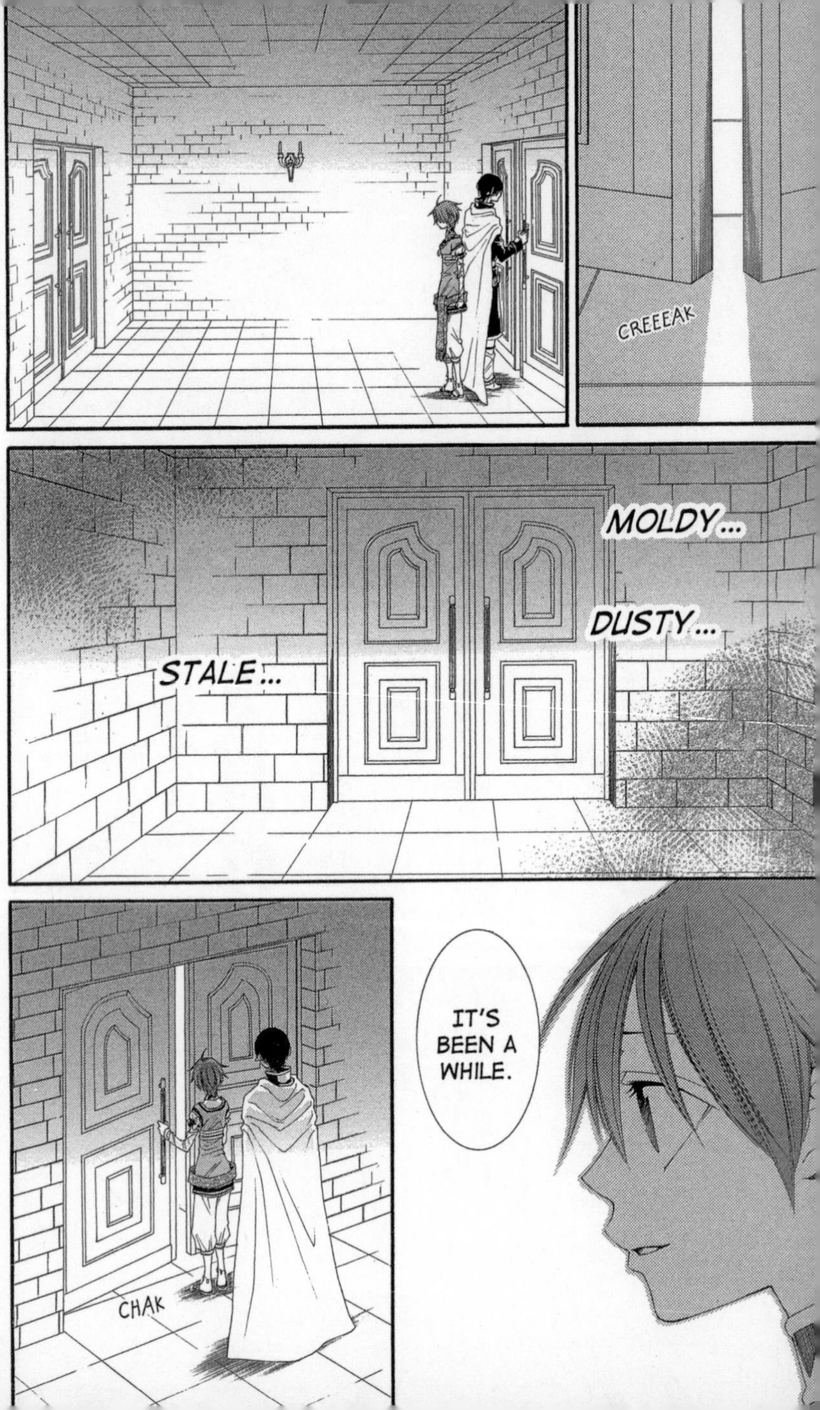
CREEEAK
MOLDY...
DUSTY...
STALE...
IT'S BEEN A WHILE.
CHAK

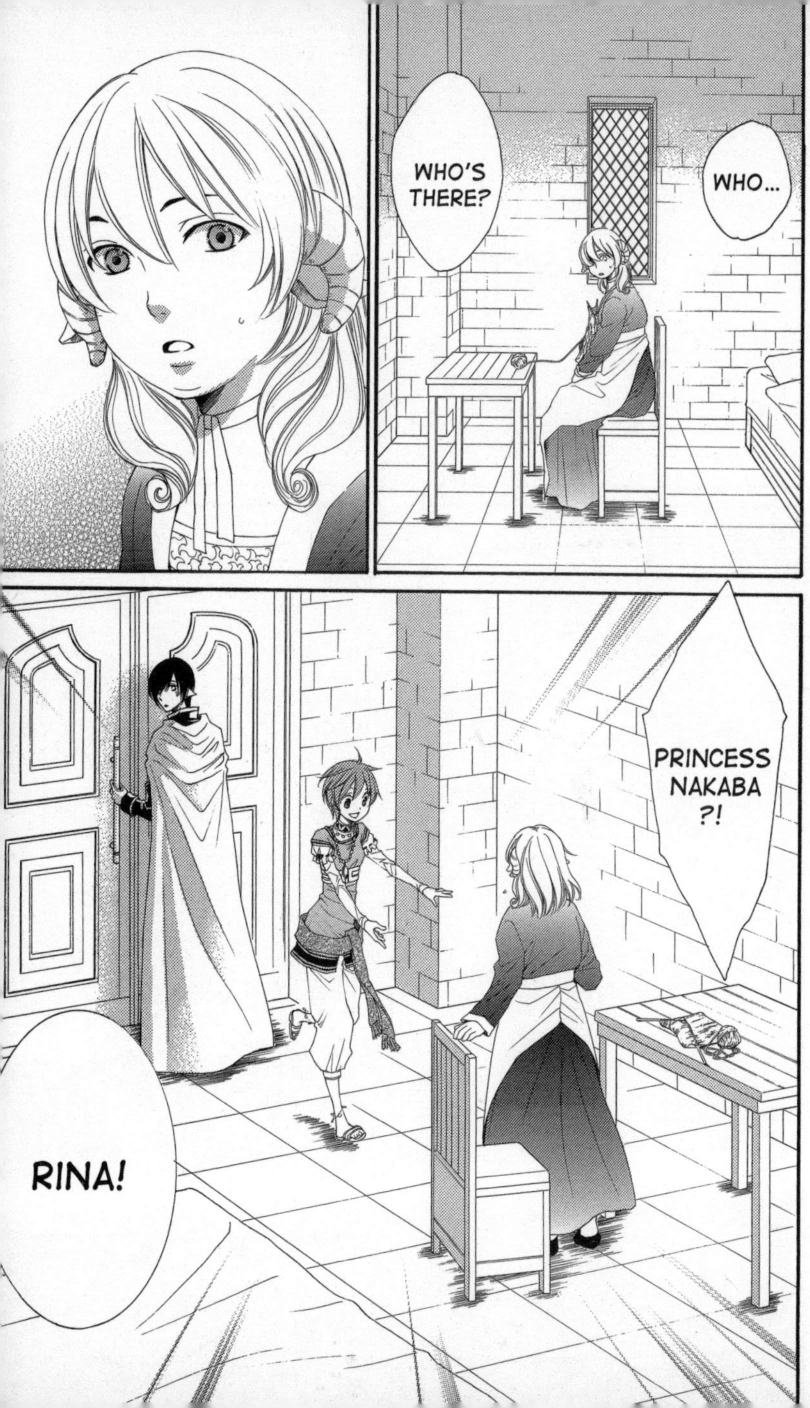
WHO...
WHO'S THERE?
PRINCESS NAKABA ?!
RINA!

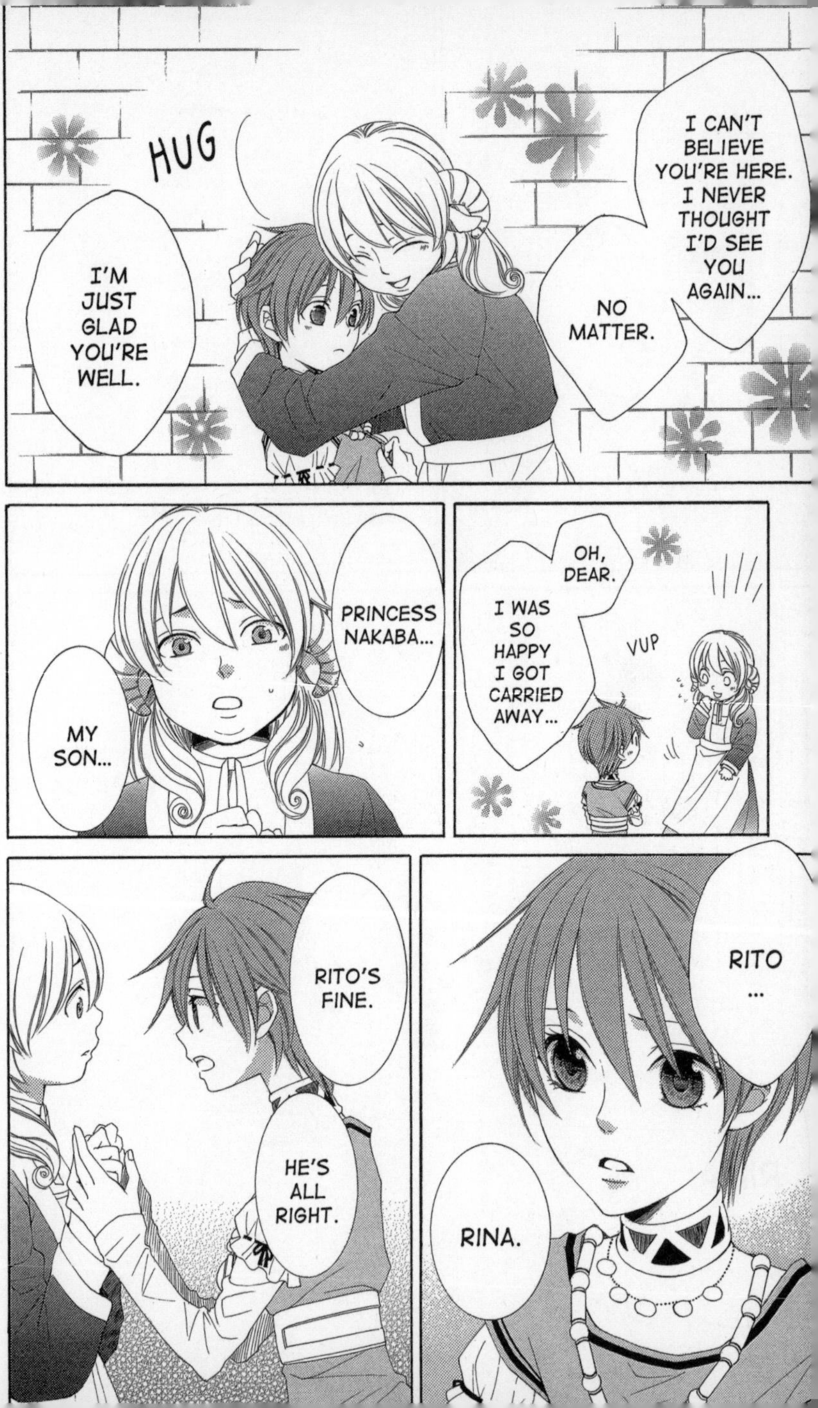
I CAN'T BELIEVE YOU'RE HERE. I NEVER THOUGHT I'D SEE YOU AGAIN...
NO MATTER.
HUG
I'M JUST GLAD YOU'RE WELL.
OH, DEAR.
I WAS SO HAPPY I GOT CARRIED AWAY...
VUP
PRINCESS NAKABA...
MY SON...
RITO ...
RINA.
RITO'S FINE.
HE'S ALL RIGHT.

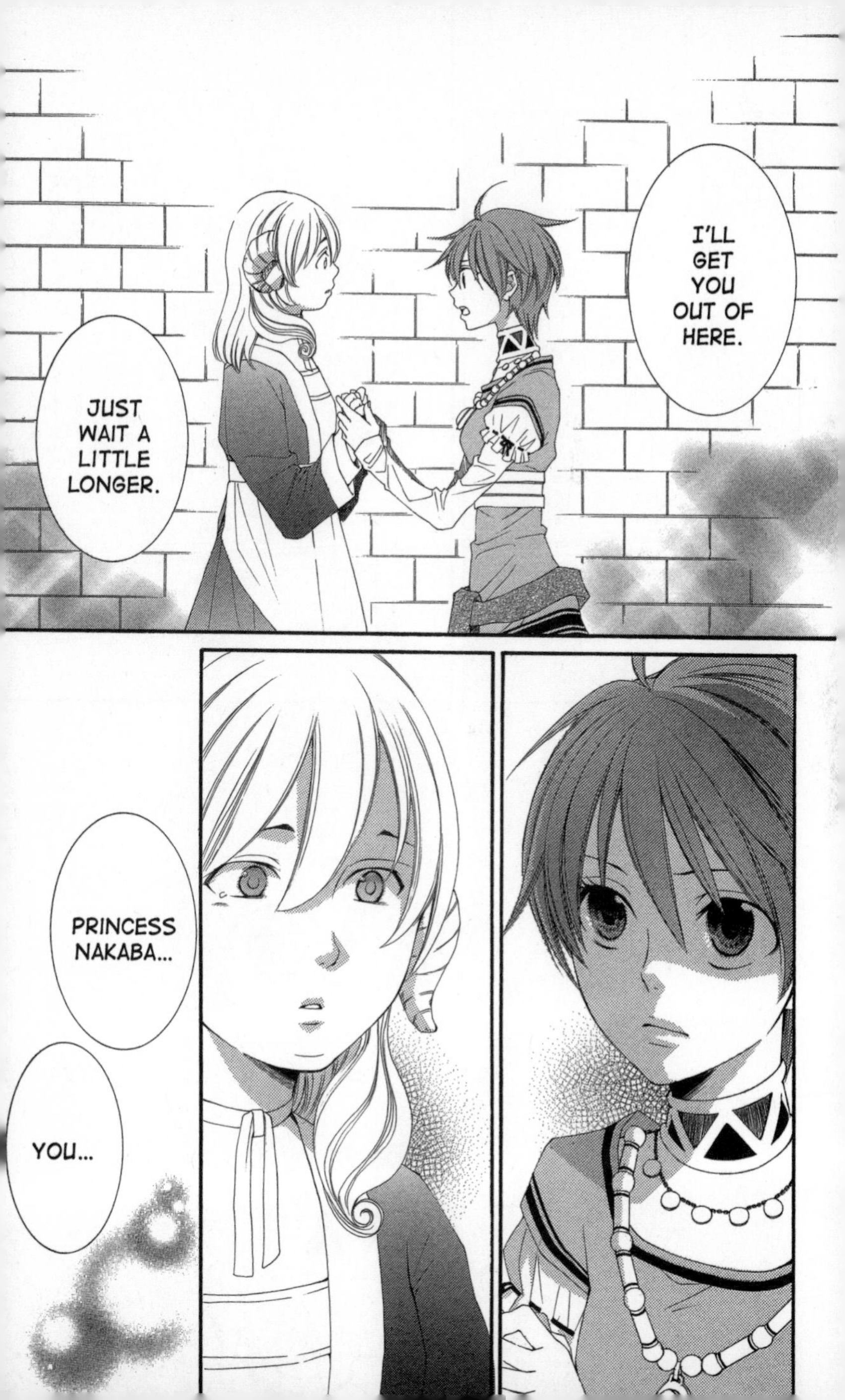
I'LL GET YOU OUT OF HERE.
JUST WAIT A LITTLE LONGER.
PRINCESS NAKABA...
YOU...

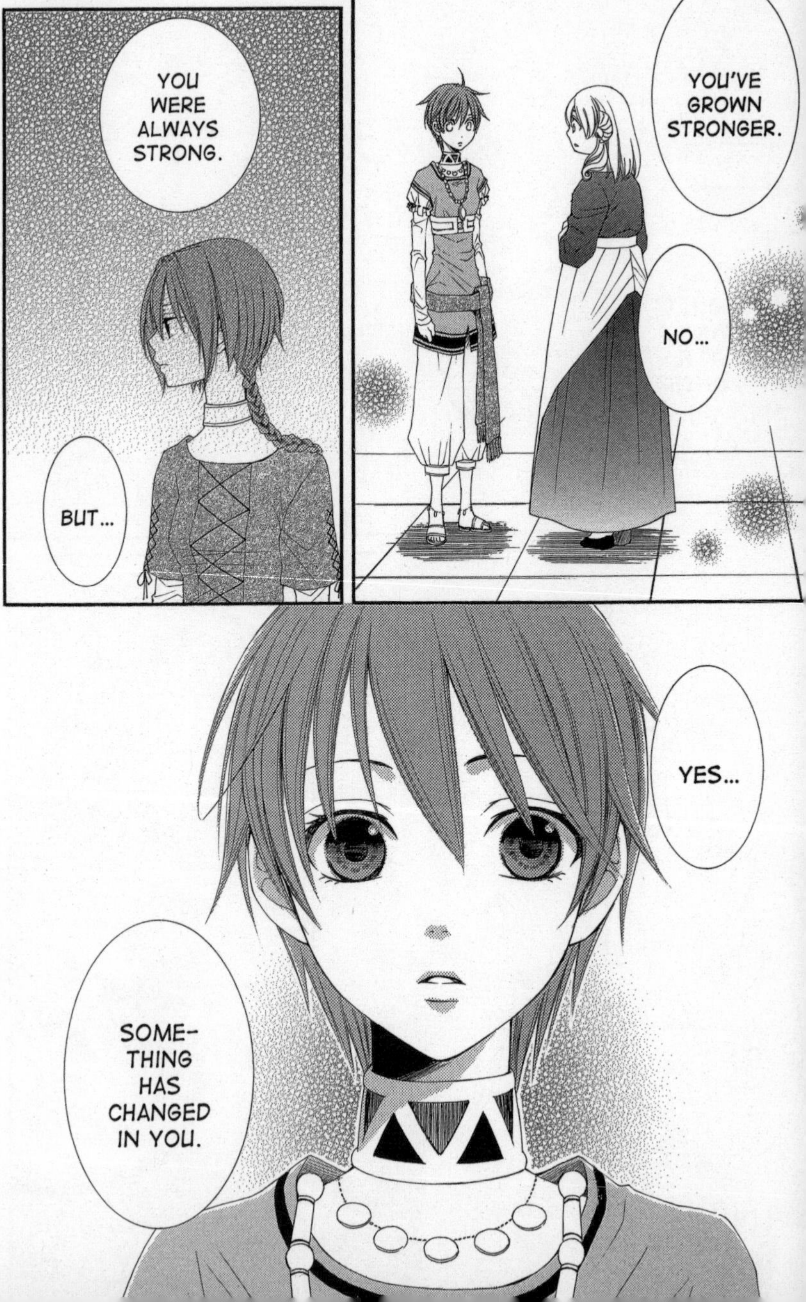
YOU'VE GROWN STRONGER.
NO...
YOU WERE ALWAYS STRONG.
BUT...
YES...
SOME-THING HAS CHANGED IN YOU.

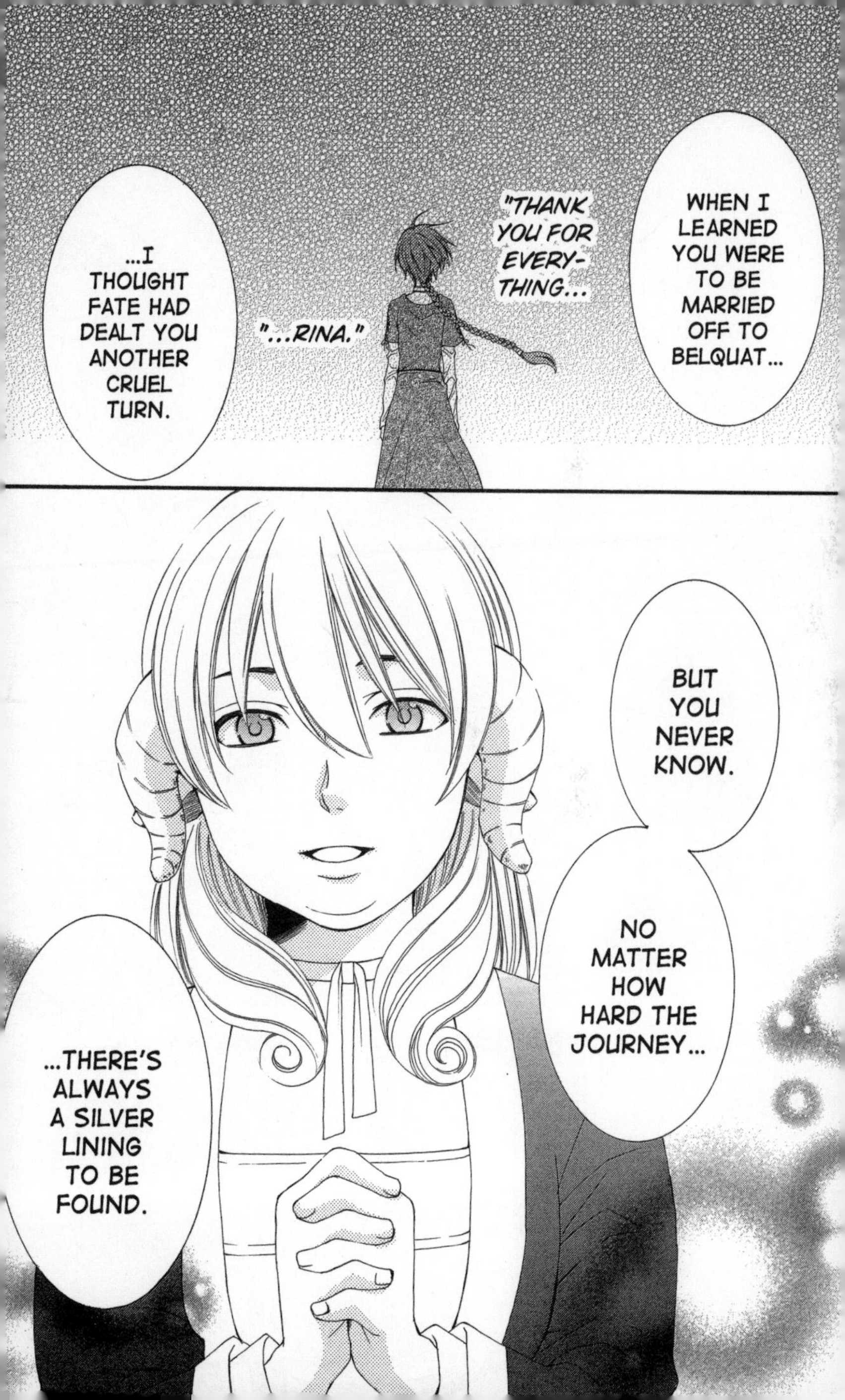
WHEN I LEARNED YOU WERE TO BE MARRIED OFF TO BELQUAT...
"THANK YOU FOR EVERY-THING...
"...RINA."
...I THOUGHT FATE HAD DEALT YOU ANOTHER CRUEL TURN.
BUT YOU NEVER KNOW.
NO MATTER HOW HARD THE JOURNEY...
...THERE'S ALWAYS A SILVER LINING TO BE FOUND.

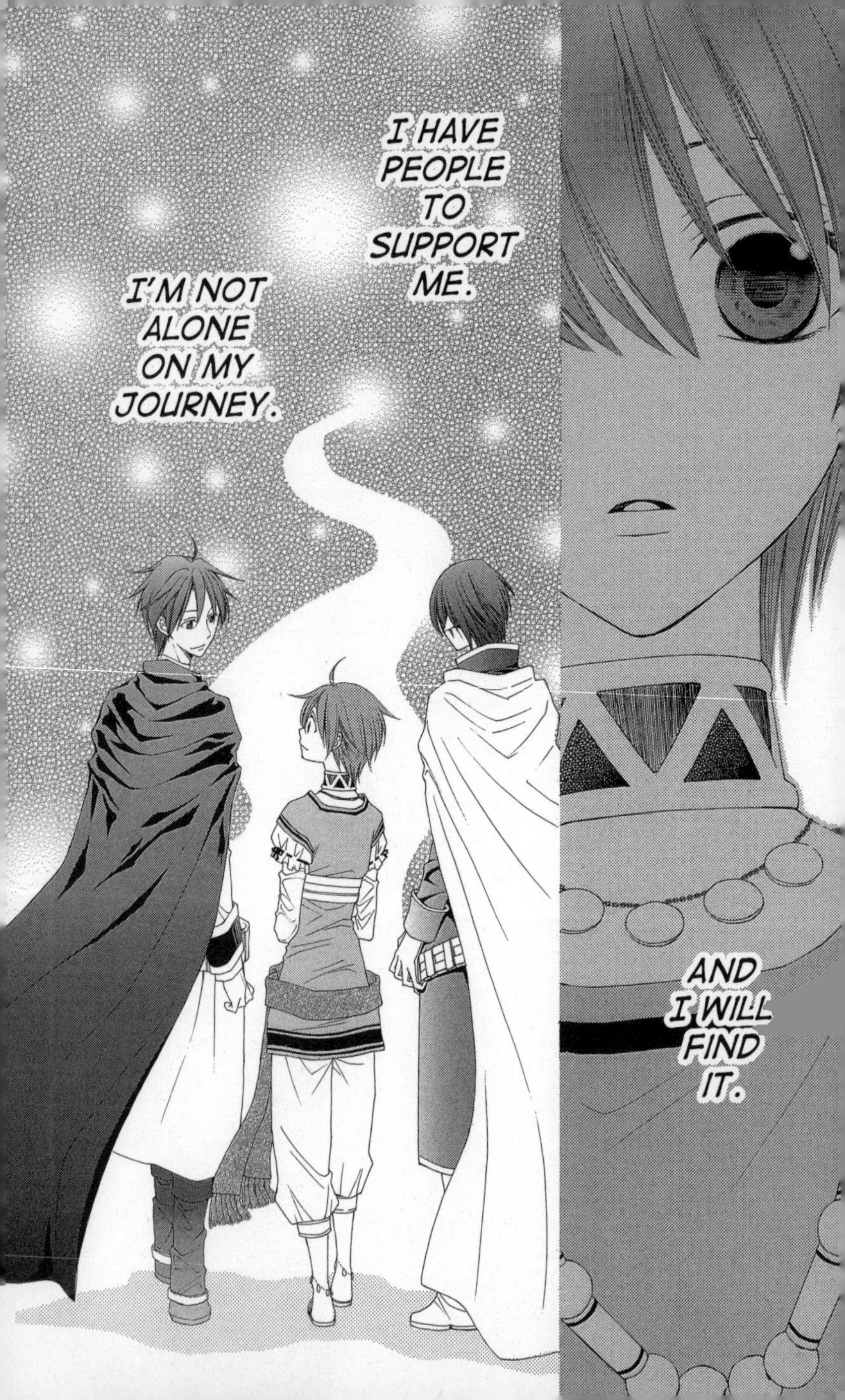
AND I WILL FIND IT.
I HAVE PEOPLE TO SUPPORT ME.
I'M NOT ALONE ON MY JOURNEY.

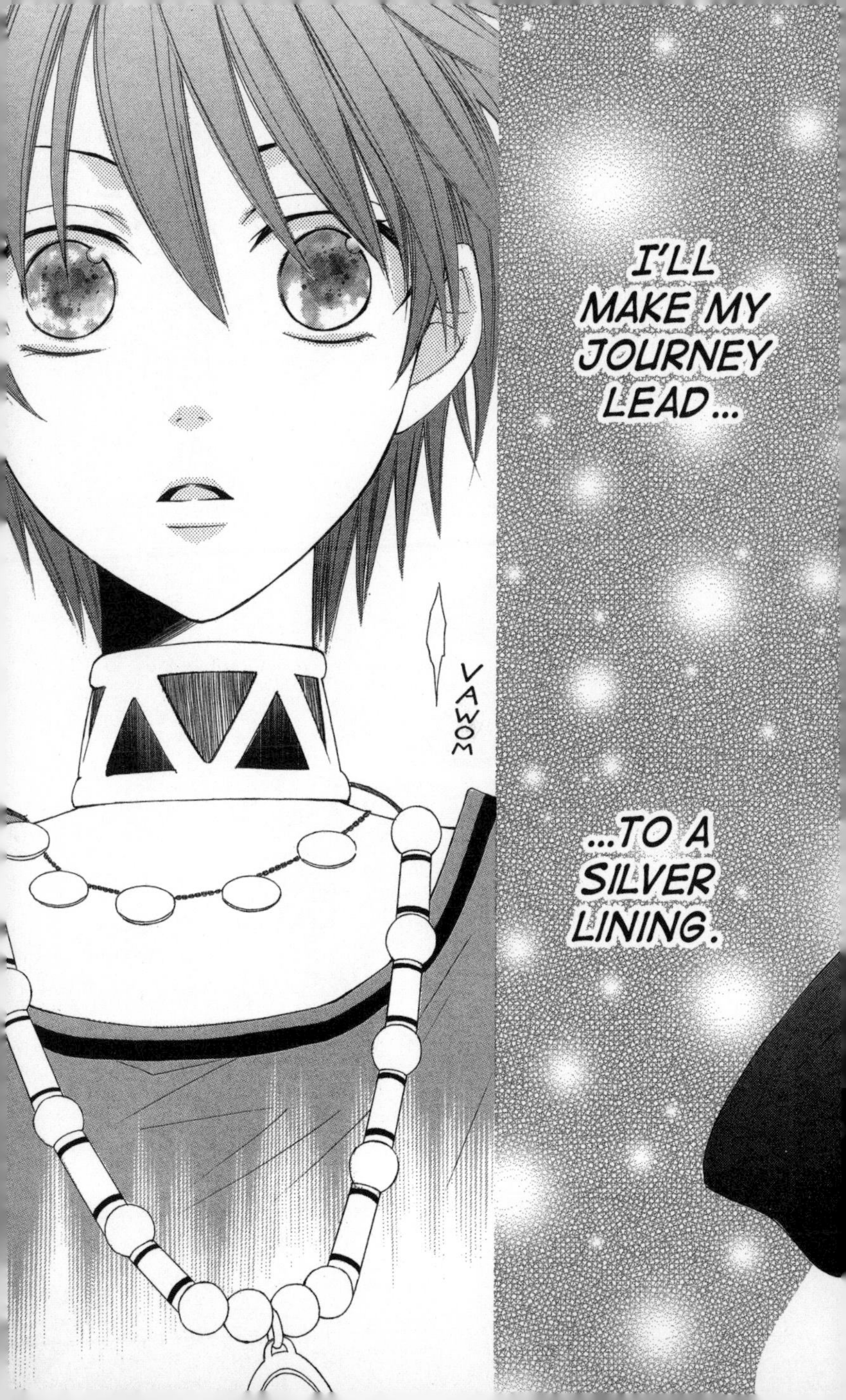
I'LL MAKE MY JOURNEY LEAD...
...TO A SILVER LINING.
VAWOM

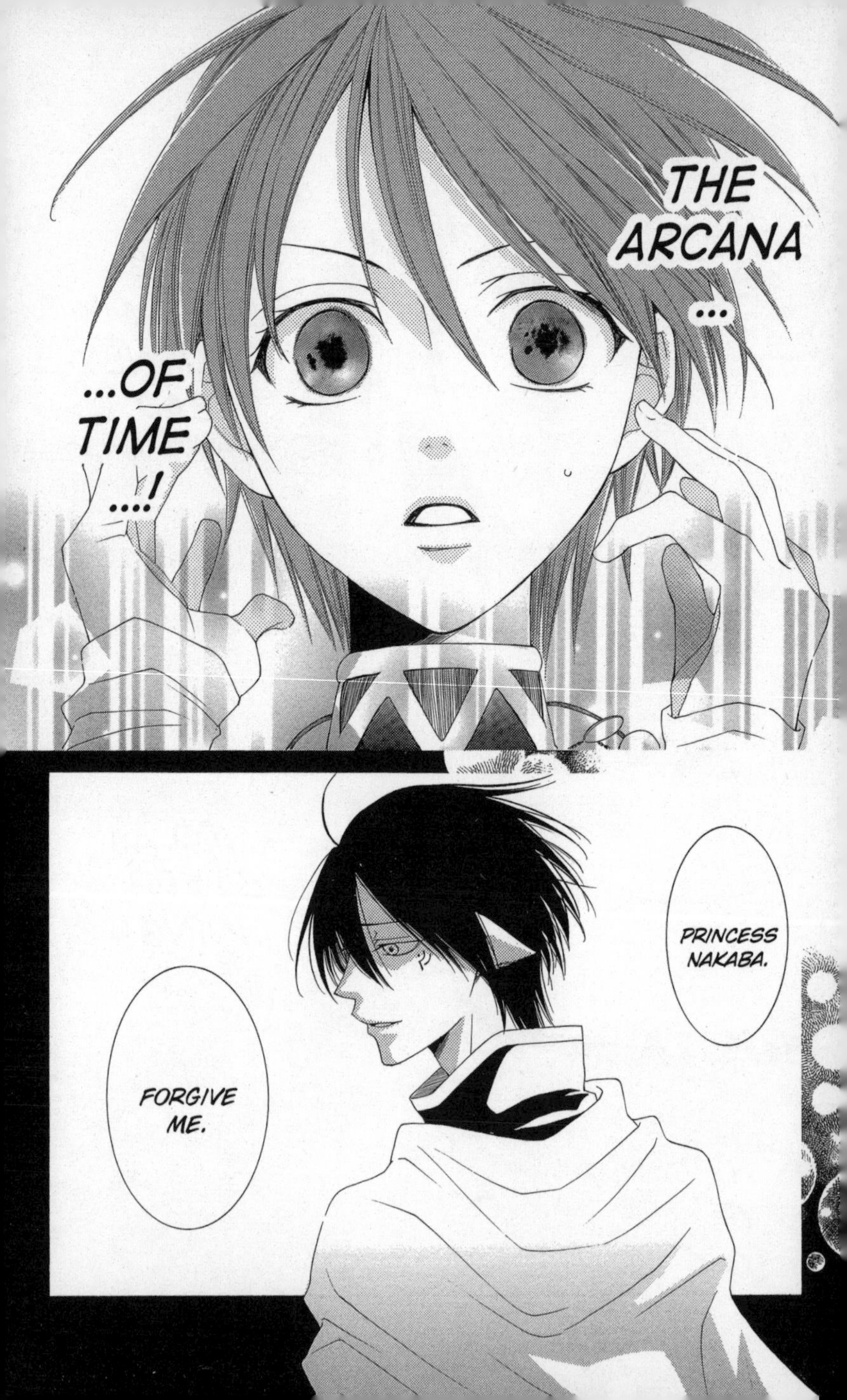
THE ARCANA ...
...OF TIME ...!
PRINCESS NAKABA.
FORGIVE ME.

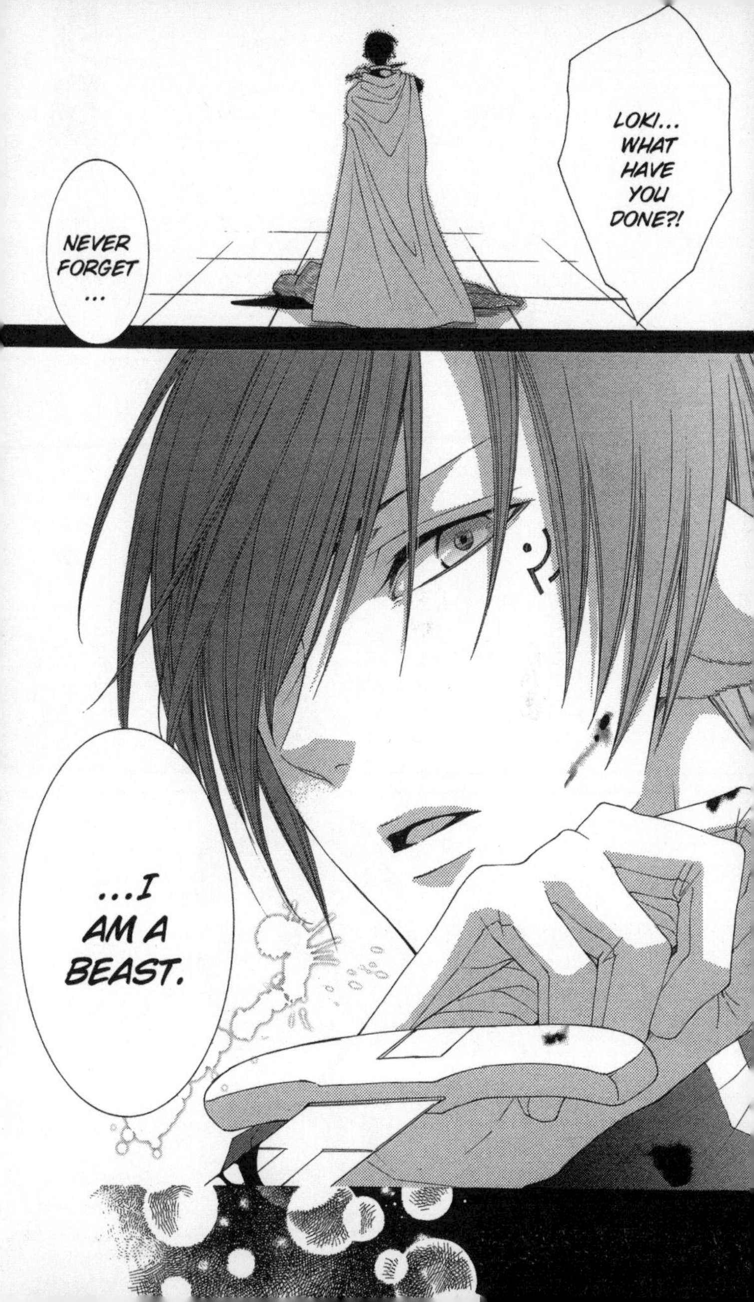
LOKI... WHAT HAVE YOU DONE?!
NEVER FORGET ...
...I AM A BEAST.

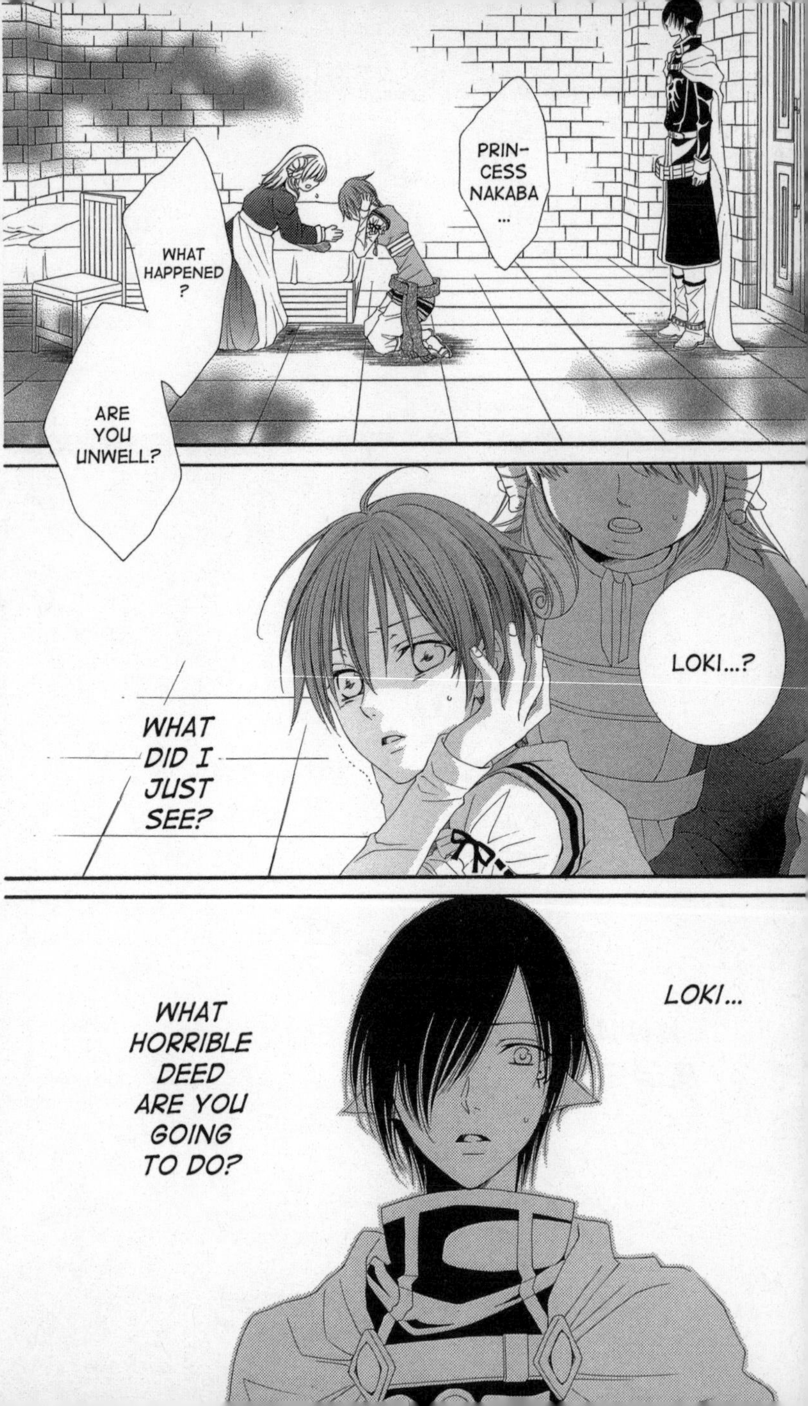
PRIN-CESS NAKABA...
WHAT HAPPENED?
ARE YOU UNWELL?
LOKI...?
WHAT DID I JUST SEE?
LOKI...
WHAT HORRIBLE DEED ARE YOU GOING TO DO?

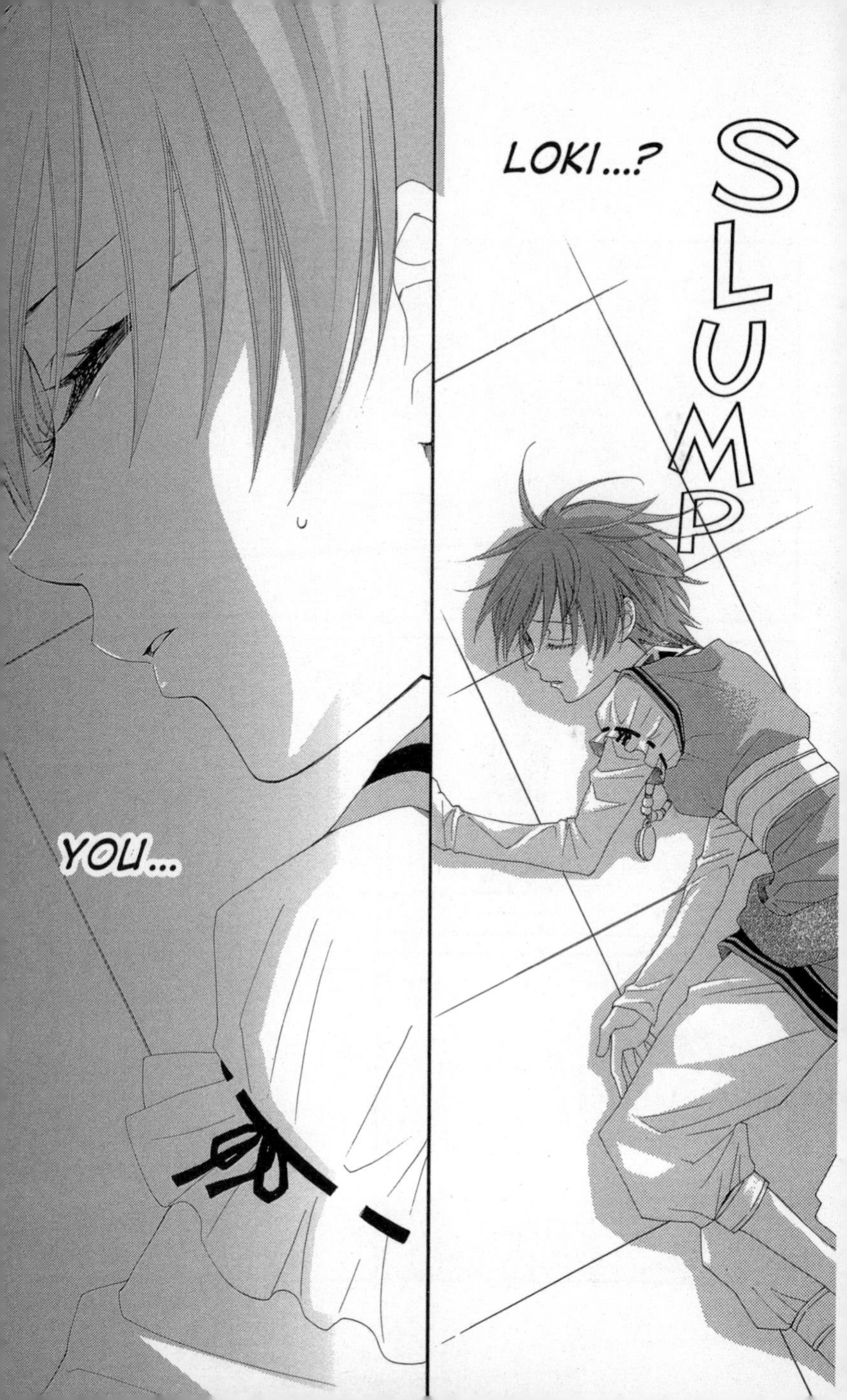
LOKI...?
SLUMP
YOU...

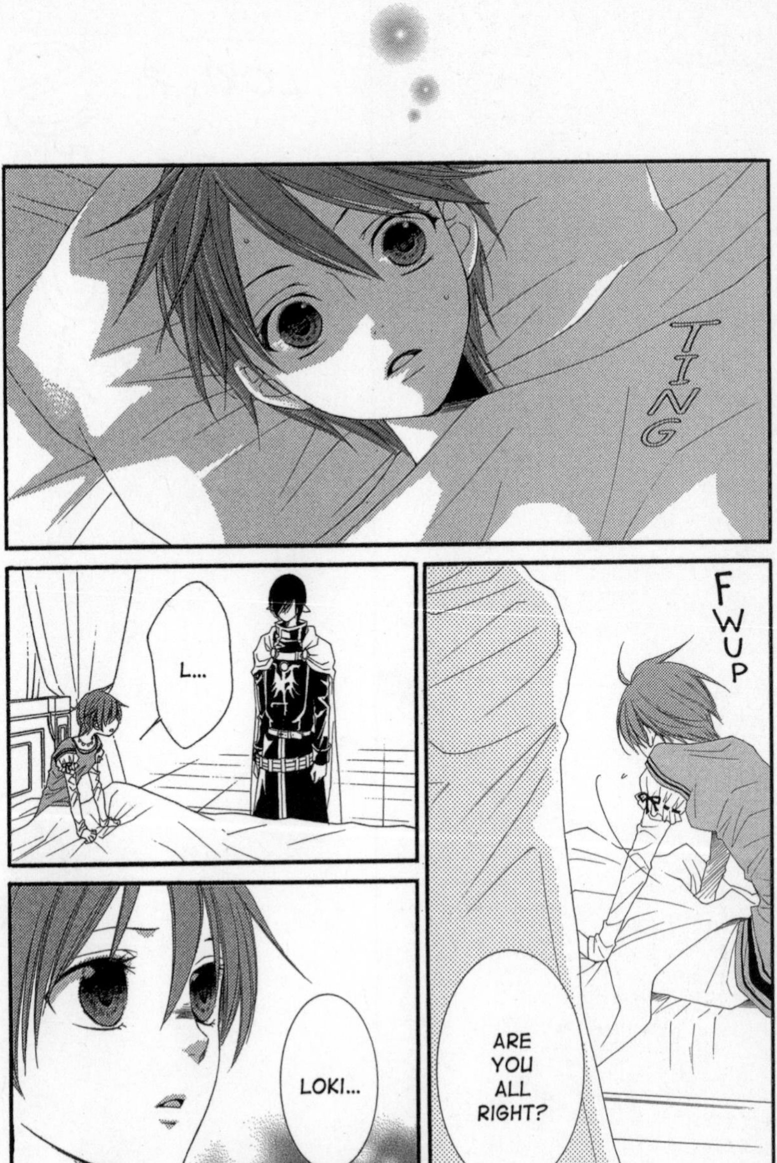
TING
FWUP
ARE YOU ALL RIGHT?
L...
LOKI...

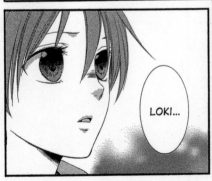

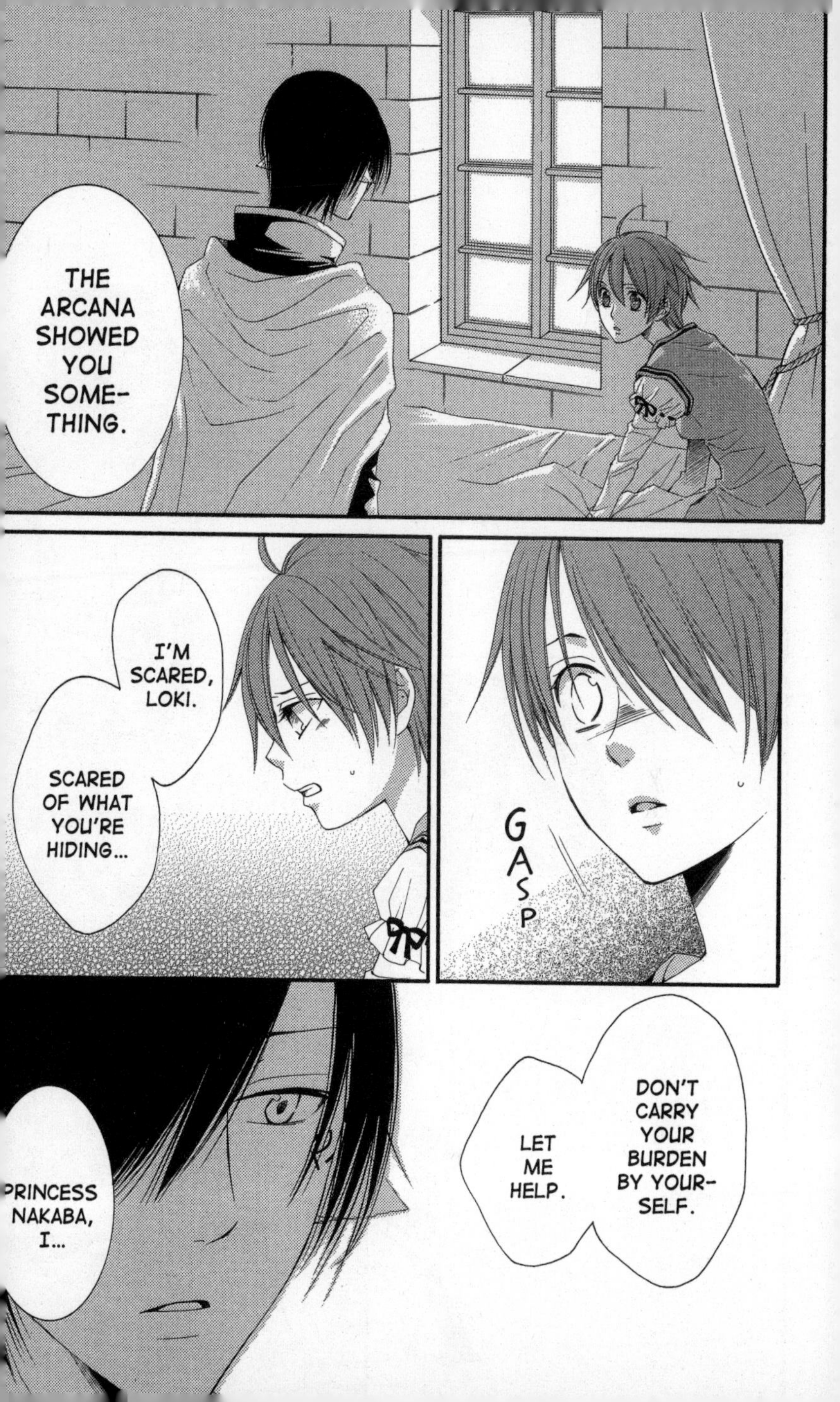
THE ARCANA SHOWED YOU SOME-THING.
GASP
I'M SCARED, LOKI.
SCARED OF WHAT YOU'RE HIDING...
DON'T CARRY YOUR BURDEN BY YOUR-SELF.
LET ME HELP.
PRINCESS NAKABA, I...

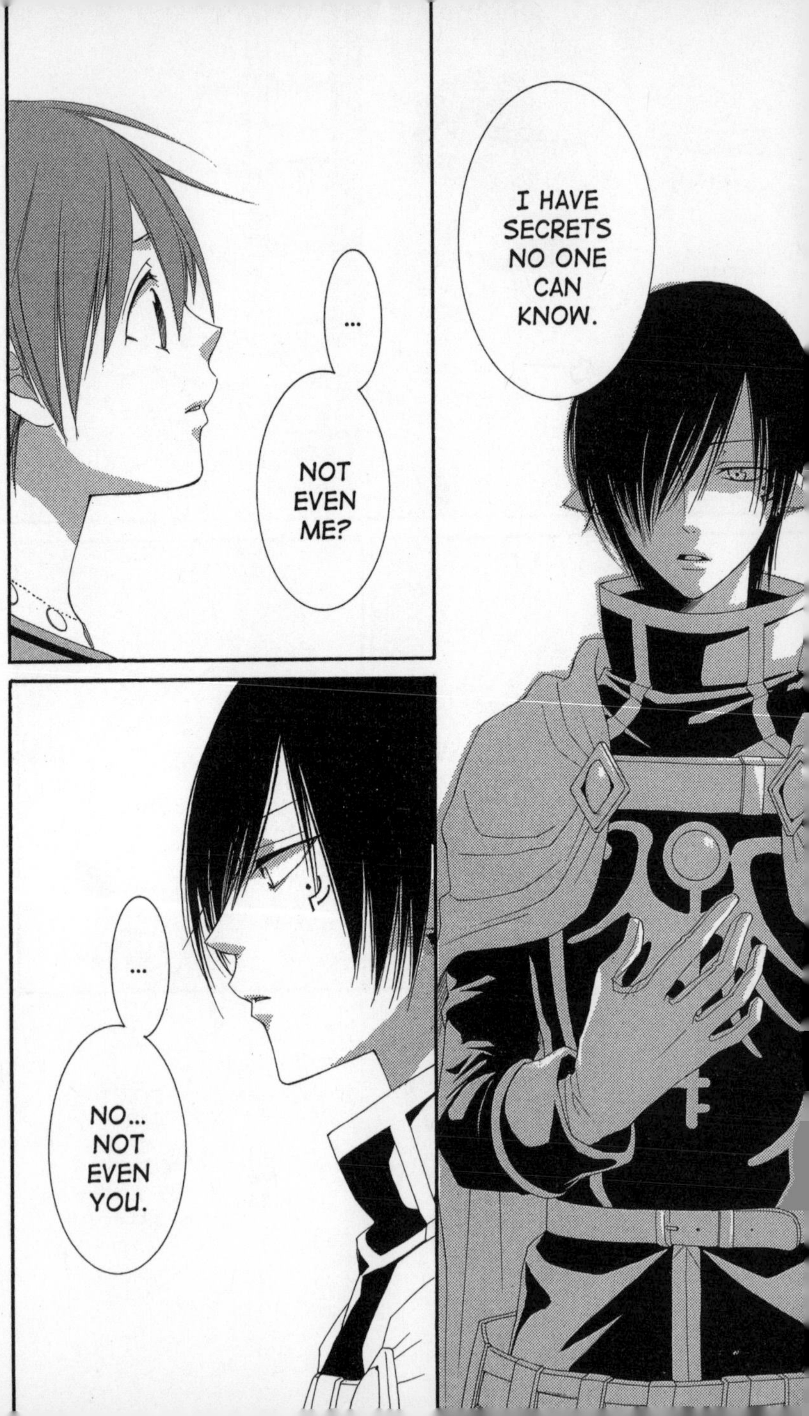
I HAVE SECRETS NO ONE CAN KNOW.
...
NOT EVEN ME?
...
NO... NOT EVEN YOU.

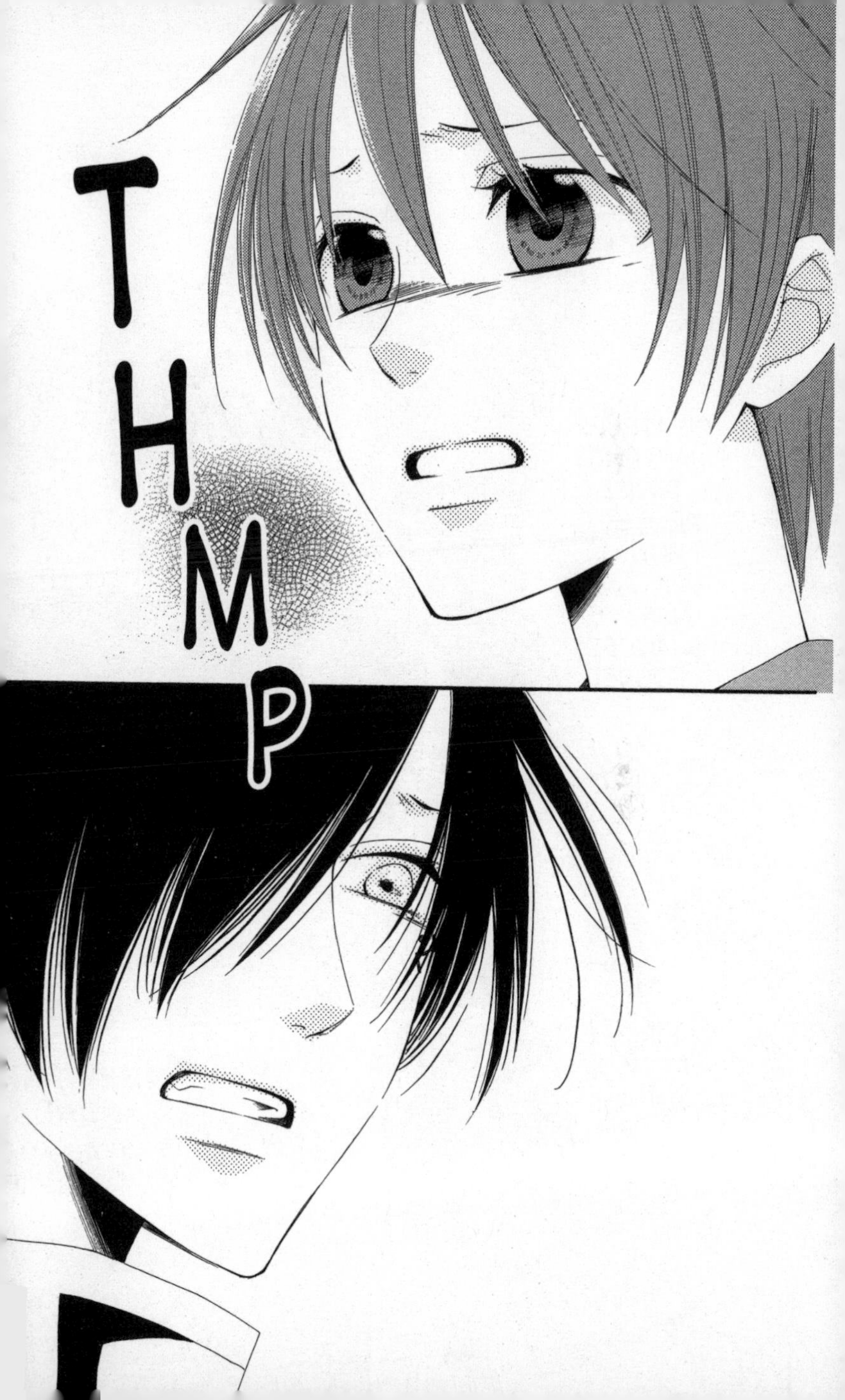
THMP

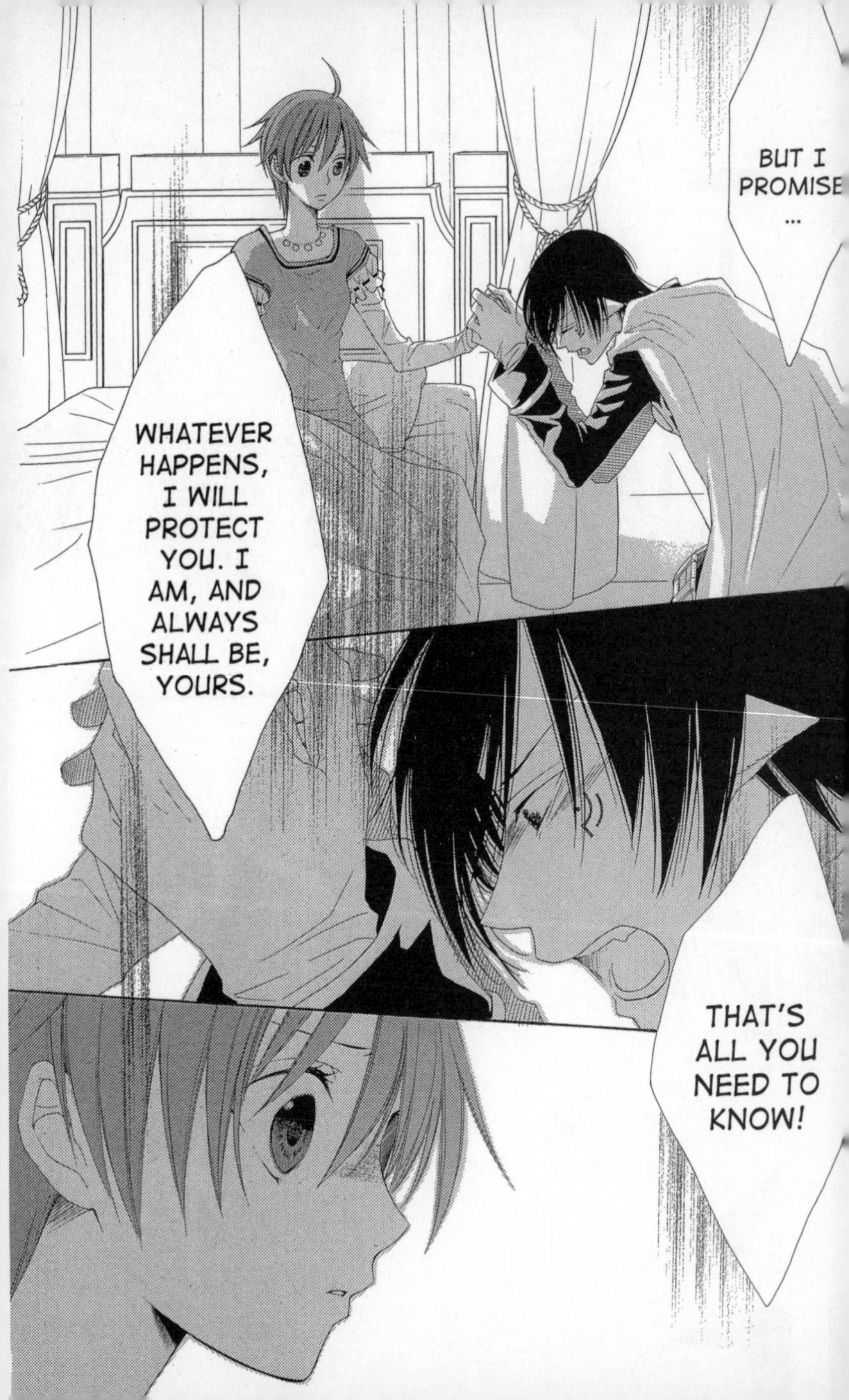
BUT I PROMISE ...
WHATEVER HAPPENS, I WILL PROTECT YOU. I AM, AND ALWAYS SHALL BE, YOURS.
THAT'S ALL YOU NEED TO KNOW!

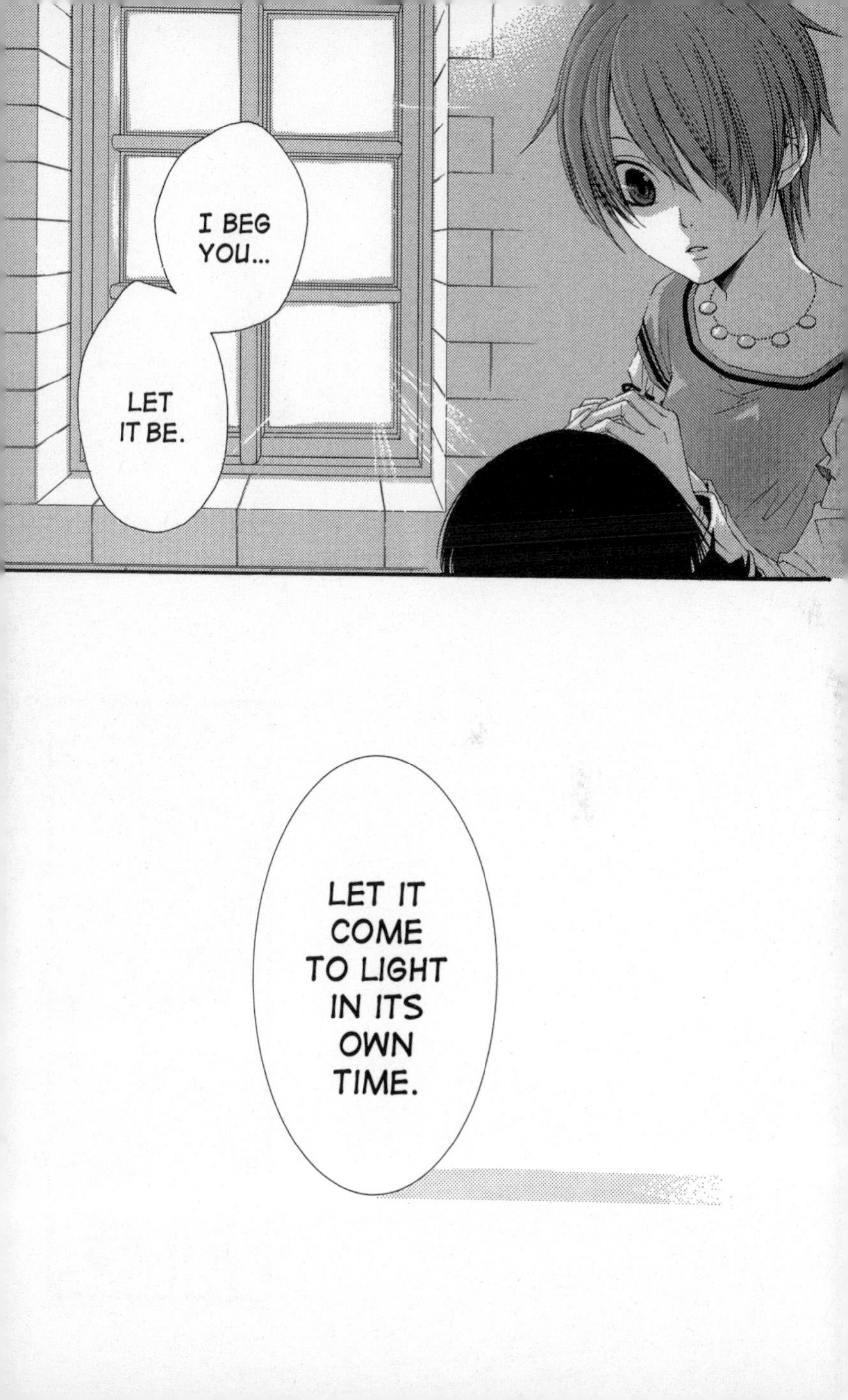
I BEG YOU...
LET IT BE.
LET IT COME TO LIGHT IN ITS OWN TIME.

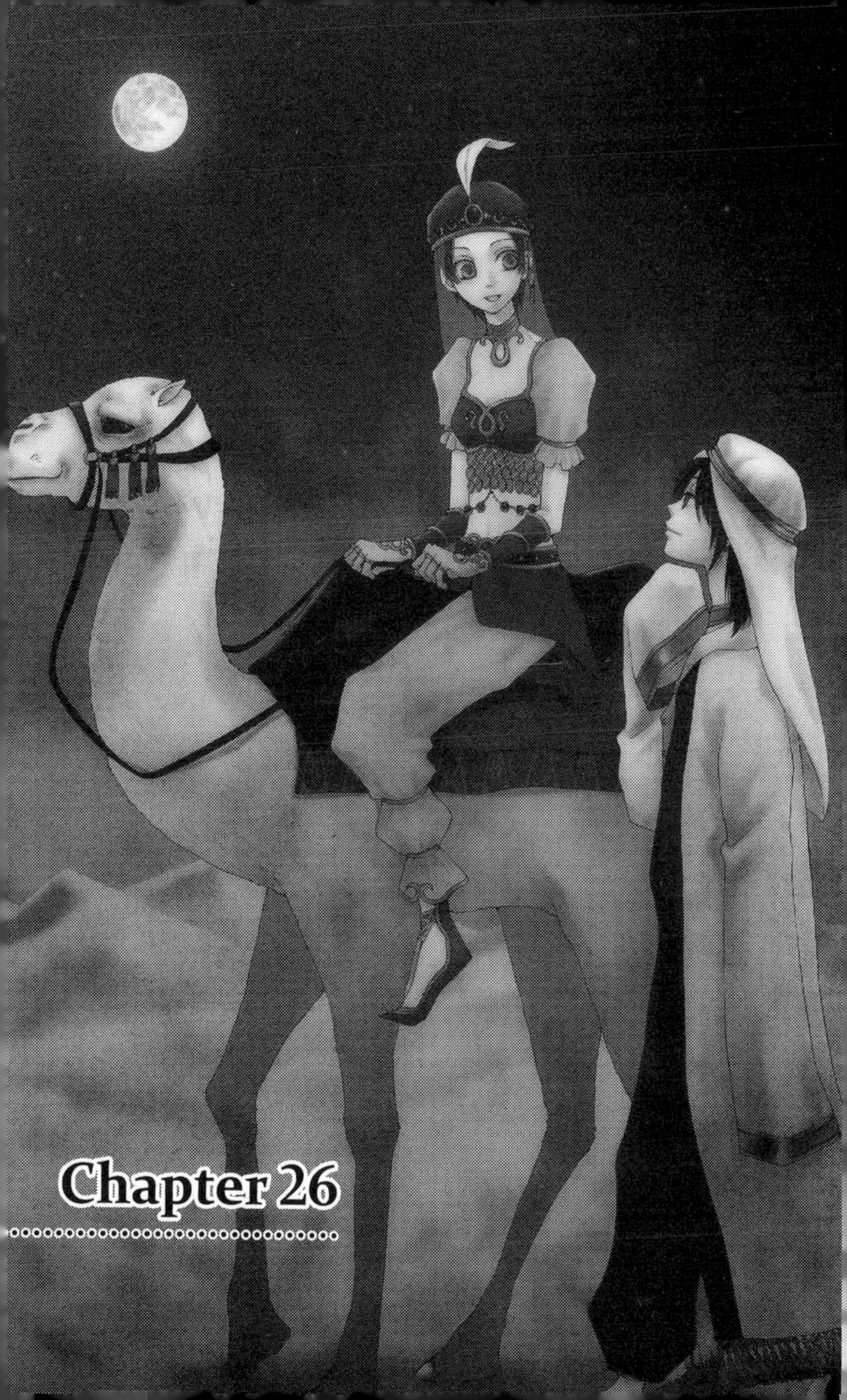
Chapter 26

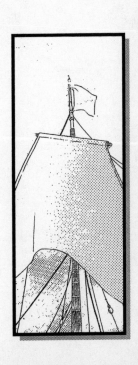

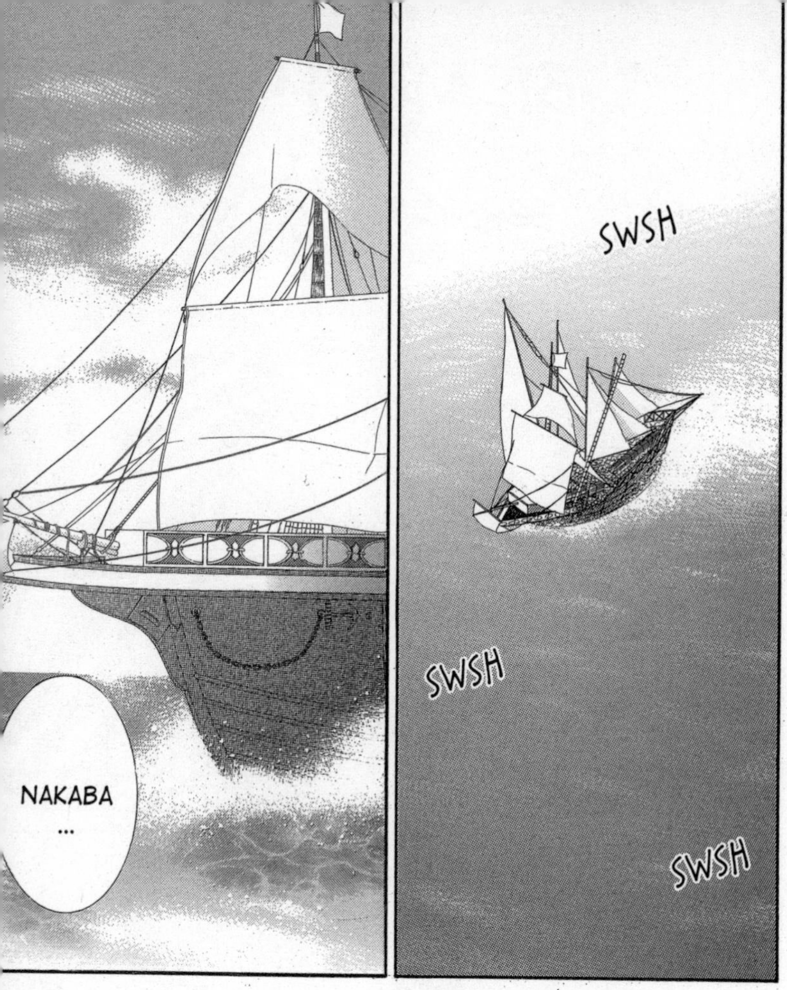
SWSH
SWSH
SWSH
NAKABA
...

Dawn of the Arcana

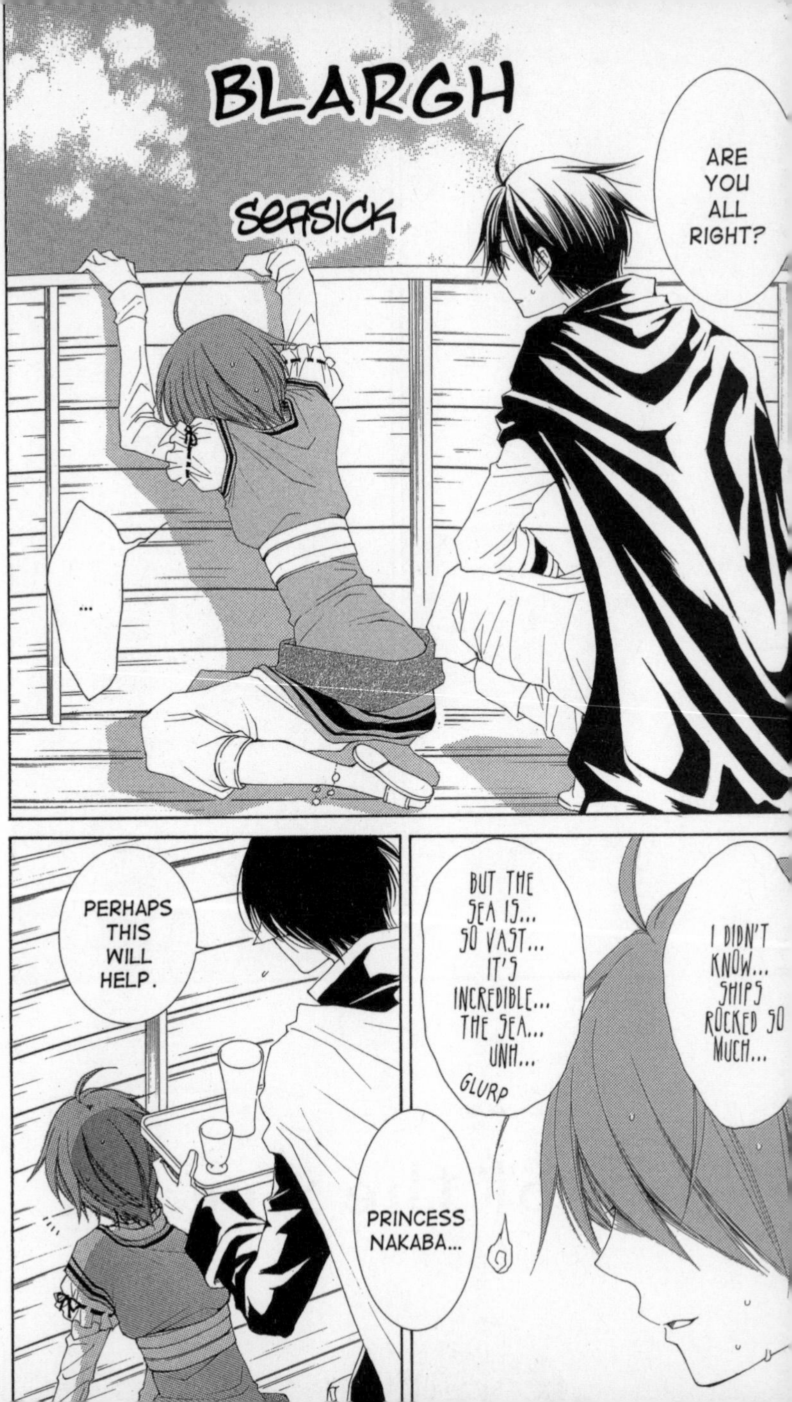
ARE YOU ALL RIGHT?
BLARGH
SEASICK
...
I DIDN'T KNOW... SHIPS ROCKED SO MUCH...
BUT THE SEA IS... SO VAST... IT'S INCREDIBLE... THE SEA... UNH...
GLURP
PRINCESS NAKABA...
PERHAPS THIS WILL HELP.

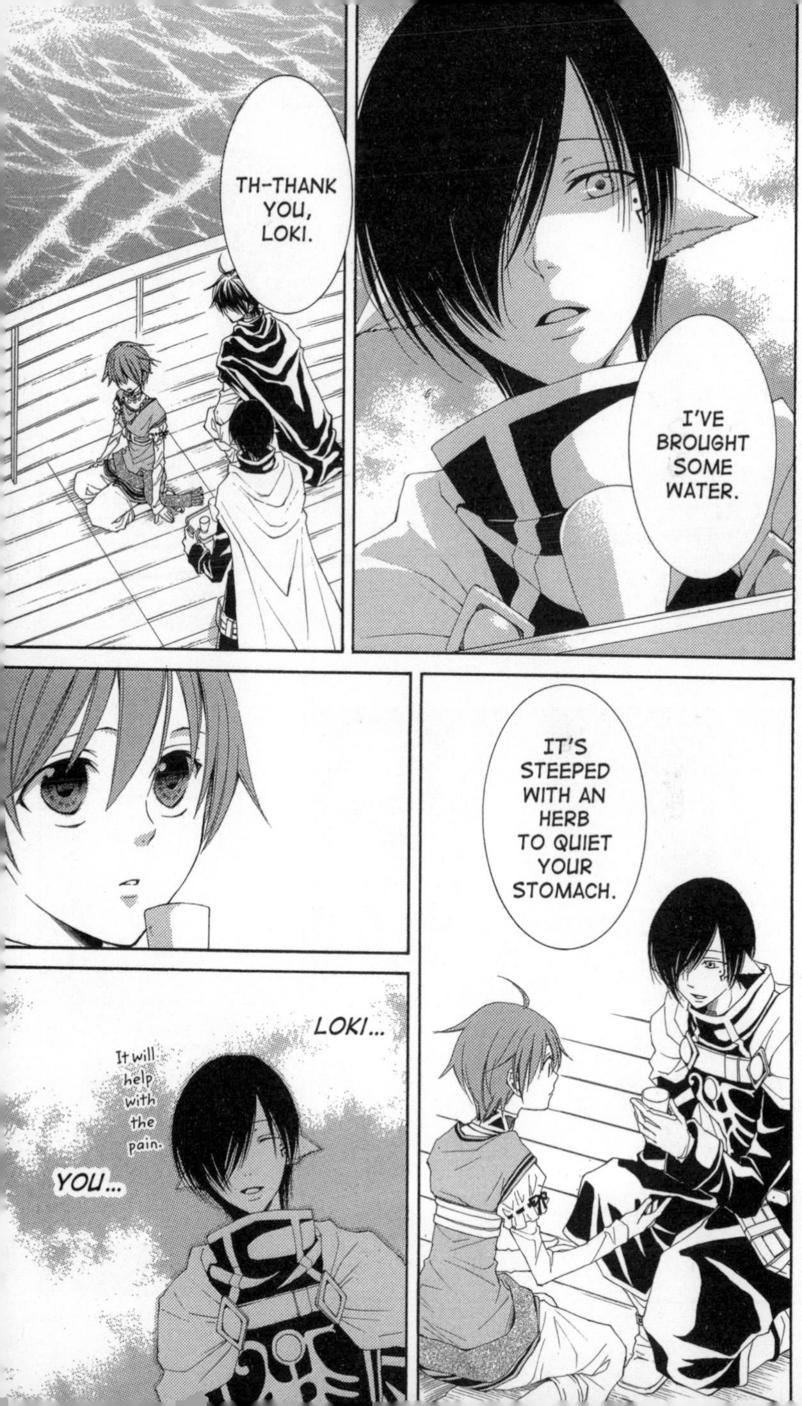
I'VE BROUGHT SOME WATER.
TH-THANK YOU, LOKI.
IT'S STEEPED WITH AN HERB TO QUIET YOUR STOMACH.
LOKI...
It will help with the pain.
YOU...

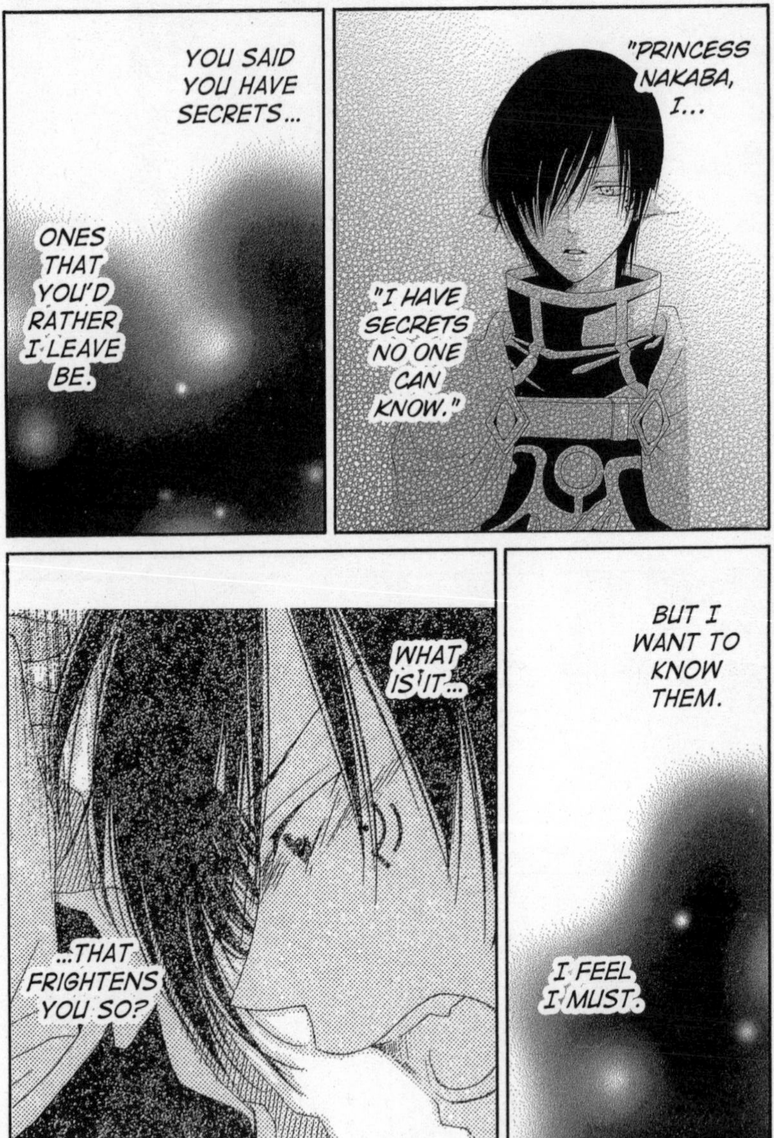
"PRINCESS NAKABA, I...
"I HAVE SECRETS NO ONE CAN KNOW."
YOU SAID YOU HAVE SECRETS...
ONES THAT YOU'D RATHER I LEAVE BE.
BUT I WANT TO KNOW THEM.
I FEEL I MUST.
WHAT IS IT...
...THAT FRIGHTENS YOU SO?

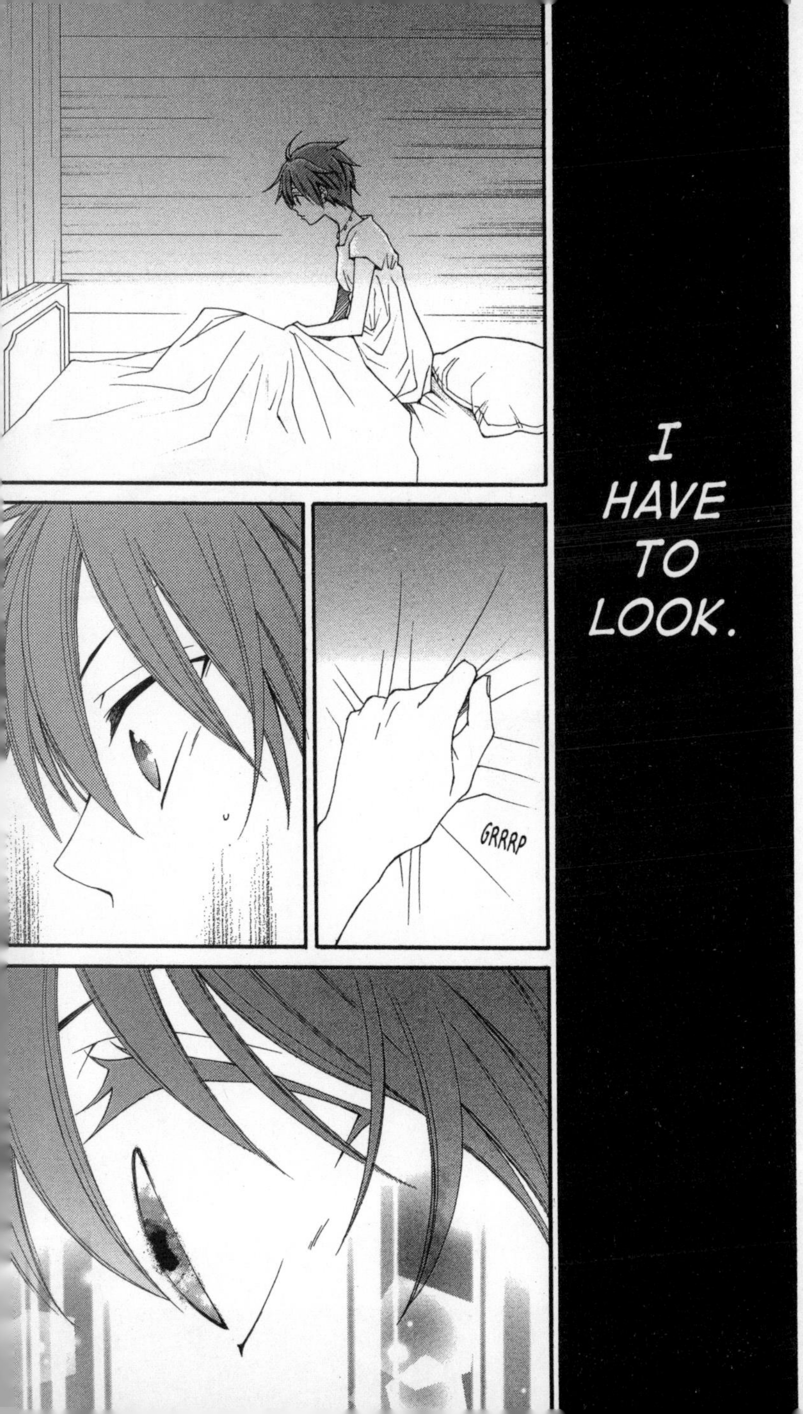
I HAVE TO LOOK.
GRRRP

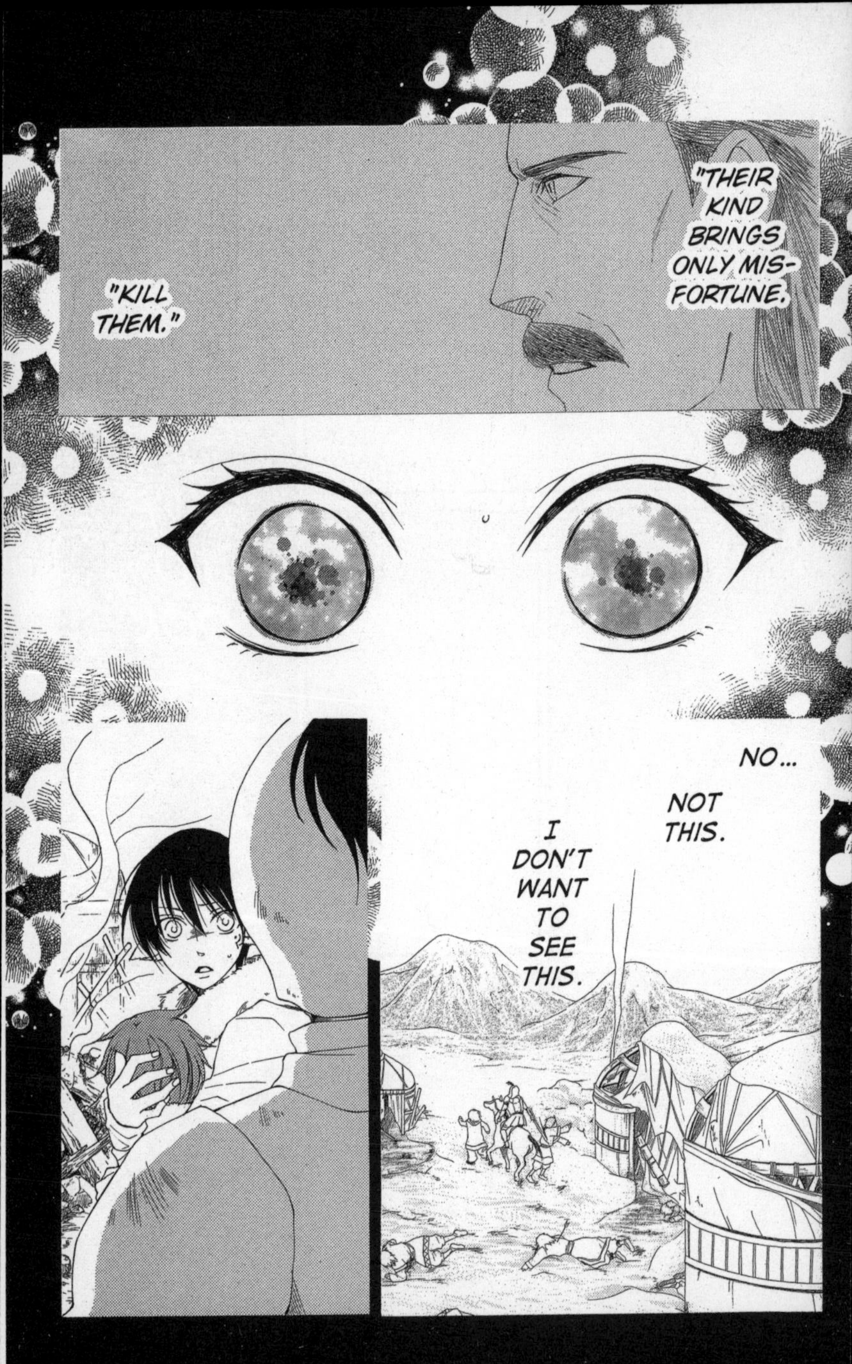
"THEIR KIND BRINGS ONLY MIS-FORTUNE.
"KILL THEM."
NO...
NOT THIS.
I DON'T WANT TO SEE THIS.

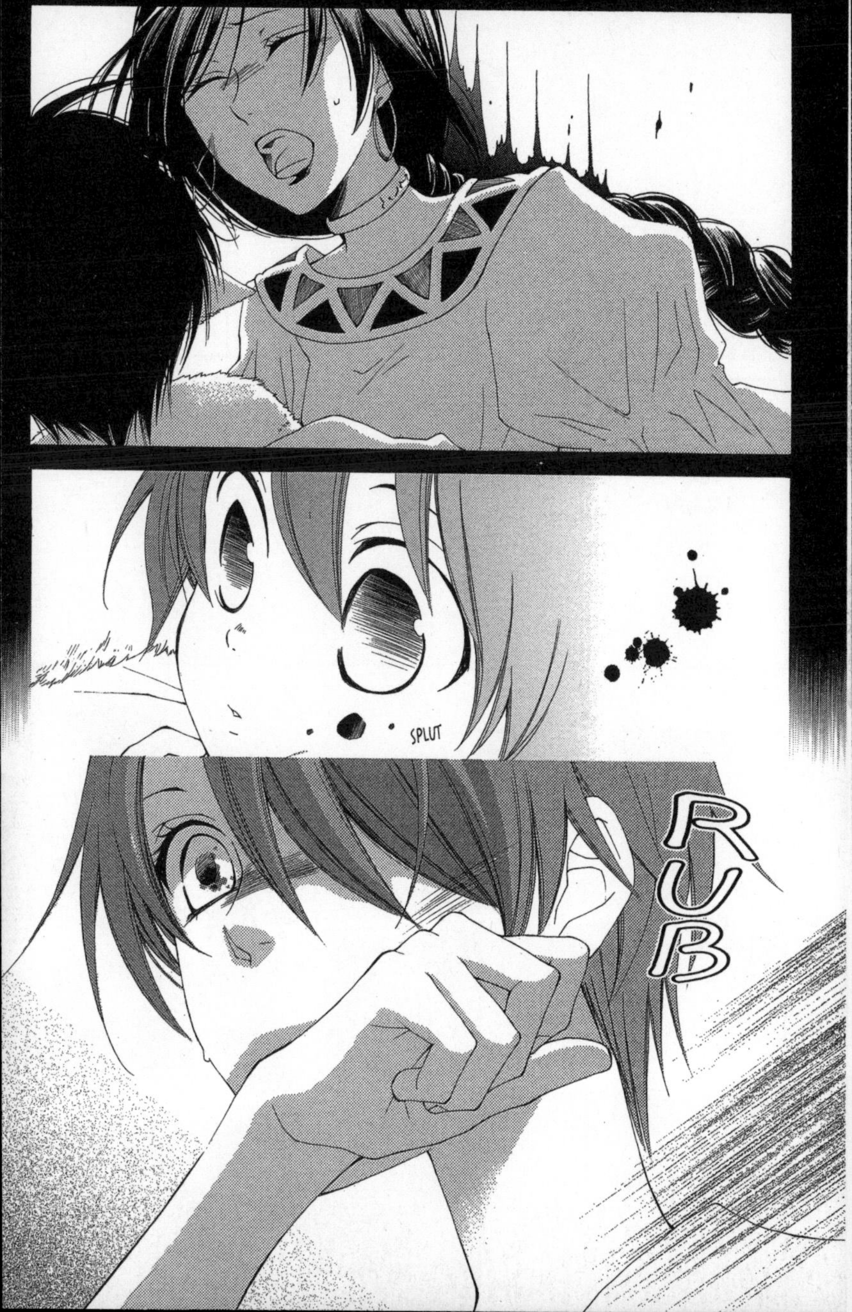
SPLUT
RUB

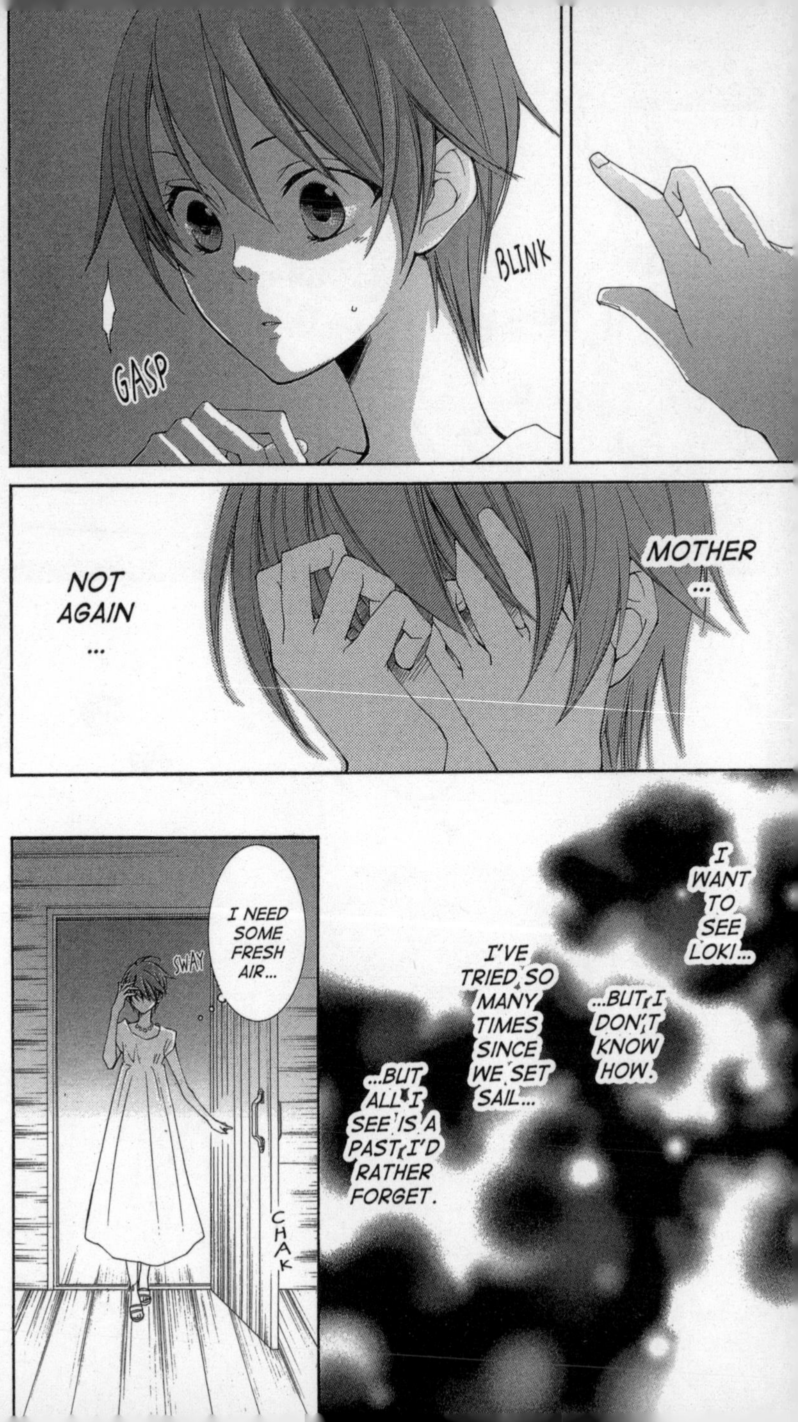
BLINK
GASP
MOTHER...
NOT AGAIN...
I WANT TO SEE LOKI...
...BUT I DON'T KNOW HOW.
I'VE TRIED SO MANY TIMES SINCE WE SET SAIL...
...BUT ALL I SEE IS A PAST I'D RATHER FORGET.
I NEED SOME FRESH AIR...
SWAY
CHAK

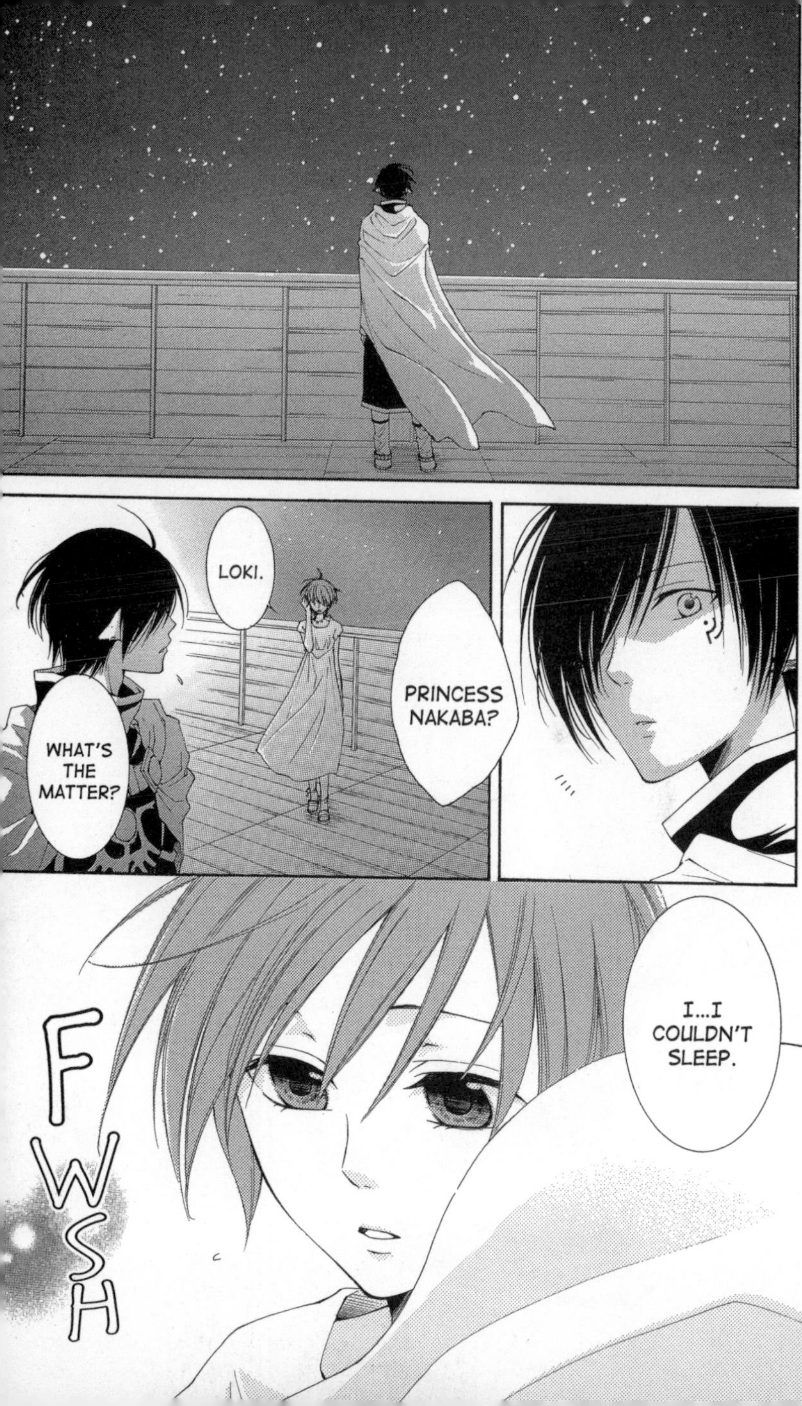
LOKI.
PRINCESS NAKABA?
WHAT'S THE MATTER?
I...I COULDN'T SLEEP.
FWSH

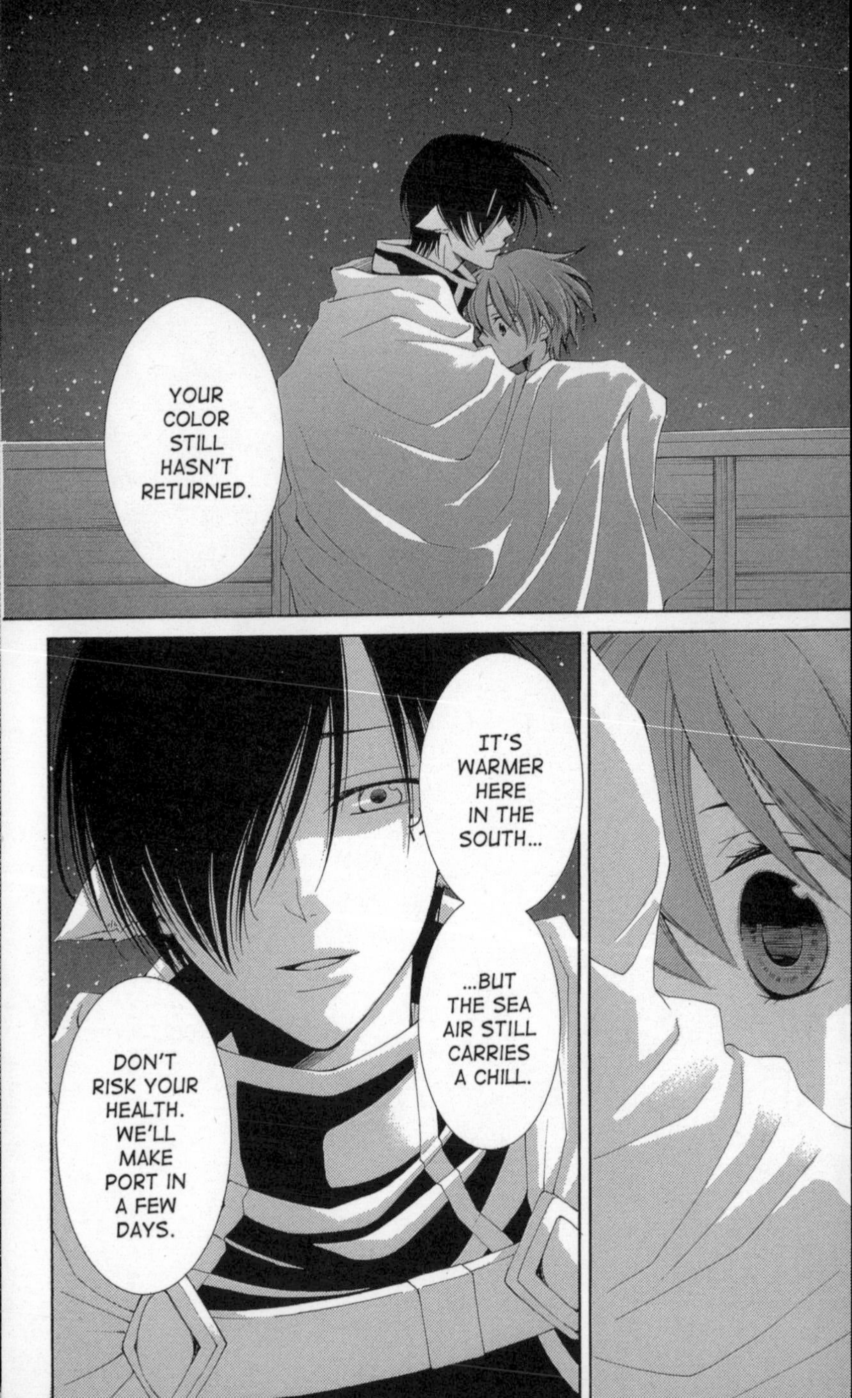
YOUR COLOR STILL HASN'T RETURNED.
IT'S WARMER HERE IN THE SOUTH...
...BUT THE SEA AIR STILL CARRIES A CHILL.
DON'T RISK YOUR HEALTH. WE'LL MAKE PORT IN A FEW DAYS.

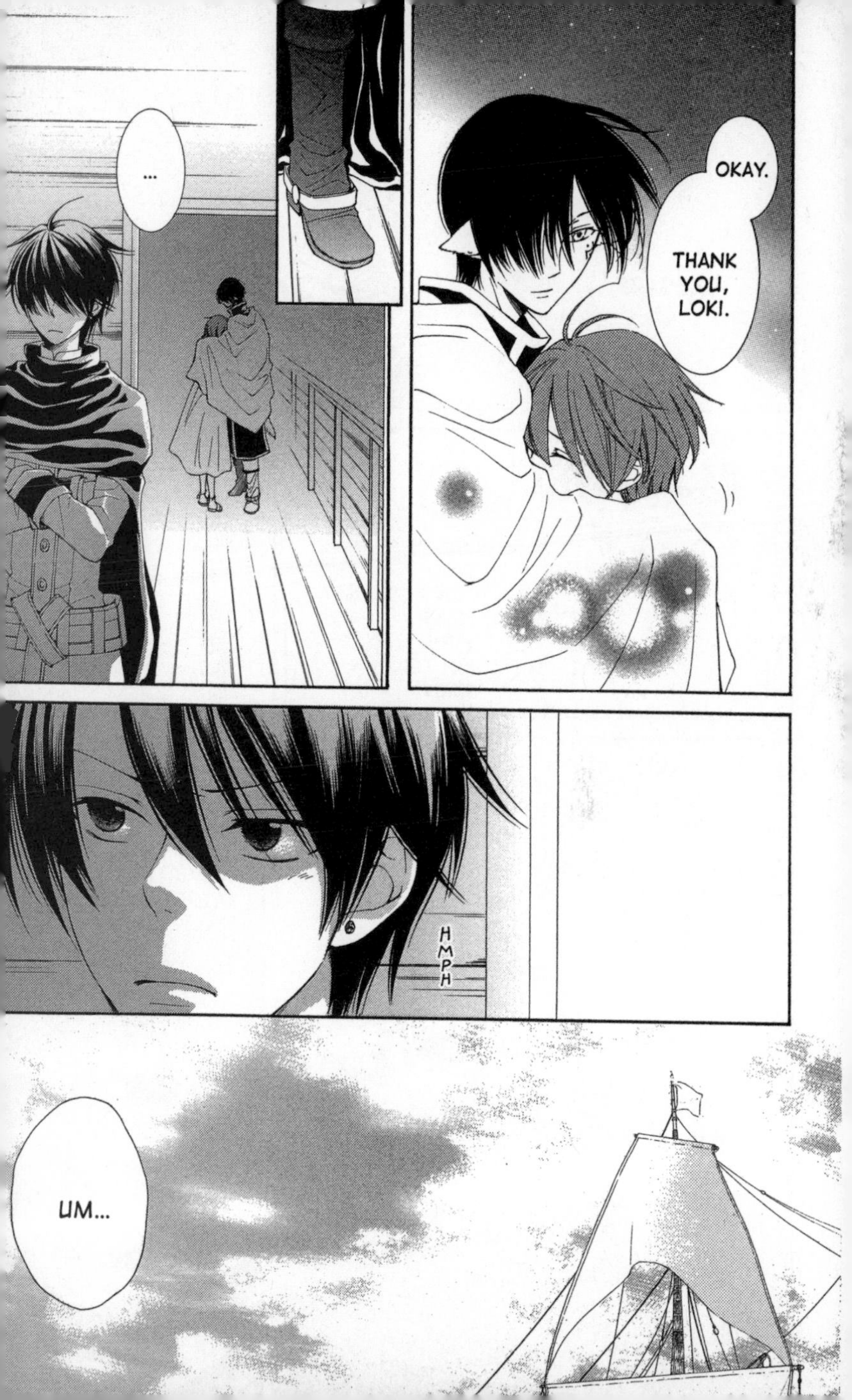
OKAY.
THANK YOU, LOKI.
...
HMPH
UM...

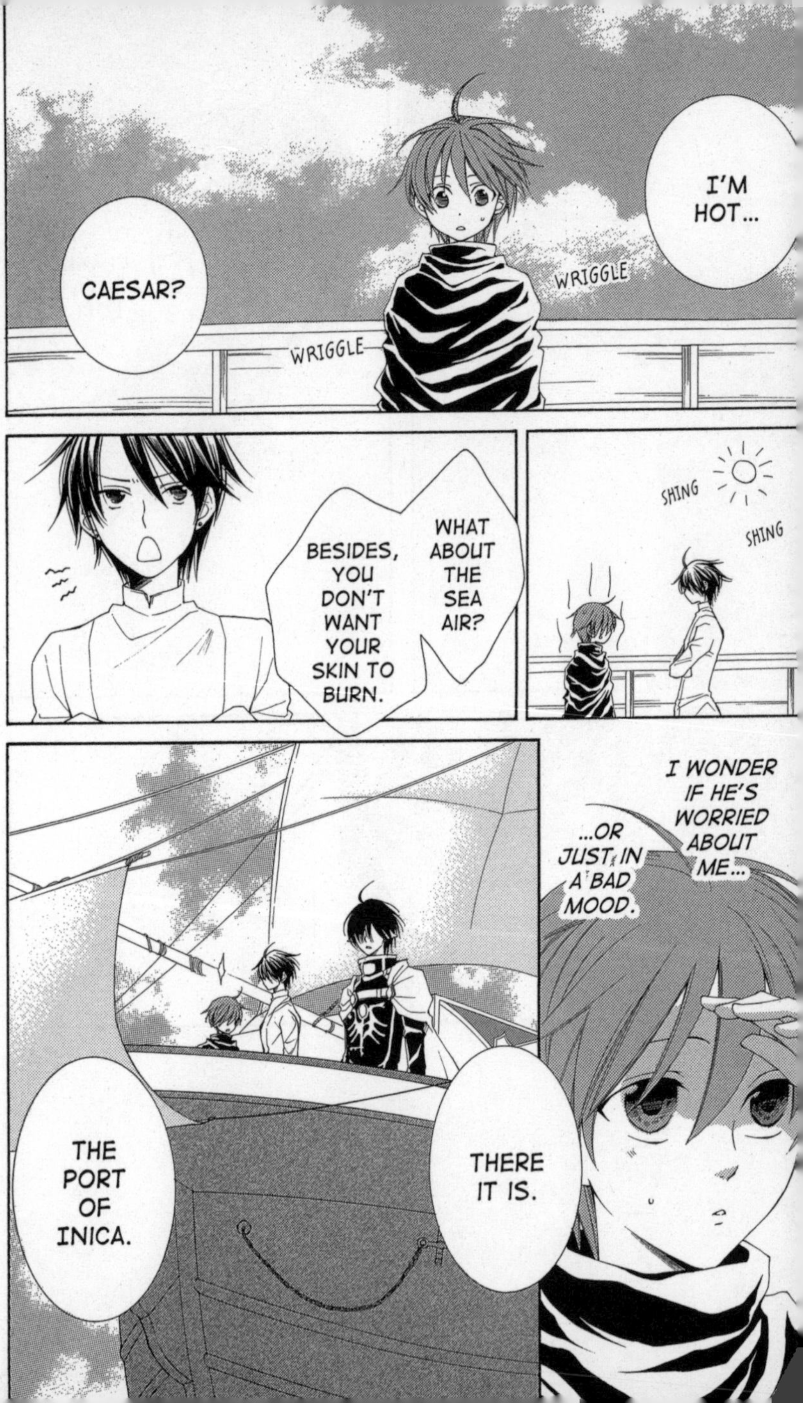
I'M HOT...
WRIGGLE
CAESAR?
WRIGGLE
SHING
SHING
WHAT ABOUT THE SEA AIR?
BESIDES, YOU DON'T WANT YOUR SKIN TO BURN.
I WONDER IF HE'S WORRIED ABOUT ME...
...OR JUST IN A BAD MOOD.
THERE IT IS.
THE PORT OF INICA.

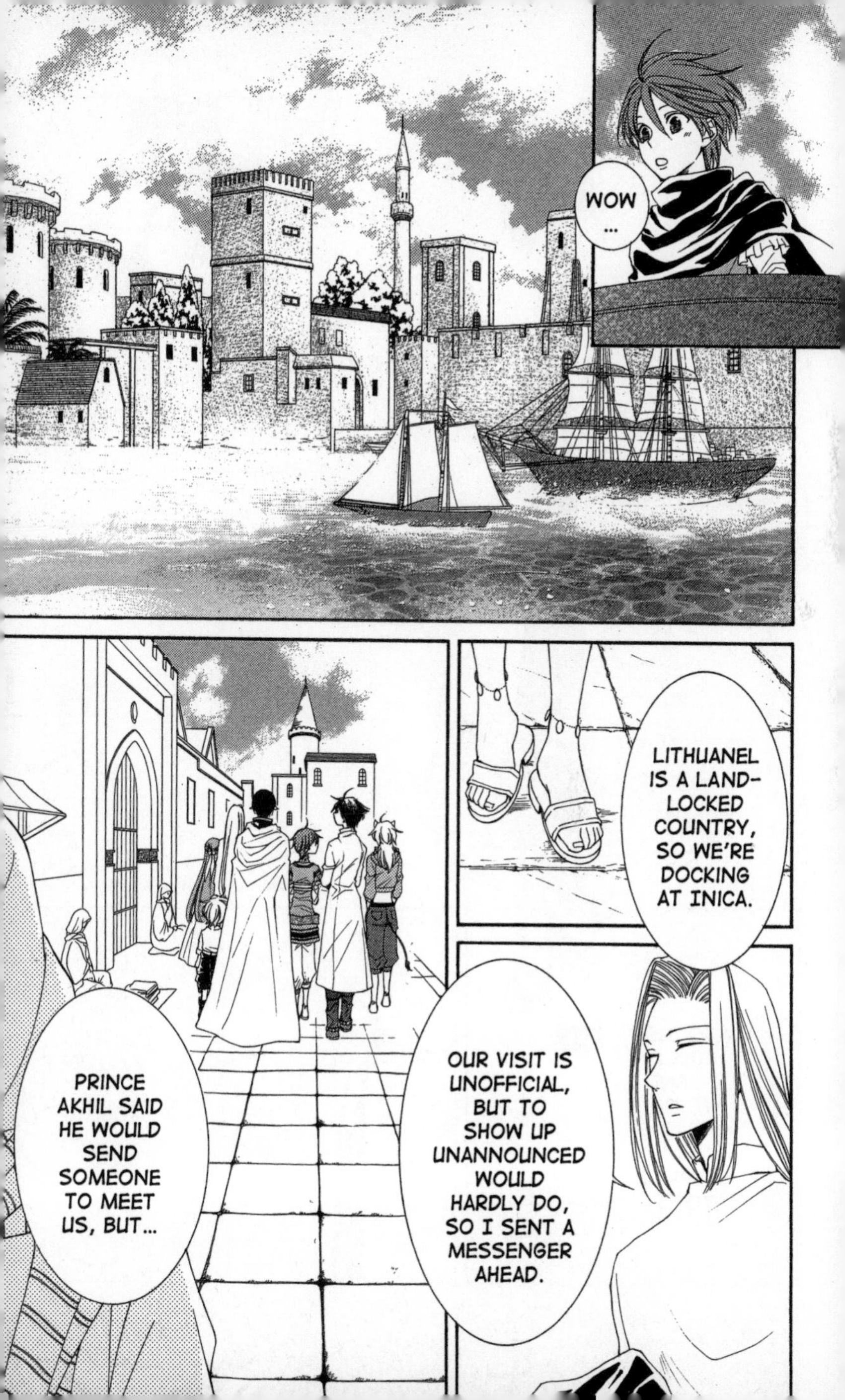
WOW ...
LITHUANEL IS A LAND-LOCKED COUNTRY, SO WE'RE DOCKING AT INICA.
OUR VISIT IS UNOFFICIAL, BUT TO SHOW UP UNANNOUNCED WOULD HARDLY DO, SO I SENT A MESSENGER AHEAD.
PRINCE AKHIL SAID HE WOULD SEND SOMEONE TO MEET US, BUT...

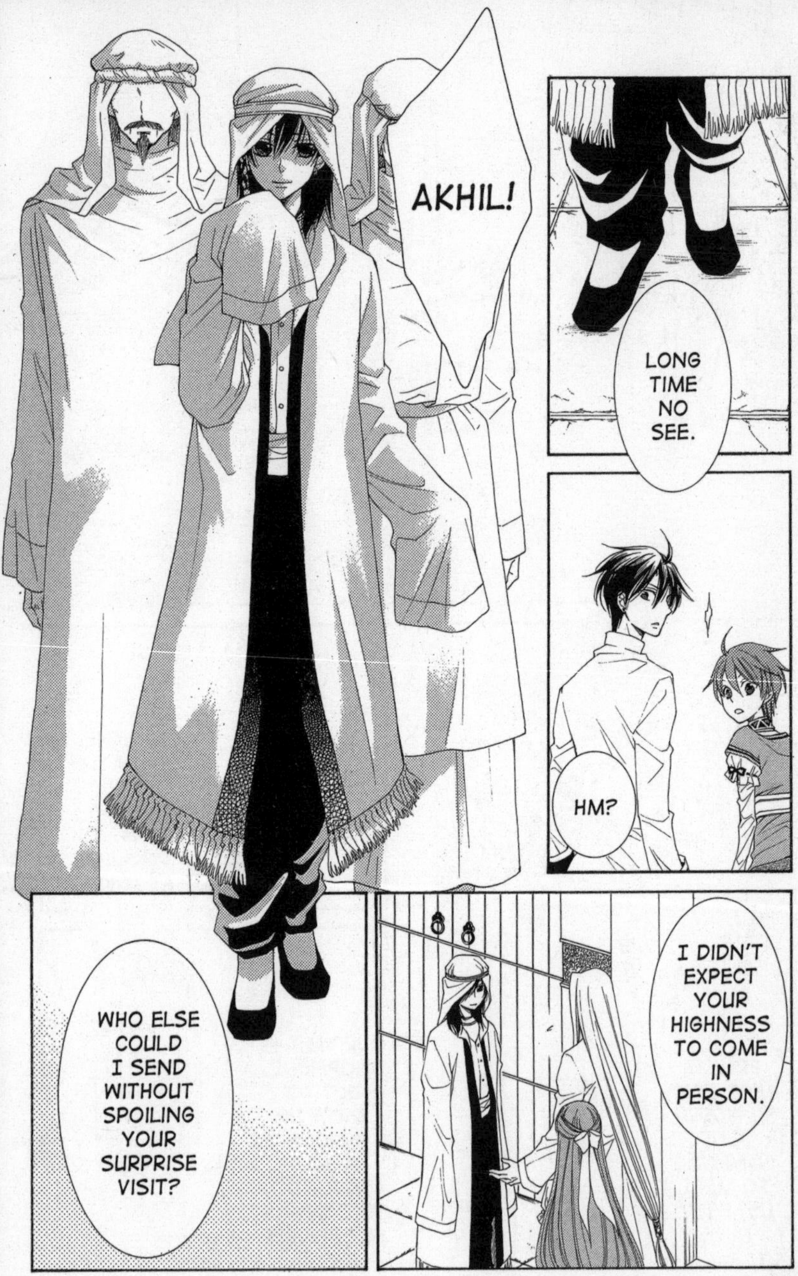
LONG TIME NO SEE.
HM?
AKHIL!
I DIDN'T EXPECT YOUR HIGHNESS TO COME IN PERSON.
WHO ELSE COULD I SEND WITHOUT SPOILING YOUR SURPRISE VISIT?

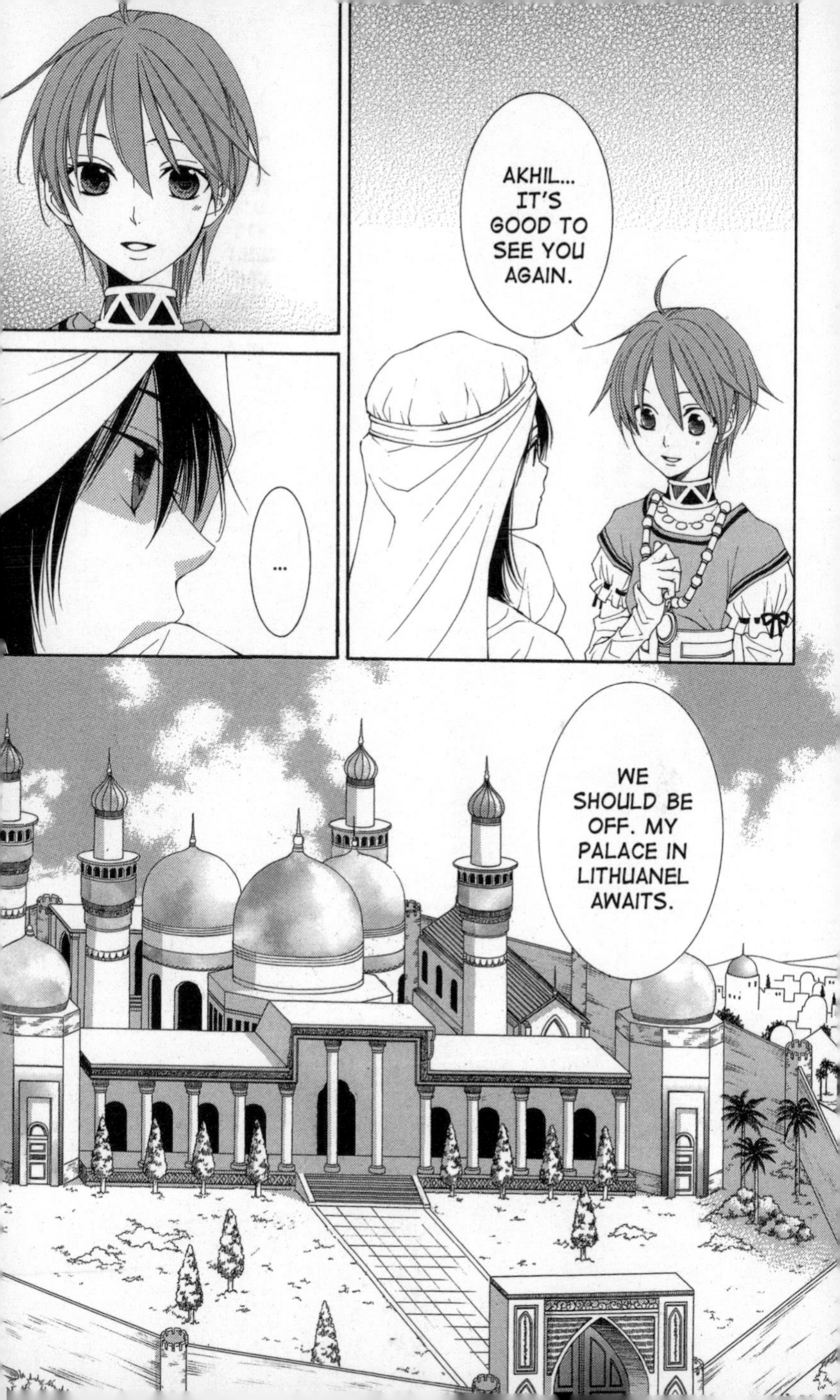
AKHIL... IT'S GOOD TO SEE YOU AGAIN.
...
WE SHOULD BE OFF. MY PALACE IN LITHUANEL AWAITS.

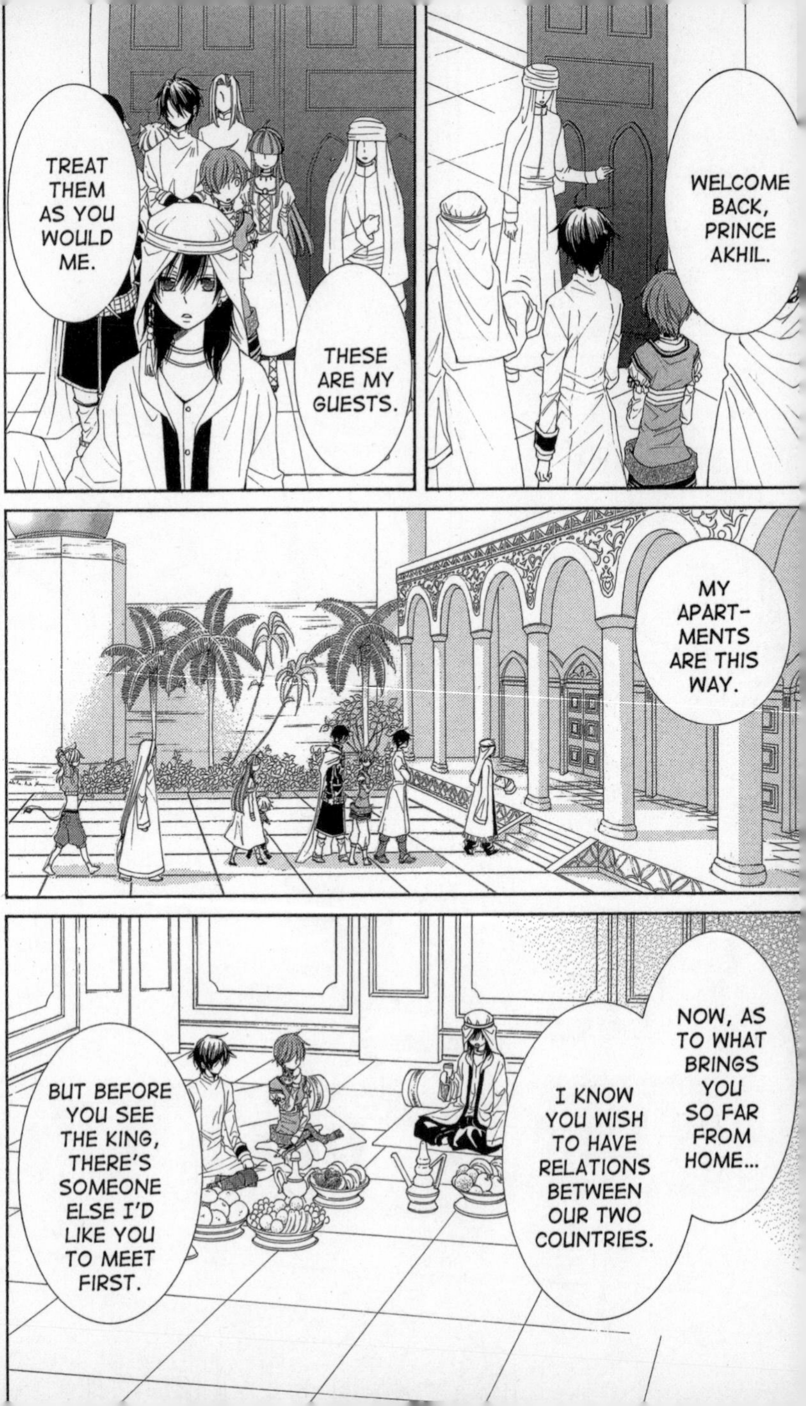
WELCOME BACK, PRINCE AKHIL.
THESE ARE MY GUESTS.
TREAT THEM AS YOU WOULD ME.
MY APART-MENTS ARE THIS WAY.
NOW, AS TO WHAT BRINGS YOU SO FAR FROM HOME...
I KNOW YOU WISH TO HAVE RELATIONS BETWEEN OUR TWO COUNTRIES.
BUT BEFORE YOU SEE THE KING, THERE'S SOMEONE ELSE I'D LIKE YOU TO MEET FIRST.

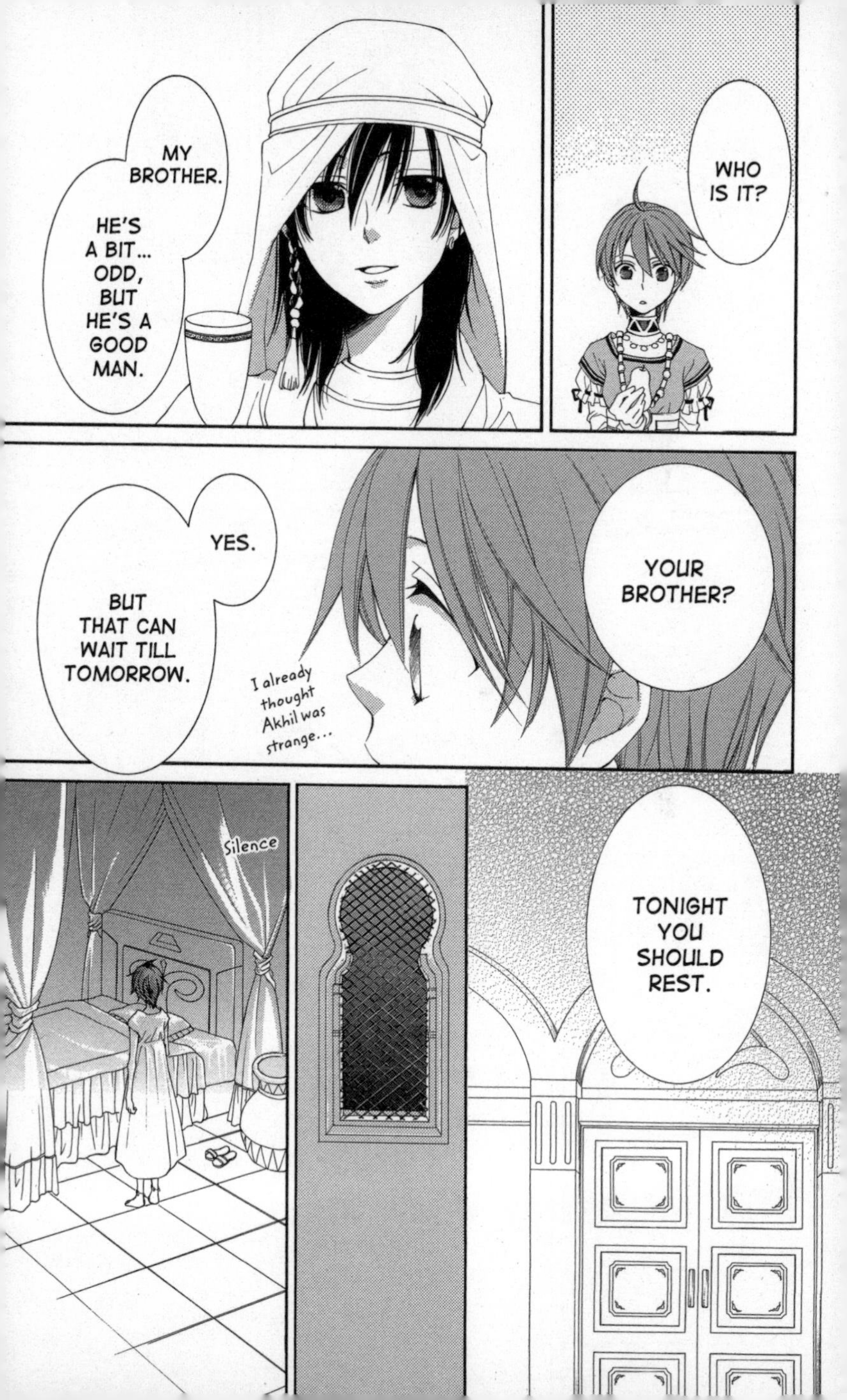
WHO IS IT?
MY BROTHER.
HE'S A BIT... ODD, BUT HE'S A GOOD MAN.
YOUR BROTHER?
YES.
BUT THAT CAN WAIT TILL TOMORROW.
I already thought Akhil was strange...
TONIGHT YOU SHOULD REST.
Silence

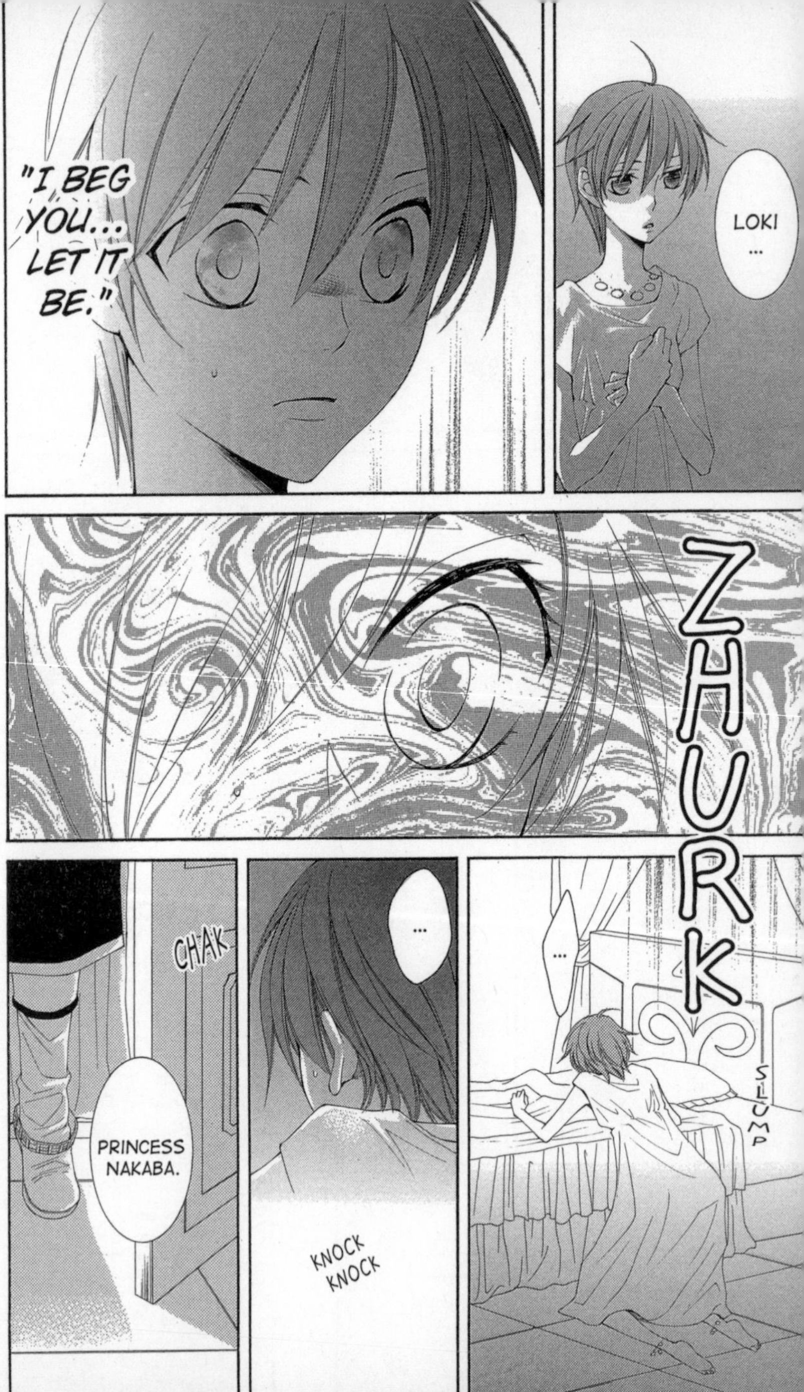
LOKI ...
"I BEG YOU... LET IT BE."
ZHURK
...
SLUMP
...
KNOCK KNOCK
CHAK
PRINCESS NAKABA.

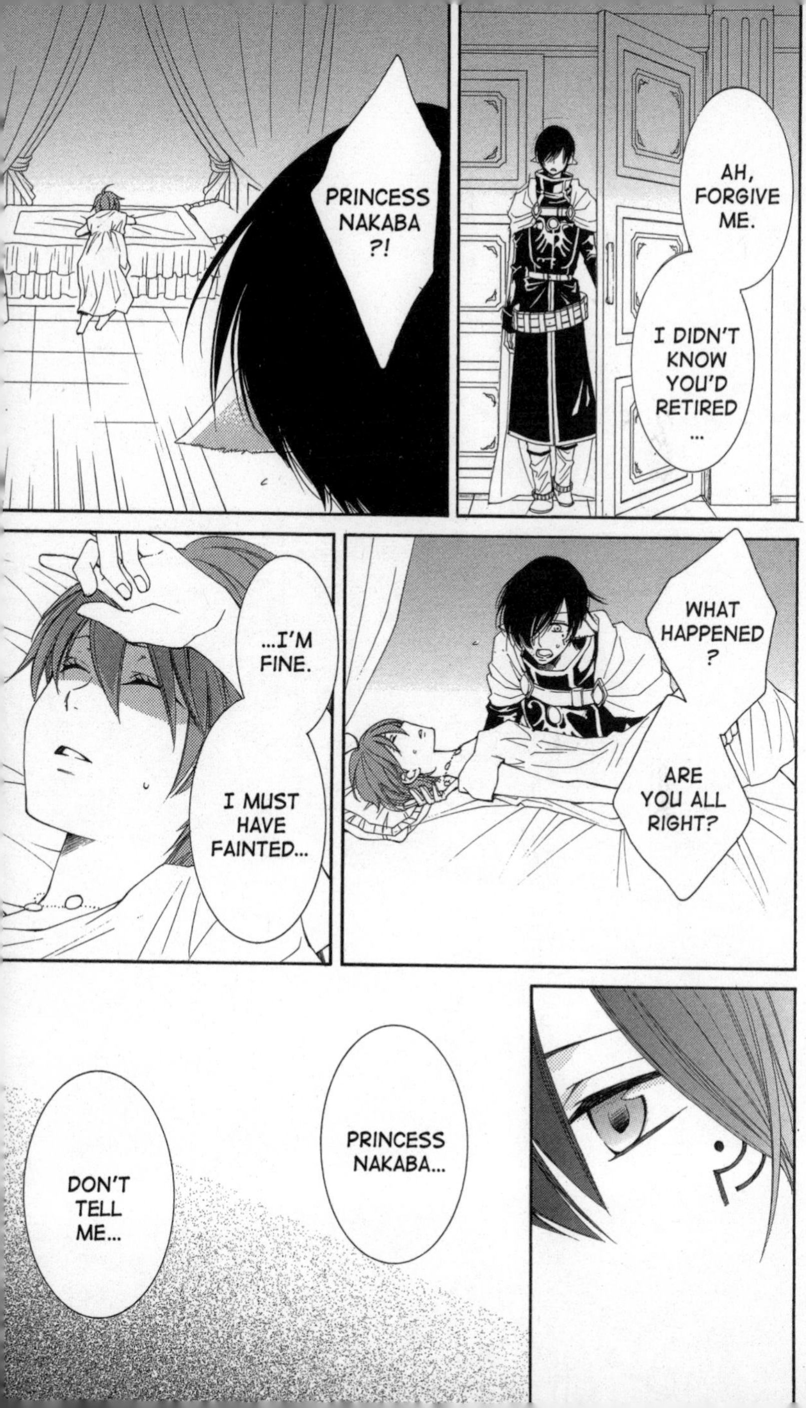
AH, FORGIVE ME.
I DIDN'T KNOW YOU'D RETIRED ...
PRINCESS NAKABA ?!
WHAT HAPPENED ?
ARE YOU ALL RIGHT?
...I'M FINE.
I MUST HAVE FAINTED...
PRINCESS NAKABA...
DON'T TELL ME...

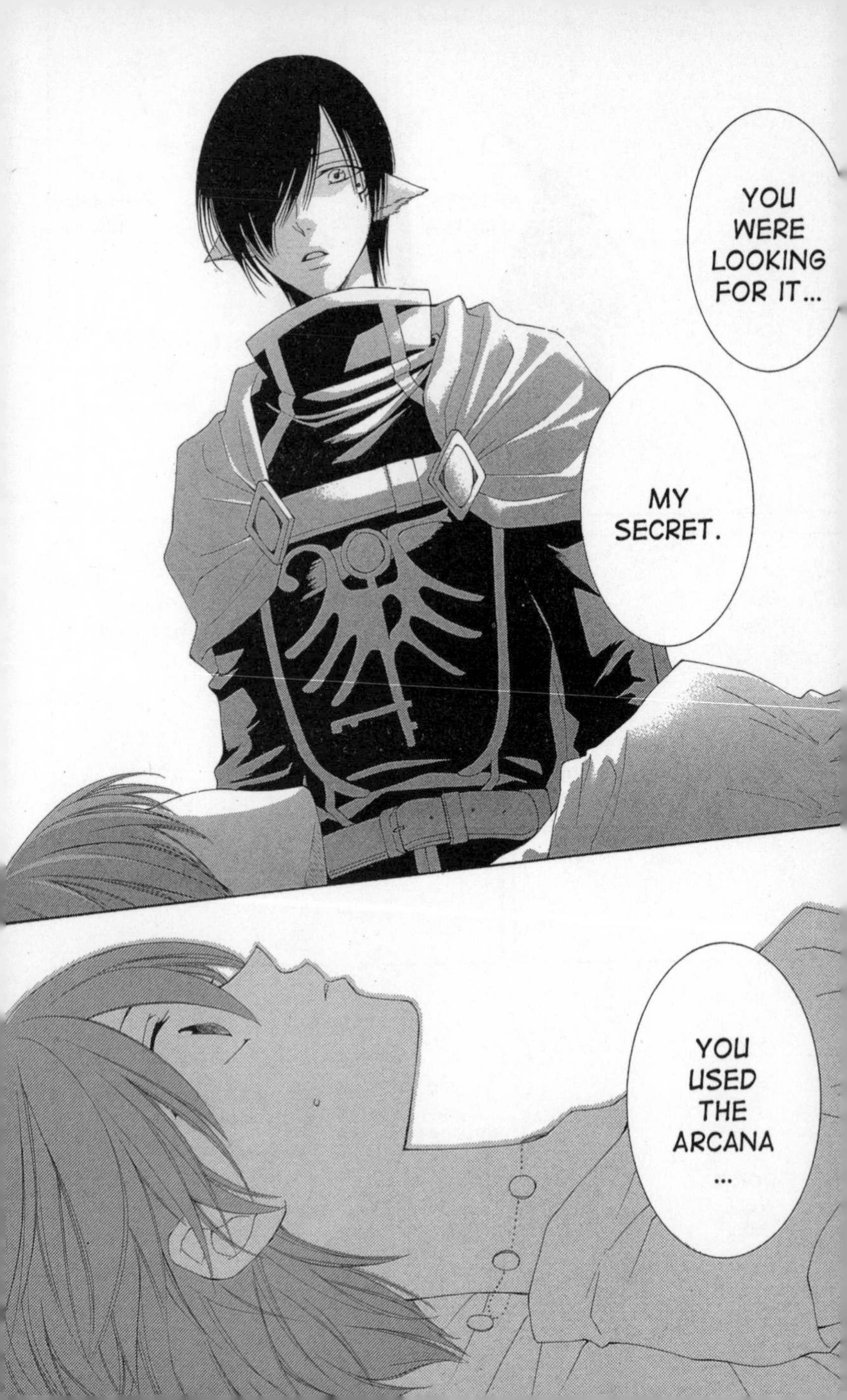
YOU WERE LOOKING FOR IT...
MY SECRET.
YOU USED THE ARCANA ...

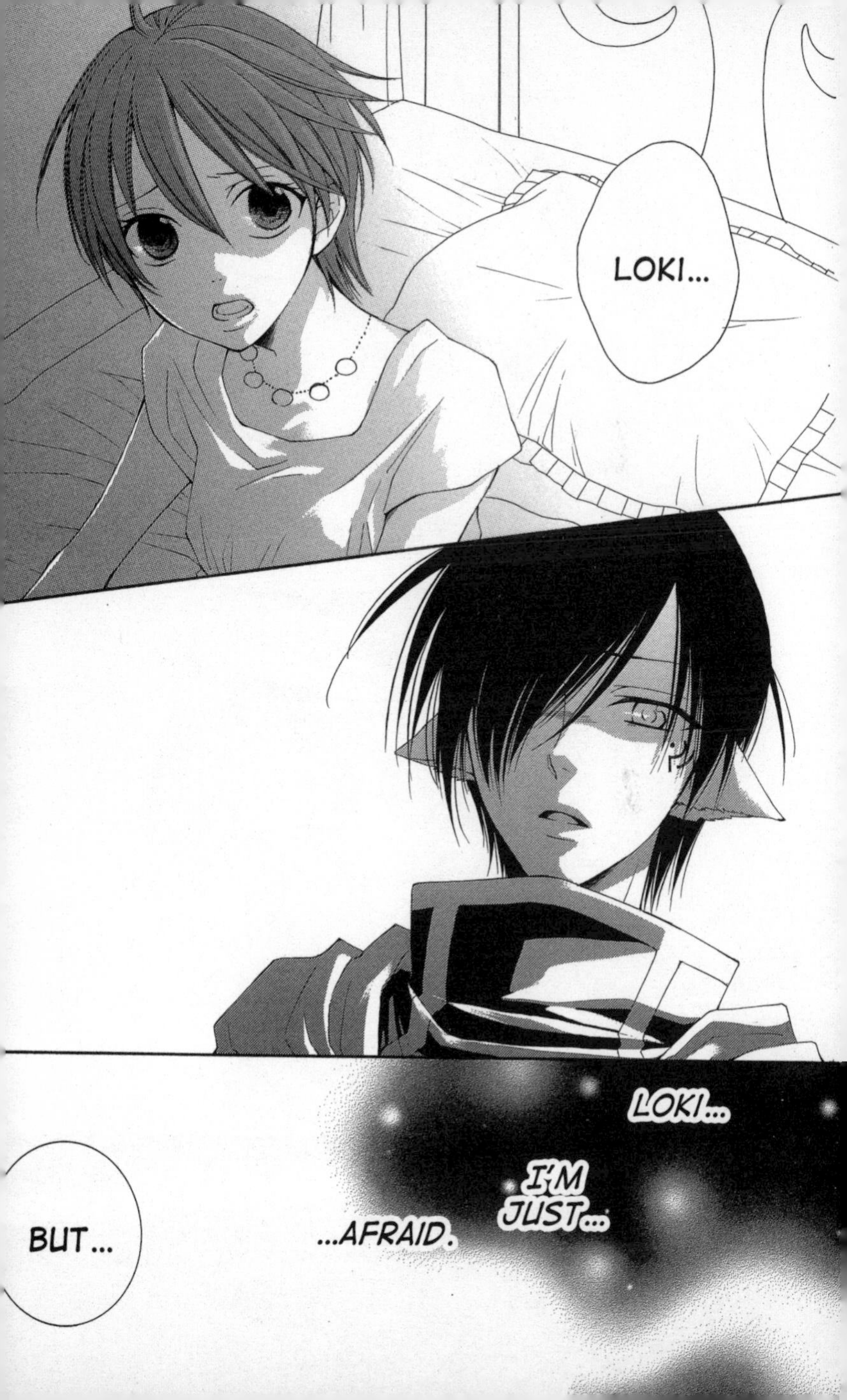
LOKI...
LOKI...
I'M JUST...
...AFRAID.
BUT...

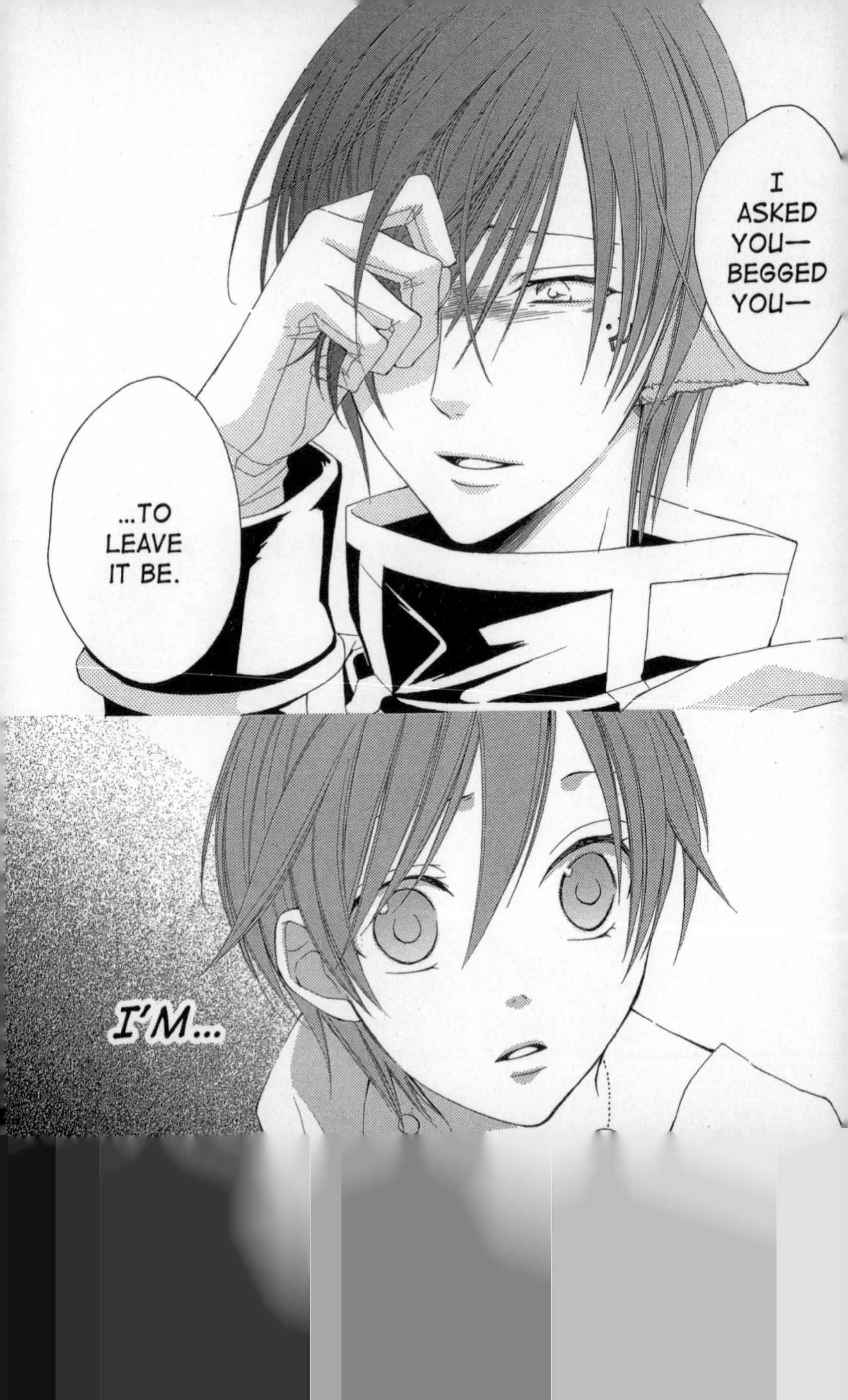
I ASKED YOU—BEGGED YOU—
...TO LEAVE IT BE.
I'M...

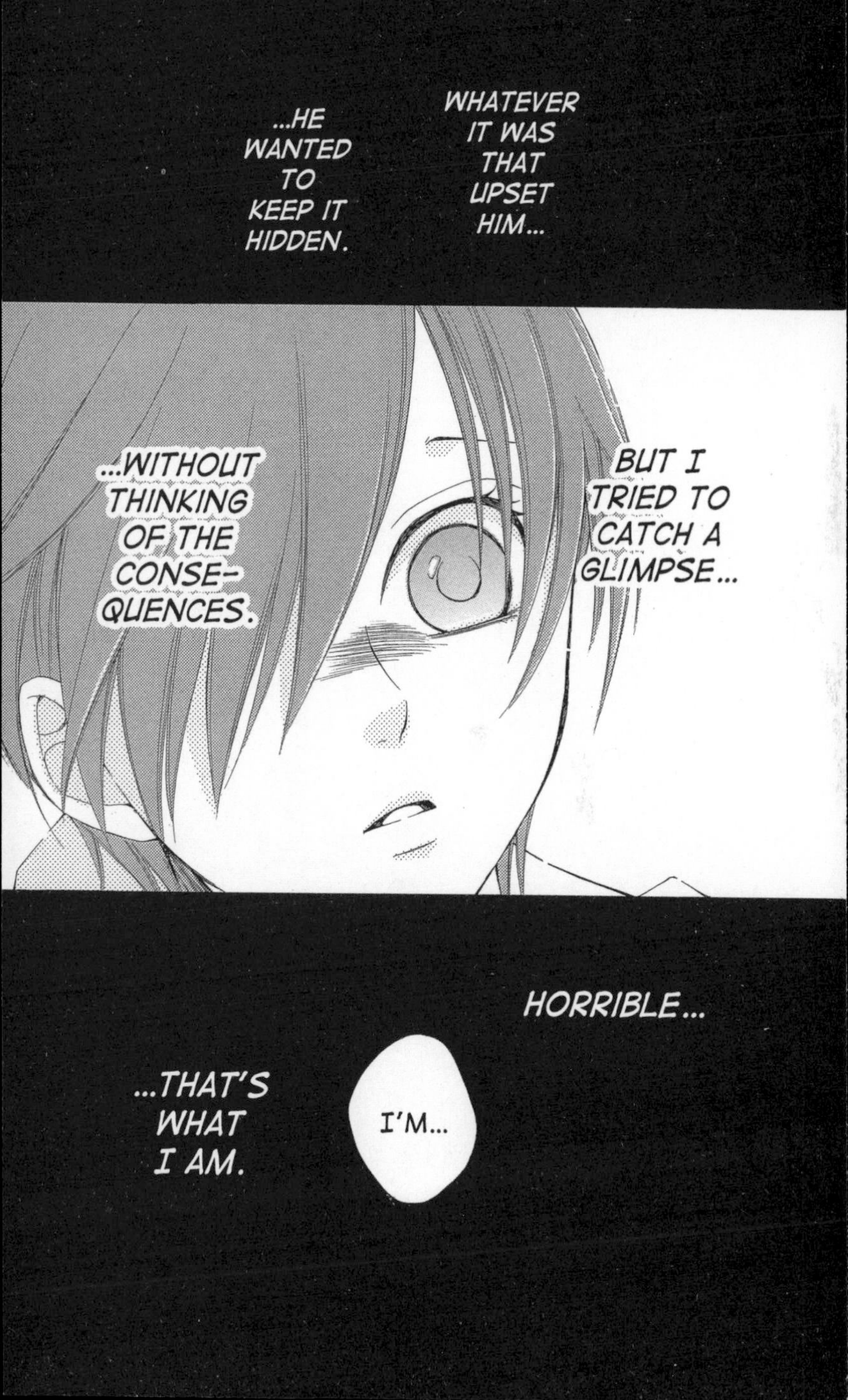
WHATEVER IT WAS THAT UPSET HIM...
...HE WANTED TO KEEP IT HIDDEN.
BUT I TRIED TO CATCH A GLIMPSE...
...WITHOUT THINKING OF THE CONSE-QUENCES.
HORRIBLE...
I'M...
...THAT'S WHAT I AM.

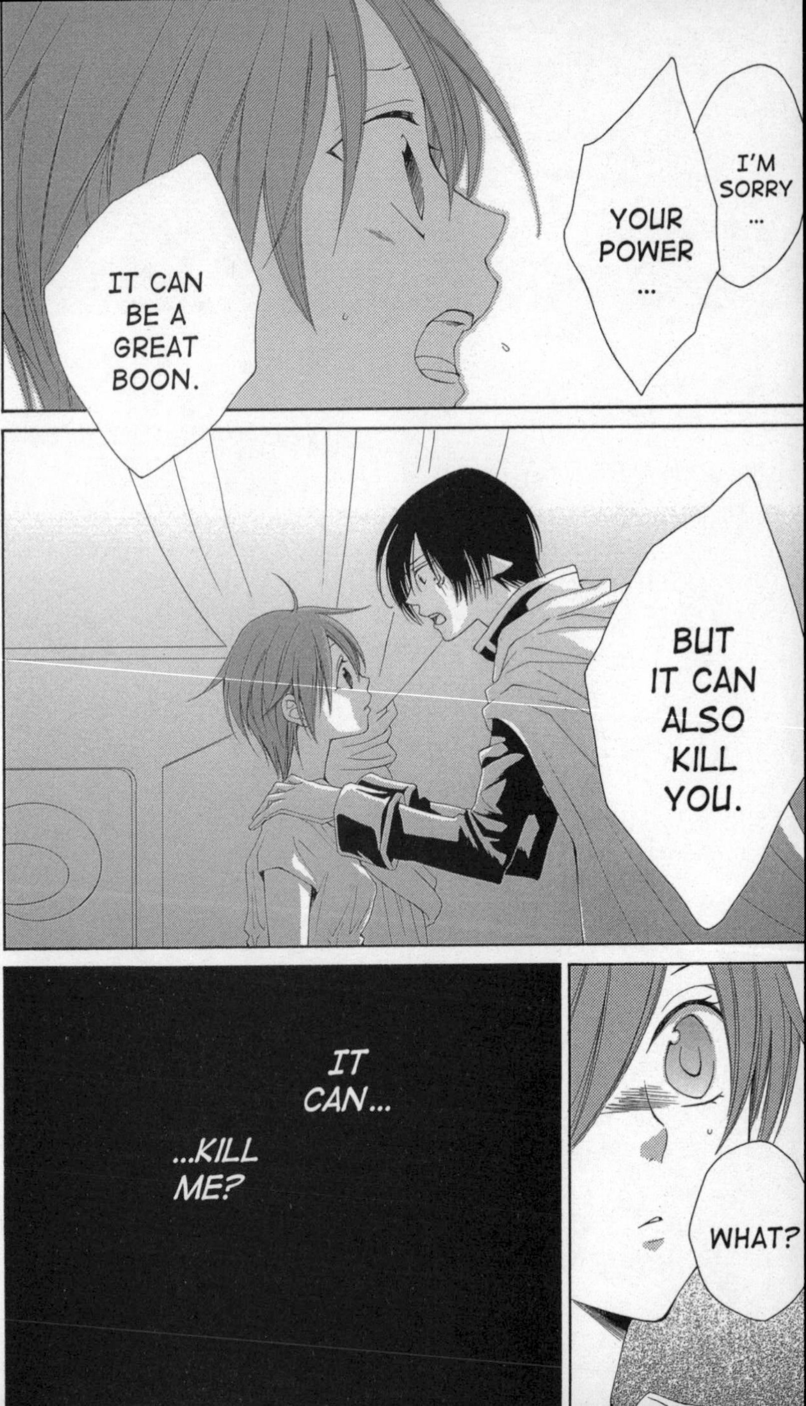
I'M SORRY ...
YOUR POWER ...
IT CAN BE A GREAT BOON.
BUT IT CAN ALSO KILL YOU.
WHAT?
IT CAN...
...KILL ME?

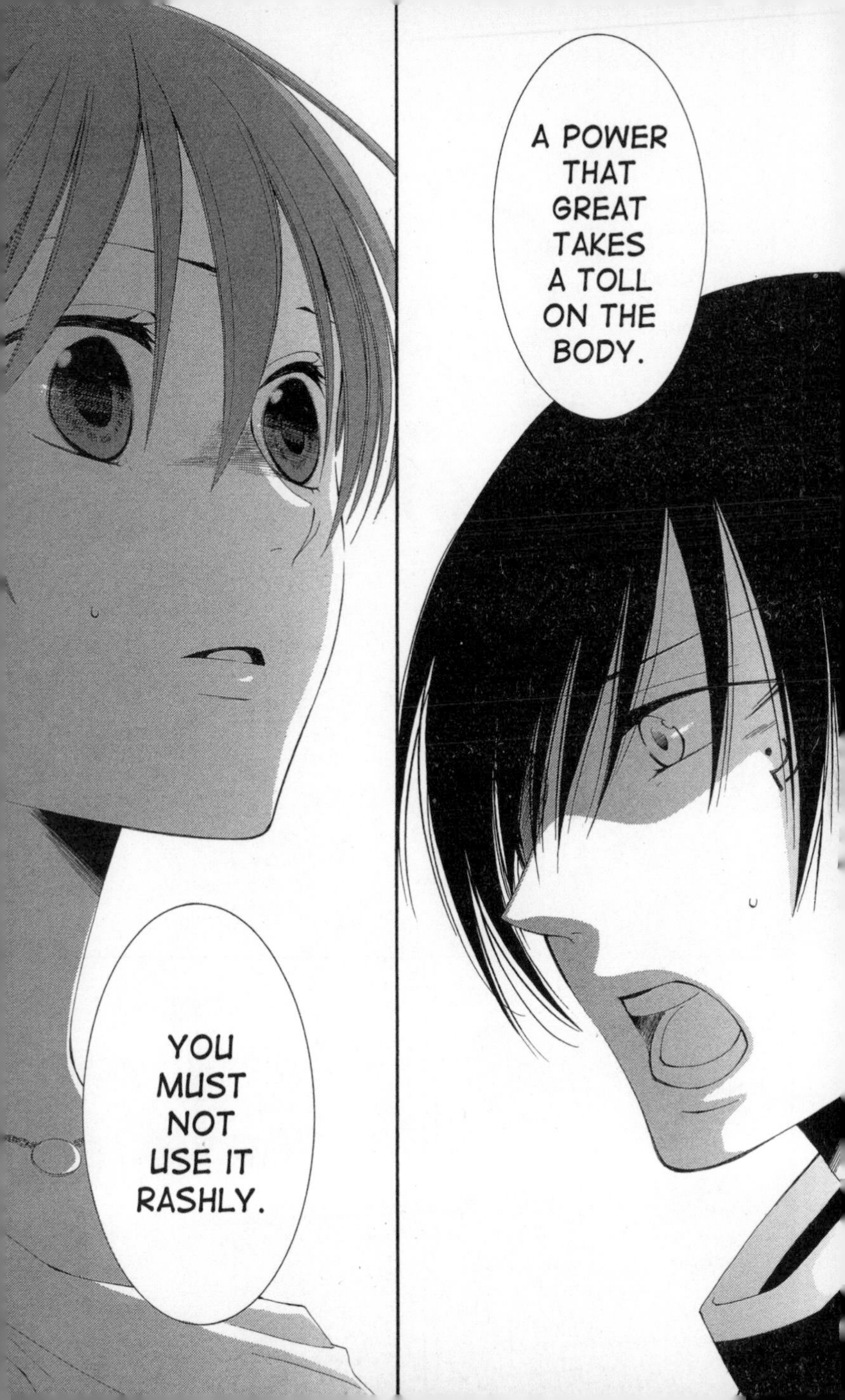
A POWER THAT GREAT TAKES A TOLL ON THE BODY.
YOU MUST NOT USE IT RASHLY.

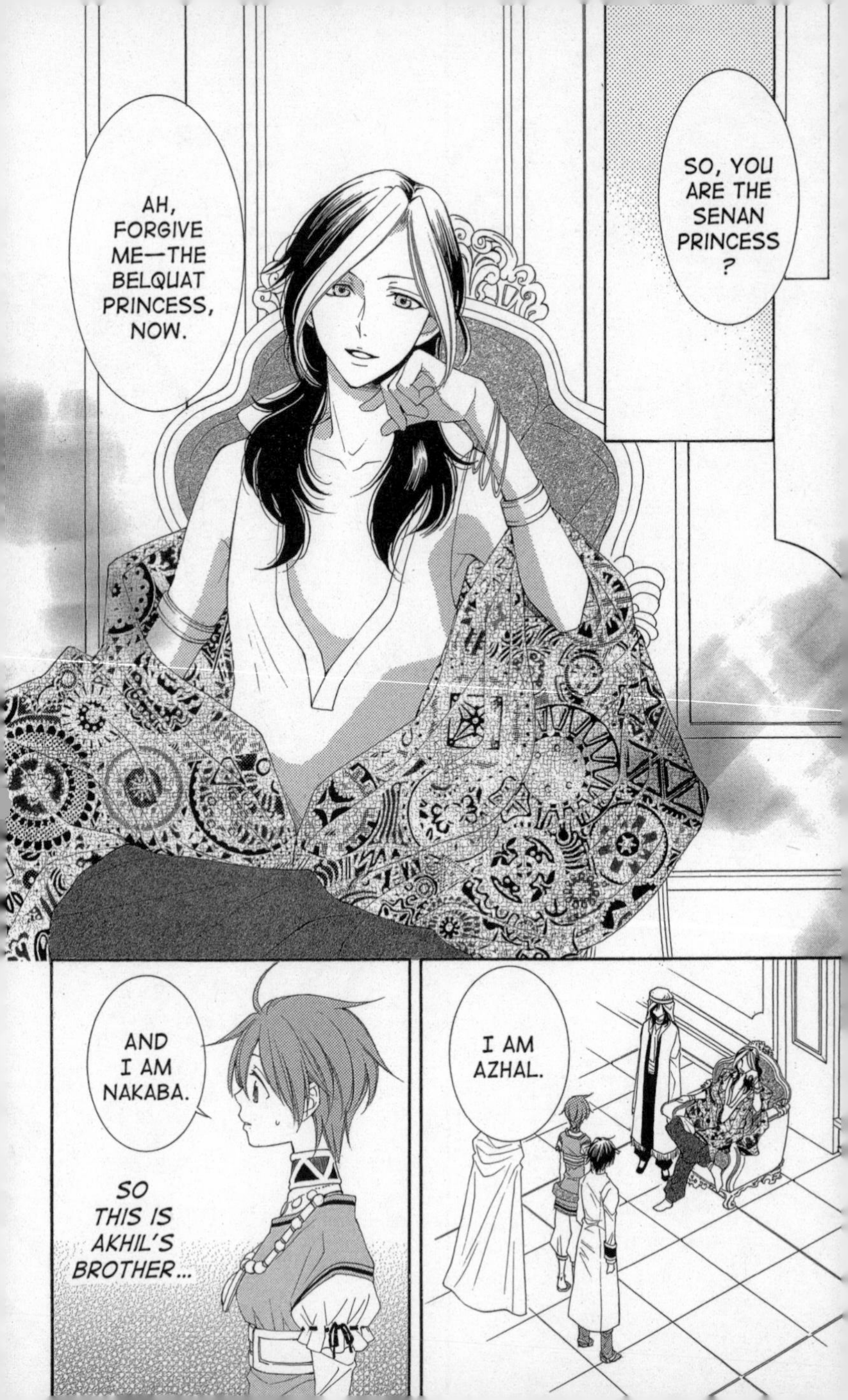
SO, YOU ARE THE SENAN PRINCESS?
AH, FORGIVE ME—THE BELQUAT PRINCESS, NOW.
I AM AZHAL.
AND I AM NAKABA.
SO THIS IS AKHIL'S BROTHER...

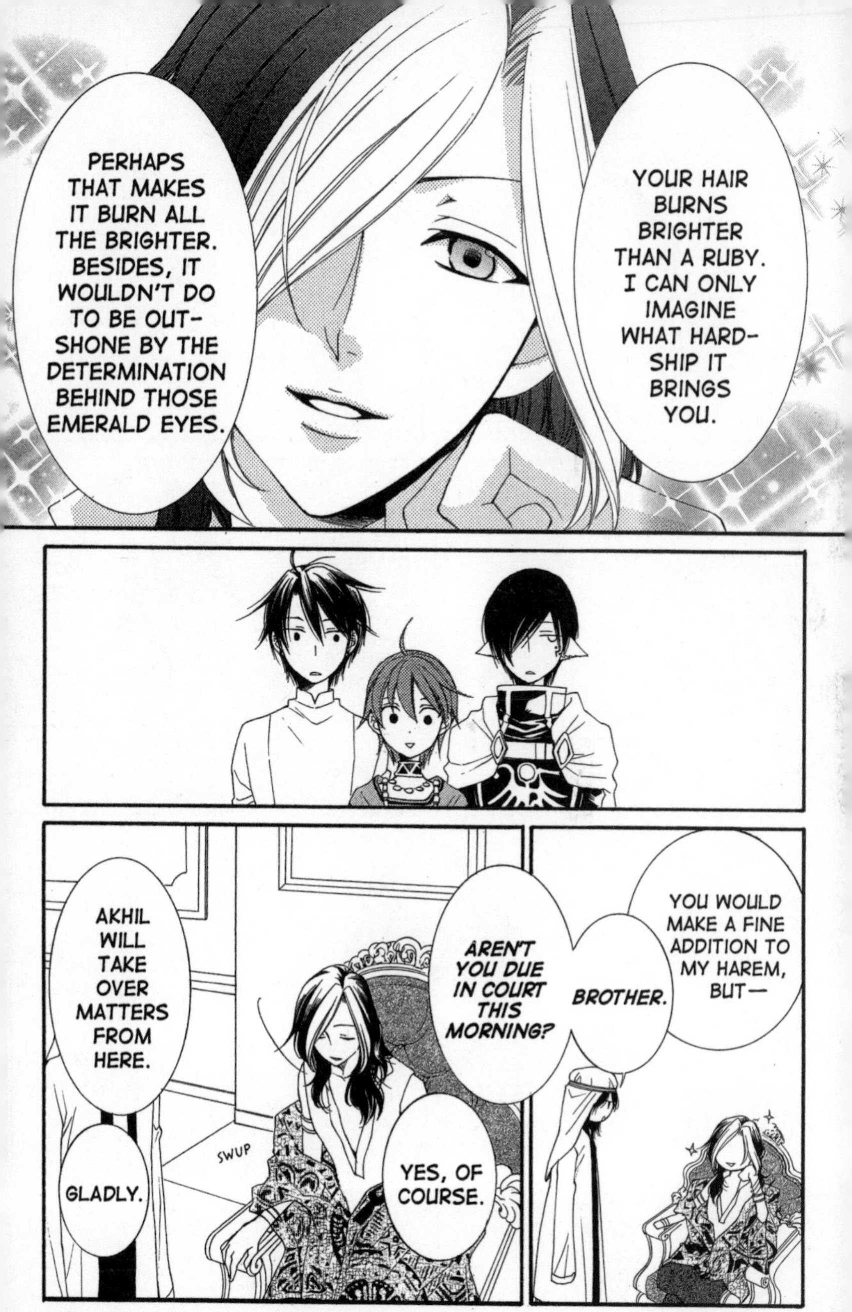
YOUR HAIR BURNS BRIGHTER THAN A RUBY. I CAN ONLY IMAGINE WHAT HARDSHIP IT BRINGS YOU.
PERHAPS THAT MAKES IT BURN ALL THE BRIGHTER. BESIDES, IT WOULDN'T DO TO BE OUTSHONE BY THE DETERMINATION BEHIND THOSE EMERALD EYES.
YOU WOULD MAKE A FINE ADDITION TO MY HAREM, BUT—
BROTHER.
AREN'T YOU DUE IN COURT THIS MORNING?
AKHIL WILL TAKE OVER MATTERS FROM HERE.
SWUP
YES, OF COURSE.
GLADLY.

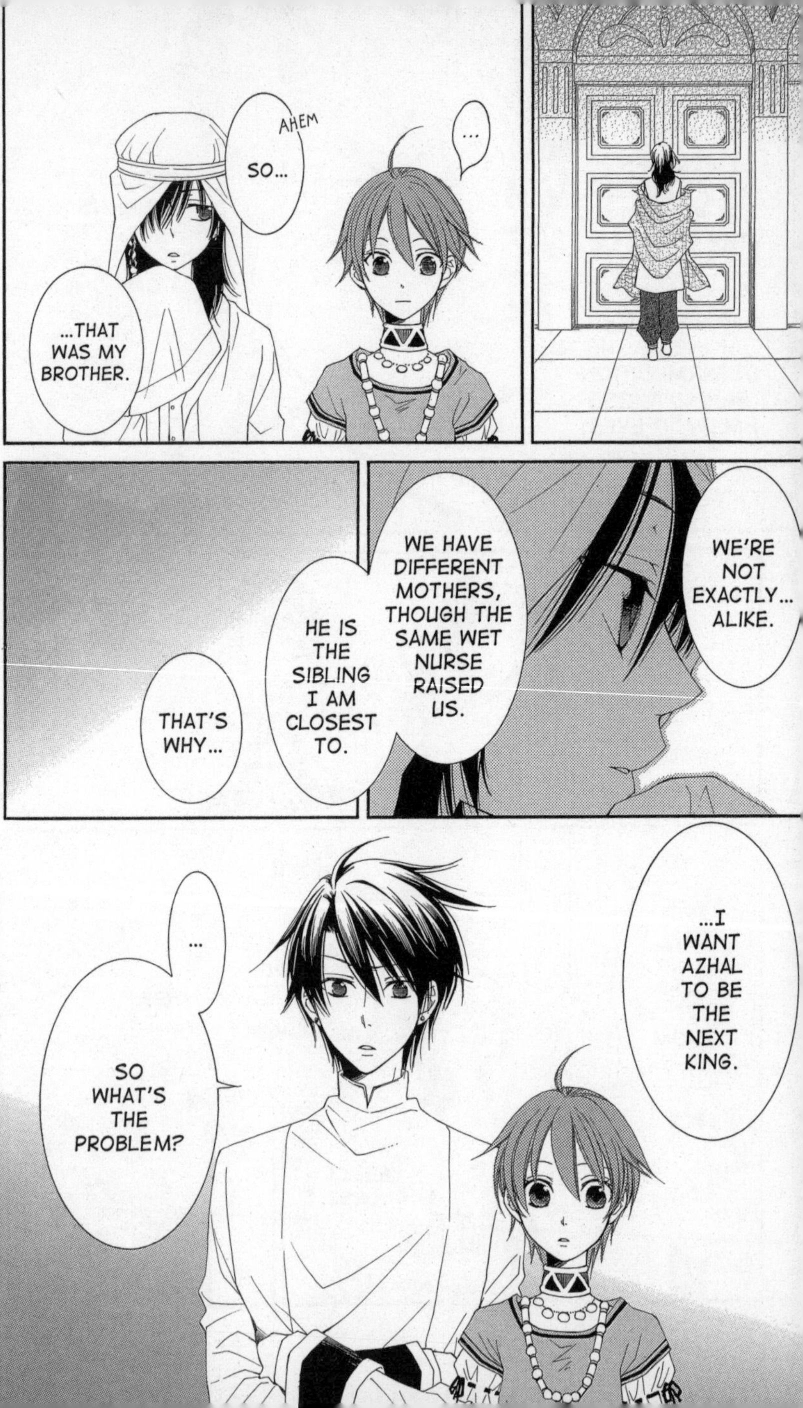
...
AHEM
SO...
...THAT WAS MY BROTHER.
WE'RE NOT EXACTLY... ALIKE.
WE HAVE DIFFERENT MOTHERS, THOUGH THE SAME WET NURSE RAISED US.
HE IS THE SIBLING I AM CLOSEST TO.
THAT'S WHY...
...I WANT AZHAL TO BE THE NEXT KING.
...
SO WHAT'S THE PROBLEM?

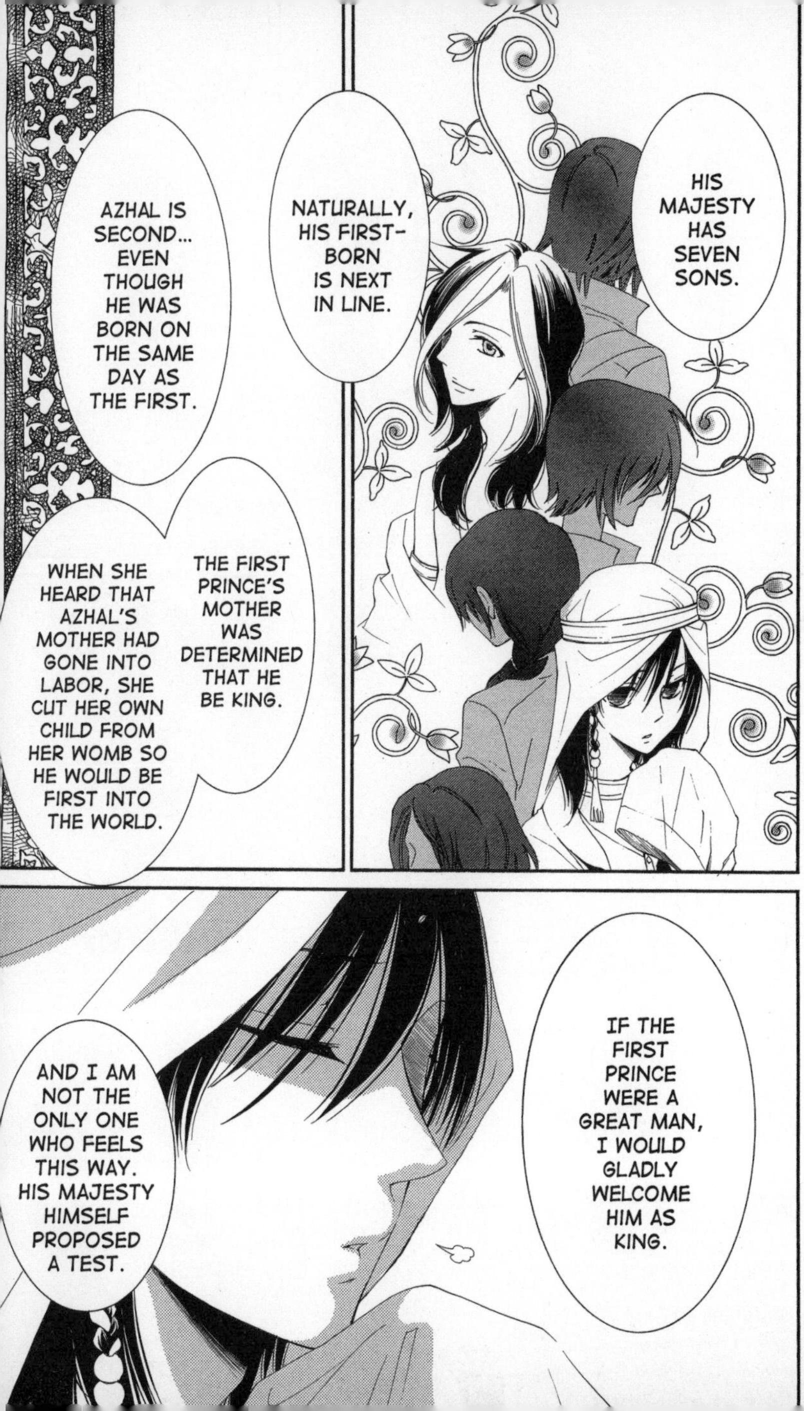
HIS MAJESTY HAS SEVEN SONS.
NATURALLY, HIS FIRST-BORN IS NEXT IN LINE.
AZHAL IS SECOND... EVEN THOUGH HE WAS BORN ON THE SAME DAY AS THE FIRST.
THE FIRST PRINCE'S MOTHER WAS DETERMINED THAT HE BE KING.
WHEN SHE HEARD THAT AZHAL'S MOTHER HAD GONE INTO LABOR, SHE CUT HER OWN CHILD FROM HER WOMB SO HE WOULD BE FIRST INTO THE WORLD.
IF THE FIRST PRINCE WERE A GREAT MAN, I WOULD GLADLY WELCOME HIM AS KING.
AND I AM NOT THE ONLY ONE WHO FEELS THIS WAY. HIS MAJESTY HIMSELF PROPOSED A TEST.

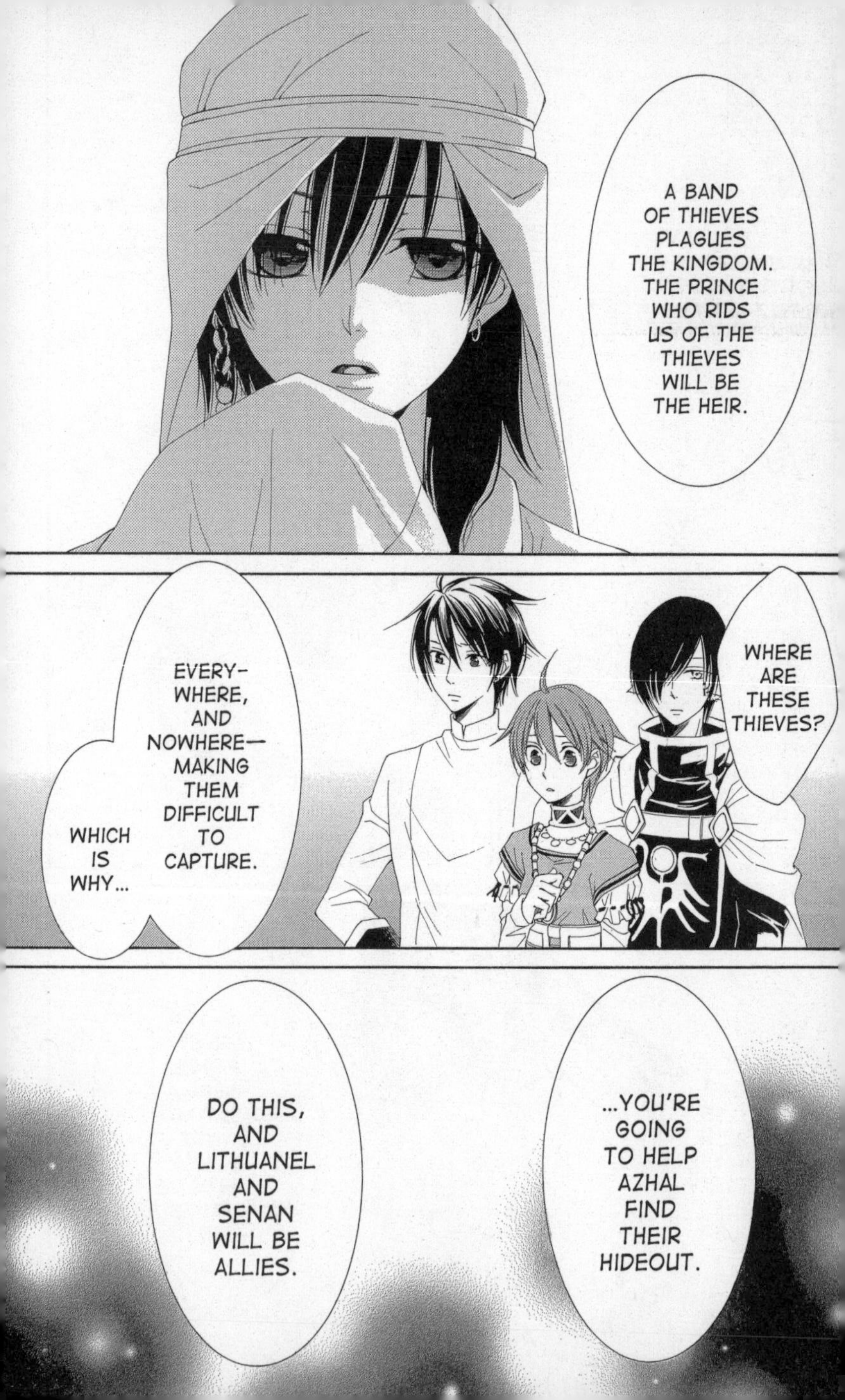
A BAND OF THIEVES PLAGUES THE KINGDOM. THE PRINCE WHO RIDS US OF THE THIEVES WILL BE THE HEIR.
WHERE ARE THESE THIEVES?
EVERY-WHERE, AND NOWHERE—MAKING THEM DIFFICULT TO CAPTURE.
WHICH IS WHY...
...YOU'RE GOING TO HELP AZHAL FIND THEIR HIDEOUT.
DO THIS, AND LITHUANEL AND SENAN WILL BE ALLIES.

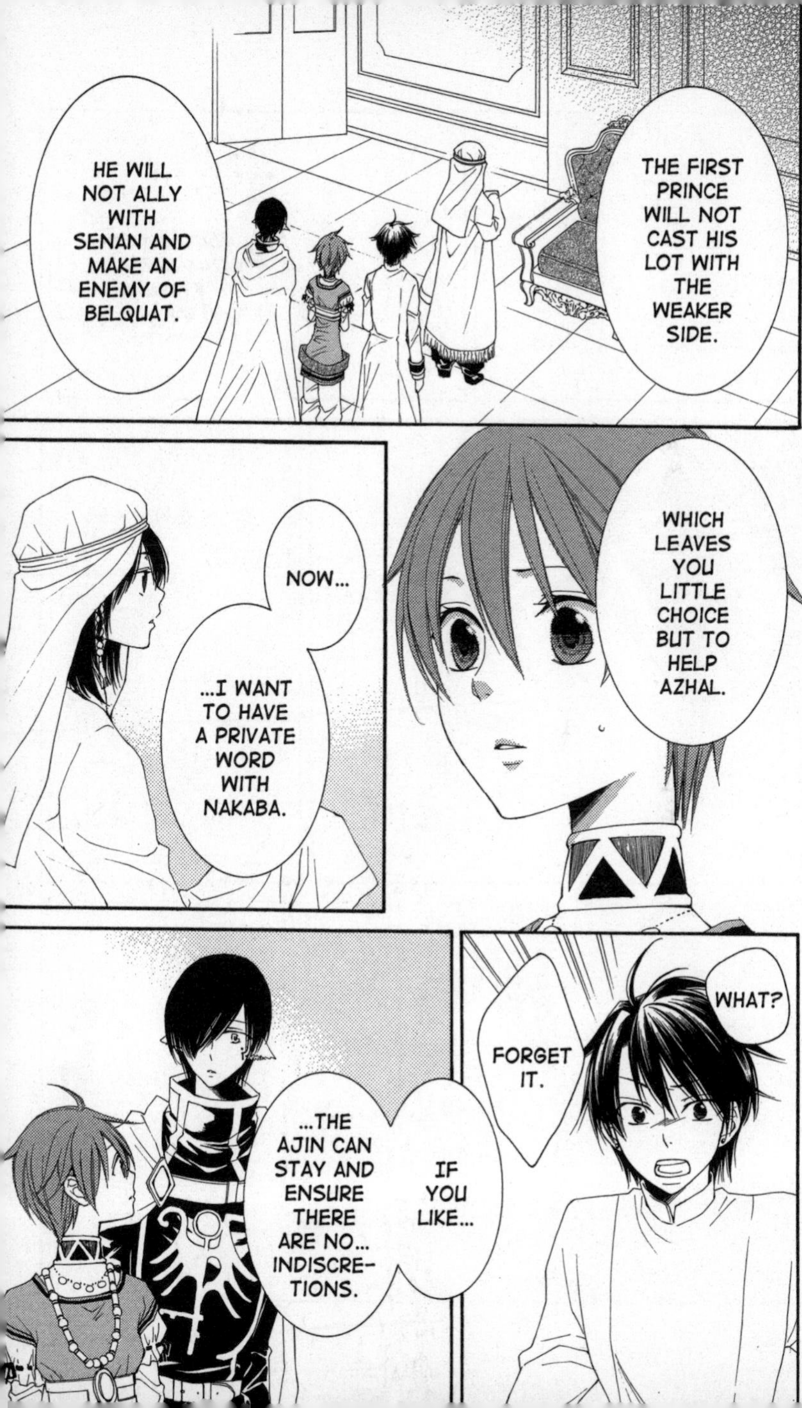
THE FIRST PRINCE WILL NOT CAST HIS LOT WITH THE WEAKER SIDE.
HE WILL NOT ALLY WITH SENAN AND MAKE AN ENEMY OF BELQUAT.
WHICH LEAVES YOU LITTLE CHOICE BUT TO HELP AZHAL.
NOW...
...I WANT TO HAVE A PRIVATE WORD WITH NAKABA.
WHAT?
FORGET IT.
IF YOU LIKE...
...THE AJIN CAN STAY AND ENSURE THERE ARE NO... INDISCRE-TIONS.

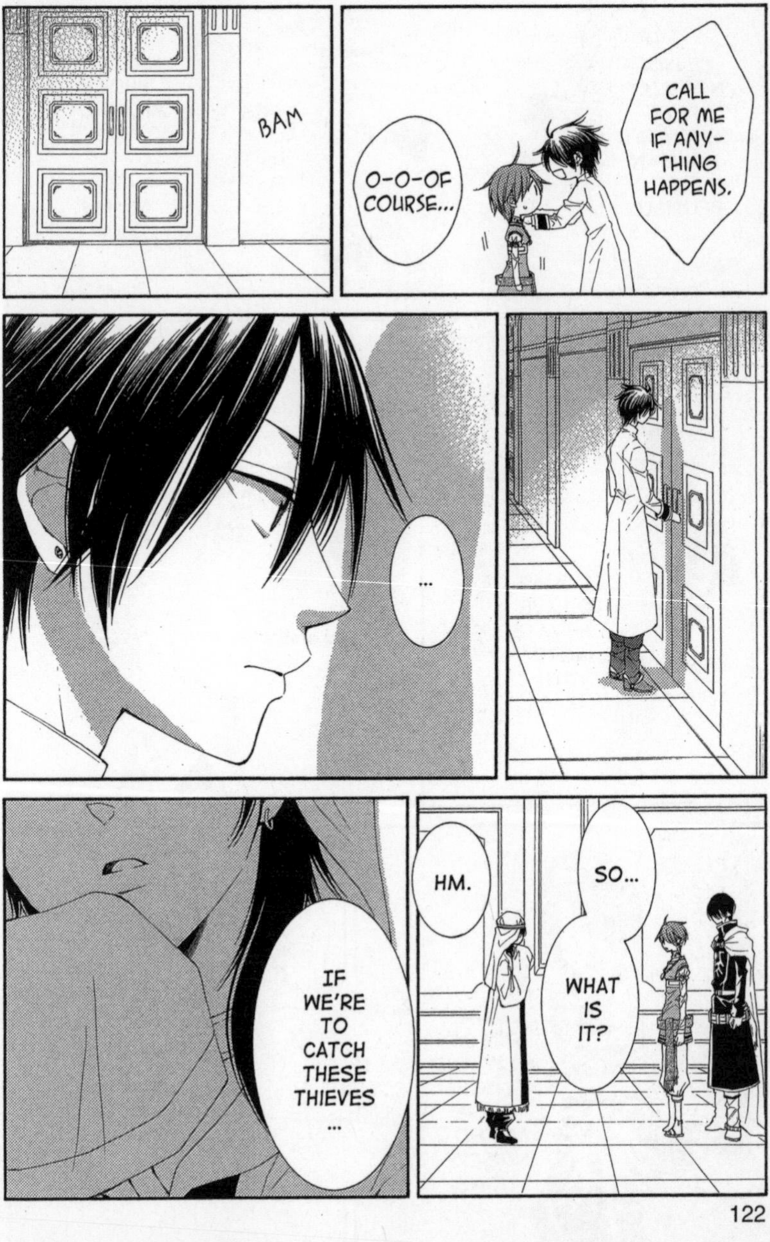
CALL FOR ME IF ANY-THING HAPPENS.
O-O-OF COURSE...
BAM
...
SO...
WHAT IS IT?
HM.
IF WE'RE TO CATCH THESE THIEVES ...

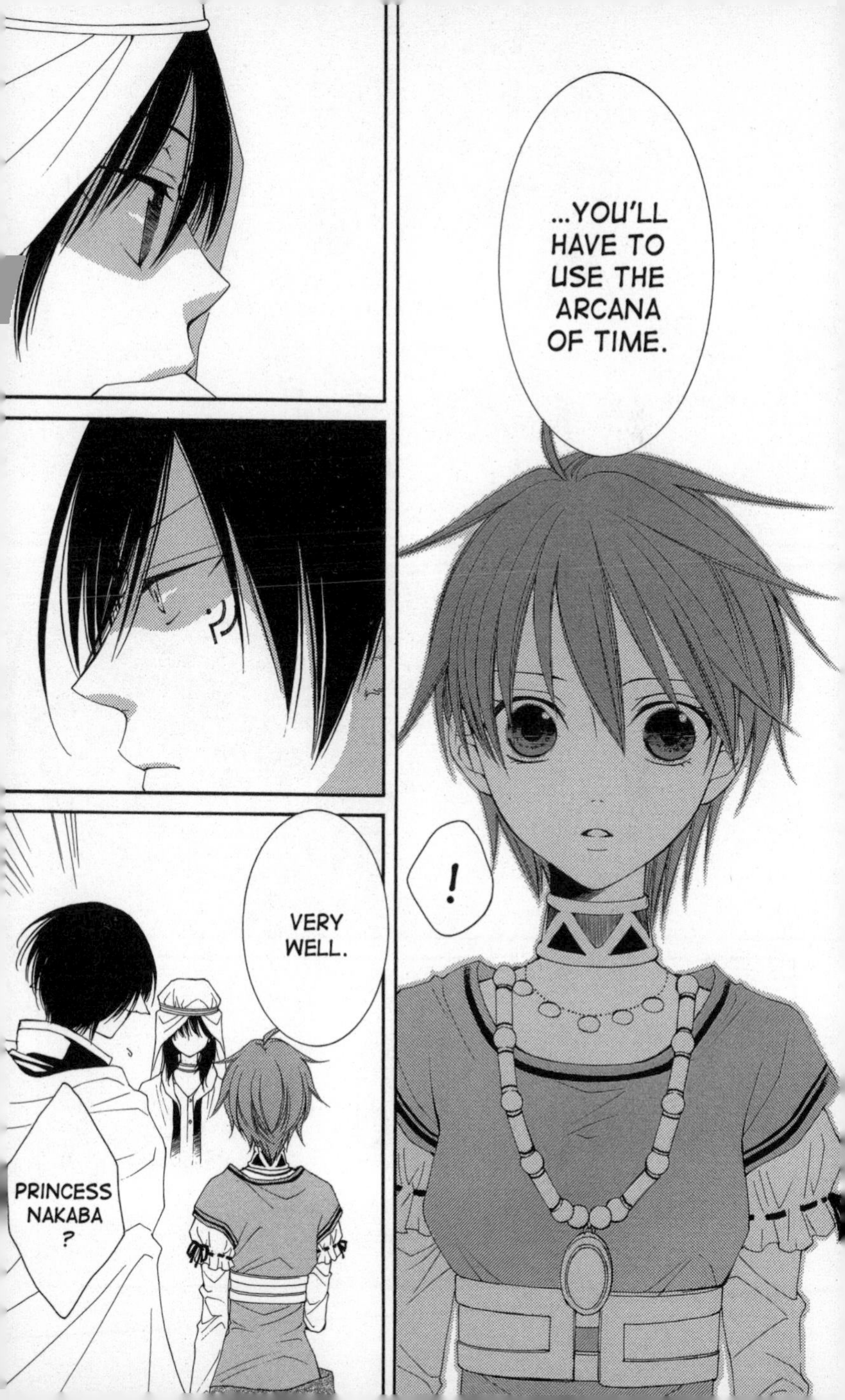
...YOU'LL HAVE TO USE THE ARCANA OF TIME.
!
VERY WELL.
PRINCESS NAKABA ?

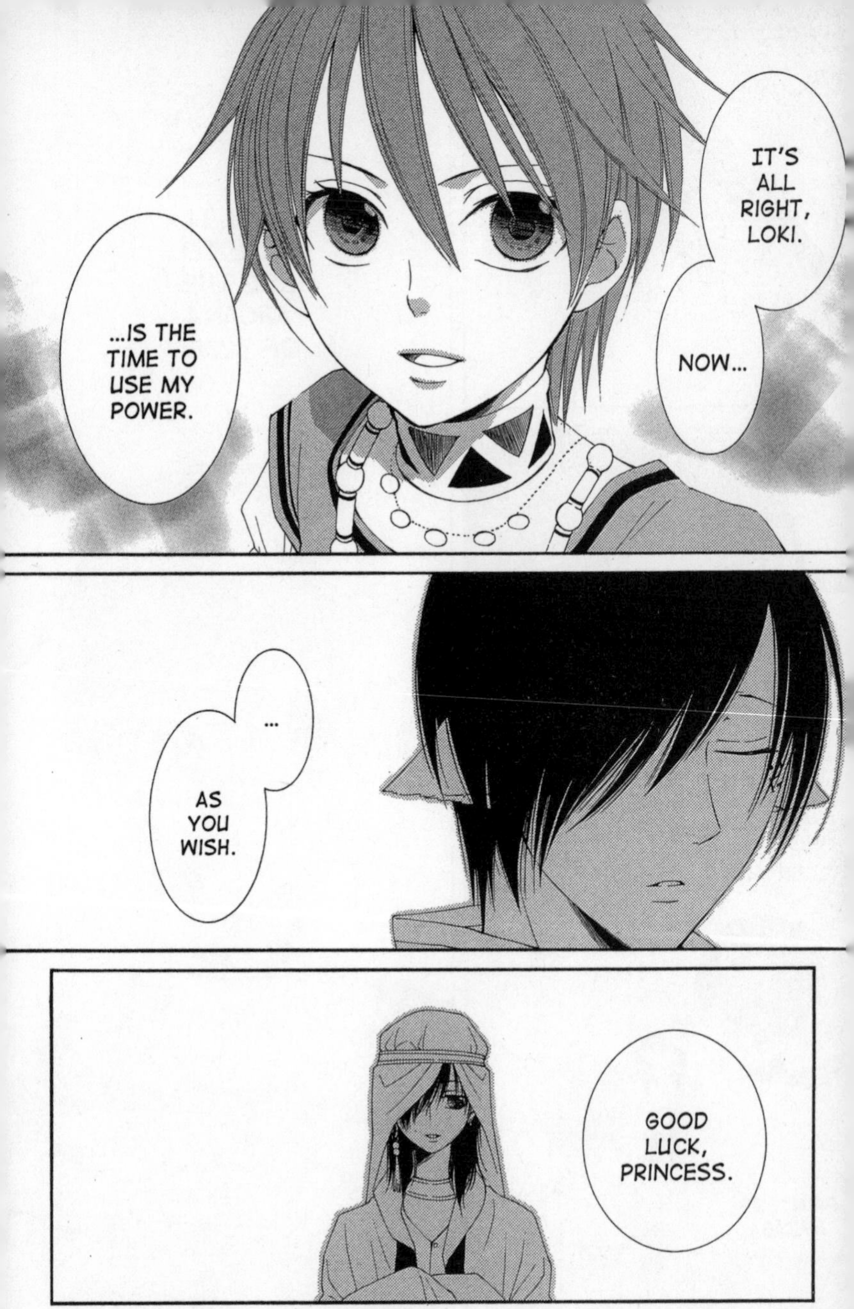
IT'S ALL RIGHT, LOKI.
NOW...
...IS THE TIME TO USE MY POWER.
...
AS YOU WISH.
GOOD LUCK, PRINCESS.

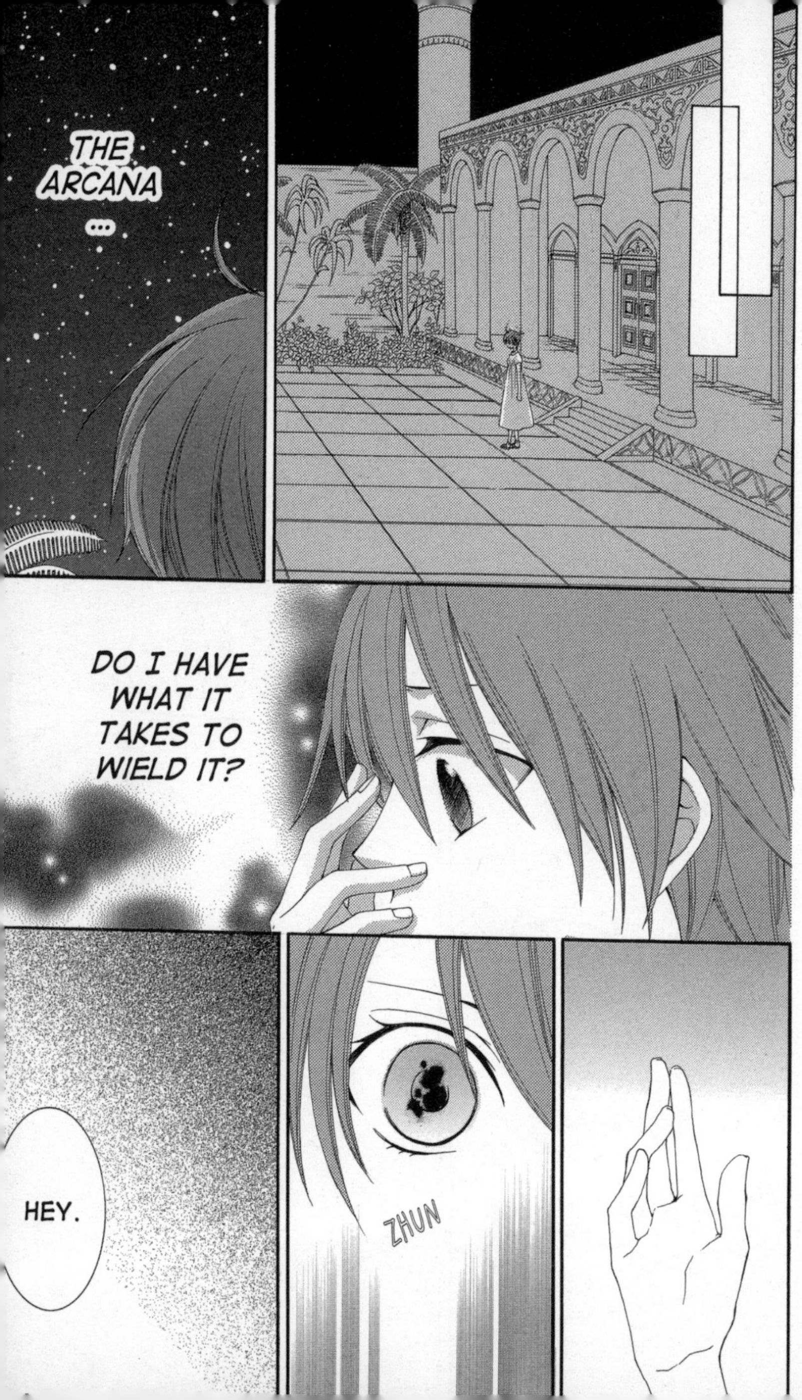
THE ARCANA ...
DO I HAVE WHAT IT TAKES TO WIELD IT?
ZHUN
HEY.

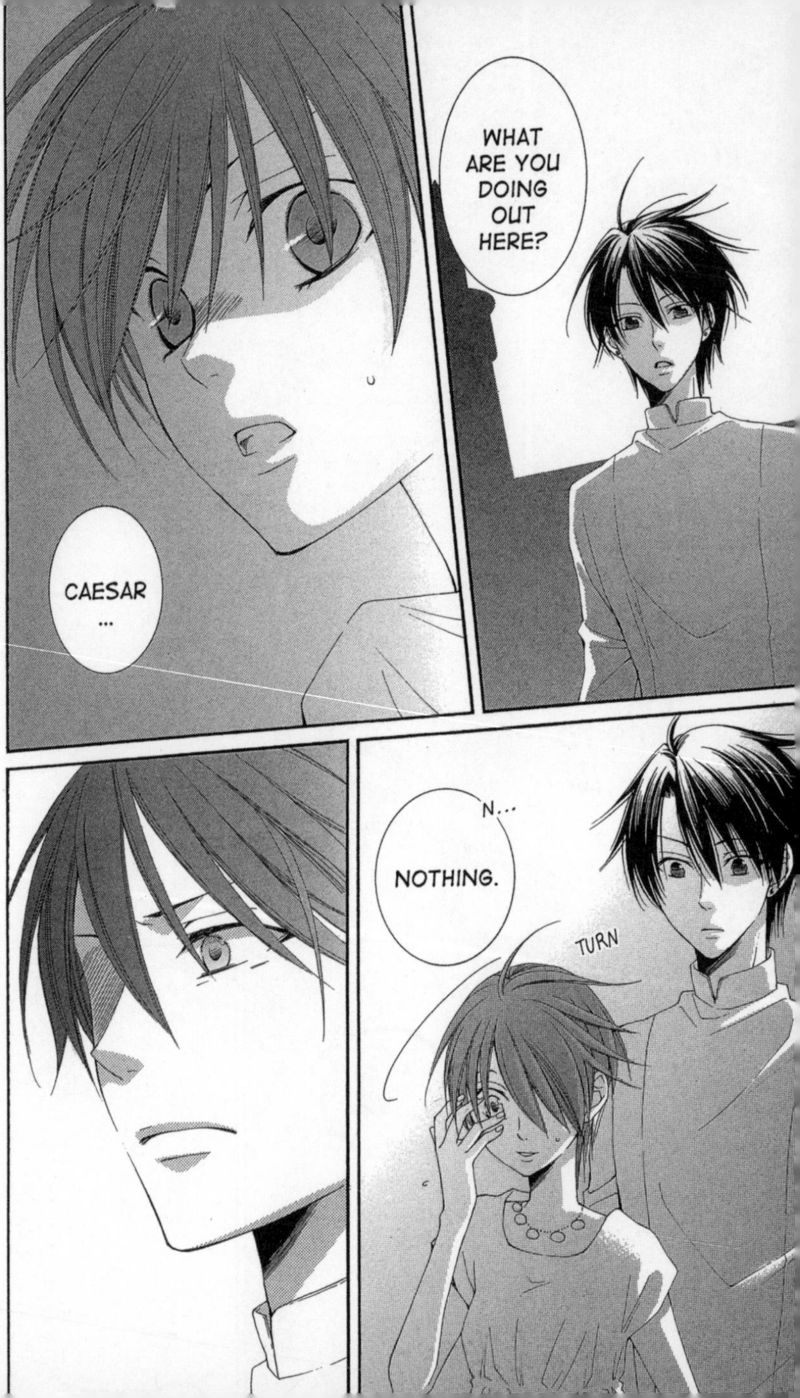
WHAT ARE YOU DOING OUT HERE?
CAESAR ...
N... NOTHING.
TURN

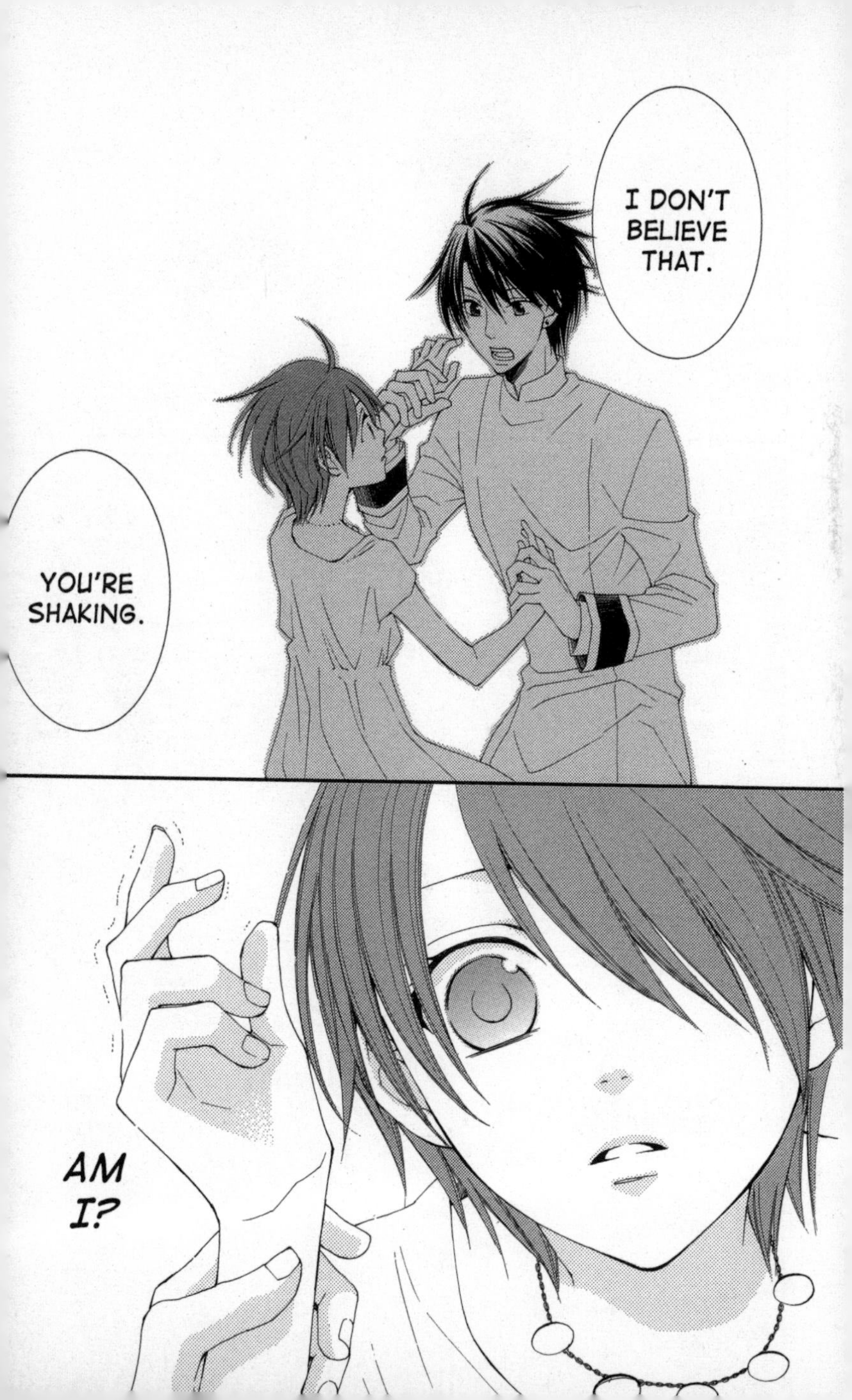
I DON'T BELIEVE THAT.
YOU'RE SHAKING.
AM I?

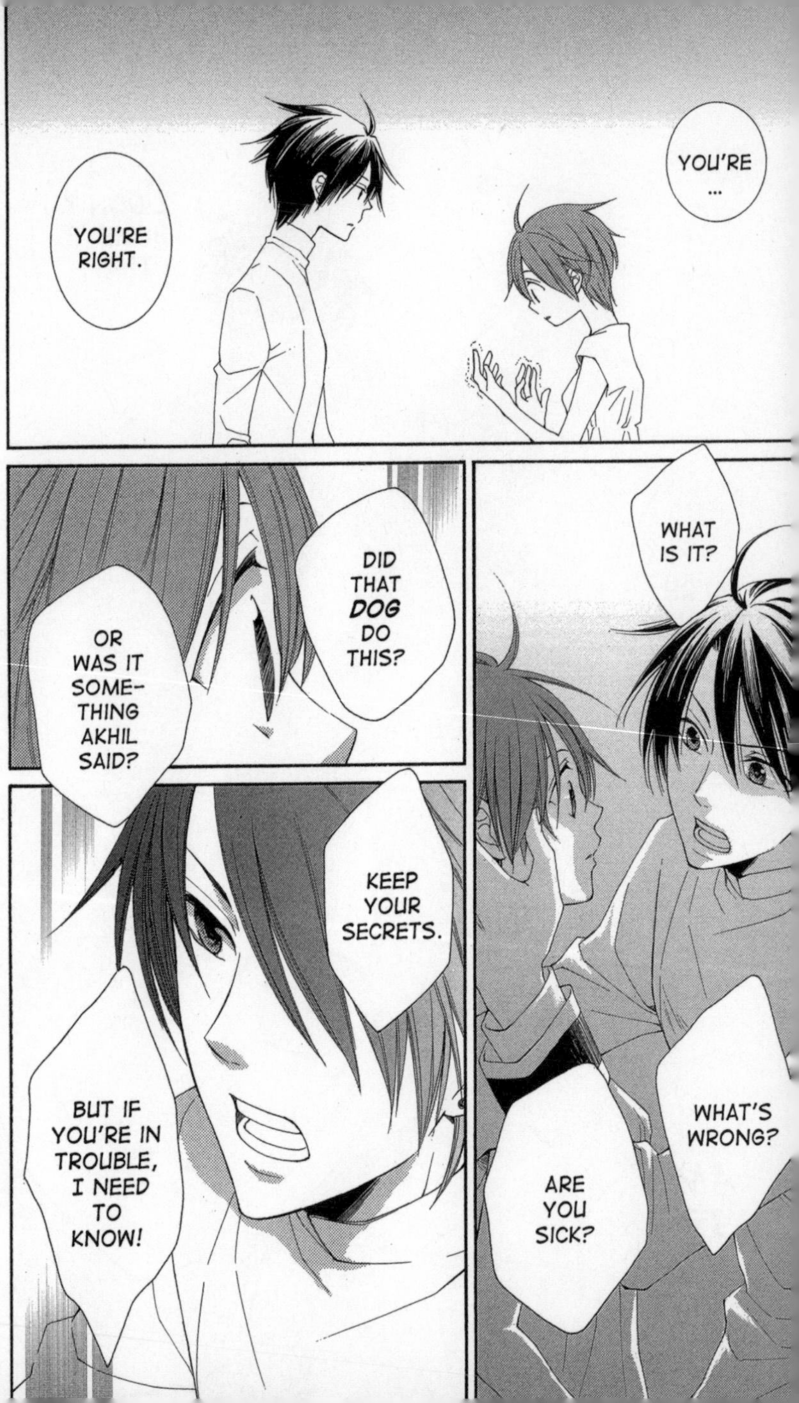
YOU'RE ...
YOU'RE RIGHT.
WHAT IS IT?
WHAT'S WRONG?
ARE YOU SICK?
DID THAT *DOG* DO THIS?
OR WAS IT SOME-THING AKHIL SAID?
KEEP YOUR SECRETS.
BUT IF YOU'RE IN TROUBLE, I NEED TO KNOW!

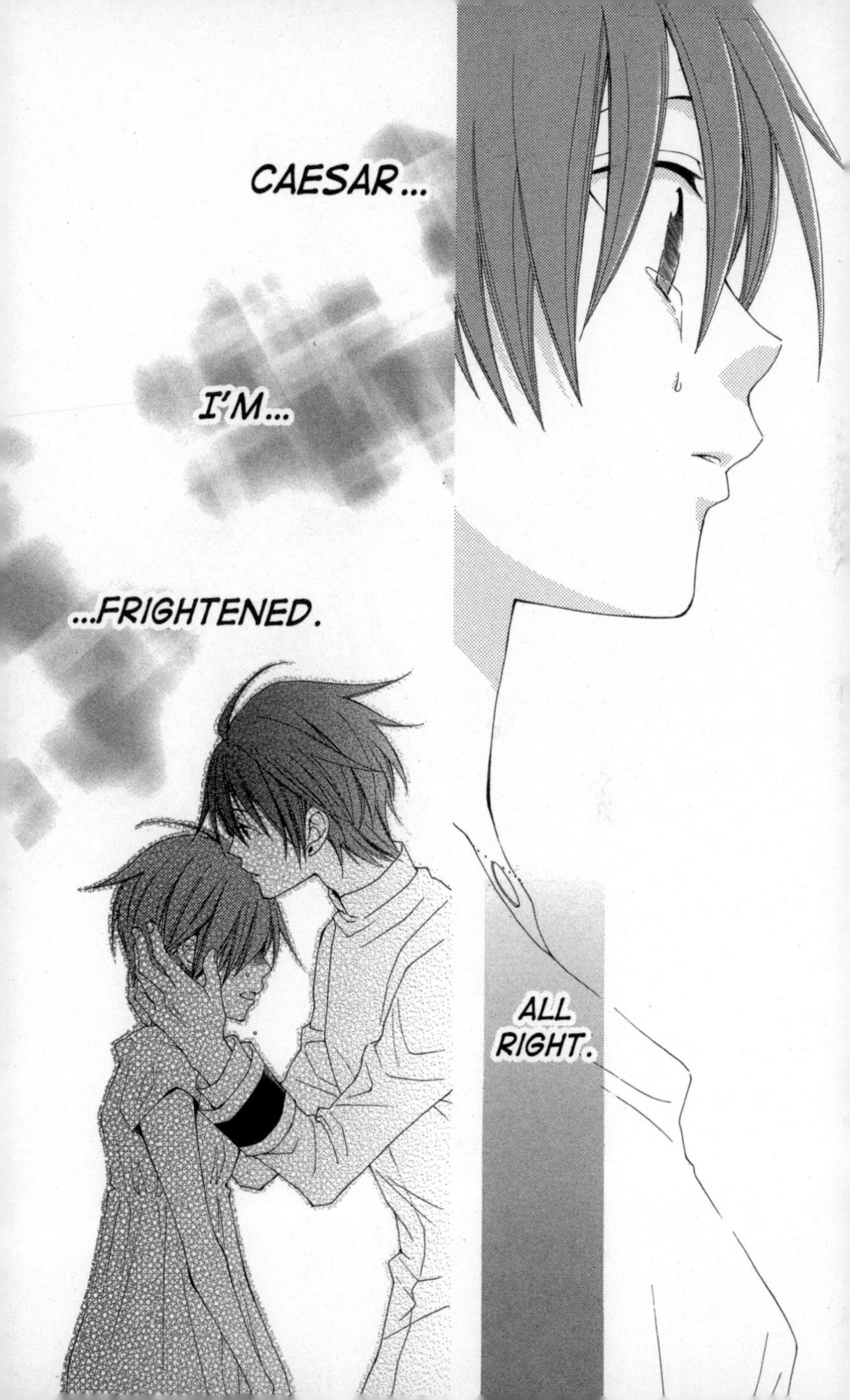
ALL RIGHT.
CAESAR...
I'M...
...FRIGHTENED.

Specialty: Sloppy eating.

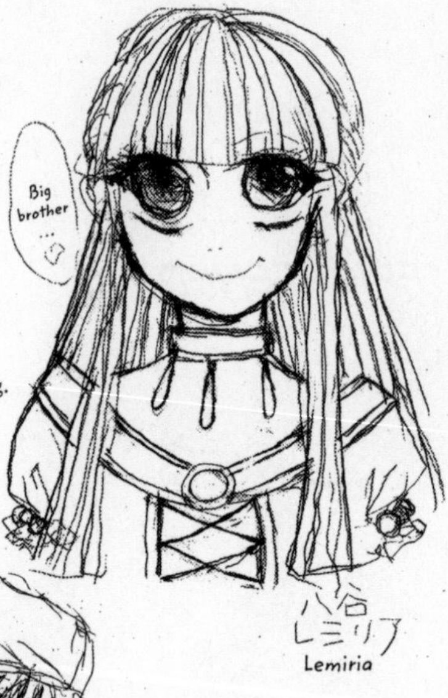
Big brother ...
Lemiria

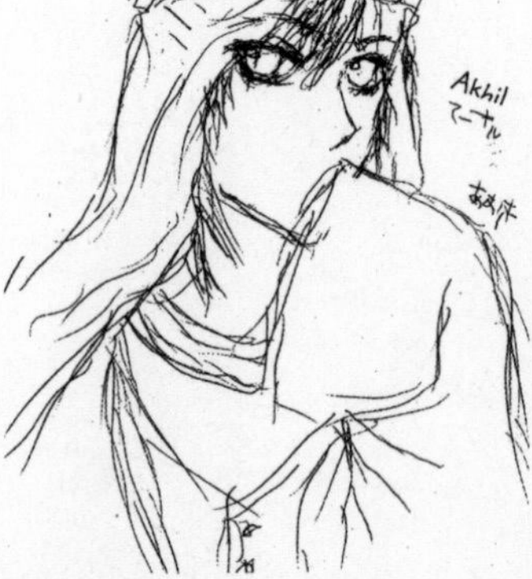
Akhil

Weakness: He's a ladies' man.

Chapter 27

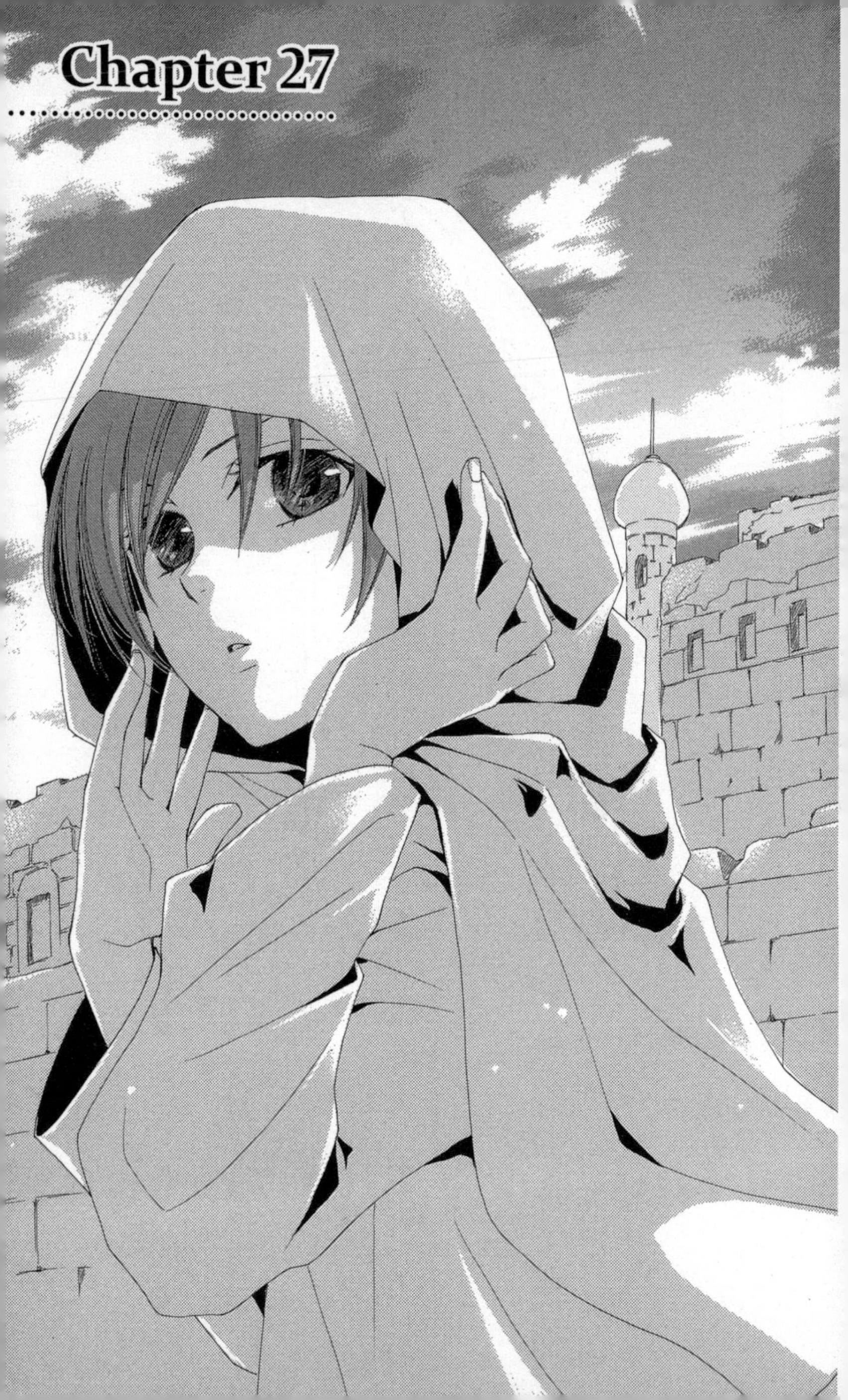

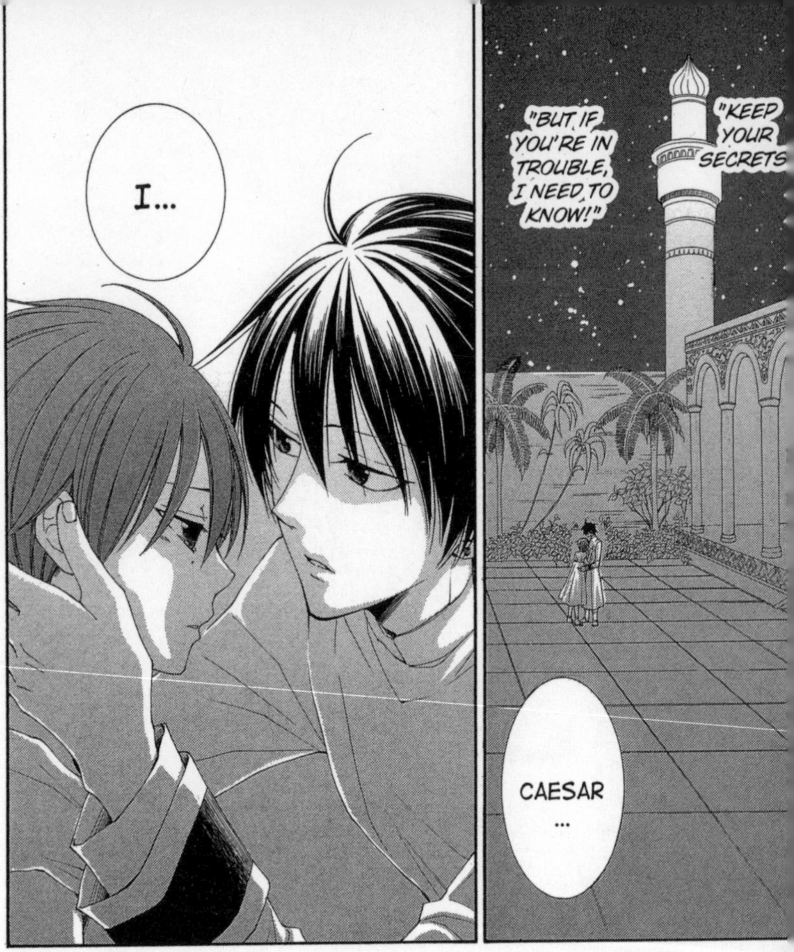
"KEEP YOUR SECRETS
"BUT IF YOU'RE IN TROUBLE, I NEED TO KNOW!"
CAESAR ...
I...

Dawn of the Arcana

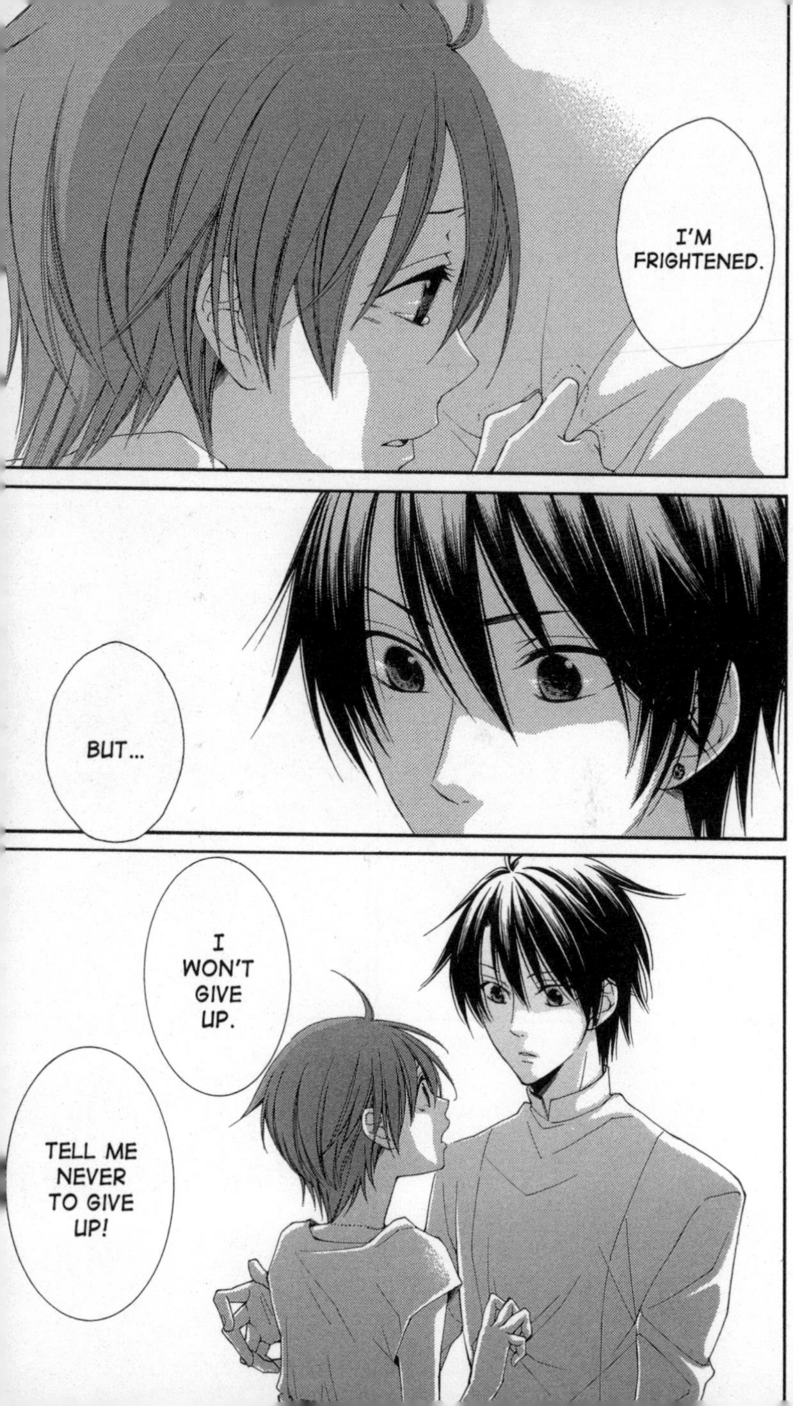
I'M FRIGHTENED.
BUT...
I WON'T GIVE UP.
TELL ME NEVER TO GIVE UP!

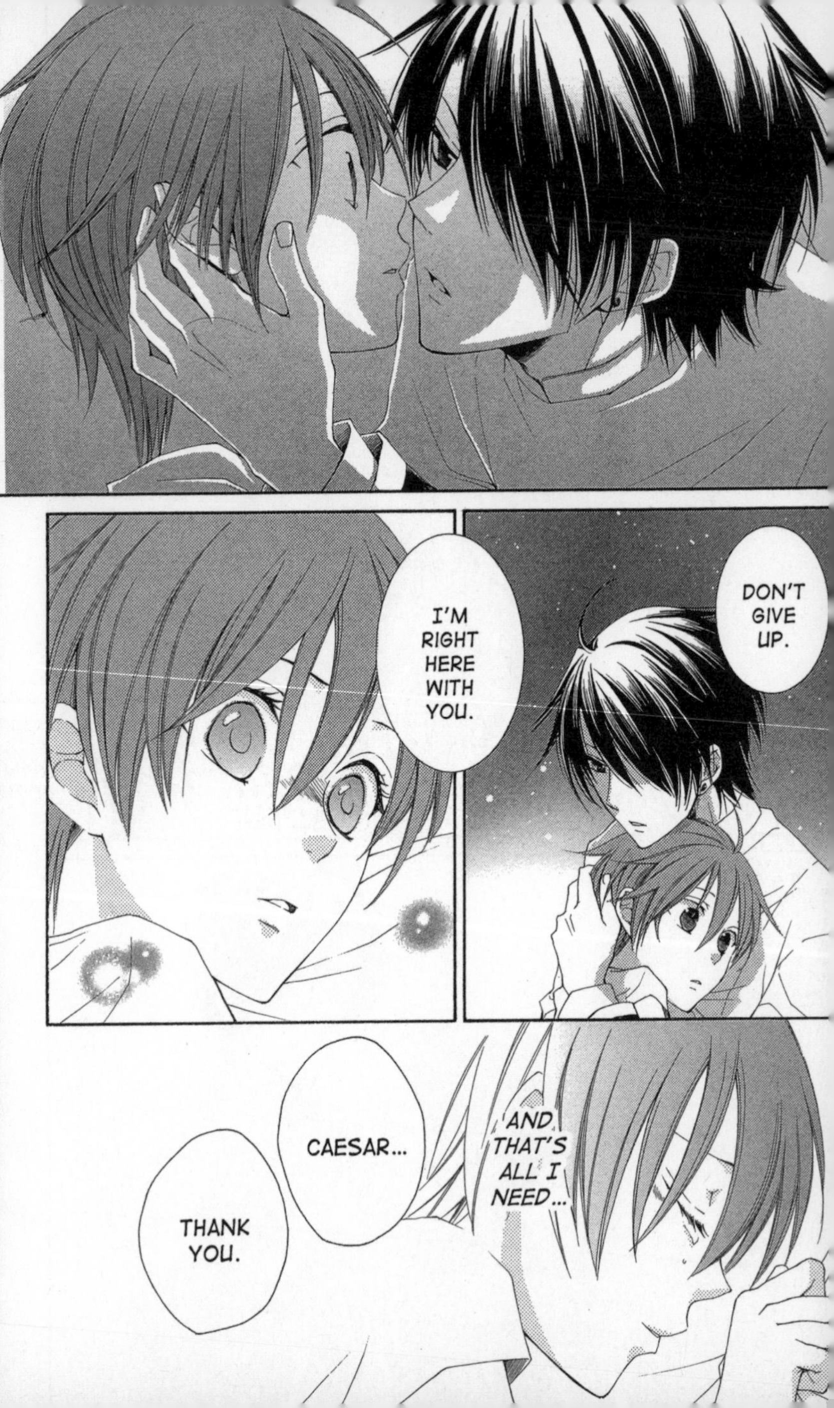
DON'T GIVE UP.
I'M RIGHT HERE WITH YOU.
AND THAT'S ALL I NEED...
CAESAR...
THANK YOU.

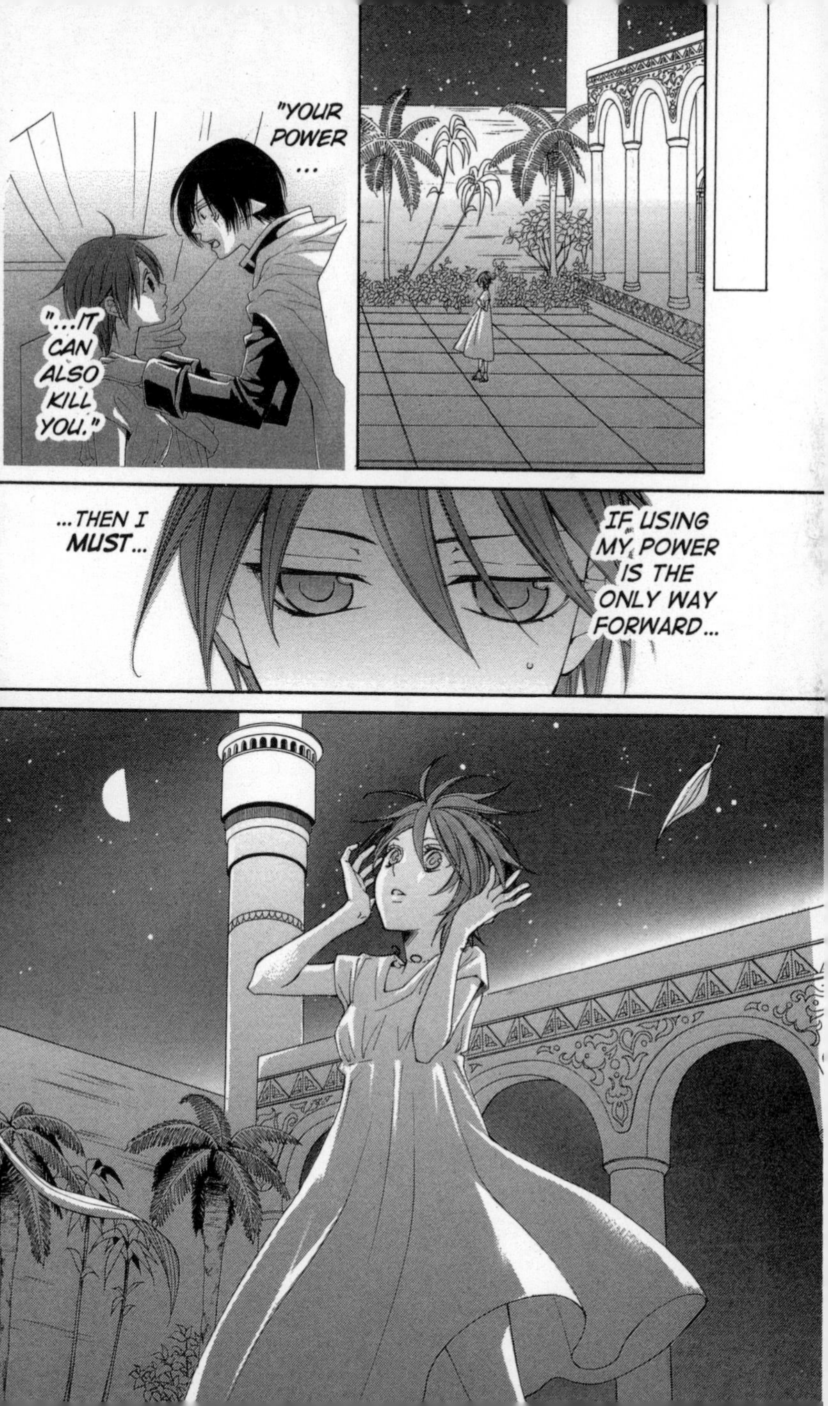
"YOUR POWER ...
"...IT CAN ALSO KILL YOU."
IF USING MY POWER IS THE ONLY WAY FORWARD...
...THEN I MUST...

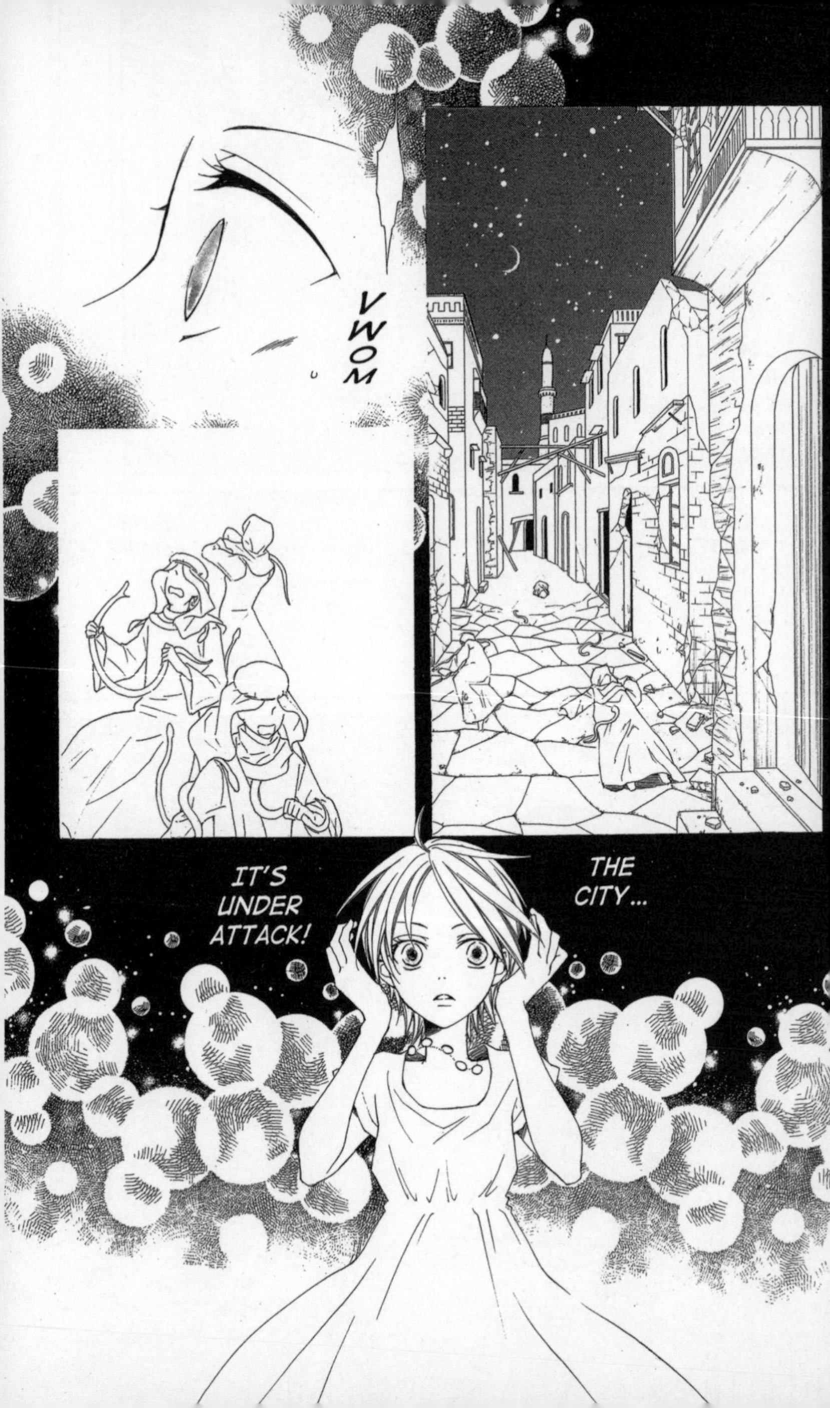
VWOM
THE CITY...
IT'S UNDER ATTACK!

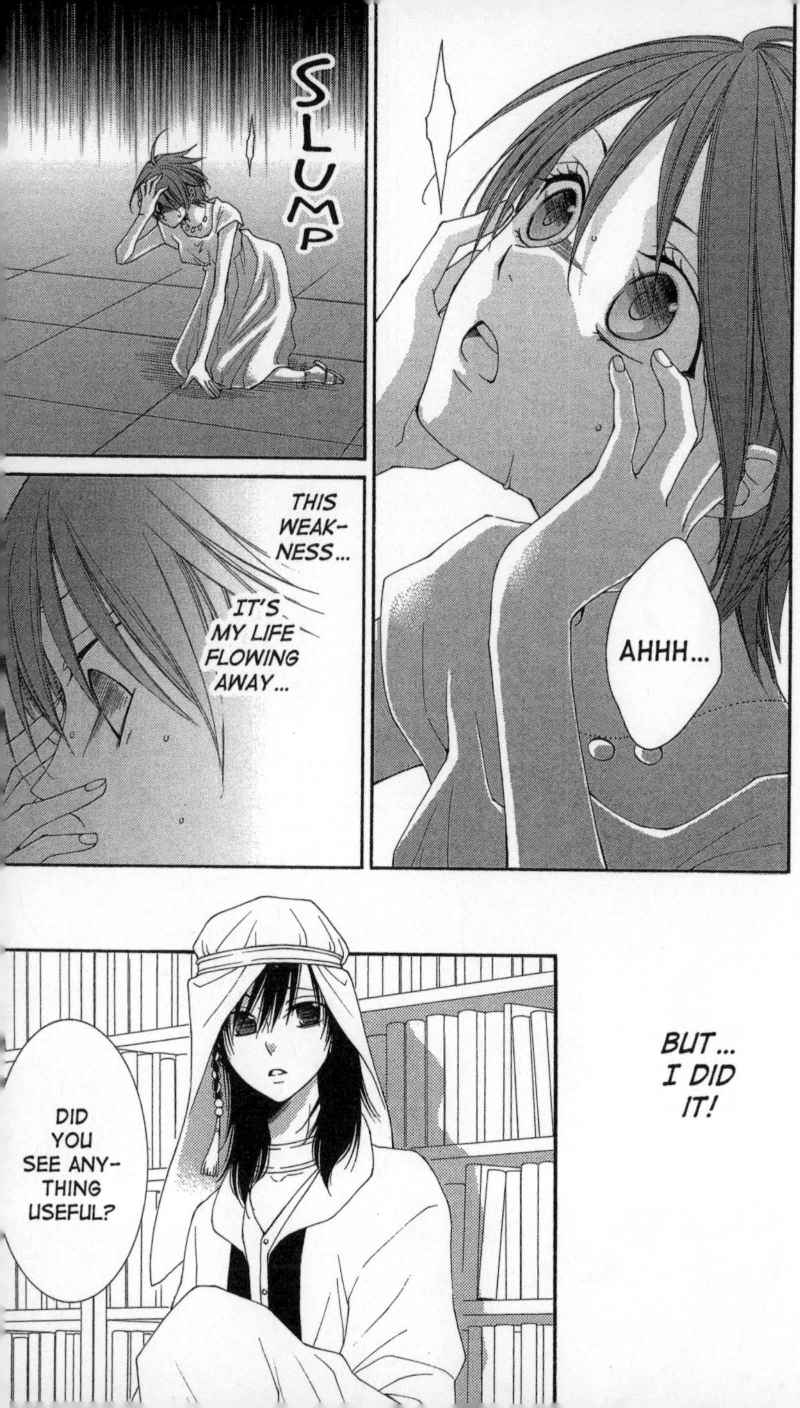
AHHH...
SLUMP
THIS WEAKNESS...
IT'S MY LIFE FLOWING AWAY...
BUT... I DID IT!
DID YOU SEE ANYTHING USEFUL?

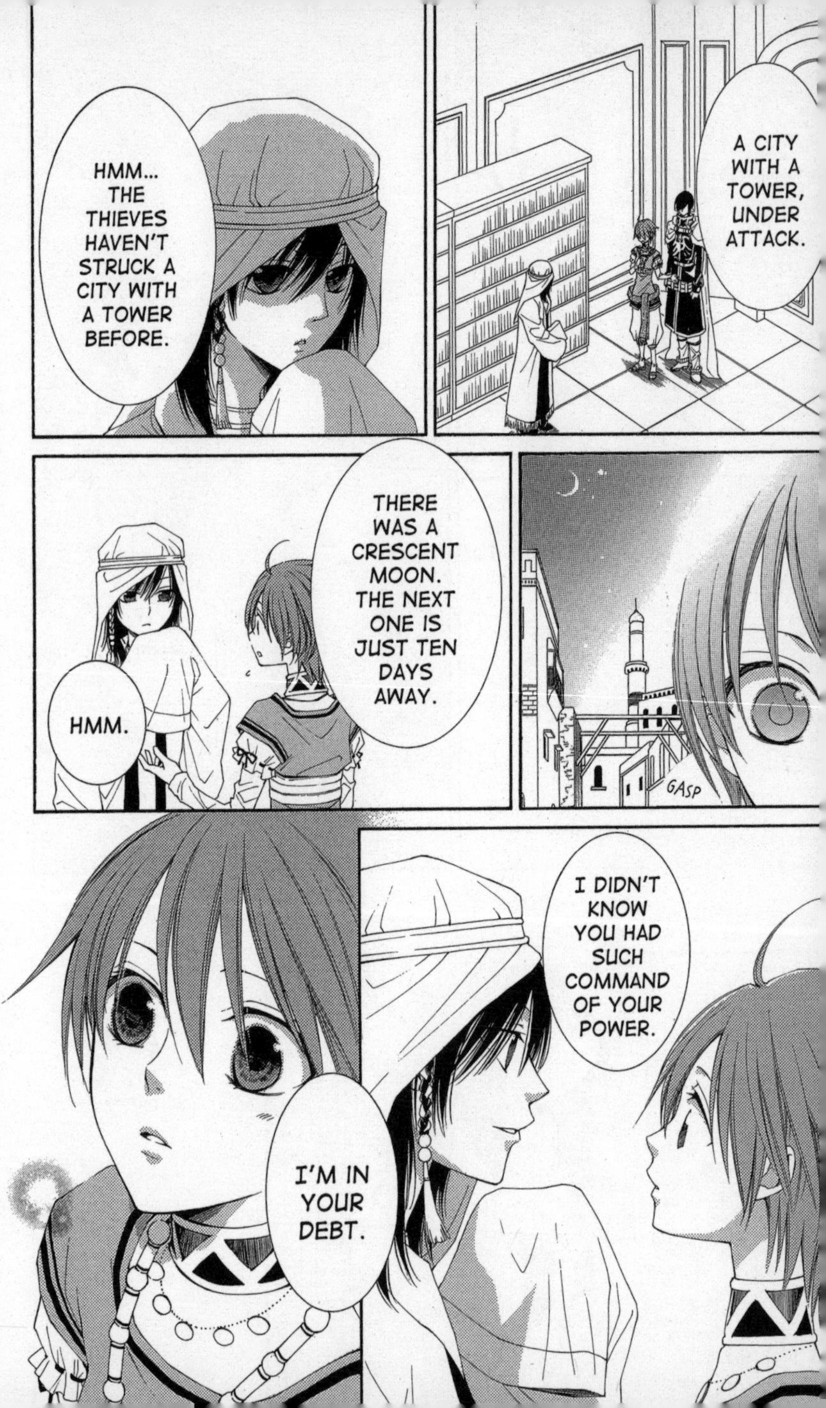
A CITY WITH A TOWER, UNDER ATTACK.
HMM... THE THIEVES HAVEN'T STRUCK A CITY WITH A TOWER BEFORE.
GASP
THERE WAS A CRESCENT MOON. THE NEXT ONE IS JUST TEN DAYS AWAY.
HMM.
I DIDN'T KNOW YOU HAD SUCH COMMAND OF YOUR POWER.
I'M IN YOUR DEBT.

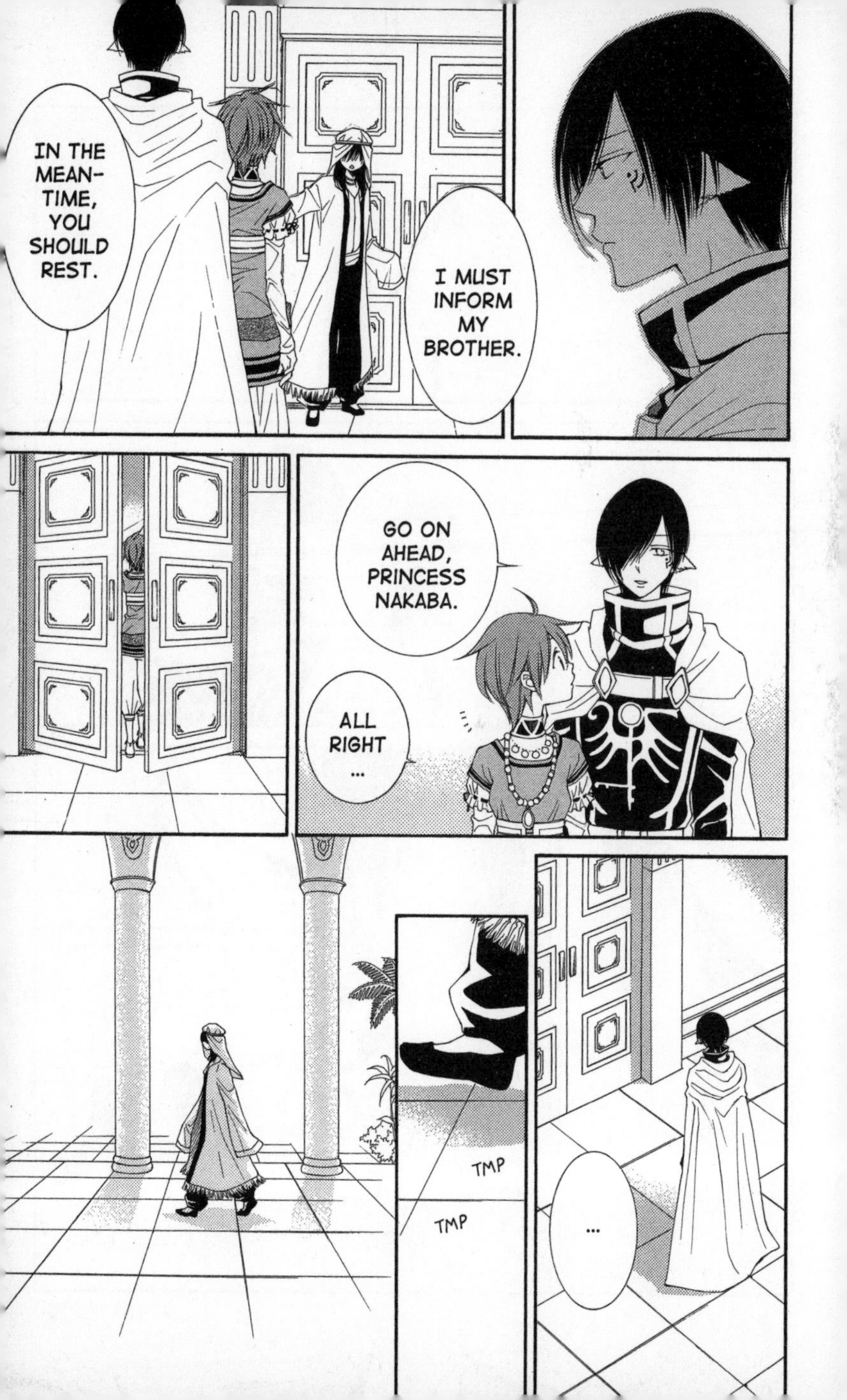
I MUST INFORM MY BROTHER.
IN THE MEAN-TIME, YOU SHOULD REST.
GO ON AHEAD, PRINCESS NAKABA.
ALL RIGHT ...
...
TMP
TMP

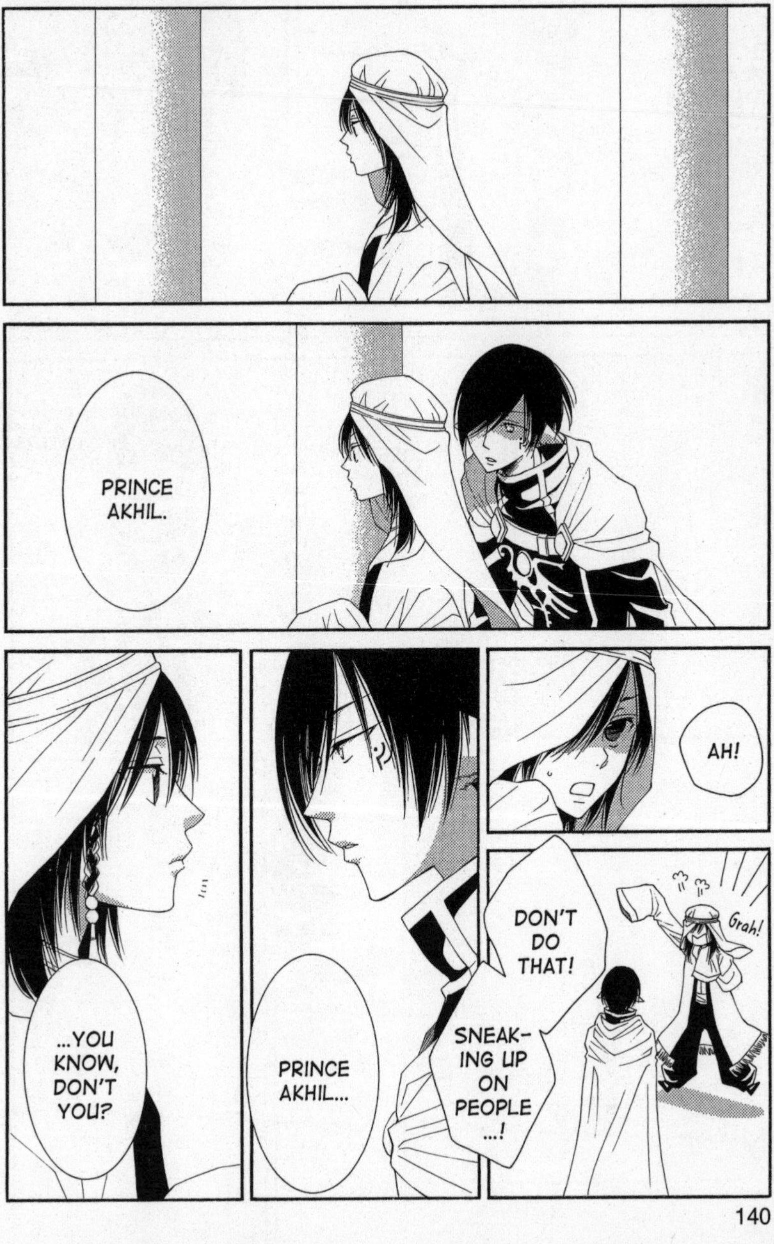
PRINCE AKHIL.
AH!
Grah!
DON'T DO THAT!
SNEAK-ING UP ON PEOPLE ...!
PRINCE AKHIL...
...YOU KNOW, DON'T YOU?

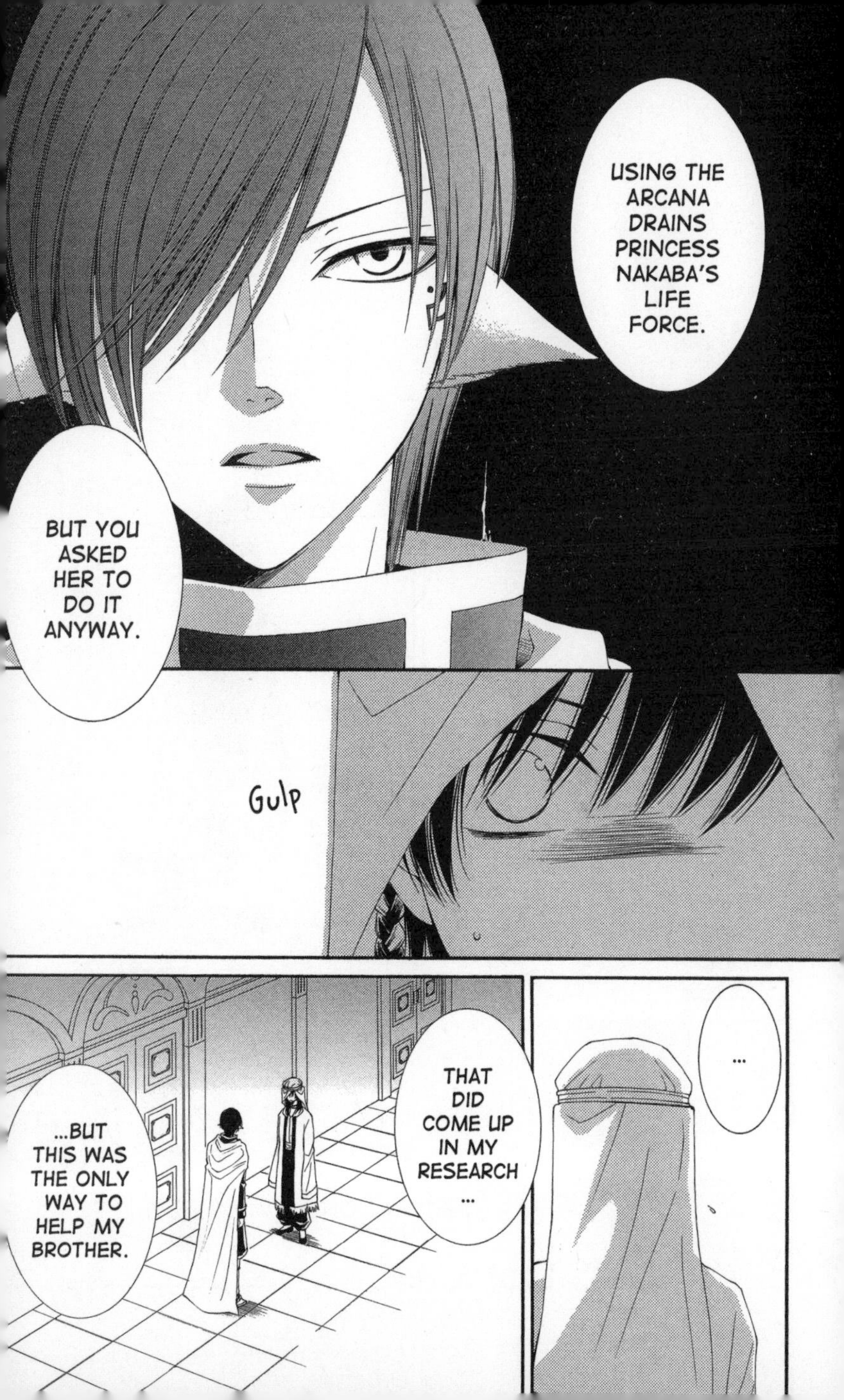
USING THE ARCANA DRAINS PRINCESS NAKABA'S LIFE FORCE.
BUT YOU ASKED HER TO DO IT ANYWAY.
Gulp
...
THAT DID COME UP IN MY RESEARCH ...
...BUT THIS WAS THE ONLY WAY TO HELP MY BROTHER.

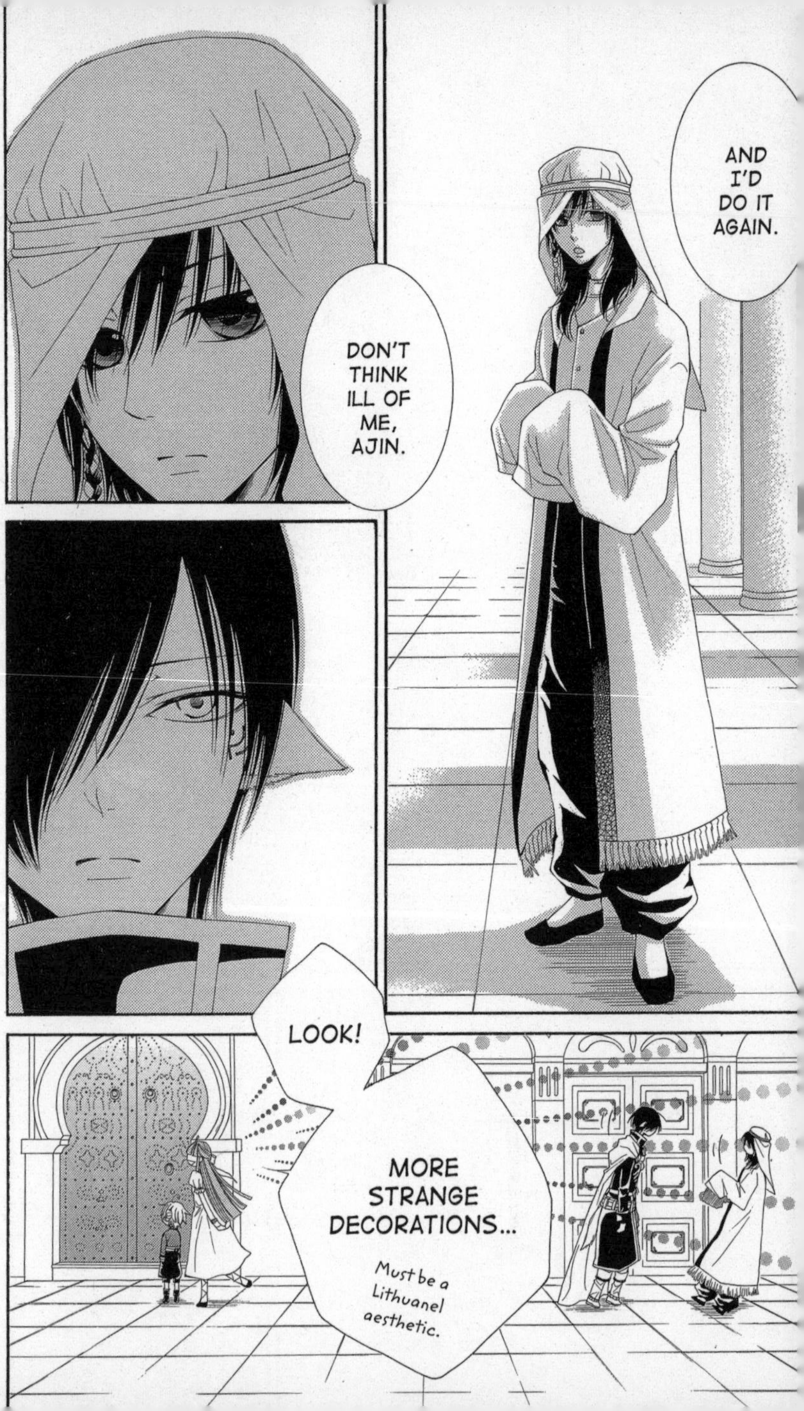

AND I'D DO IT AGAIN.
DON'T THINK ILL OF ME, AJIN.
LOOK!
MORE STRANGE DECORATIONS...
Must be a Lithuanel aesthetic.

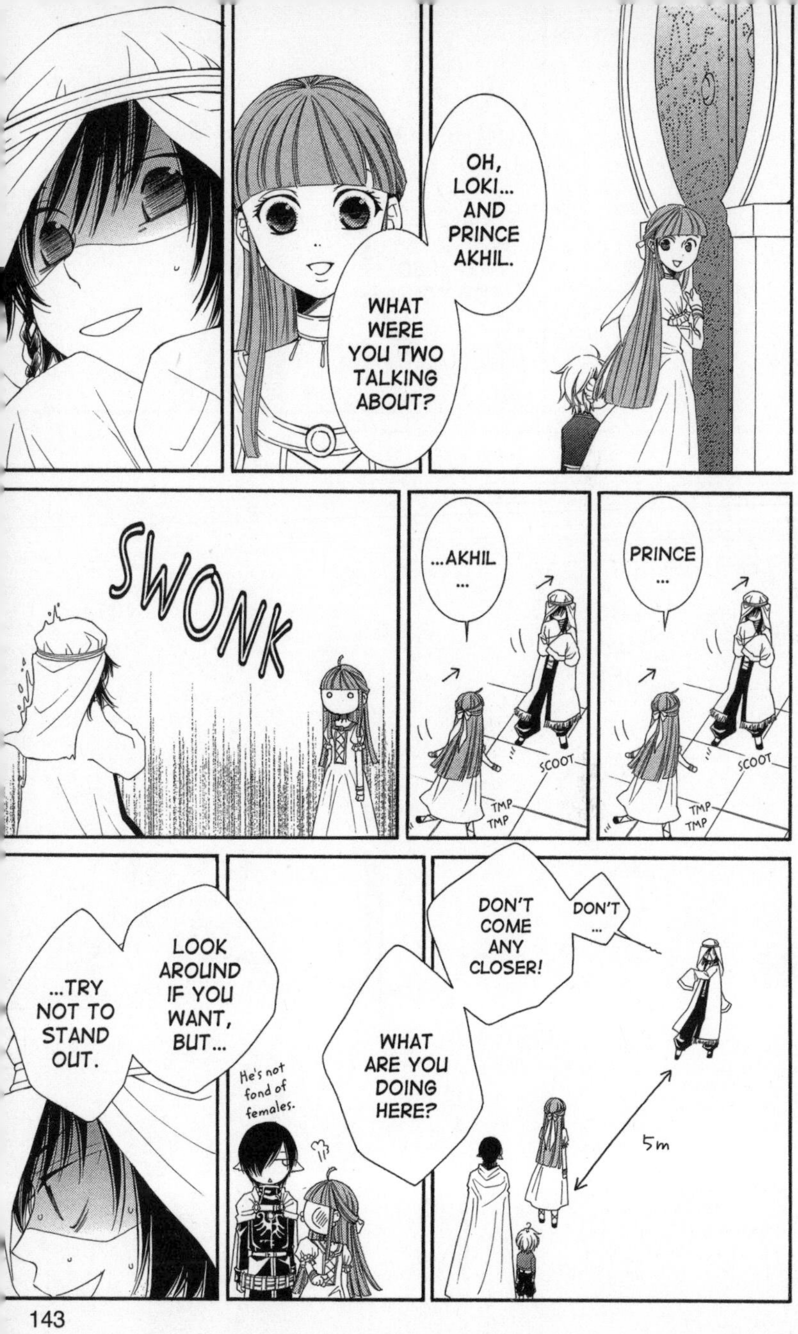
OH, LOKI... AND PRINCE AKHIL.
WHAT WERE YOU TWO TALKING ABOUT?
PRINCE ...
SCOOT
TMP TMP
...AKHIL ...
SCOOT
TMP TMP
SWONK
DON'T ...
DON'T COME ANY CLOSER!
WHAT ARE YOU DOING HERE?
5m
He's not fond of females.
LOOK AROUND IF YOU WANT, BUT...
...TRY NOT TO STAND OUT.

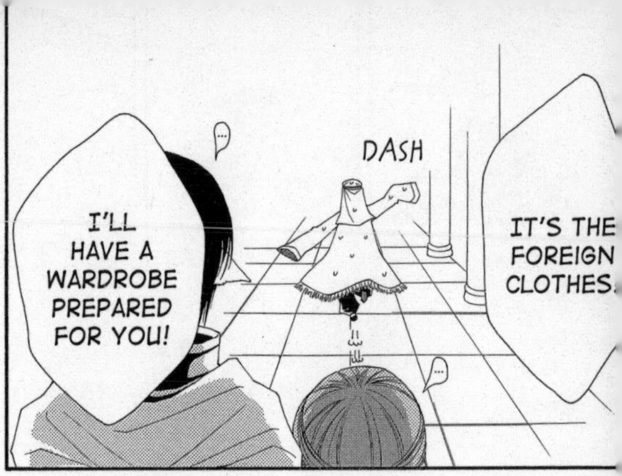
IT'S THE FOREIGN CLOTHES.
DASH
...
I'LL HAVE A WARDROBE PREPARED FOR YOU!
...

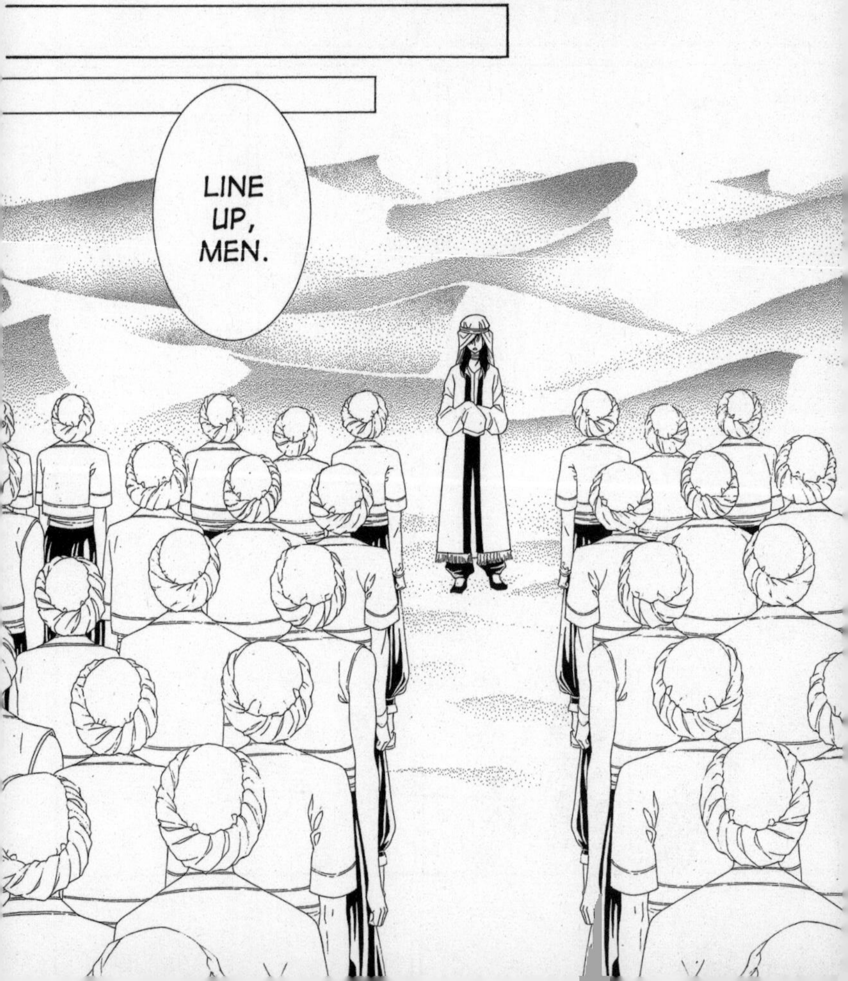
LINE UP, MEN.

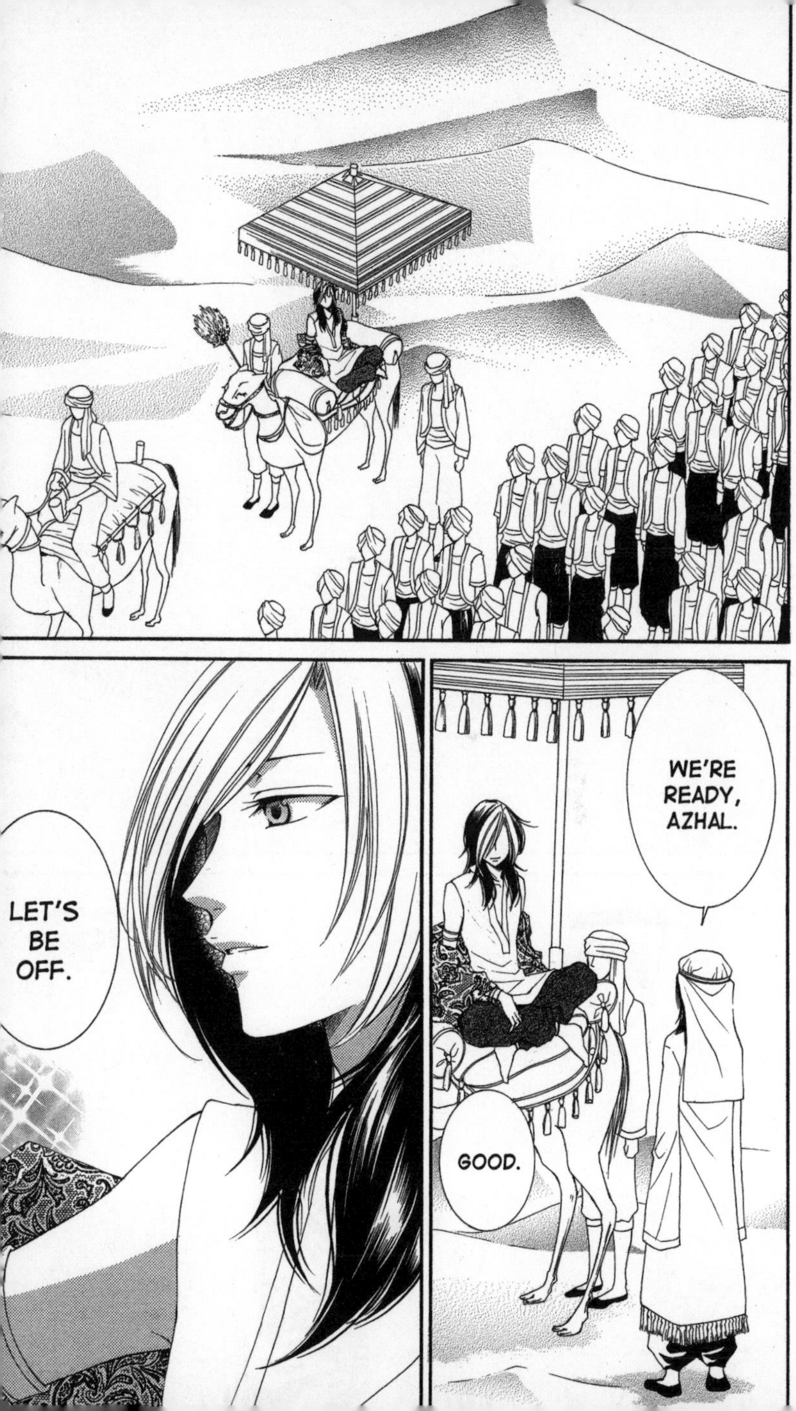
WE'RE READY, AZHAL.
GOOD.
LET'S BE OFF.

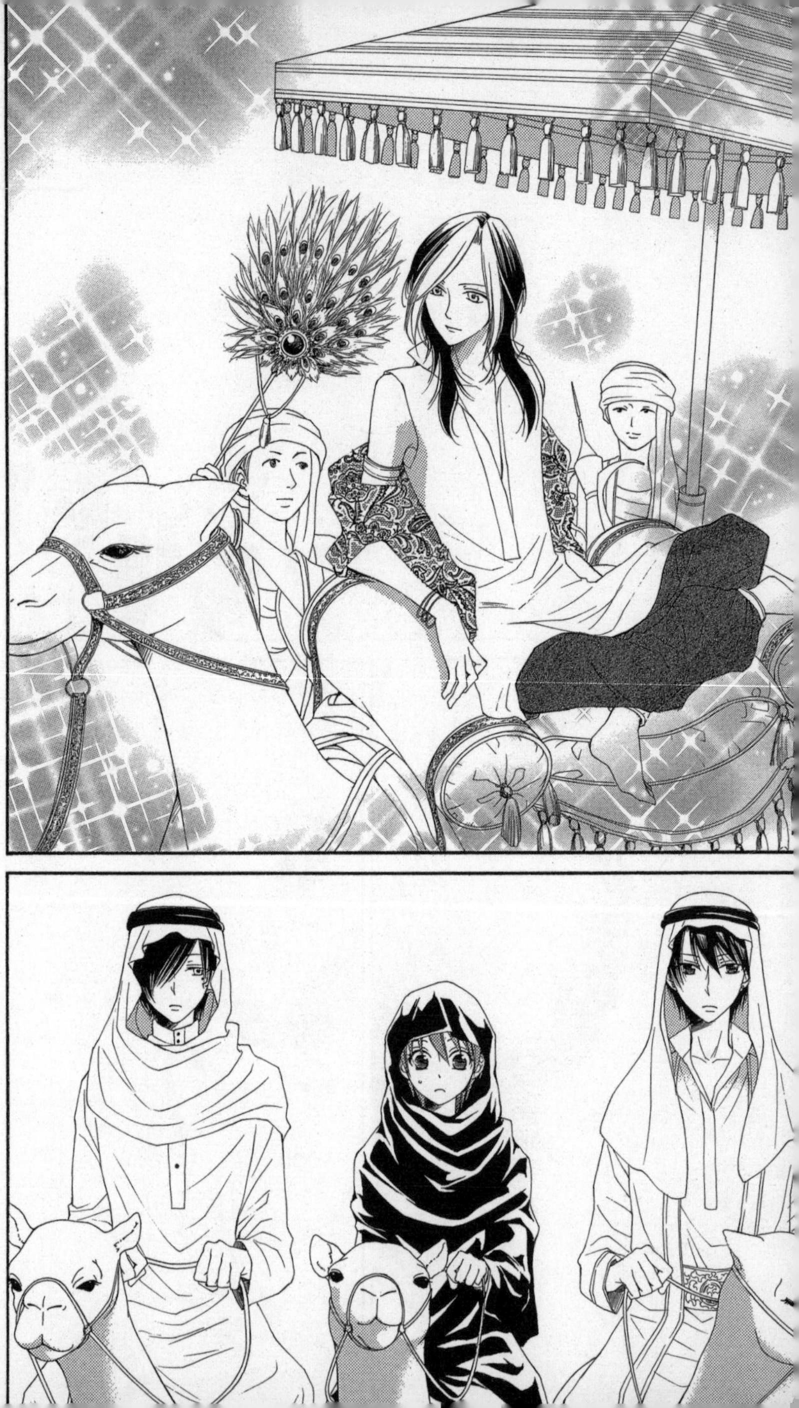

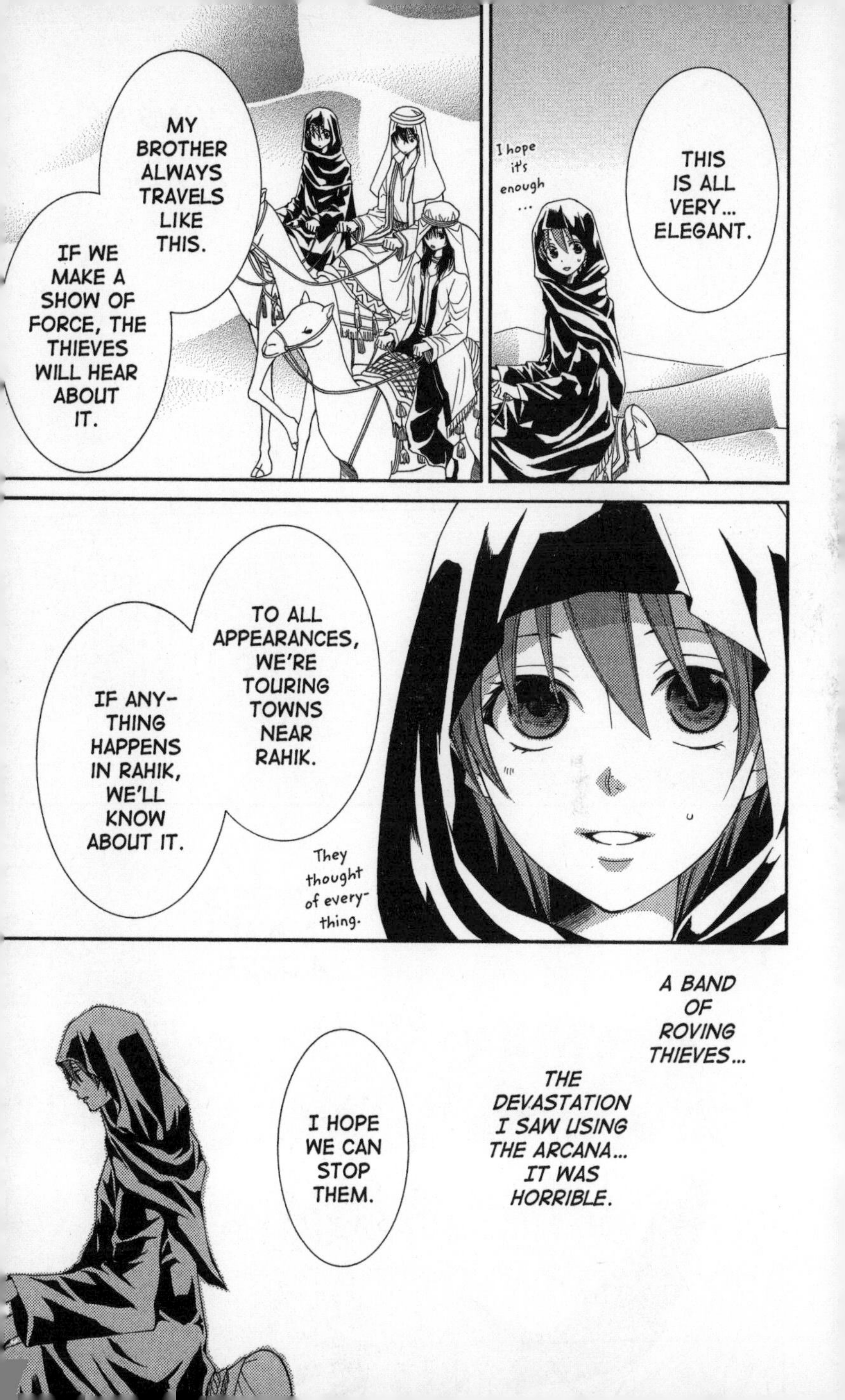
THIS IS ALL VERY... ELEGANT.
I hope it's enough...
MY BROTHER ALWAYS TRAVELS LIKE THIS.
IF WE MAKE A SHOW OF FORCE, THE THIEVES WILL HEAR ABOUT IT.
TO ALL APPEARANCES, WE'RE TOURING TOWNS NEAR RAHIK.
IF ANY-THING HAPPENS IN RAHIK, WE'LL KNOW ABOUT IT.
They thought of every-thing.
A BAND OF ROVING THIEVES...
THE DEVASTATION I SAW USING THE ARCANA... IT WAS HORRIBLE.
I HOPE WE CAN STOP THEM.

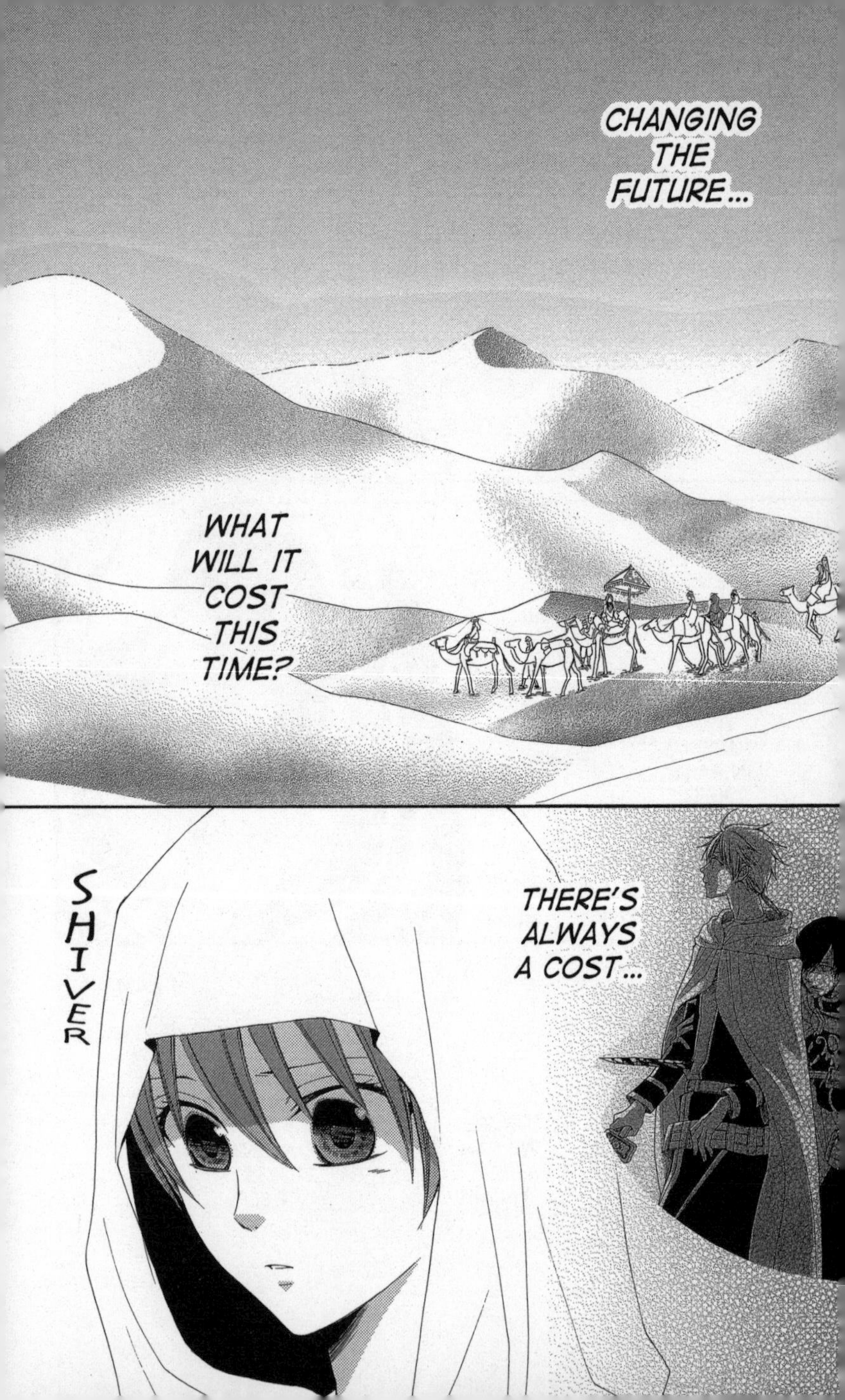
CHANGING THE FUTURE...
WHAT WILL IT COST THIS TIME?
THERE'S ALWAYS A COST...
SHIVER

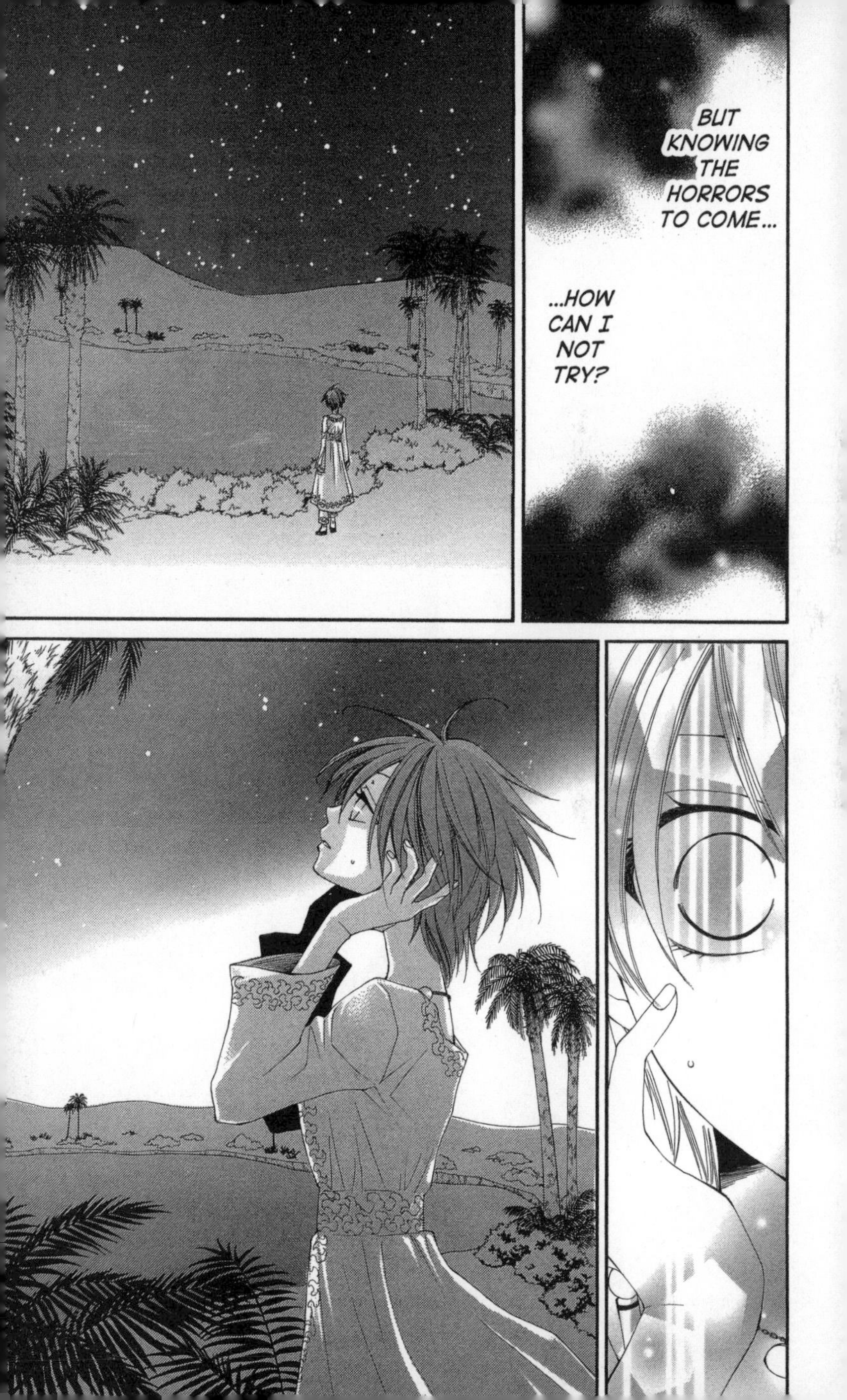
BUT KNOWING THE HORRORS TO COME...
...HOW CAN I NOT TRY?

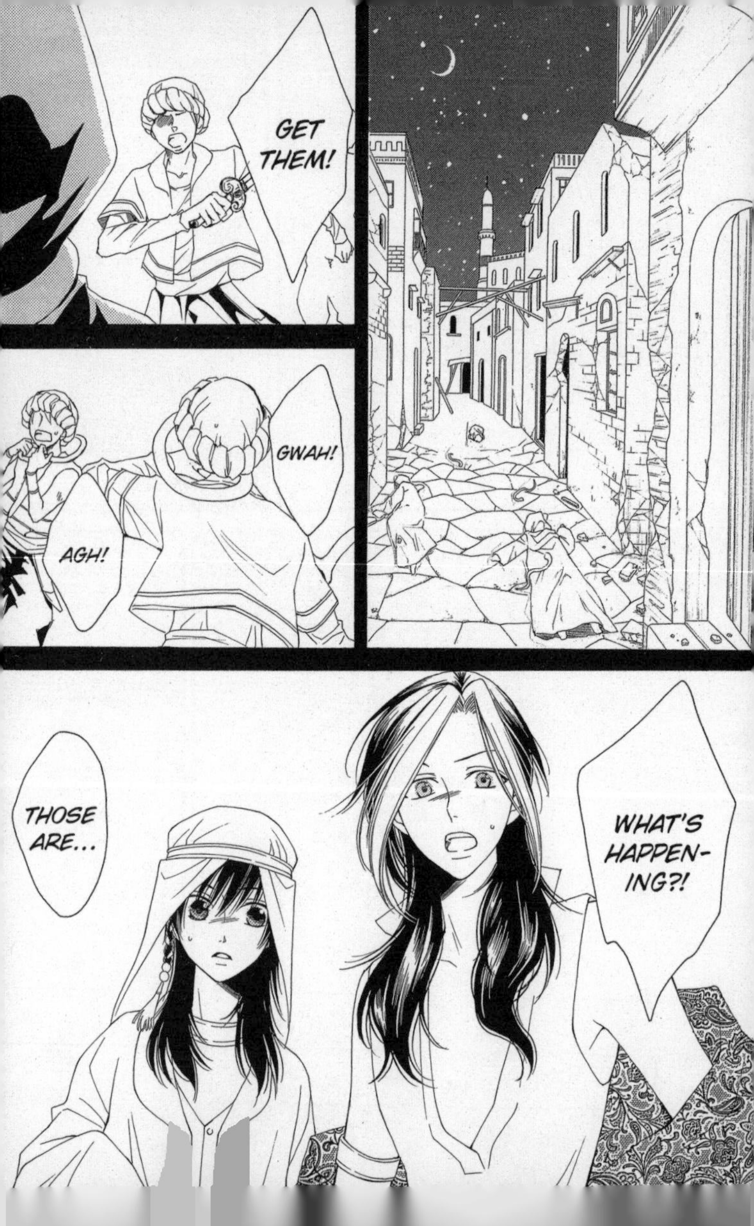
GET THEM!
GWAH!
AGH!
WHAT'S HAPPEN-ING?!
THOSE ARE...

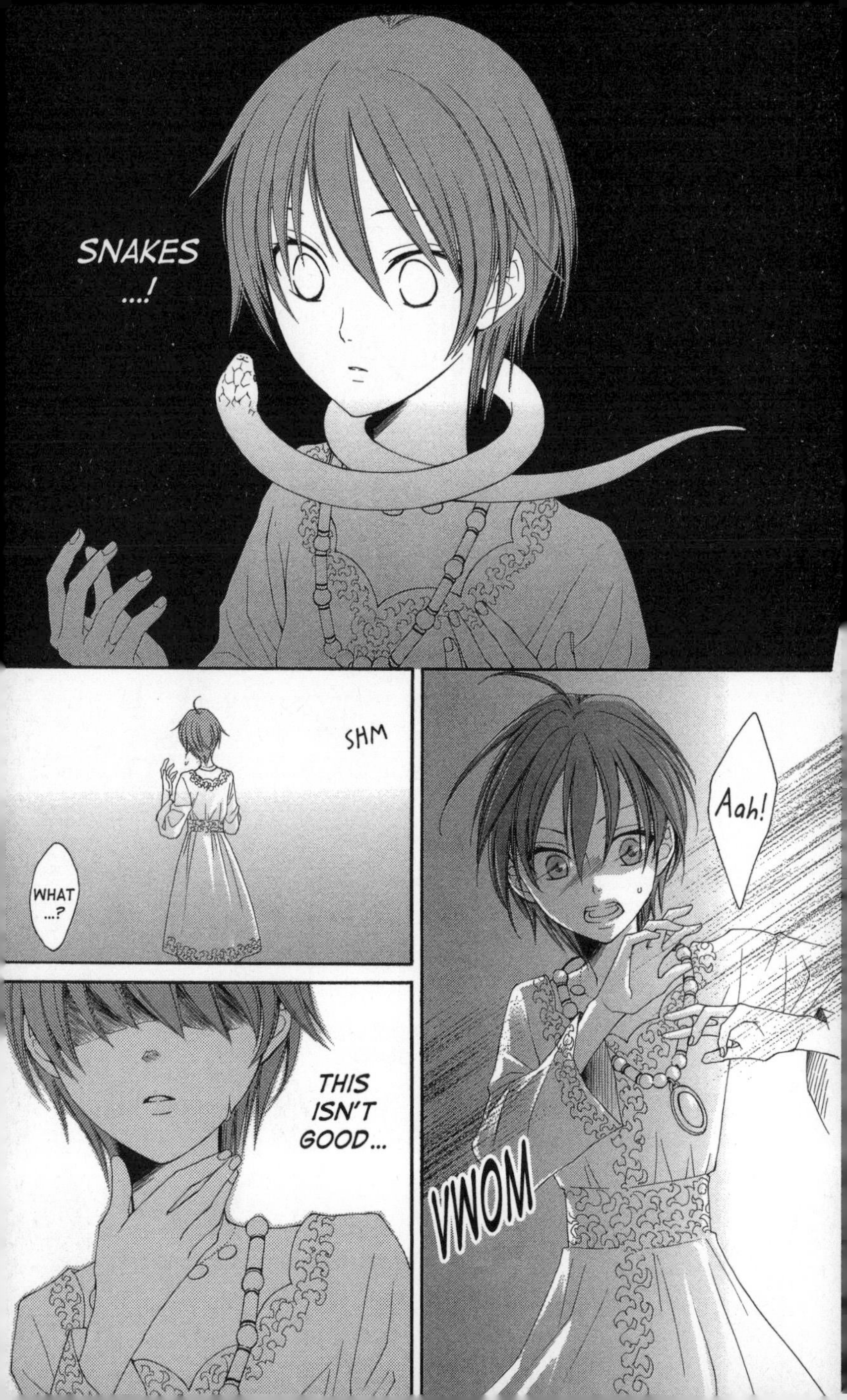
SNAKES ...!
Aah!
VWOM
SHM
WHAT ...?
THIS ISN'T GOOD...

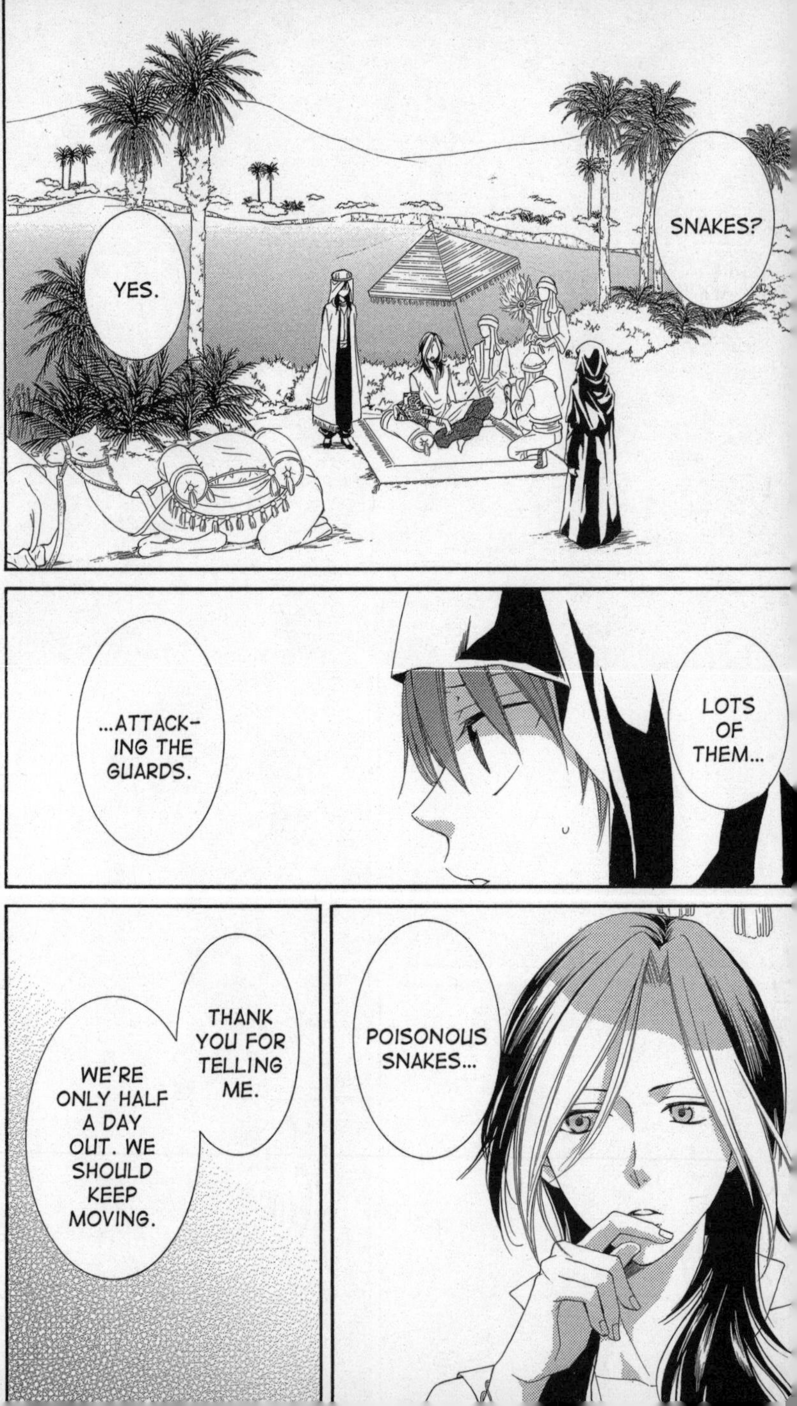
SNAKES?
YES.
LOTS OF THEM...
...ATTACK-ING THE GUARDS.
POISONOUS SNAKES...
THANK YOU FOR TELLING ME.
WE'RE ONLY HALF A DAY OUT. WE SHOULD KEEP MOVING.

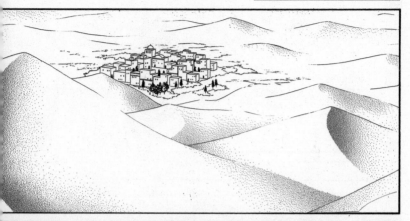

THAT'S RINA-BAN.

THE CITY BEYOND IT IS RAHIK.

AS YOU CAN SEE, WE'RE JUST A STONE'S THROW FROM RINABAN.

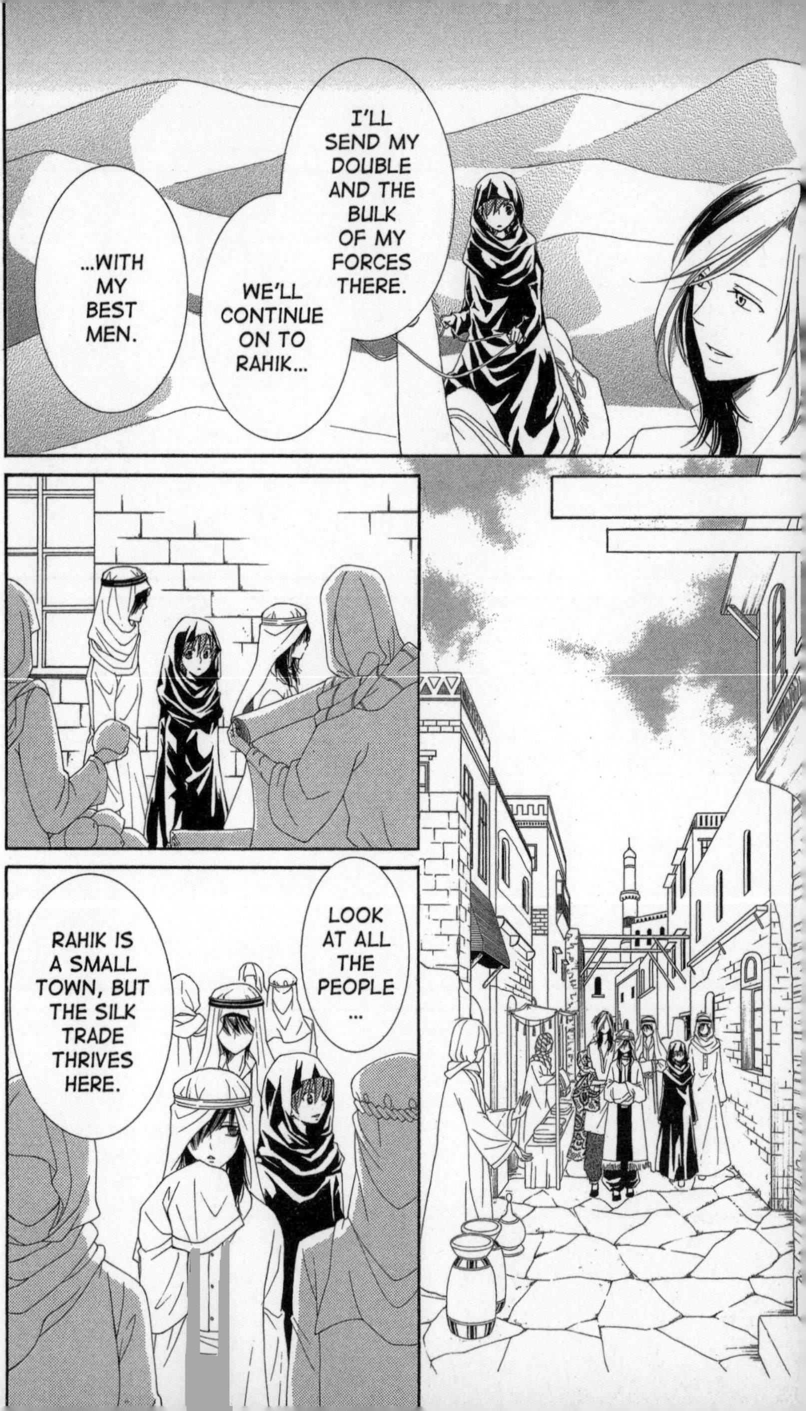
I'LL SEND MY DOUBLE AND THE BULK OF MY FORCES THERE.
WE'LL CONTINUE ON TO RAHIK...
...WITH MY BEST MEN.
LOOK AT ALL THE PEOPLE ...
RAHIK IS A SMALL TOWN, BUT THE SILK TRADE THRIVES HERE.

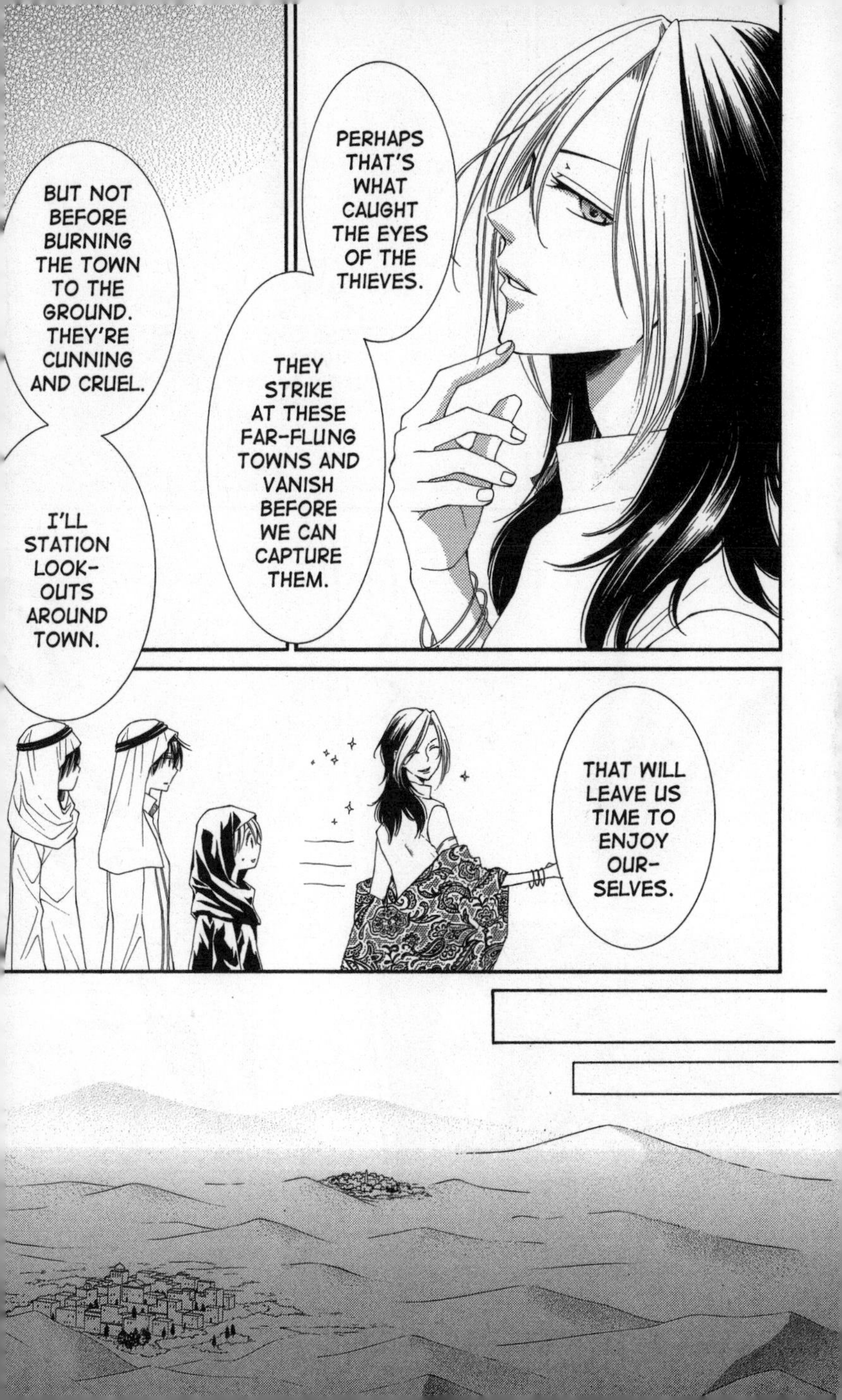
PERHAPS THAT'S WHAT CAUGHT THE EYES OF THE THIEVES.
THEY STRIKE AT THESE FAR-FLUNG TOWNS AND VANISH BEFORE WE CAN CAPTURE THEM.
BUT NOT BEFORE BURNING THE TOWN TO THE GROUND. THEY'RE CUNNING AND CRUEL.
I'LL STATION LOOK-OUTS AROUND TOWN.
THAT WILL LEAVE US TIME TO ENJOY OUR-SELVES.

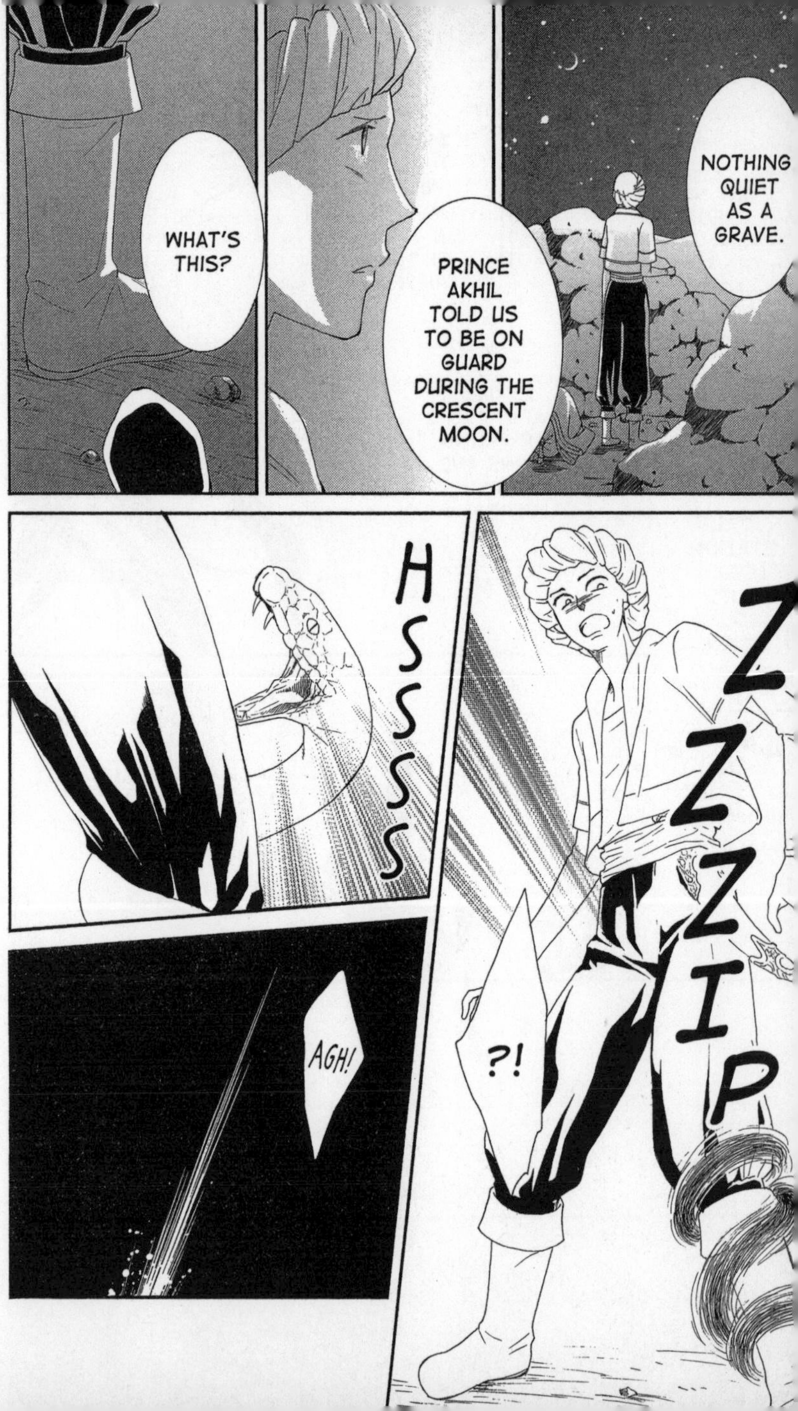
NOTHING QUIET AS A GRAVE.
PRINCE AKHIL TOLD US TO BE ON GUARD DURING THE CRESCENT MOON.
WHAT'S THIS?
ZZZIP
?!
HSSSS
AGH!

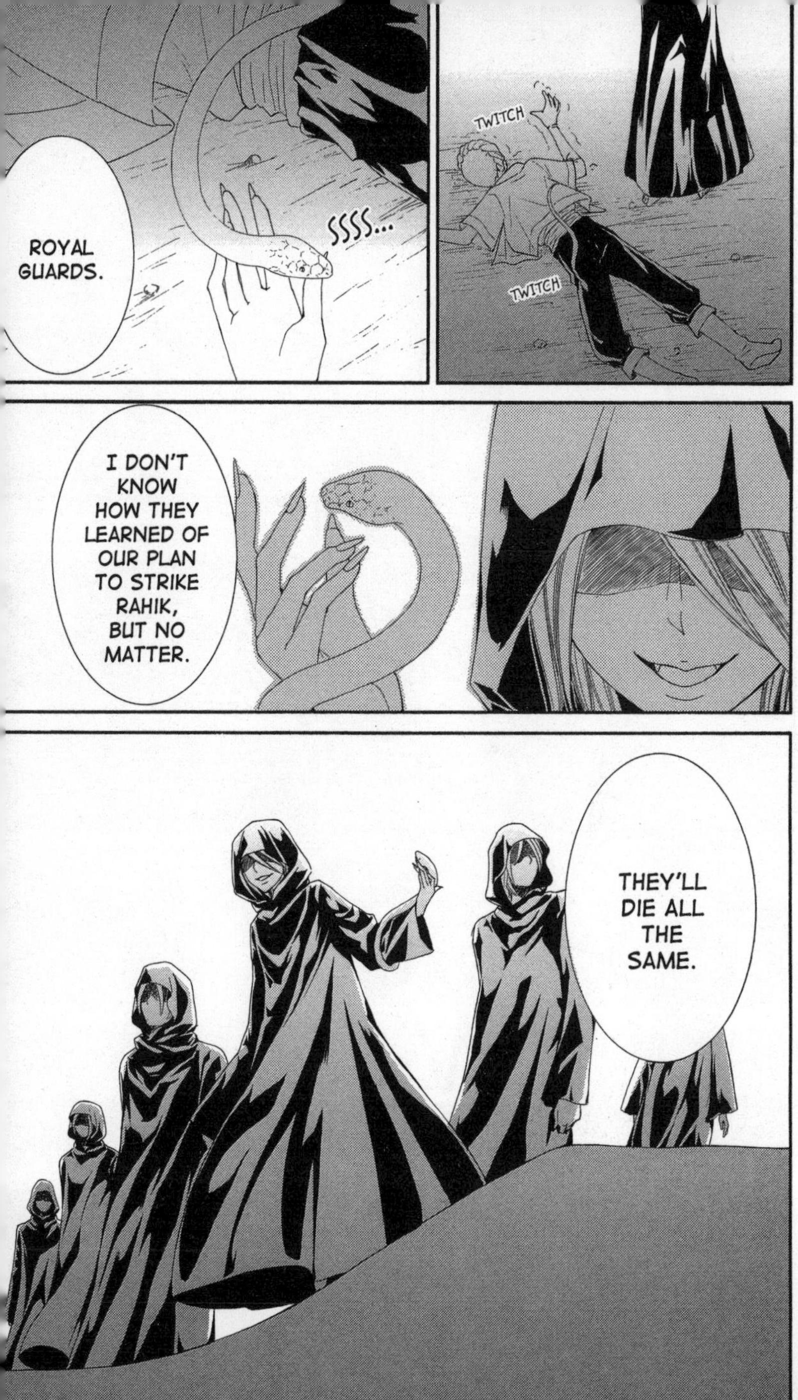
TWITCH
TWITCH
SSSS...
ROYAL GUARDS.
I DON'T KNOW HOW THEY LEARNED OF OUR PLAN TO STRIKE RAHIK, BUT NO MATTER.
THEY'LL DIE ALL THE SAME.

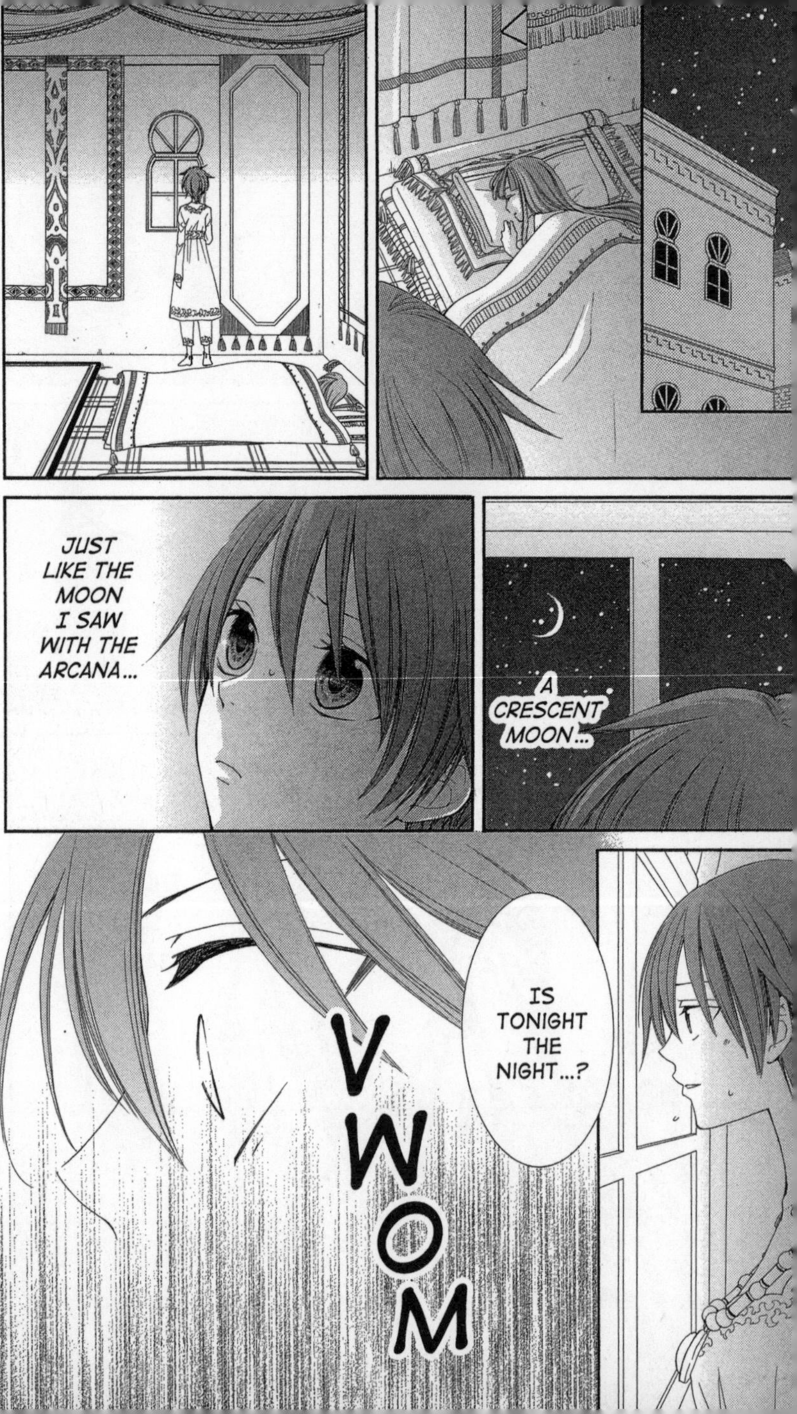
A CRESCENT MOON...
JUST LIKE THE MOON I SAW WITH THE ARCANA...
IS TONIGHT THE NIGHT...?
VWOM

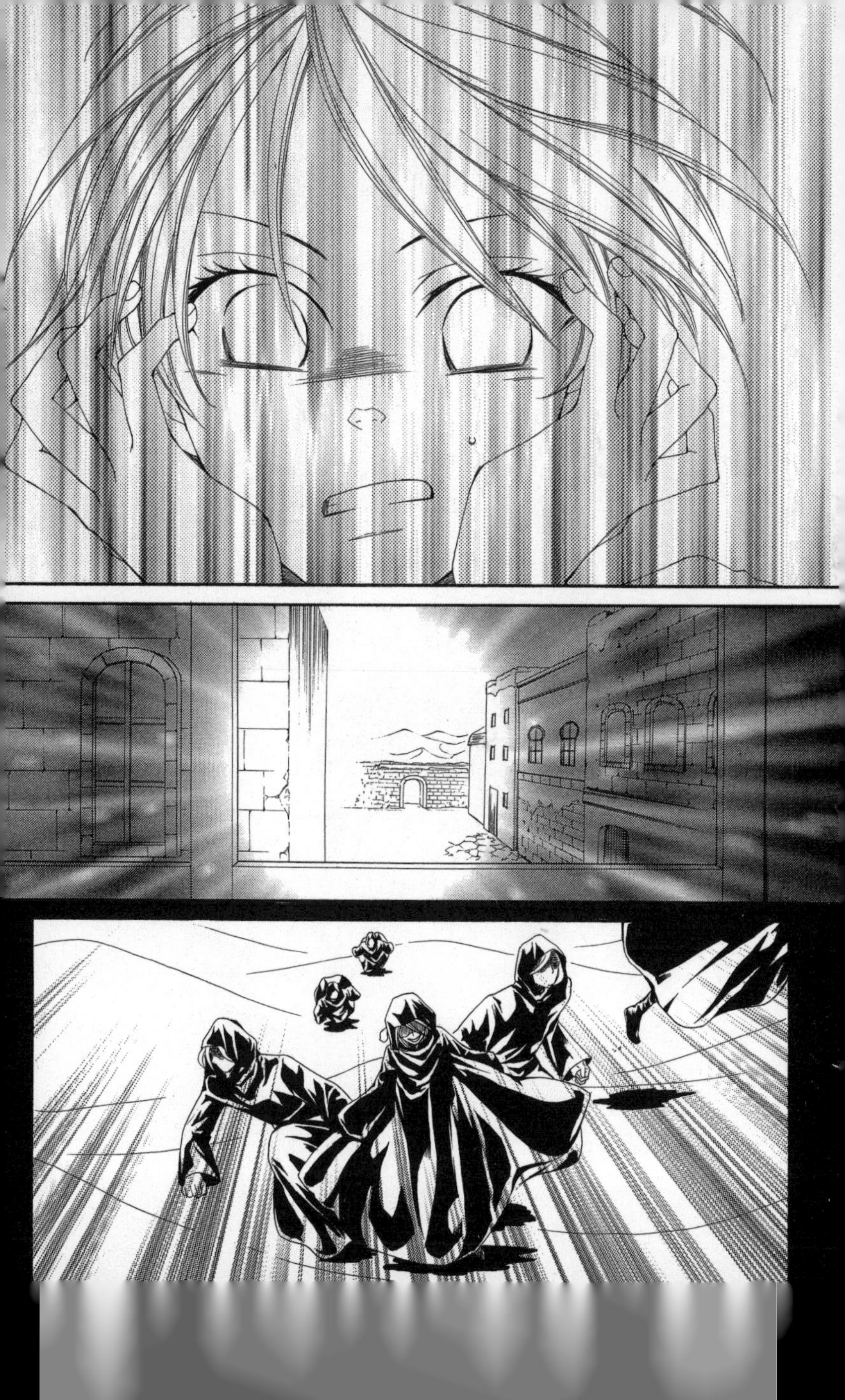

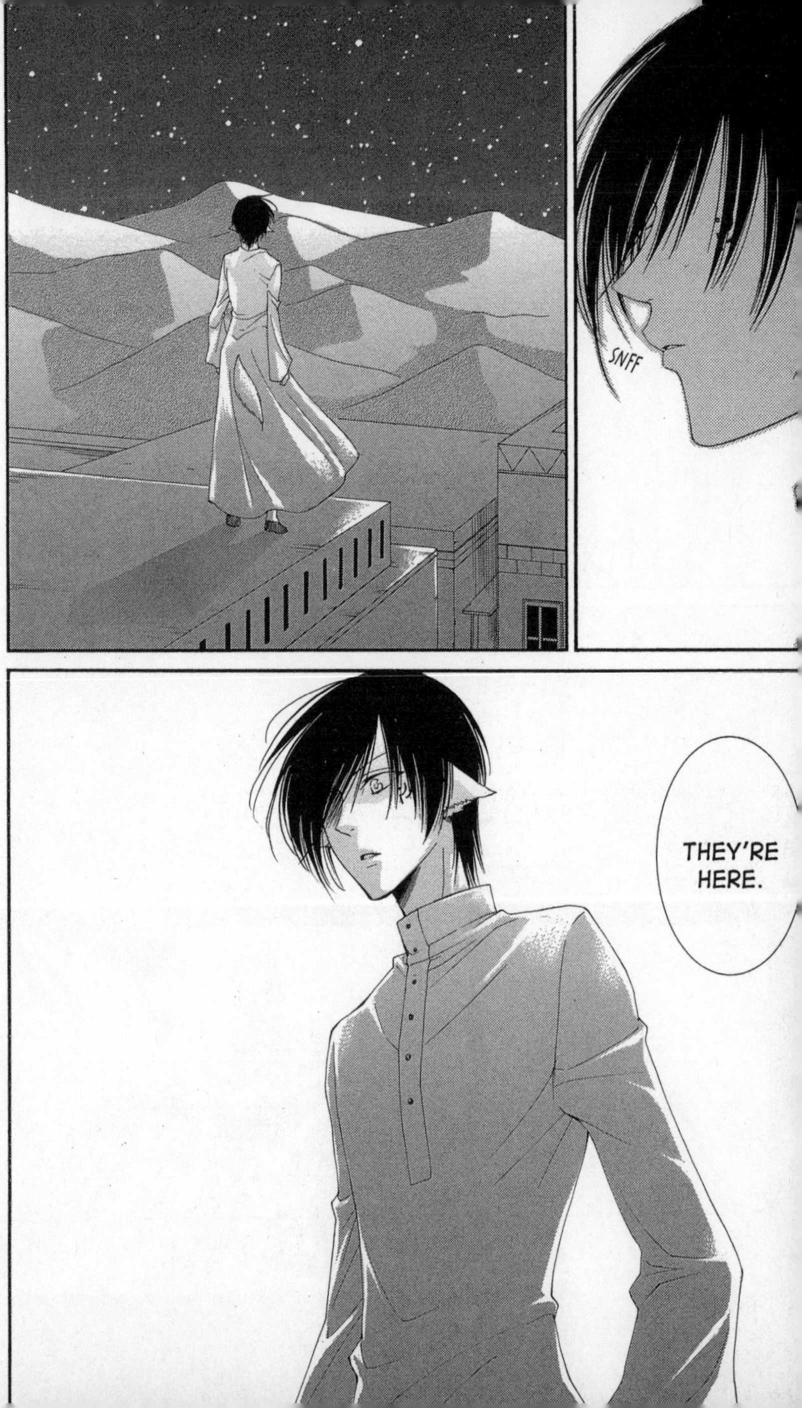
SNFF
THEY'RE HERE.

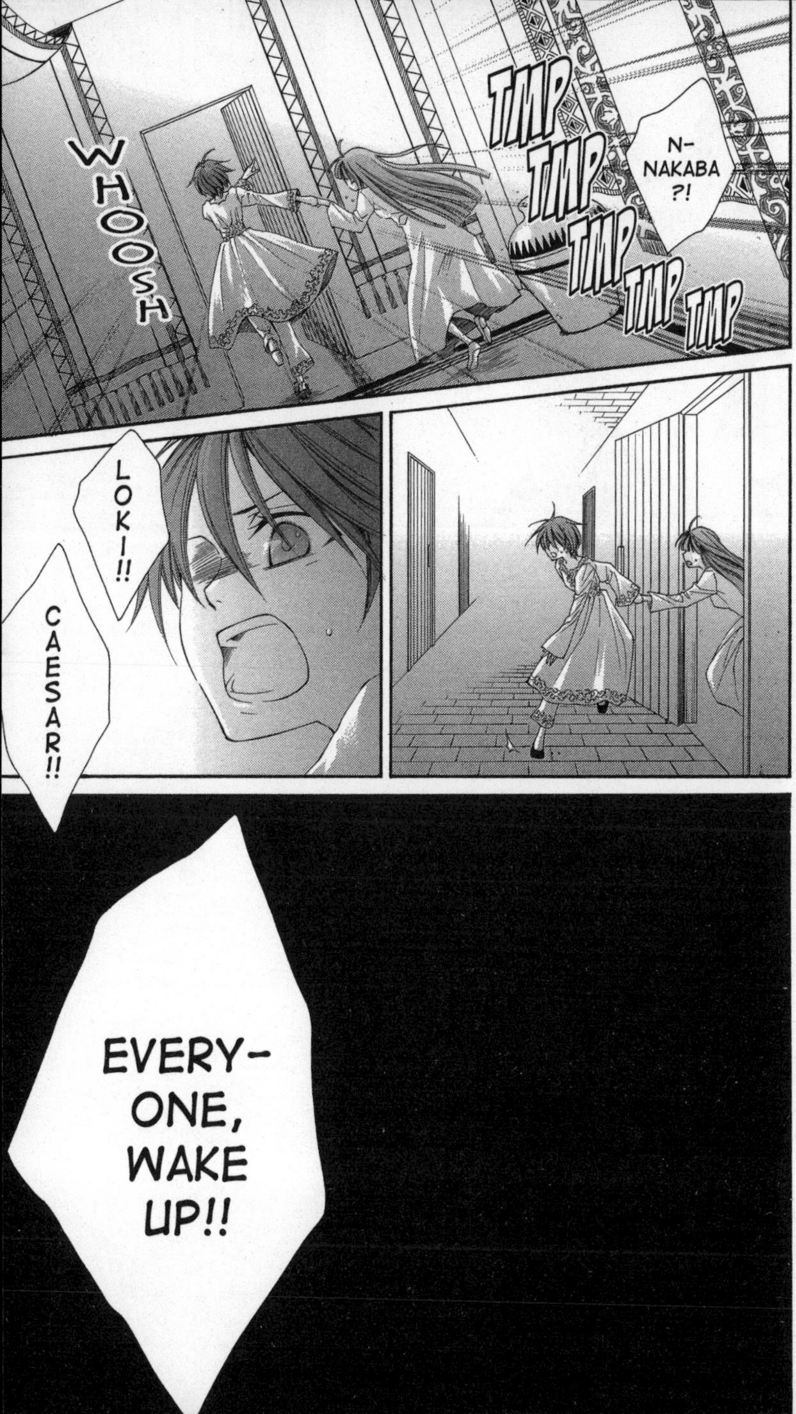
N-NAKABA?!
TMP TMP TMP TMP TMP
WHOOSH
LOKI!!
CAESAR!!
EVERY-ONE, WAKE UP!!

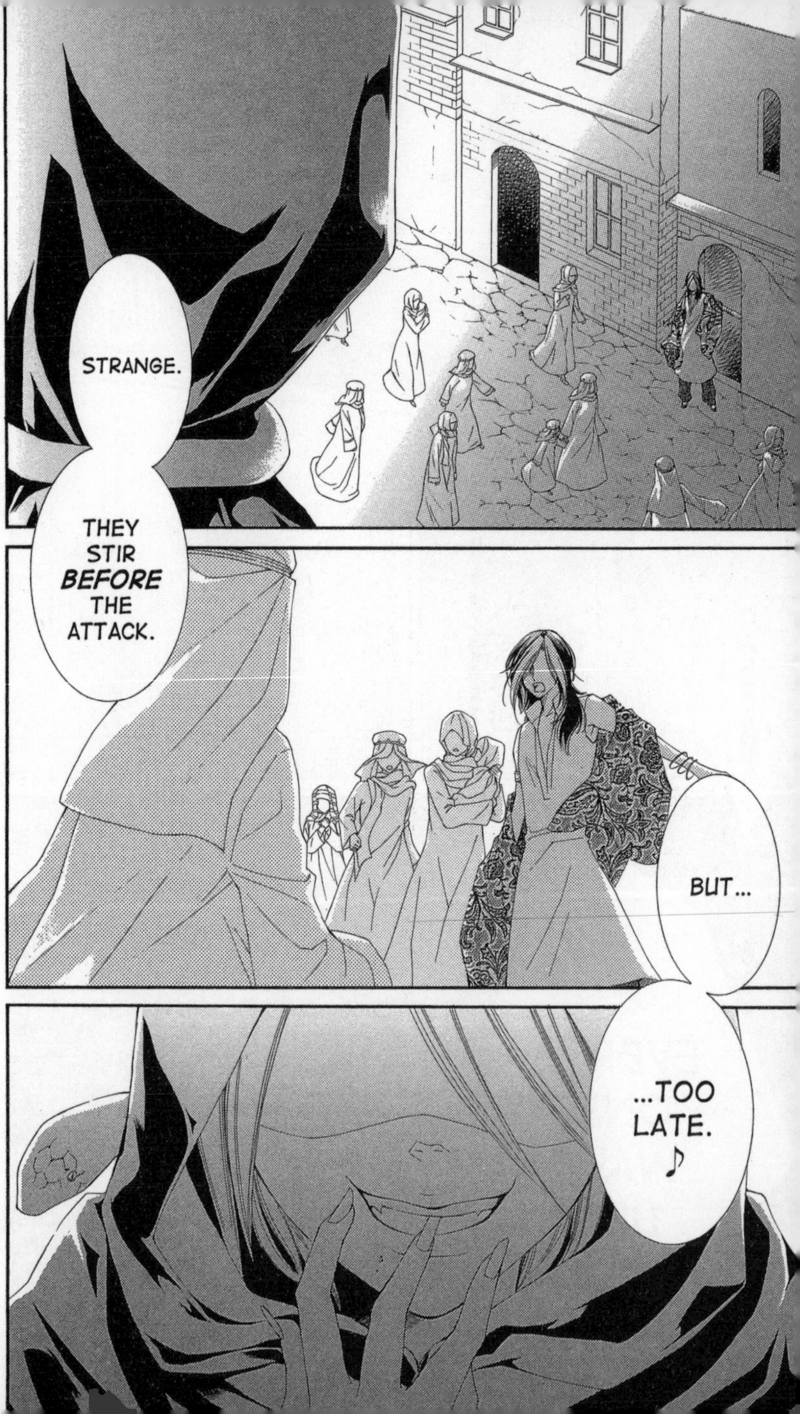
STRANGE.
THEY STIR *BEFORE* THE ATTACK.
BUT...
...TOO LATE. ♪

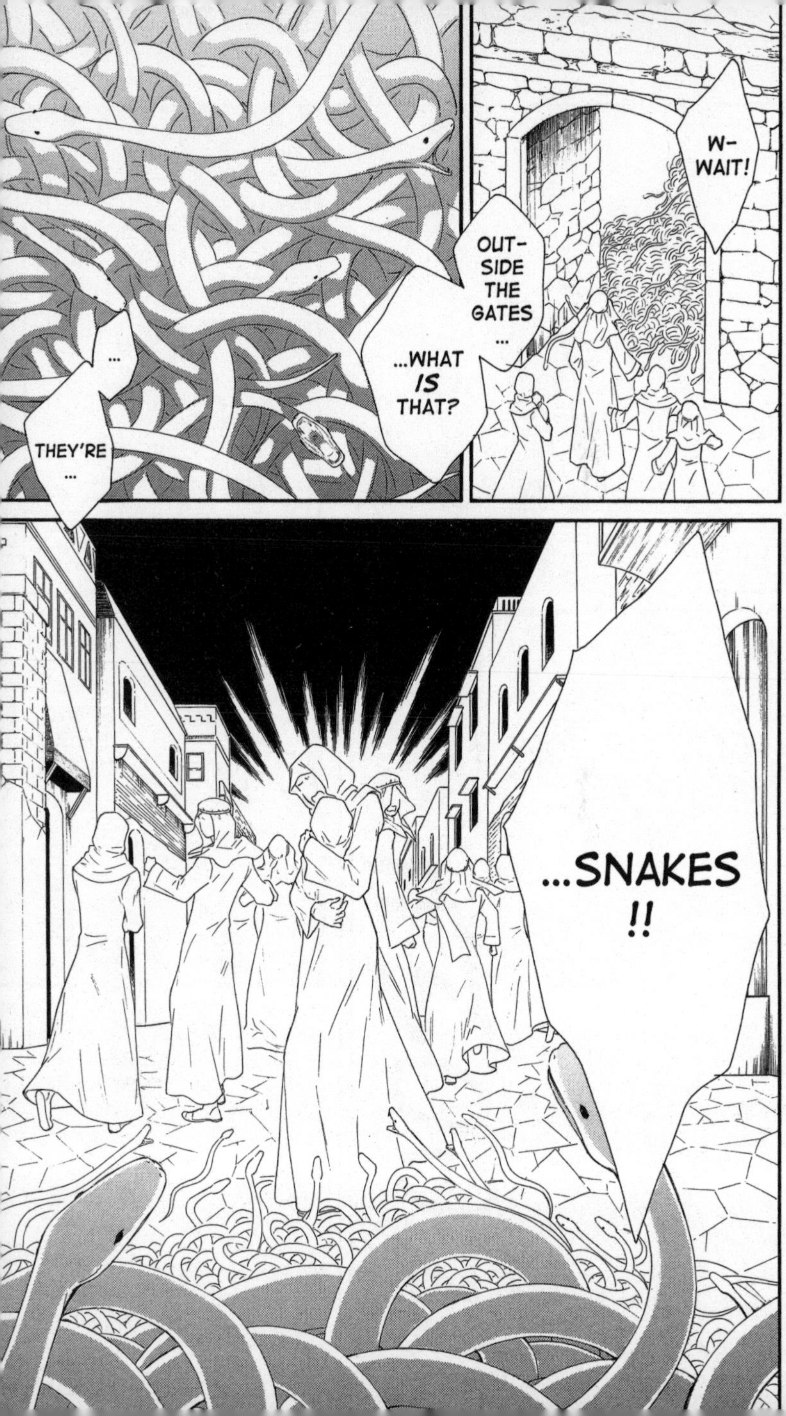
W-WAIT!
OUT-SIDE THE GATES...
...WHAT *IS* THAT?
...
THEY'RE...
...SNAKES!!

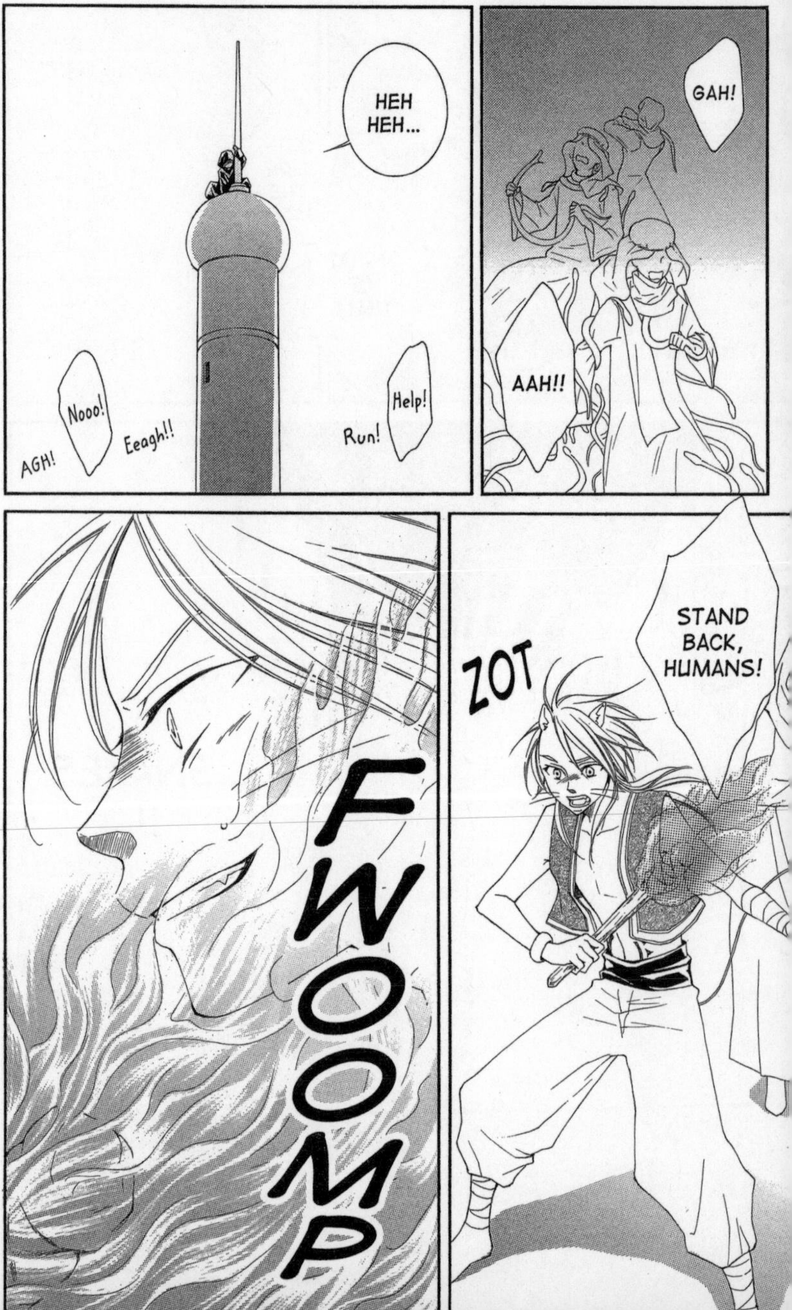
GAH!
AAH!!
HEH HEH...
Help!
Run!
Nooo!
Eeagh!!
AGH!
STAND BACK, HUMANS!
ZOT
FWOOMP

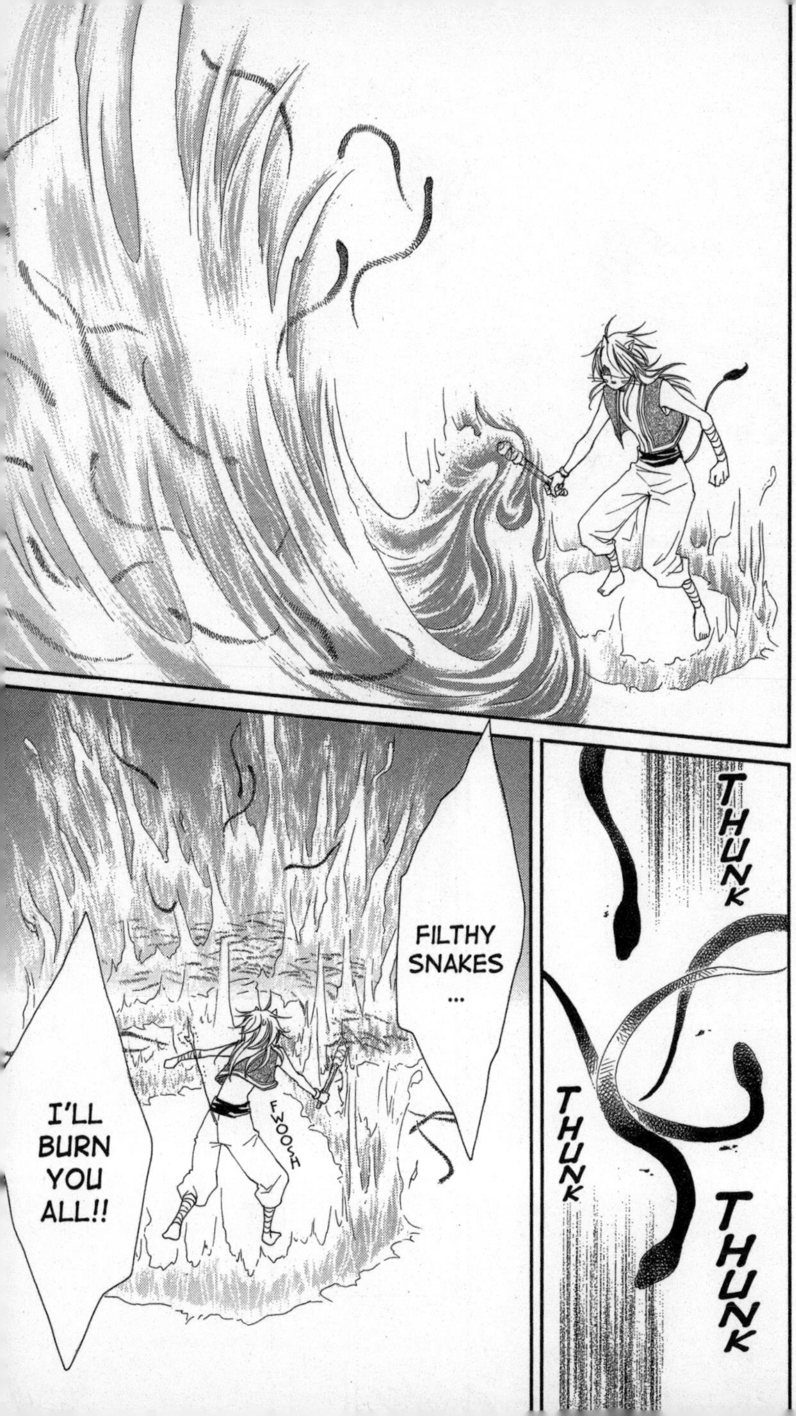
THUNK
THUNK
THUNK
FILTHY SNAKES ...
FWOOSH
I'LL BURN YOU ALL!!

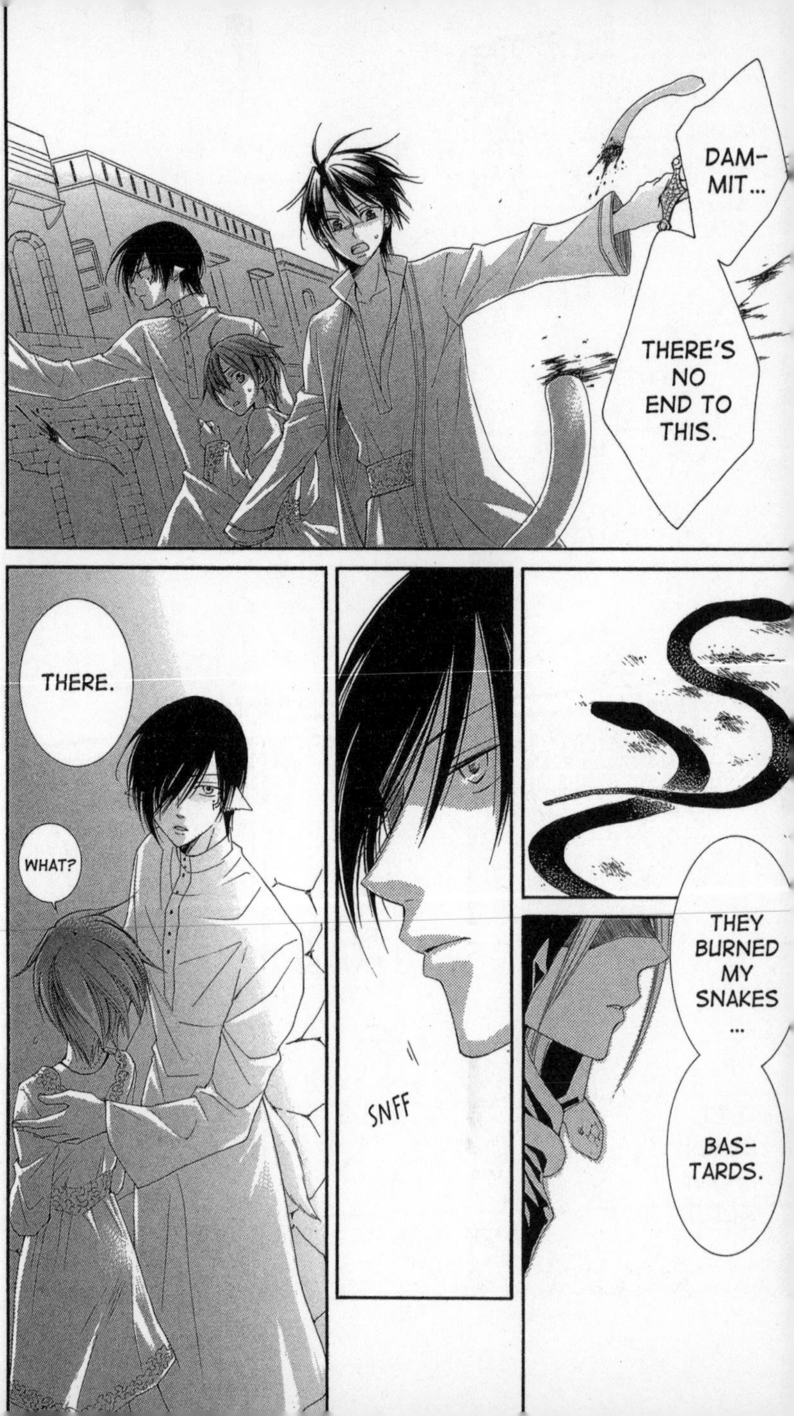
DAM-MIT...
THERE'S NO END TO THIS.
THEY BURNED MY SNAKES ...
BAS-TARDS.
SNFF
THERE.
WHAT?

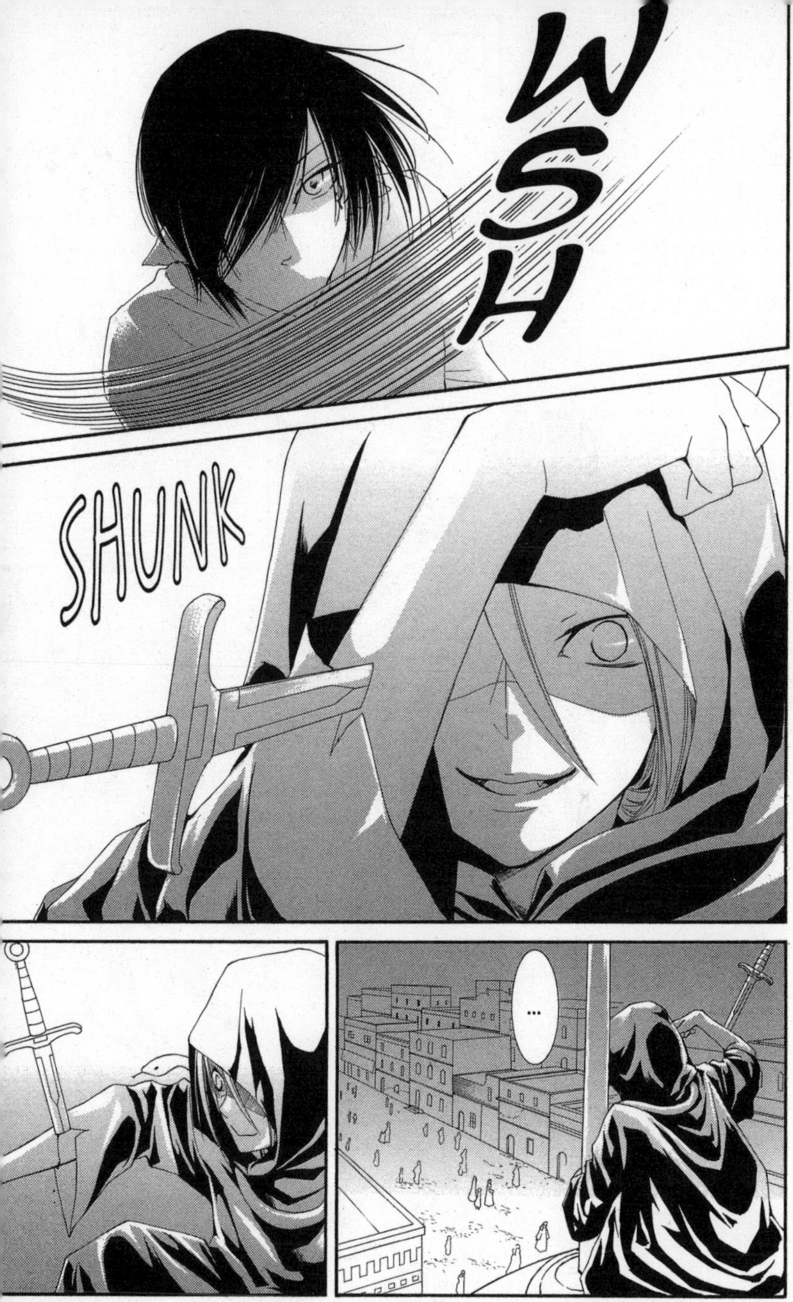
WSH
SHUNK
...

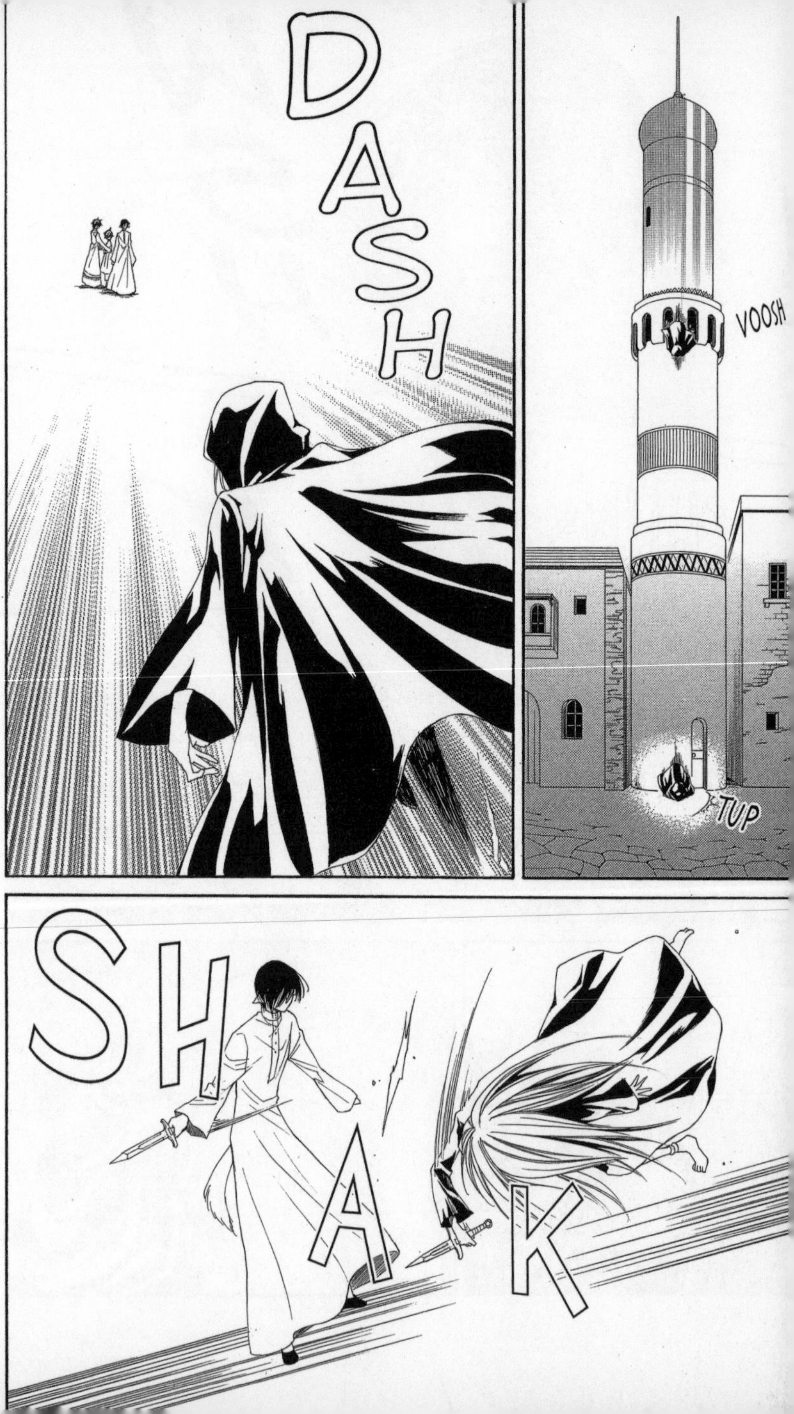
VOOSH
TUP
DASH
SHAK

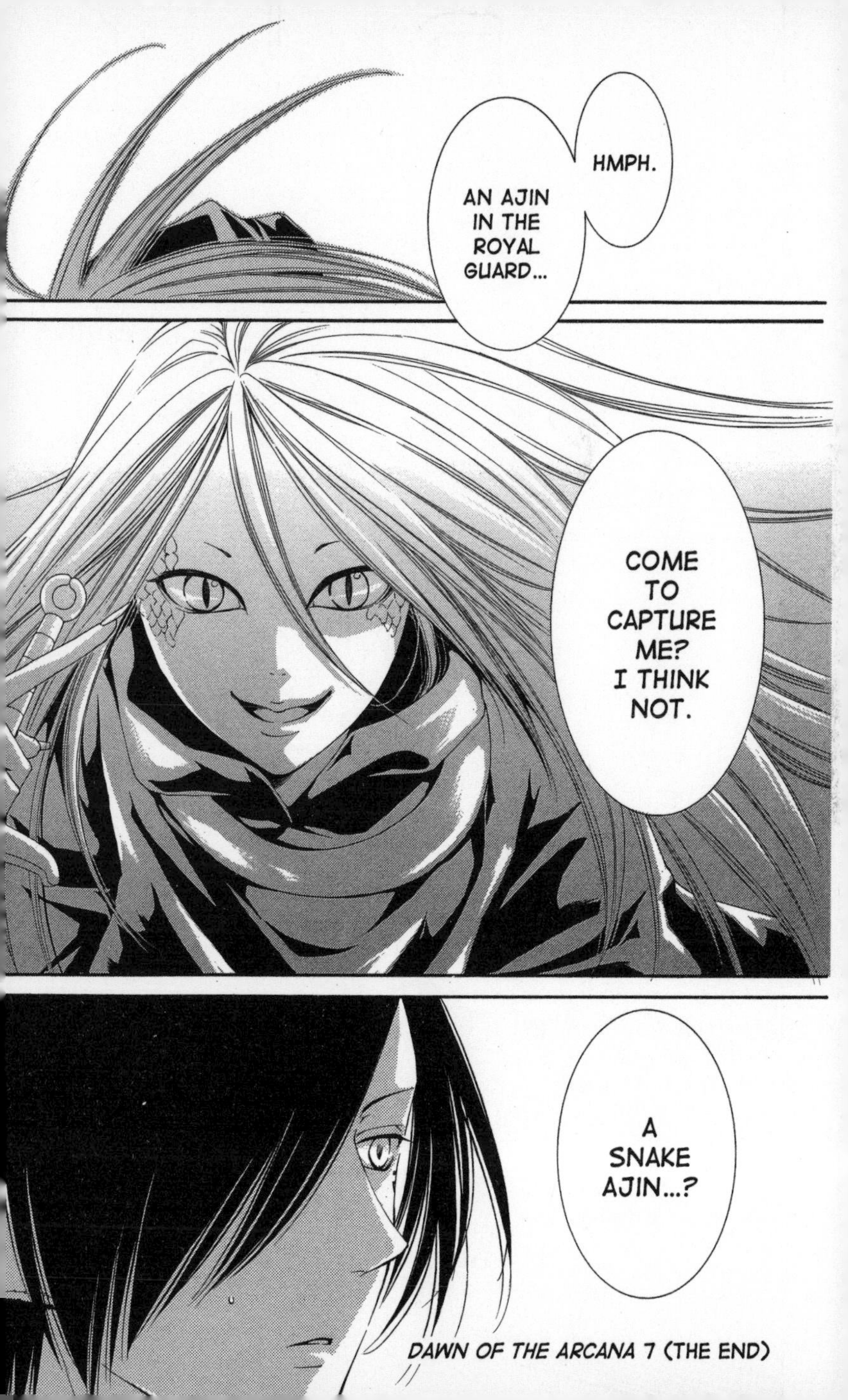
HMPH.
AN AJIN IN THE ROYAL GUARD...
COME TO CAPTURE ME? I THINK NOT.
A SNAKE AJIN...?
DAWN OF THE ARCANA 7 (THE END)

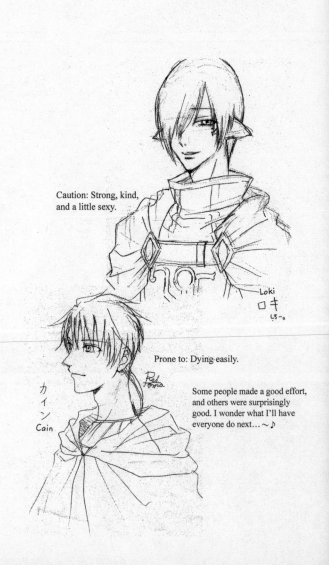

Caution: Strong, kind,
and a little sexy.

Loki
ロキ
LS-o

Prone to: Dying easily.

カイン
Cain

Some people made a good effort,
and others were surprisingly
good. I wonder what I'll have
everyone do next...～♪

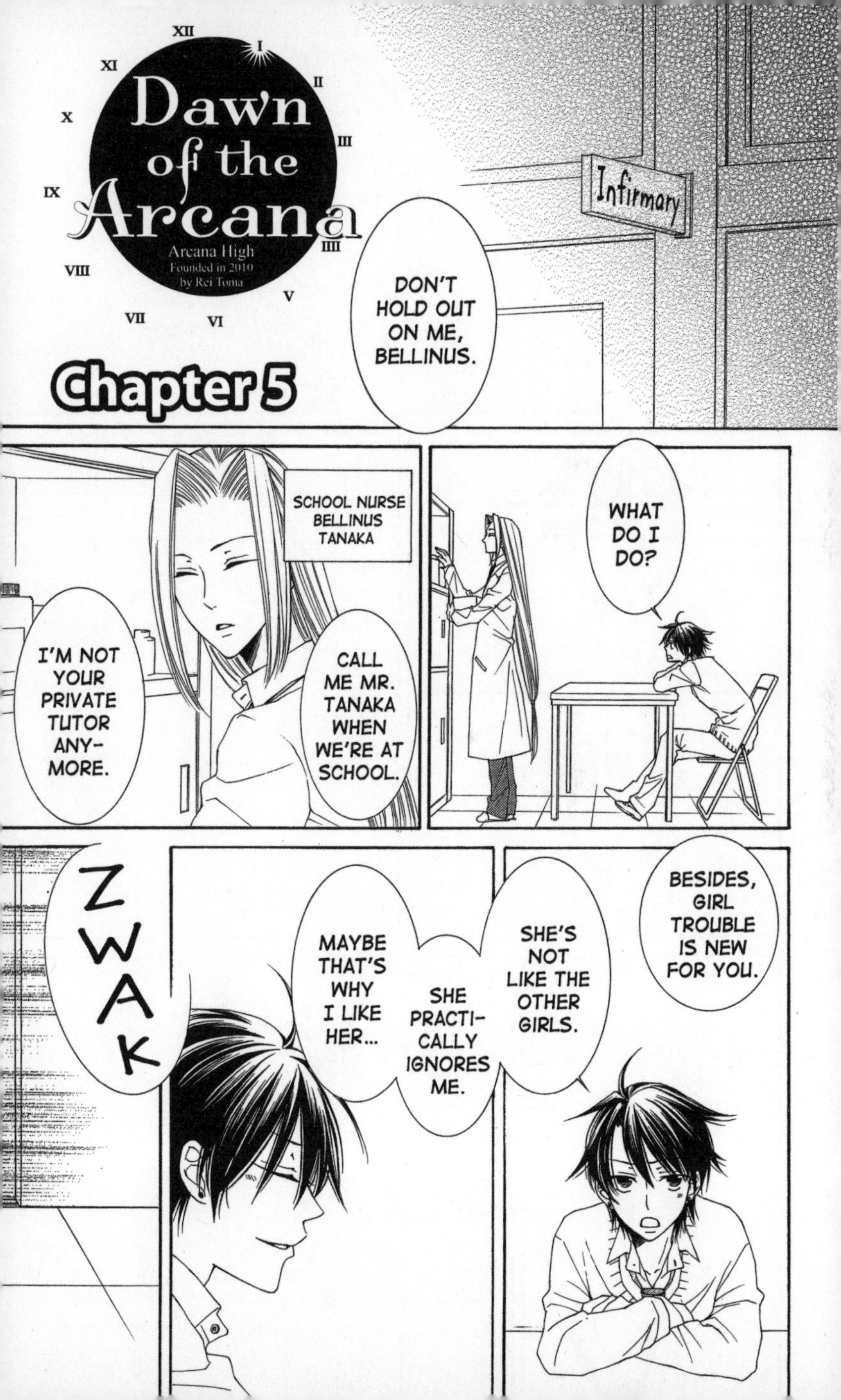

Infirmary
DON'T HOLD OUT ON ME, BELLINUS.
Dawn of the Arcana
Arcana High Founded in 2010 by Rei Toma
Chapter 5
WHAT DO I DO?
SCHOOL NURSE BELLINUS TANAKA
CALL ME MR. TANAKA WHEN WE'RE AT SCHOOL.
I'M NOT YOUR PRIVATE TUTOR ANYMORE.
BESIDES, GIRL TROUBLE IS NEW FOR YOU.
SHE'S NOT LIKE THE OTHER GIRLS.
SHE PRACTICALLY IGNORES ME.
MAYBE THAT'S WHY I LIKE HER...
ZWAK

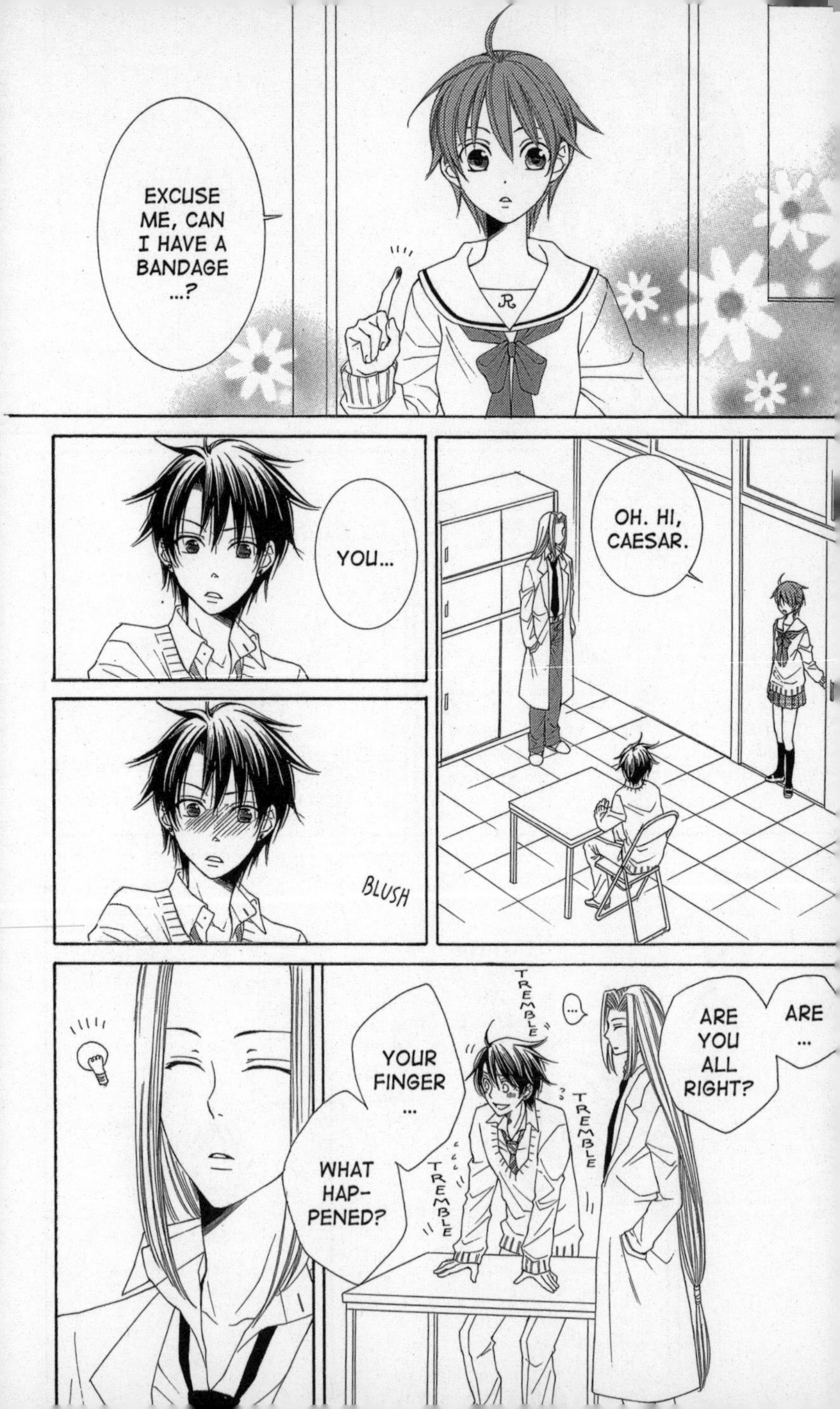
EXCUSE ME, CAN I HAVE A BANDAGE ...?
OH. HI, CAESAR.
YOU...
BLUSH
ARE ...
ARE YOU ALL RIGHT?
...
TREMBLE
YOUR FINGER ...
TREMBLE
WHAT HAP-PENED?
TREMBLE

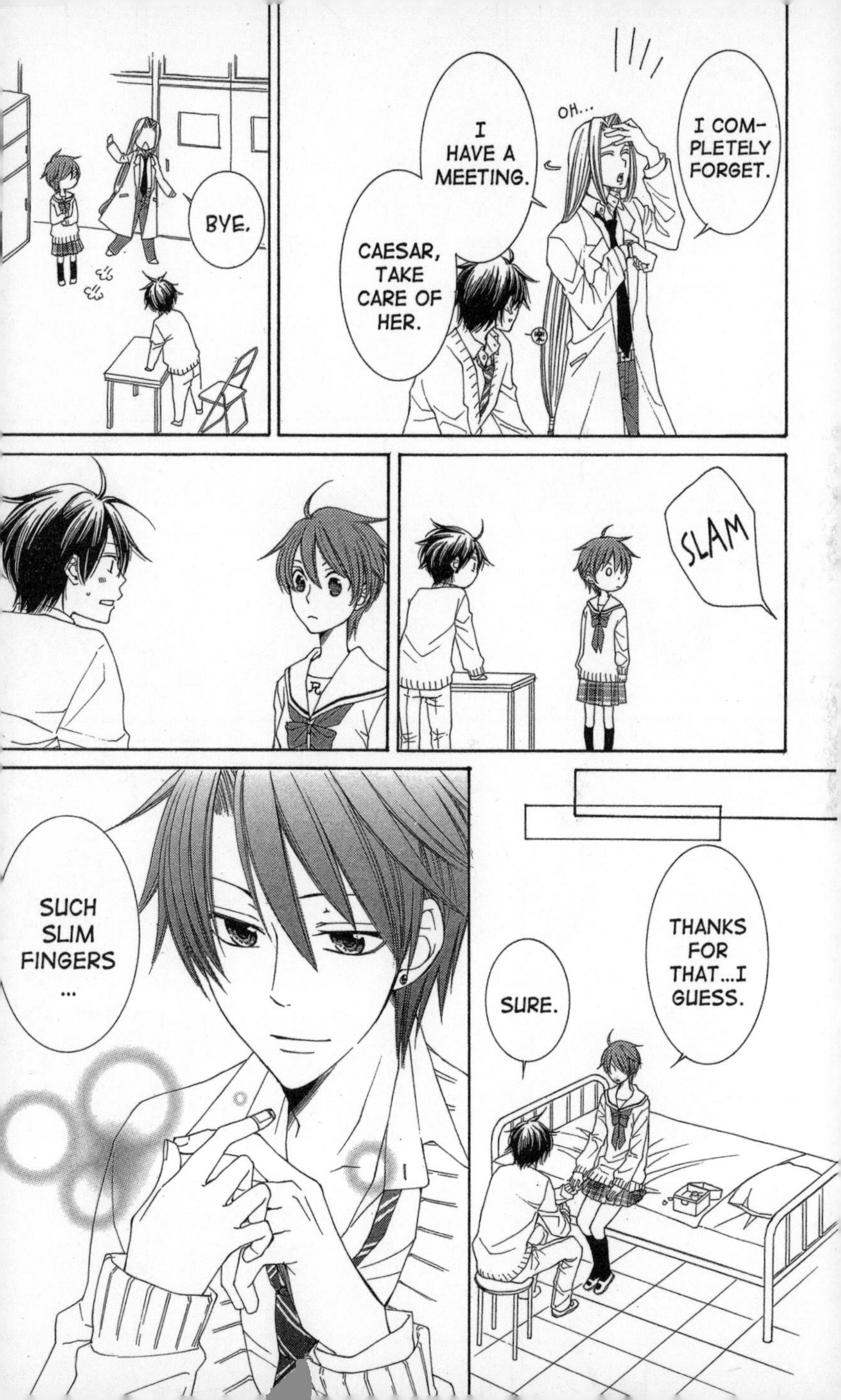
I COM-PLETELY FORGET.
OH...
I HAVE A MEETING.
CAESAR, TAKE CARE OF HER.
BYE.
SLAM
THANKS FOR THAT...I GUESS.
SURE.
SUCH SLIM FINGERS ...

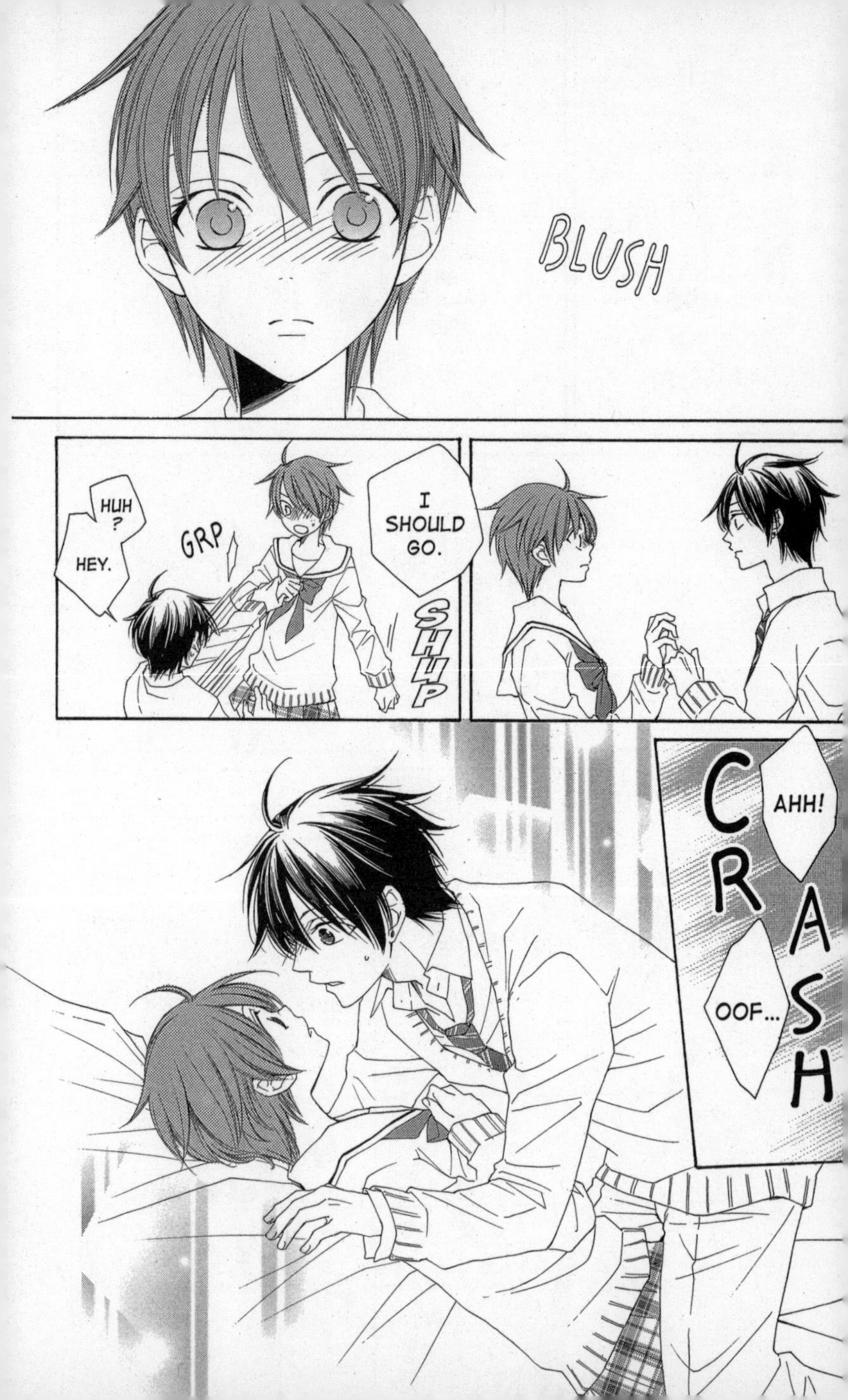
BLUSH
I SHOULD GO.
SHUP
GRP
HUH?
HEY.
CRASH
AHH!
OOF...

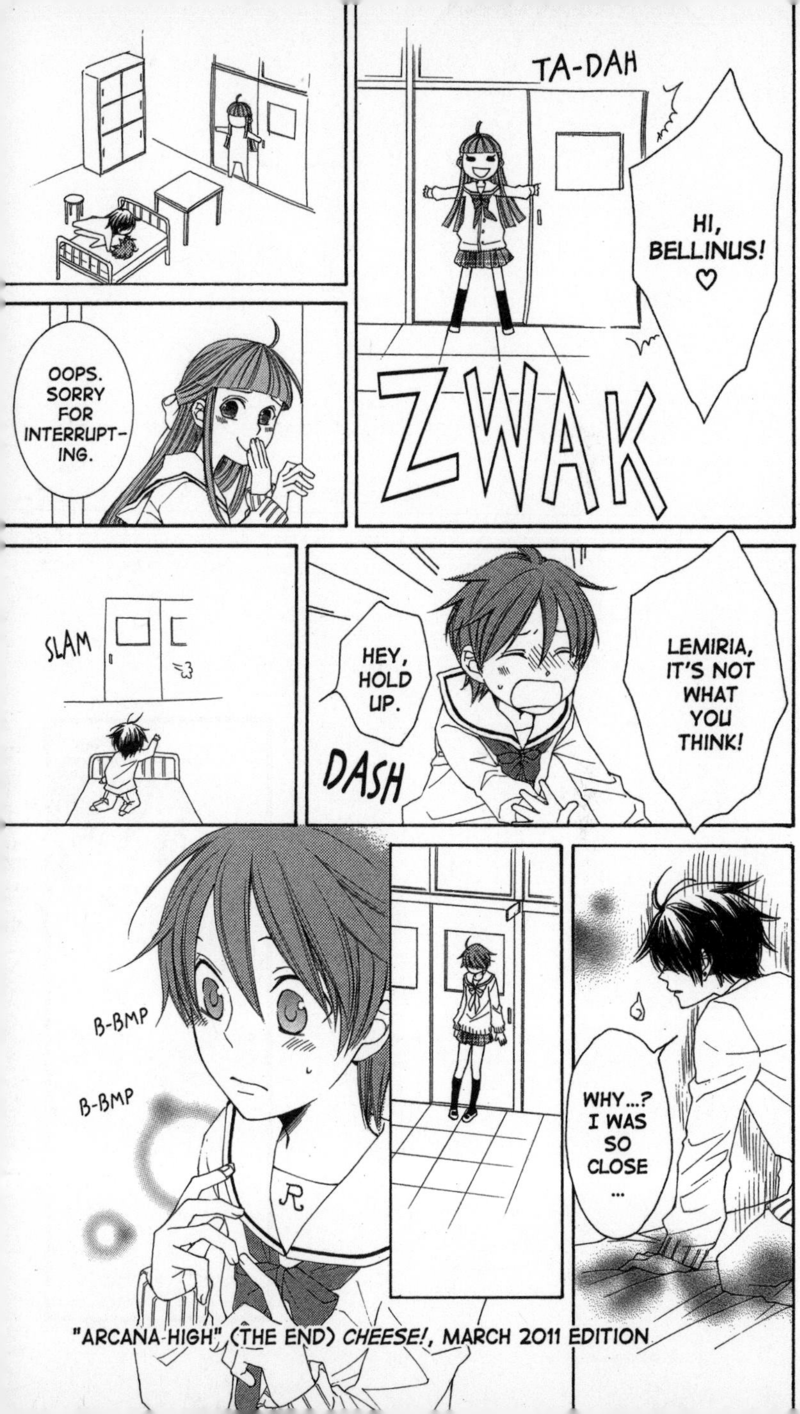
TA-DAH
HI, BELLINUS! ♡
ZWAK
OOPS. SORRY FOR INTERRUPT-ING.
LEMIRIA, IT'S NOT WHAT YOU THINK!
HEY, HOLD UP.
DASH
SLAM
WHY...? I WAS SO CLOSE ...
B-BMP
B-BMP

"ARCANA HIGH" (THE END) *CHEESE!*, MARCH 2011 EDITION

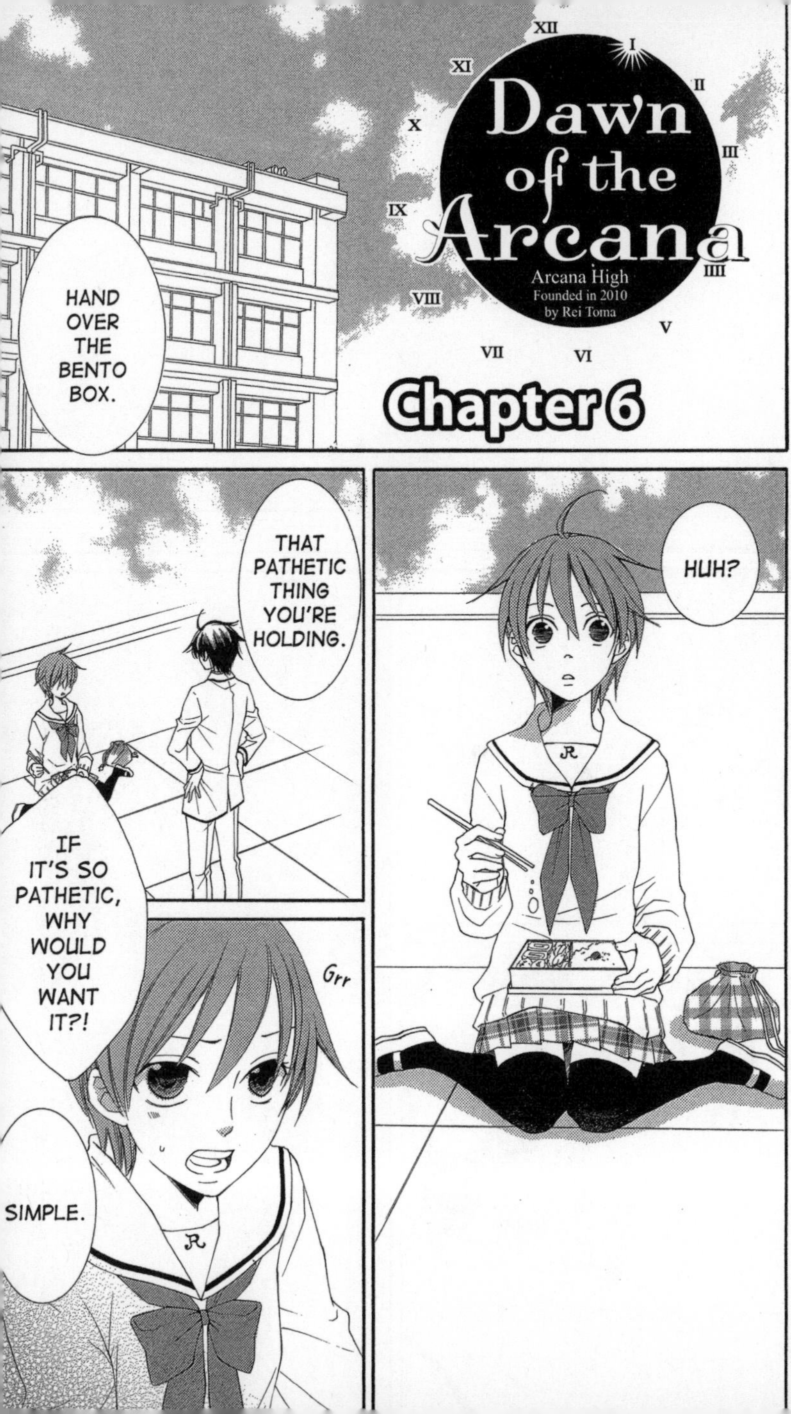

Dawn of the Arcana
Arcana High
Founded in 2010
by Rei Toma
Chapter 6
HAND OVER THE BENTO BOX.
HUH?
THAT PATHETIC THING YOU'RE HOLDING.
IF IT'S SO PATHETIC, WHY WOULD YOU WANT IT?!
Grr
SIMPLE.

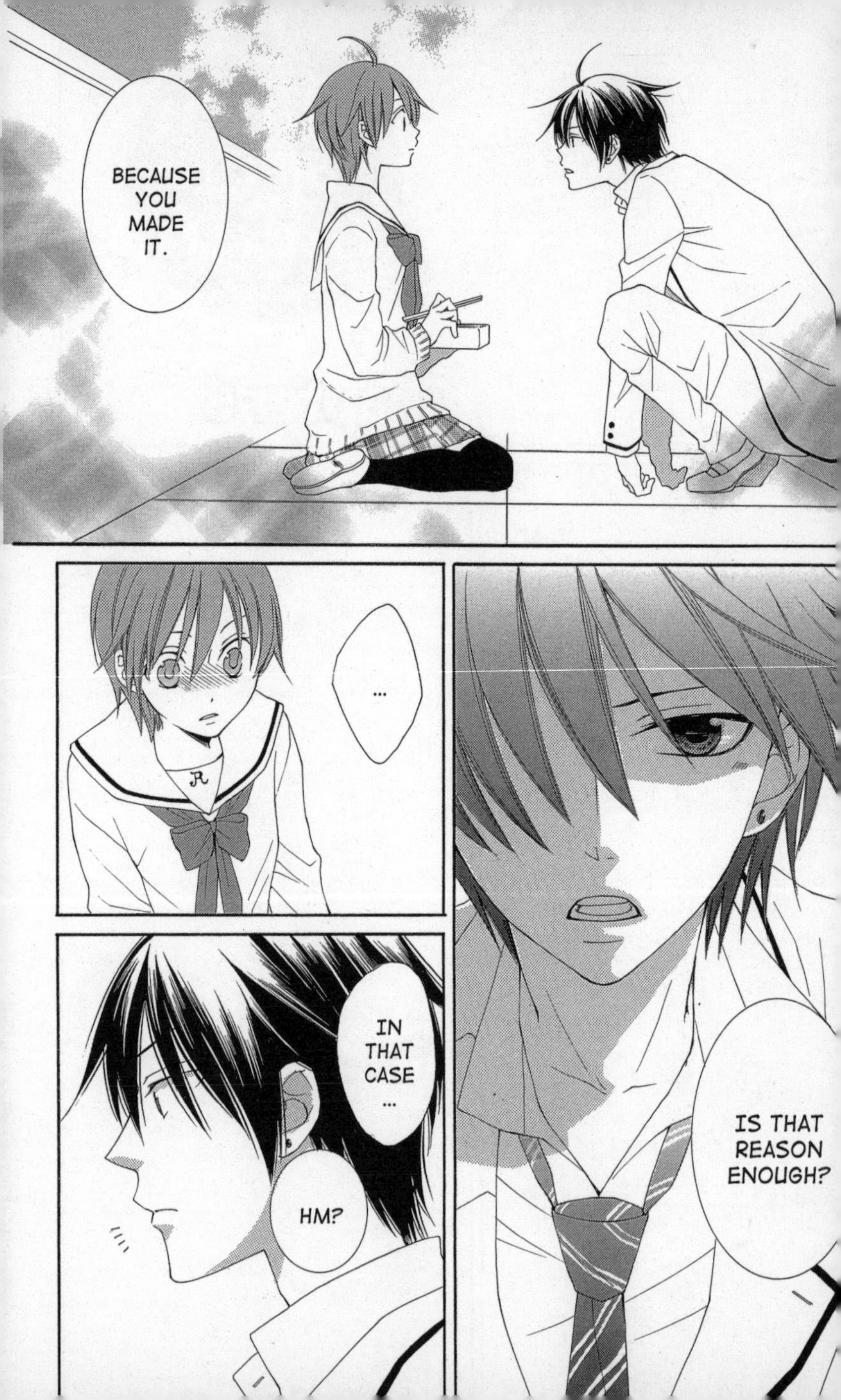
BECAUSE YOU MADE IT.
IS THAT REASON ENOUGH?
...
IN THAT CASE ...
HM?

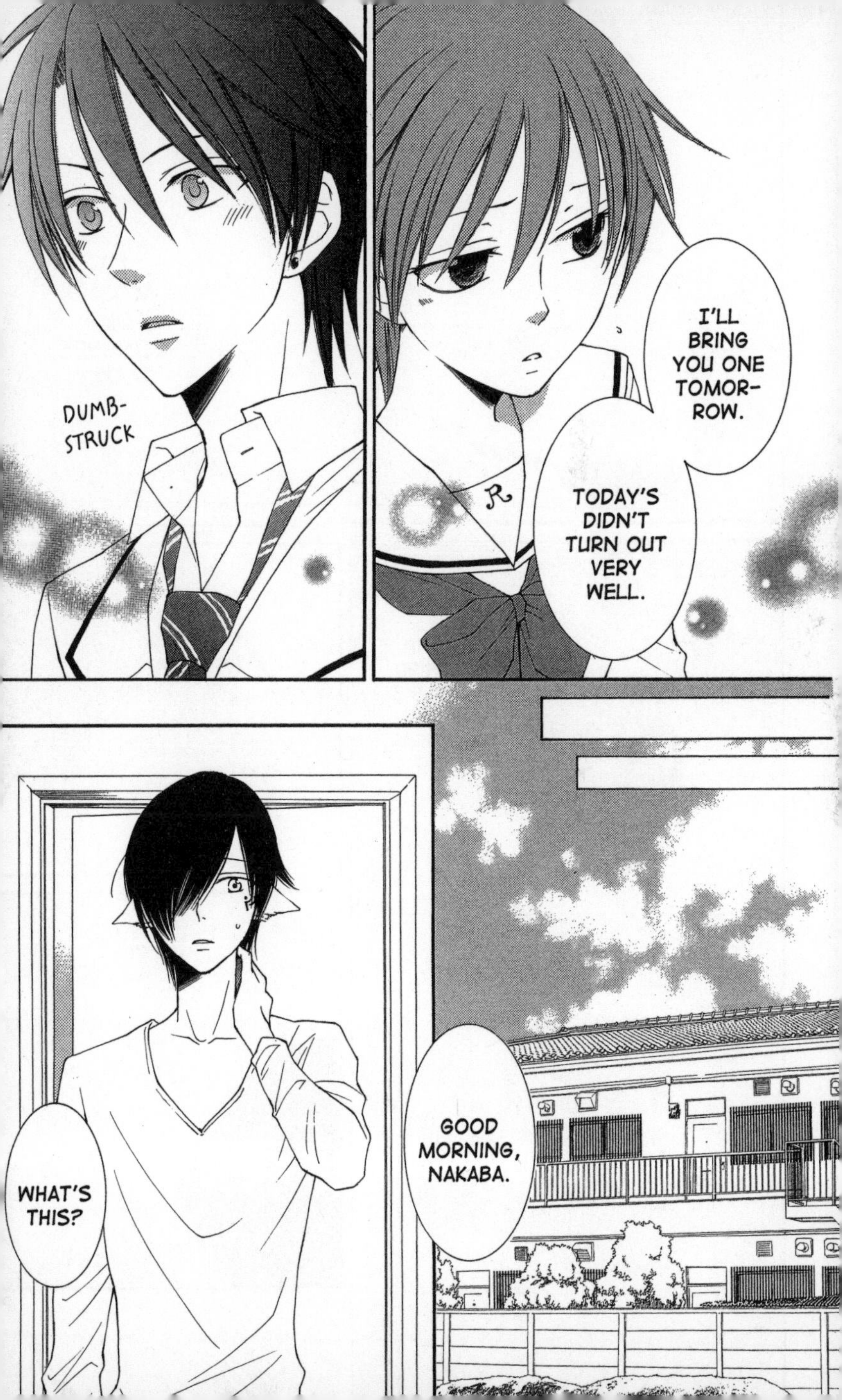
I'LL BRING YOU ONE TOMOR-ROW.
TODAY'S DIDN'T TURN OUT VERY WELL.
DUMB-STRUCK
GOOD MORNING, NAKABA.
WHAT'S THIS?

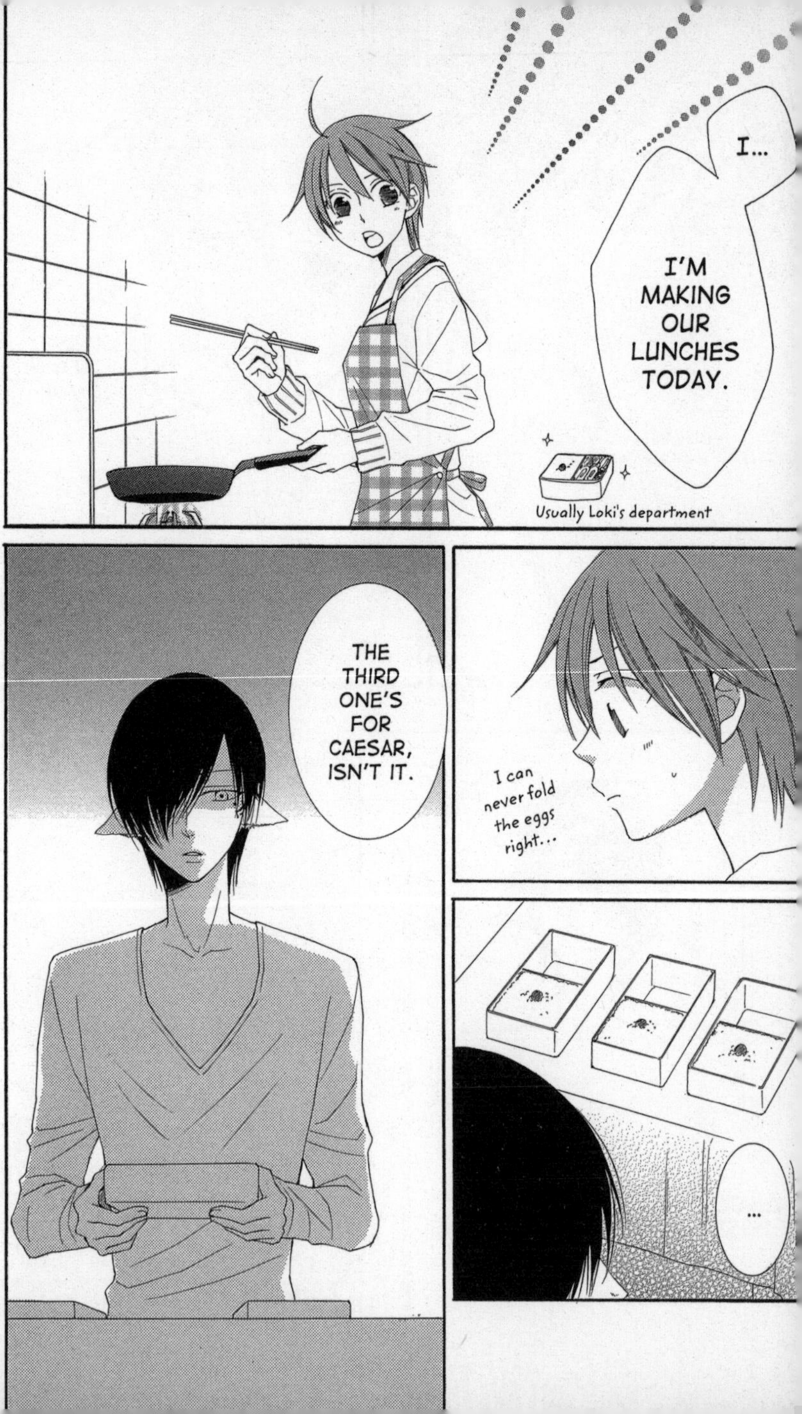
I...
I'M MAKING OUR LUNCHES TODAY.
Usually Loki's department
I can never fold the eggs right...
THE THIRD ONE'S FOR CAESAR, ISN'T IT.
...

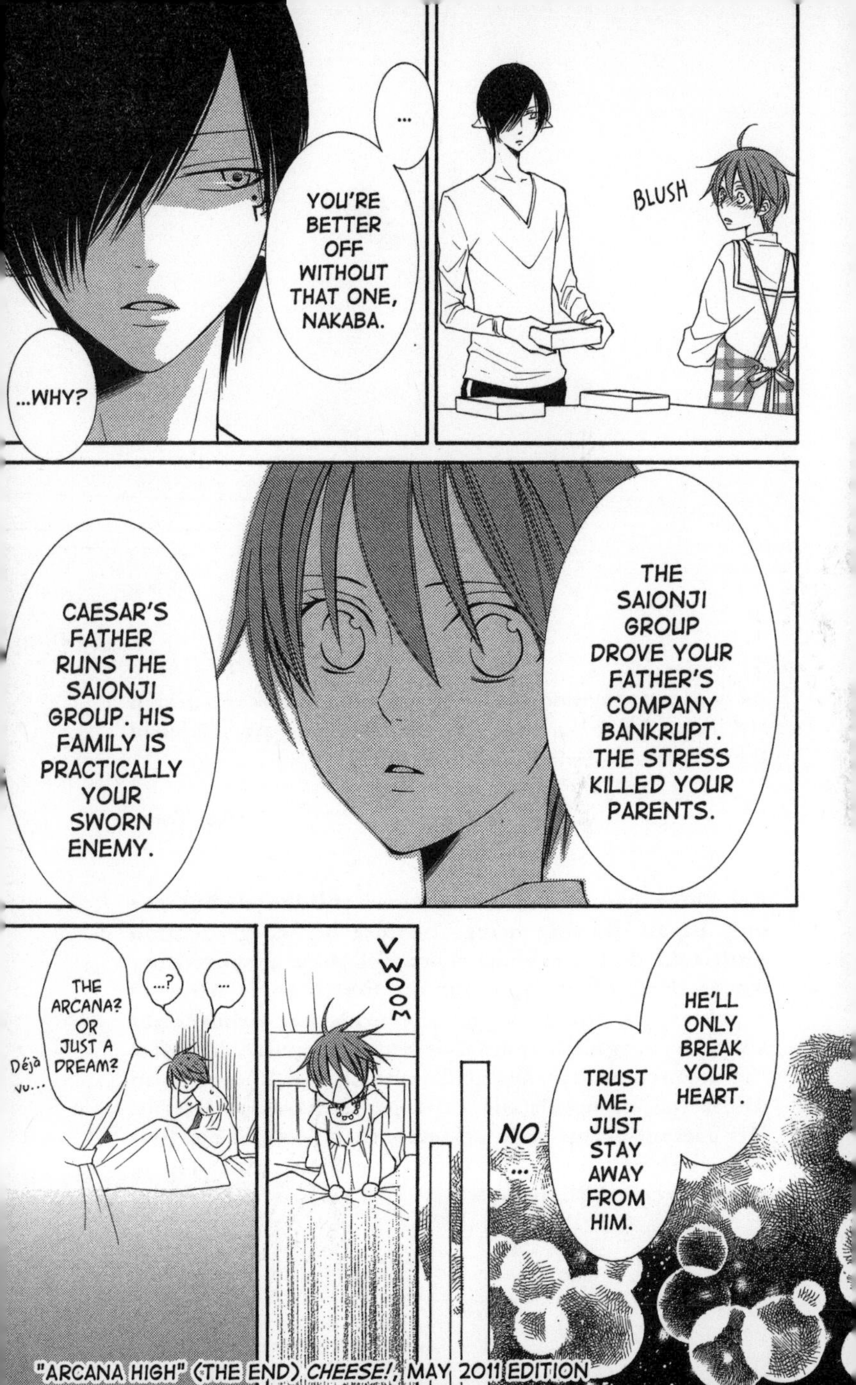
BLUSH
...
YOU'RE BETTER OFF WITHOUT THAT ONE, NAKABA.
...WHY?
THE SAIONJI GROUP DROVE YOUR FATHER'S COMPANY BANKRUPT. THE STRESS KILLED YOUR PARENTS.
CAESAR'S FATHER RUNS THE SAIONJI GROUP. HIS FAMILY IS PRACTICALLY YOUR SWORN ENEMY.
HE'LL ONLY BREAK YOUR HEART.
TRUST ME, JUST STAY AWAY FROM HIM.
NO...
VWOOM
...
...?
THE ARCANA? OR JUST A DREAM?
Déjà vu...

"ARCANA HIGH" (THE END) *CHEESE!*, MAY 2011 EDITION

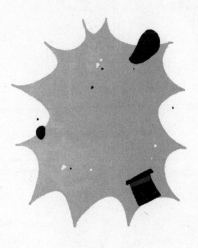

As you may have noticed, I've changed the cover design starting with this volume! To the fans who are saddened that it wasn't a Bellinus cover... Sorry!

–Rei Toma

Rei Toma has been drawing since childhood, but she only began drawing manga because of her graduation project in design school. When she drew a short-story manga, *Help Me, Dentist,* for the first time, it attracted a publisher's attention and she made her debut right away. Her magnificent art style became popular, and after she debuted as a manga artist, she became known as an illustrator for novels and video game character designs. Her current manga series, *Dawn of the Arcana,* is her first long-running manga series, and it has been a hit in Japan, selling over a million copies.

DAWN OF THE ARCANA
VOLUME 7
Shojo Beat Edition

STORY AND ART BY
REI TOMA

© 2009 Rei TOMA/Shogakukan
All rights reserved.
Original Japanese edition "REIMEI NO ARCANA"
published by SHOGAKUKAN Inc.

Translation & Adaptation/Kajiya Productions
Touch-up Art & Lettering/Freeman Wong
Design/Yukiko Whitley
Editor/Amy Yu

Printed in the U.S.A.

Published by VIZ Media, LLC
P.O. Box 77010
San Francisco, CA 94107

10 9 8 7 6 5 4 3 2
First printing, December 2012
Second printing, November 2015

www.viz.com   www.shojobeat.com

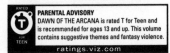

This is the last page.

In keeping with the original Japanese comic format, this book reads from right to left—so action, sound effects, and word balloons are completely reversed. This preserves the orientation of the original artwork—plus, it's fun! Check out the diagram shown here to get the hang of things, and then turn to the other side of the book to get started!

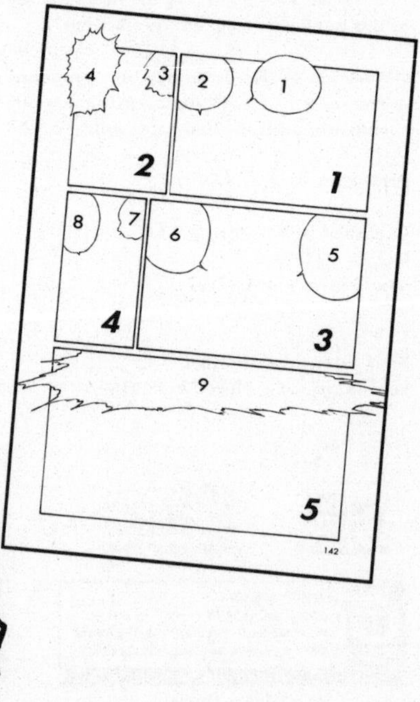
1
2
1
3
4
2
5
6
3
7
8
4
9
5
142

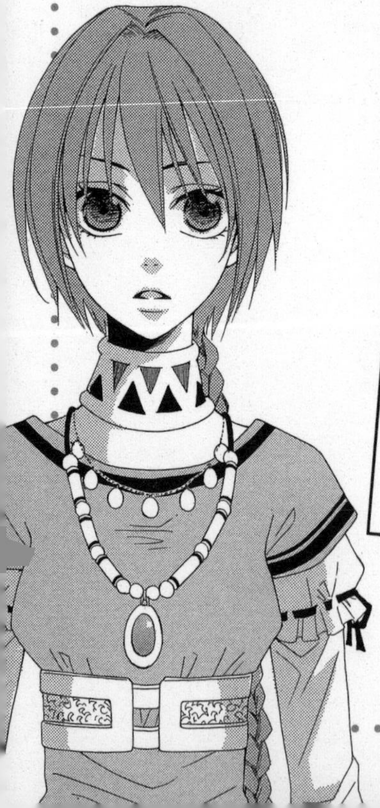